Science
and Football
III

Science and Football III

Edited by

T. Reilly
J. Bangsbo
and
M. Hughes

Proceedings of the
Third World Congress of
Science and Football
Cardiff, Wales
9-13 April 1995

E & FN SPON
An Imprint of Chapman & Hall

London · Weinheim · New York · Tokyo · Melbourne · Madras

Published by E & FN Spon, an imprint of Chapman & Hall,
2–6 Boundary Row, London SE1 8HN, UK

Chapman & Hall, 2–6 Boundary Row, London SE1 8HN, UK

Chapman & Hall GmbH, Pappelallee 3, 69469 Weinheim, Germany

Chapman & Hall USA, 115 Fifth Avenue, New York, NY 10003, USA

Chapman & Hall Japan, ITP-Japan, Kyowa Building,
3F, 2-2-1 Hirakawacho, Chiyoda-ku, Tokyo 102, Japan

Chapman & Hall Australia, 102 Dodds Street, South Melbourne, Victoria 3205, Australia

Chapman & Hall India, R. Seshadri, 32 Second Main Road, CIT East, Madras 600 035, India

First edition 1997

© 1997 E & FN Spon

Printed in Great Britain by St Edmundsbury Press Ltd, Bury St Edmunds, Suffolk

ISBN 0 419 22160 3

A catalogue record for this book is available from the British Library

∞ Printed on permanent acid-free text paper, manufactured in accordance with ANSI/NISO
Z39.48-1992 and ANSI/NISO Z39.48-1984 (Permanence of Paper).

Third World Congress on Science and Football
Cardiff, Wales, 9-13 April 1995

Congress Organiser

Mike Hughes

Scientific Committee

T. Reilly (Chair)
J. Bangsbo
J. Clarys
I. Franks
M. Hughes

Contents

Preface   **xiii**

Introduction   **xv**

PART ONE   Fitness Test Profiles of Footballers

1. A comparison of fitness characteristics of elite
    and non-elite Gaelic football players   3
    S. Keane, T. Reilly and A. Borrie

2. Profile of elite female touch football players   7
    D. O'Connor

3. Fitness profile of professional Rugby League
    players   11
    D. O'Connor

4. A comparison of upper body strength in
    collegiate Rugby players   16
    R.J. Tong and G.L. Wood

5. Aerobic and anaerobic field testing of soccer
    players   21
    K. Odetoyinbo and R. Ramsbottom

6. Fitness profiles of English professional and
    semi-professional soccer players using a
    battery or field tests   27
    G.M.J. Dunbar and K. Power

7. Comparison of the physiological charactersitics
    of the First, Second and Third League Turkish
    soccer players   32
    G. Tiryaki, F. Tuncel, F. Yamaner, S.A. Agaoglu,
    H. Gumubdad and M.F. Acar

8. Physiological characteristics of Turkish female
    soccer players   37
    K. Tamer, M. Gunay, G. Tiryaki, I. Cicioolu and
    E. Erol

PART TWO   Metabolism and Nutrition

9. The physiology of intermittent activity in
    football   43
    J. Bangsbo

10. Fluid loss and replacement in English Premier
    League soccer players   54
    P.D. Davies, C.B. Cooke and R.F.G.J. King

11. The influence of water ingestion on repeated
    sprint performance during a simulated soccer
    match   60
    *J.L. Fallowfield, A.G. Jackson, D.M. Wilkinson
    and J.J.H. Harrison*

12. The influence of carbohydrate ingestion on
    repeated sprint performance during a
    simulated soccer match   66
    *D.M. Wilkinson, J. Garner, J.L. Fallowfield
    and J.J.H. Harrison*

13. The lipid profile of a Rugby Union football
    squad   72
    C.P. O'Brien and J.F. Fielding

14. Pattern of alcohol use in Rugby players and
    Rugby referees   77
    C.P. O'Brien and J.F. Fielding

15. Iron supplements are not required for Rugby
    Union football   81
    C.P. O'Brien and J.F. Fielding

PART THREE   Football Training

16. Resistance training by senior Rugby Union
    players - just what do coaches think they're
    doing?   89
    J. McKenna

17. Rugby Union players' resistance training - an
    application of the transtheoretical model   94
    J. McKenna and A. Muckle

18. The effect of pre-season training on the physiological characteristics of international rugby players 98
R.J. Tong and R. Mayes

19. Effects of different pre-season preparations on lactate kinetics in professional soccer players 103
C. Islegen, M.F. Acar, A. Cecen, T. Erding, R. Varol, G. Tiryaki and O. Karamizrak

20. Endurance capacity of soccer players pre-season and during the playing season 106
A.N. Rebelo and J.M.C. Soares

21. Fitness profiles of professional soccer players before and after pre-season conditioning 112
T.H. Mercer, N.P. Gleeson and J. Mitchell

22. An investigation into the fitness of professional soccer players over two seasons 118
K. Brady, A. Maile and B. Ewing

PART FOUR   Medical Aspects of Football

23. Footballers' body clocks 125
T. Reilly

24. Injuries in American Football 132
D.T. Kirkendall, K.P. Speer and W.E. Garrett Jr

25. Lumbar spine abnormalities in American Football linemen 139
K.P. Speer, H. Pavlov and R.F. Warren

26. The diagnosis and treatment of pulmonary pneumothorax in grid-iron football 142
A.S. Levy, K. Speer, F. Bassett and S. Lintner

27. Cervical spines of middle-aged soccer players: radiographic findings and computer simulation 145
H. Kurosawa and T. Yamanoi

28. Knee ligament injuries in soccer players 150
J. Ekstrand

29. Injuries in Rugby football   156
    D.A.D. MacLeod

30. Effect of a fatigue task on absolute and
    relavitised indices of isokinetic leg strength
    in female collegiate soccer players   162
    N. Gleeson, T. Mercer and I. Campbell

31. Training and retraining muscle strength   168
    J.P. Clarys, E. Zinzen, D. Caboor and
    P. Van Roy

32. Isokinetic assessment of Rugby League
    players with groin problems   176
    D. O'Connor

PART FIVE   Paediatric Science and Football

33. Sports injuries and physical fitness in
    adolescent soccer players   185
    T. Kohno, N. O'Hata, M. Ohara,
    T. Shirahata, Y. Endo, M. Satoh,
    Y. Kimura and Y. Nakajima

34. High-school soccer summer tournaments
    in Japan - comparison of laboratory data
    of the players in summer and winter   190
    M. Kobayashi, H. Aoki, S. Ikeda,
    T. Katsumata, T. Kohno, K. Shiono, J. Seki,
    T. Takagi, T. Takei, J. Tanaka, K. Nabeshima,
    K. Nomura, S. Fukaya, T. Fukubayashi,
    S. Miyakawa, T. Murakami, T. Morikawa,
    T. Morimoto, F. Yamashita, M. Wakayama
    and N. O'Hata

35. Heart rate responses of children during
    soccer play   196
    B. Drust and T. Reilly

36. Developing and acquiring football skills   201
    L. Burwitz

PART SIX   Match Analysis

37. Use of match analysis by coaches   209
    E. Olsen and O. Larsen

38. An analysis of the playing patterns of the
    Japan national team in the 1994 World Cup
    qualifying match for Asia   221
    K. Yamanaka, D.Y. Liang and M. Hughes

39. A new notational analysis system with
    special reference to the comparison of Brazil
    and its opponents in the World Cup 1994   229
    P.H. Luhtanen, V. Korhonen and A. Ilkka

40. Bivariate analysis of the repeatability of
    football offensive schemes   233
    C. Sforza, G. Michielon, G. Grassi,
    G. Alberti and V.F. Ferrario

41. Repeatability of the football penalty: a
    statistical evaluation by the Morphological
    Variation Analysis   240
    C. Sforza, S. Dunani, F. Mauro, L. Torri
    and V.F. Ferrario

42. Analysis of goal-scoring patterns of European
    top level soccer teams   246
    J. Garganta, J. Maia and F. Basto

43. A time analysis of men's and women's soccer   251
    S. Miyamura, S. Seto and H. Kobayashi

44. A method to analyse attacking moves in soccer   258
    J.F. Grehaigne, D. Bouthier and B. David

PART SEVEN   Psychology and Football Behaviour

45. Use of feedback by coaches and players   267
    I.M. Franks

46. Effects of exercise on the decision making
    of soccer players   279
    T. McMorris and J. Graydon

47. Stress management in male and female soccer
    players   285
    I.W. Maynard, M.J. Smith and L. Warwick-
    Evans

48. Improving anticipation of goalkeepers using
    video observation   290
    T. McMorris and B. Hauxwell

49. Physical play, foul play and violence in football:
Comparitive analysis of violent play among
professional soccer players in Italy and England   295
B.J. Peiser and T. Madsen

PART EIGHT   Management and Organisation

50. The expected economic effects of football
special events   301
S. Thompson

51. Issues of management and business arising
from the transformation of the soccer industry   308
E.D. Allcorn

52. The impact of 'youth training' on the stock
of 'contract professional' players in soccer in
England and Wales   314
J. Sutherland, G. Stewart and C. Wolsey

53. Comparison of Australian Rules football
and German professional soccer with regard
to planning and execution of training and
competition   321
W. Kuhn

54. Rugby's penalty problem - myth or reality?   330
C. Thomas

Index   337

Preface

The third World Congress on Science and Football was held at the Cardiff Institute of Higher Education, April 9-13, 1995. This event followed the inaugural Congress in Liverpool in 1987 and the Second Congress at Eindhoven, Netherlands four years later. In all instances the Congresses were under the aegis of the World Commission of Sports Biomechanics and in particular its Working Group on Science and Football (Chair T. Reilly). It was supported by the various football codes. These included American football, Australian Rules and Gaelic football, Rugby League and Rugby Union and Association football (soccer).

Patrons of the Congress included the International Council of Sports Science and Physical Education and the International Society of Biomechanics. The Congress was also supported by the European Society of Team Physicians in Football and endorsed by the British Association of Sport and Exercise Sciences.

The organisers of this Congress were fortunate to have generous support from Mars PLC for specific attention to football nutrition. This followed a consensus statement prior to the 1994 World Cup for Soccer by the world's leading sports nutritionists which was extended to the other football codes on the occasion of this Congress. Delegates at the Congress had opportunities to witness at first hand the excellent sports facilities at the Cardiff Institute. They were also able to see the outstanding demonstration of football in practice by the Wigan Rugby League Club, the Hollymount (Mayo) Gaelic football team, the Welsh Rugby Football Union and the Welsh F.A.

The philosophy underpinning the Congress is to bring together, every four years, those scientists whose research is directly related to football and practitioners of football interested in obtaining current information about its scientific aspects. In this way an attempt is made to bridge the gap between research and practice so that scientific knowledge about football can be communicated and applied. The Congress themes are related to all the football codes and the common threads among these are teased out in the formal presentations, workshops and seminars of the Congress programme.

Overall the Congress programme included keynote addresses, oral communications, posters, demonstrations, symposia and workshops. The detailed requirements of the scientific programme were adroitly handled by the local organiser Mike Hughes. The symposia provided a Celtic flavour to the social events which included local sports competitions.

Delegates from all over the world attended the Congress. For its five days, football in its various forms was the topic of debate until the early hours of each morning. The debate is likely to continue at the Fourth World Congress of Science and Football when it is convened at Sydney, Australia in 1999.

The papers published in this volume constitute the preceedings of the Third Congress. They represent the material, either invited addresses or formal communications, that was submitted for publication and passed successfully through the peer review process. Collectively they provide a flavour of the work currently underway in research in football and give an indication of the present state of knowledge in the area. Hopefully the content will stimulate further research into Science and Football and encourage practitioners to impliment some of the findings.

Thomas Reilly, April 1996
Chair, Steering Group on Football of the
World Commission of Sport Biomechanics
(a service group of the International
Council for Sport Science and Physical
Education and the International Society
of Biomechanics)

Introduction

This is the third volume in the 'Science and Football' series. It is a testimony to the growth of sport and exercise science which has matured sufficiently to generate a body of knowledge applicable to the football codes. Volumes 1 and 2 confirmed the growing interest in bridging the gap between the theory and practice of the various branches of football and the increased awareness of the value of a scientific approach to these games. This volume, Science and Football III, represents the Proceedings of the Third World Congress of Science and Football held at Cardiff, Wales, and provides a record of selected research reports related to the football games.

The proceedings indicate current research work in football and provide markers of the topics that researchers are currently addressing. Less than half of the contributions to the conference programme are reproduced here. Researchers either failed to meet the deadlines set by the editors or the quality control standards set for publication. The manuscripts selected for publication provide a reasonable balance of the topics covered within the Congress programme.

The book is divided into eight parts, each containing a group of related papers. This is less than in the previous volumes, although the titles of the parts have been retained where possible. Since the publication of Science and Football I and Science and Football III, it is reassuring to note the large number of citations of papers published in the series. Clearly the proceedings constitute a unique repository of data on football and footballers that would not otherwise be collated.

The papers within each Part are related by theme or disciplinary approach. In a few cases contributions cross disciplinary boundaries. A few others could sit comfortably in more than one Part and its location was based on its main theme.

The editors are grateful to the contributors for their painstaking preparation of manuscripts to comply with the publisher's guidelines and our deadlines. We are equally indebted to the office staff at Cardiff Institute of Higher Education and at Liverpool John Moores University (notably Joanna Rowlands) for their skilful assistance with word-processing. The impact of other members of the Steering Group on Science and Football (Brian Dawson and Ian Franks) in refereeing papers alongside various referees was invaluable.

It is our aim that these Proceedings should function as an up-to-date reference for researchers in football and yield important current information for football practitioners. The material may motivate others to embark on research programmes, prior to the Forth World Congress of Science and Football in Sydney, Australia, in 1999.

Thomas Reilly
Jens Bangsbo
Mike Hughes

PART ONE

Fitness Test Profiles of Footballers

A COMPARISON OF FITNESS CHARACTERISTICS OF ELITE AND NON-ELITE GAELIC FOOTBALL PLAYERS

S. KEANE, T. REILLY and A. BORRIE
Centre for Sport and Exercise Sciences, Liverpool John Moores University,
Mountford Building, Byrom Street, Liverpool L3 3AF, England.

1 Introduction

Gaelic Football is one of the national sports in Ireland. It is a field sport played by two teams of 15 players, in which a round ball may be caught and/or kicked from the ground or the hands. Comparatively little scientific data are available concerning the physiological and fitness characteristics of players at elite (inter-county) or non-elite (senior club) standards. Such information is important as it provides reference values to which coaches may compare their players' performance in training. This information can then be used to develop and monitor new training programmes. A comparison with the reference values and those attained by players may help coaches to assess the ability of their players. The motivation of the players may be increased as a result of having an exact target to aim for, i.e. to attain similar figures to those reported here.

Physiological profiles have been commonplace in a number of sports, including soccer and rugby (Reilly, 1990), both of which have common threads with Gaelic football. Useful information, for the coach, may be obtained by a comparison of results.

The aim of this study was to establish and compare a number of fitness characteristics for elite and non-elite players.

2 Methods

Between 37 to 35 inter-county players and 34 to 40 senior club players participated in this study. Because players were tested on eight different occasions during the season, while training with their county or club, the number of subjects taking part in each fitness test varied. The highest overall test value were then recorded for each subject.

Anthropometric measures included height, body mass and the body mass index. The horizontal and vertical jump tests were used as indices of "explosive" performance of the leg muscles (Clarke, 1967). The maximal oxygen uptake (VO_2 max) was estimated, in an outdoor setting, on a grass surface, from performance on a progressive 20 m shuttle run test (Leger and Lambert, 1982). Cooper's (1968) 12 min run was conducted in a outdoor setting. Subjects ran around a 500 m grass circuit, which was marked out in 20 m intervals. Subjects were informed of the elapsed time as they ran. A whistle was blown after 12 min and subjects were instructed to stop and move to the nearest marking cone. The total distance completed was then calculated for each player. The sprint test results are the mean times for the five sprints. Each sprint was a straight line 100 m run, undertaken from a standing start. Subjects had a 2 min recovery between each sprint(in which time they walked back to the starting position)and completed 5 sprints in total.

The results were analysed using multivariate analysis (MANOVA) to investigate overall differences between the two groups. The highest overall values for each subject, from the eight separate test occasions, were used in this analysis. Further analysis (univariate analysis) was also undertaken.

3 Results and Discussion

Elite players were significantly taller and had a higher body mass than their club counterparts, although the body mass index was not significantly different. This suggests a similar body build, but with the requirement of being heavier and taller to compete at elite level. This may reflect the more robust nature of competition at elite level. The poorer performances in the power tests (vertical and horizontal jump) by the club players suggest lower muscularity than that of elite players. This is further underlined by the difference in the sprint test times, with the inter-county players being significantly quicker.

The aerobic fitness, as indicated by the shuttle run and 12 min run tests were significantly higher for elite players. This suggests a higher aerobic level of fitness, which may be consistent with a higher work-rate during competition.

Table 1. Performance on selected tests for elite and club players

	Inter-county	Senior club	
Age (years)	23.5 (±4.9) n=37	26.8 (±3.9) n=40	(a)
Height (cm)	181 (±4.0) n=37	175 (±6.4) n=40	(a)
Body mass (kg)	82.6 (±4.8) n=37	76.5 (±6.7) n=40	(a)
Body mass index	25.3 (±1.5) n=37	24.9 (±1.7) n=40	
Horizontal jump (m)	2.44 (±0.2) n=37	2.28 (±0.1) n=40	(a)
Vertical jump (cm)	58.4 (±6.4) n=36	51.6 (±6.5) n=40	(a)
Estimate VO$_2$max (ml/kg/min)	54.1 (±3.2) n=37	51.4 (±5.8) n=35	(c)
Cooper's 12 min run (m)	2990 (±182) n=35	2866 (±207) n=34	(b)
Sprint test mean (s)	13.44 (±0.4) n=35	14.11 (±0.5) n=33	(a)

(a)significantly different ($P<0.001$) (b)significantly different ($P<0.01$) (c) significantly different ($P<0.05$)

Values reported by Kirgan and Reilly (1993) for Gaelic footballers playing in the English county leagues are lower than those reported here. The Irish club players had a higher VO_2 max (51.4 ml/kg/min to 47.6 ml/kg/min), horizontal jump (2.28 m to 2.10 m) and vertical jump (51.6 cm to 48.6 cm). Irish players were slightly taller (175 cm to 174 cm) and heavier (76.5 kg to 73.3 kg) than their English club counterparts. These differences reflect the systematic training and competition of players domicile in Ireland, which is not always available to English club players.

The results in this study are similar to those reported by Young and Murphy (1993) for Ulster inter-county players. The Ulster champions were smaller (178 cm to 181 cm), lighter (80.7 kg to 82.6 kg), and had a higher estimated VO_2 max during the pre-season (57.1 ml/kg/min), but a similar value during the off-season (54.1 ml/kg/min), to the elite subjects reported here. The Ulster players also had a shorter horizontal jump (2.29 m to 2.44 m).

Inter-county player, when compared to English professional soccer players are taller and heavier, and have higher values for the explosive power tests (Thomas and Reilly, 1979). This may be the result of having to compete for possession of the ball in the air as well as on the ground. The soccer players did show a higher cardiovascular fitness (Raven et al., 1976), as indicated by the VO_2 max values (54 ml/kg/min to 58.4 ml/kg/min), but a lower distance was covered by the soccer players in Cooper's 12 min run (2990 m to 2970 m).

These results are surprising when the amateur status of Gaelic football players is taken into consideration. Although Gaelic Football matches are between 20 min and 30 min shorter than soccer games, it seems that the level of fitness required to play at an elite level approaches that called for in soccer. This reflects a high degree of commitment and dedication on behalf of elite players to their sport.

4 References

Clarke, H.H. (1967) **Application of Measurement to Health and Physical Education**. Prentice-Hall, New Jersey.

Cooper, K.H. (1968) A means of assessing maximal oxygen intake correlating between field are treadmill running. **Journal of the American Medical Association**, 203, 201-204.

Kirgan, B. and Reilly, T. (1993) A fitness evaluation of Gaelic football club players, in **Science and Football** (eds T.Reilly, J.Clarys and A.Stibbe), E. and F.N. Spon, London, pp. 59-61.

Leger, L. and Lambert, J. (1982) A maximal multistage 20 m shuttle run test to predict VO_2 max. **European Journal of Applied Physiology**, 49, 1-5.

Raven, P.B., Gettman, L.R., Pollock, M.L. and Cooper, K.H. (1976) A physiological evaluation of professional soccer players. **British Journal of Sports Medicine**, 10, 209-216.

Reilly, T. (1990) Football, in **Physiology of Sports** (eds T.Reilly, N.Secher, P.Snell and C.Williams), E. and F.N. Spon, London, pp. 371-425.

Thomas, V. and Reilly T. (1979) Fitness assessment of English league soccer players through the competitive season. **British Journal of Sports Medicine**, 13, 103-109.

Young, E. and Murphy, M.H. (1993) Off season and pre-season fitness profiles of the 1993 Ulster Gaelic football champions. **Communication to BASES**, Nov. 4-7.

PROFILE OF ELITE FEMALE TOUCH FOOTBALL PLAYERS

DONNA O'CONNOR
Human Movement and Health Education, University of Sydney, 2006, Sydney.
Australia.

1 Introduction

Touch football is one of the fastest growing sports in Australia with over 180,000 registered participants in 1993 and a growth rate of 20% per annum. Despite the popularity Touch football enjoys in Australia, comparatively little scientific information is available on the fitness characteristics of the elite player. Touch football involves intermittent activity of varying intensities from walking to a sequence of forwards and backwards runs or all-out-sprints. The game consists of two 25 minute halves. The physiological fitness levels depend on the work-rate demands of the game. These demands increase as the standard of competition improves.

Australia is the leading nation in Touch football. Consequently, knowledge of the physical and physiological characteristics of Australian female Touch football players participating at an international level, will aid coaches in designing and evaluating training programmes and implementing talent identification programmes.

Australia is the World champion team, having won the previous two world titles and all Trans-Tasman tests (Australia v New Zealand). Somatotype for Australian female players was assessed at 2.9 - 3.0 - 2.2 prior to the 1993 Trans-Tasman test (O'Connor, 1993). There was no significant difference between playing position in somatotype.

The purpose of this study was to outline the fitness profile of elite female Touch football players and document their training regime prior to the World Cup.

2 Methods

A fitness assessment was conducted on the Australian Women's squad (n=25) nine weeks prior to the Third World Cup held in Hawaii in March, 1995.

Session one involved testing in the laboratory. This included height (cm), body mass (kg), sum of seven skinfolds (biceps, triceps, subscapular, suprailiac, abdominal, thigh, calf) and isokinetic assessment using the Cybex 340 dynamometer. The knee flexors and extensors were evaluated at an angular velocity of 1.05 rad/s. Gravity correction was performed prior to testing. After two submaximal repetitions and two maximal repetitions for familiarisation, the test protocol consisted of four maximal repetitions.

Session two consisted of the following field tests: 10 m and 40 m sprint using timing gates; the "defensive agility test" performed to the left and then to the right (Fig. 1); "glycolytic agility test" (O'Connor, 1992) followed by lactate testing; speed-recovery (8x7 second sprint with 23 seconds recovery; total distance in metres and fatigue decrement percent were recorded); the multistage fitness test was used to estimate the players' maximal aerobic power (Leger and Lambert, 1982). All players had 20 minutes recovery prior to the speed-recovery test and the aerobic power test.

```
    *  * Attacker           Player commences at *1 and
                            effects a 'Touch' on the
    *  *1                   attacker which indicates
                            the commencement of the test.
5 m                         The objective is for the player
                            to run backwards and then to the
       *  *                 side 5 m (L or R) as quickly as
 *L             *R          possible while keeping eye
                            contact with the attacker.
```

Figure 1. Defensive agility test.

3 Results and Discussion

Mean values and standard deviations for each test item are displayed in Table 1.

Table 1. Assessment results

	Mean	SD
Height (cm)	162.5	7.6
Body mass (kg)	56.8	4.2
Skinfolds (mm)	71.3	11.8
Age (years)	22.1	3.2
10 metres (s)	1.82	0.09
40 metres (s)	5.71	0.22
Glycolytic agility (s)	45.8	1.7
Maximum aerobic power (ml/kg/min)	50.8	3.2
Speed recovery		
Distance (m)	38	8.5
Decrement (%)	38	5.1
Knee extension peak torque (Nm)	145.8	24.1
Knee flexion peak torque (Nm)	88.5	21.9
Hamstring:Quads PT ratio (%)	60	8.0
Lactate reading (mM)	11.2	2.8

Training demands at a national level have increased as coaches require players to be fitter to execute correct strategies and minimise errors. The speed of the game has consequently increased over the years. Estimated maximal aerobic power was recorded at 50.8 ml/kg/min which was slightly lower than that found by Allen (1989) for elite Touch football players using a treadmill protocol. This figure is slightly higher than those reported for female soccer (47.9 ml/kg/min; Colquhon and Chad, 1986), hockey (47.9 ml/kg/min) and rugby (46.4 ml/kg/min, Townsend et al., 1992; 43.8-47.3 ml/kg/min, Kirby and Reilly, 1993) which all used the multistage fitness test. It must be noted that the game of Touch football (50 minutes) is shorter in duration than any of the sports listed above. Players also continually interchange every 2-4 minutes thereby only actively participating for 40-60% of the game. Consequently the players are relying on both the aerobic and anaerobic energy system. Recovery commences when the player is on the sideline rather than on the field which enables the team to maintain play at a high intensity for a longer duration.

An international or national level game of Touch football is played at a fast pace with minimum ball handling errors. The increase in skill level tends to produce strategies by coaches where they are willing to play "attacking Touch" which again increases the physical demands of the game. An attacking team aims to get the opposition back-pedalling and then strike before the opponents have time to set themselves properly in defence. Consequently speed, agility and timing are of paramount importance.

Allen (1989) found that the average distance sprinted in a game was 10 metres. Consequently speed and power are important variables for optimising performance. The results from this study show that the players are quicker than those registered by male British rugby Union players (5.8-6.4 s for 40 m, Rigg and Reilly, 1988) and similar to those of male professional soccer players (1.8 s for 10 m, Kollath and Quade, 1991). The average "glycolytic agility" result of 45.8 seconds is approximately three seconds slower than that recorded for the men's open squad. Mean lactate readings of 11.2 mM were similar for both sexes.

The speed-recovery results (38 m and 38 % decrement) suggest that players cannot maintain maximal speed over several sprints. This indicates the game would be played at a slower pace where there is more walking and jogging and less sprinting. For this reason it would be imperative that player interchanges occurred quickly and frequently. This component was identified as a main focus area for subsequent training programmes.

The Hamstring:Quadriceps torque ratio is within the recommended range according to the literature (Appen and Duncan, 1986).

4 References

Allen, G. (1989) Activity patterns and physiological responses of elite Touch players during competition. **Journal of Human Movement Studies, 17**, 207-215.

Appen, L. and Duncan, P.W. (1986) Strength relationship of the knee musculature:Effects of gravity and sport. **Journal of Orthopaedic and Sports Physical Therapy, 7(5)**,232-235.

Colquhoun, D. and Chad, K.L. (1986) Physiological characteristics of Australian female soccer players after a competitive season. **Australian Journal of Science and Medicine in Sport, 18** (3), 9-12.

Kirby, W. and Reilly, T. (1993) Anthropometric and fitness profiles of elite female rugby union players, in **Science and Football II** (eds T. Reilly, J. Clarys and A. Stibbe), E. and F.N. Spon, London, pp.27-30.

O'Connor, D. (1993) Body composition of elite Touch players. (Abstract). **International Conference of Science, Medicine and Sport**, Melbourne, October.

O'Connor, D. (1992) Glycolytic agility for rugby league and Touch. **Sports Coach, 15**(4), 8-12.

Rigg, P. and Reilly, T (1988) A fitness profile and anthropometric analysis of first and second class Rugby Union players, in **Science and Football** (eds T. Reilly, A. Lees, K. Davids and W.J. Murphy), E. and F.N. Spon, London, pp. 194-200.

Townsend, M.B., Sauers, R.J and Weiss, C.B (1992) Physical fitness evaluation of elite women rugby athletes. **National Strength and Conditioning Association Journal, 14** (5), 42-45.

FITNESS PROFILE OF PROFESSIONAL RUGBY LEAGUE PLAYERS

DONNA O'CONNOR
Human Movement and Health Education, University of Sydney,
2006, Sydney, Australia

1 Introduction

The innovative developments in coaching technology and increased training demands on Rugby League players continue to produce improvements in strength, speed, power and skills. With the introduction of the new 10 m rule in 1994 the games are being played at a faster pace than ever before. As a result there tends to be more emphasis on positional specialisation such as former half-backs being converted to hookers. For optimal performance it is necessary to identify any distinguishing characteristics related to successful play in the various positions and levels of participation. Positional differences in player profiles have been documented by Bell et al. (1993) and Rigg and Reilly (1988) for Rugby Union; Green (1992) and Puga et al. (1993) for soccer.

It is widely accepted that strength levels play an important role in successful performance. There are few studies of Rugby league where strength and power have been assessed isokinetically to determine bench marks for graded players. The purpose of this study was to develop a profile of professional Rugby League players, and secondly to examine any positional differences in these characteristics.

2 Methods

Fifty-four players from eight Australian Rugby League clubs were assessed both in the laboratory and in the field. All players competed in the 1994 season in either First grade (n=31), Reserves (n=9) or Under 21s (n=14). The players were divided into five positional categories for analysis: Backs (fullback, wing, centre; n=25); Halves (five-eight, halfback; n=5); Back-row (lock, second-row; n=10); Front-row (n=10) and Hookers (n=4).

The laboratory session incorporated anthropometric measurements of height (cm), body mass (kg) and sum of eight skinfolds (biceps, triceps, subscapular, suprailiac mid-axilla, abdominal, thigh and calf). The Cybex 340 isokinetic dynamometer was used to determine peak torque, power, total work, endurance and peak torque ratios of the knee flexors and extensors at 1.05 and 5.25 rad/s (340 User's manual). Calibration of the dynamometer was automatically administered at the beginning of each testing session. Gravity correction was performed with the knee in full extension. Following a to repetition submaximal and two repetition maximal warm up for familiarisation, the testing protocol consisted of four maximal knee flexion/extension contractions at 1.05 rad/s and 30 repetitions at 5.25 rad/s. The same procedure was administered to the opposite leg.

Field testing was conducted on a separate occasion and included a 10 metre and 40 metre sprint on grass using timing gates. The multistage fitness test (Leger and Lambert, 1982) was used to estimate maximal aerobic power (ml/kg/min).

The mean and standard deviation of each variable were determined in relation to each position. Significant differences between positions was determined using analysis of variance procedures with the Tukey method adopted when a significant F-ratio was found ($P \leq 0.05$).

3 Results

Anthropometric differences among playing positions can be observed in Table 1. The Front-row were the tallest players (184.4 cm) and together with the Back-row players were significantly taller ($P \leq 0.05$) than the Halves (163.3 cm) and Hookers (169 cm). This trend was also demonstrated when assessing body mass. The Halves were significantly lighter than the Front-rows and Back-rows ($P \leq 0.05$). There was no significant difference between playing position and sum of skinfolds.

Table 1. Anthropometric measurements (Mean and standard deviation)

Position	Height (cm)	Mass (kg)	Skinfolds (mm)
Backs	178.6 (5.1)	86.1 (5.6)	66.9 (11.3)
Halves	169.3 (3.9)	75.3 (4.8)	63.5 (10.2)
Back-row	183.6 (4.1) a,b	96.1 (3.5) a	78.6 (12.3)
Front-row	184.4 (4.5) a,b	101.4 (7.4) a,b	90.9 (11.4)
Hooker	169 (2.9)	83.2 (5.8)	76.0 (15.1)

a = significantly different from Halves
b = significantly different from Hookers

The Hooker's recorded the quickest time over 10 m (Table 2) and the highest maximal aerobic power although there was no significant difference between grade or position for these two parameters. The Backs and Halves were significantly quicker than the Front-rowers over 40m ($P \leq 0.01$).

Table 2. Field test results

Position	10 m (s)	40 m (s)	Maximal Aerobic Power (ml/kg/min)
Backs	1.79 (0.09)	5.19 (0.17)	54.4 (4.1)
Halves	1.81 (0.04)	5.23 (0.2)	50.2 (6.7)
Back-row	1.83 (0.09)	5.46 (0.21)	53.8 (2.7)
Front-row	1.89 (0.1)	5.59 (0.2) a,c	50.0 (4.7)
Hooker	1.76 (0.11)	5.42 (0.25)	55.9 (3.4)

a = significantly different from Halves
c = significantly different from Backs

As there were few positional differences when assessing the isokinetic data, Table 3 illustrates the means and standard deviations for all players. Peak torque for knee flexion (153.3 - 153.7 Nm) and extension (252.9-255.4 Nm) revealed no muscle imbalance at 1.05 rad/s. Total work output at 525 rad/s revealed that few players had any differences between dominant and non-dominant limbs.

Table 3. Isokinetic data

	Rad/s	Dominant Limb		Non-dominant limb	
		Mean	SD	Mean	SD
Flexion Peak Torque (Nm)	1.05	153.3	33.6	153.7	35.5
Extension Peak Torque (Nm)	1.05	255.4	52.5	252.9	46.8
Flexion power (W)	5.25	297.4	69.1	306.7	76.4
Extension power (W)	5.25	434.5	91.9	431.1	86.7
Flexion total work (J)	5.25	2469.3	604.7	2660.7	621.1
Extension total work (J)	5.25	3670.7	706.9	3669.3	654.8
Flex. endurance ratio (%)	5.25	65.8	19.5	62.9	21.1
Ext. endurance ratio	5.25	65.0	21.1	61.7	12.3
H:Q Peak Torque ratio (%)	5.25	62.8	12.7	64.0	19.3

4 Discussion

The data presented indicated that there are few major differences in player characteristics between the various playing positions. Results do indicate that the Front-row players were taller and heavier than other positions. The players with a higher body mass are more difficult to tackle, thereby increasing the workload of the defensive team. If this increase is due to higher skinfolds the player is disadvantaged as this constitutes an extra energy demand in moving his body around the field.

It is likely that Hookers have higher standards of aerobic fitness because of the greater work rate demands of that position (dummy half specialist, support player and so on). The mean aerobic power for all players tested (53.2 ± 4.5 ml/kg/min) was similar to British Rugby League players (Backs: 55.5 and Forwards: 52.5 ml/kg/min; Moran, 1994, unpublished data) yet below that found in soccer (59.7 ml/kg/min; Ekblom, 1986), Rugby Union (54.6 ml/kg/min; Maud, 1983) and Australian Rules (64 ml/kg/min; Douge, 1988). Although different test protocols were used, the lower maximal aerobic power values suggest that aerobic fitness may have been neglected in Rugby League training.

The fast sprint times recorded by the Hookers may be a reflection of the trend to convert Half-backs into Hookers due to the introduction of the 10 metre rule. The results of the 10 and 40 m sprints are compatible with the Backs' role of running with the ball compared to the Forwards. Interestingly, these times (5.36 ± 0.27 s) were superior to those recorded by first class British Rugby Union (5.8 s for backs and 6.38 s for forwards; Rigg and Reilly, 1988) and Rugby League players (5.67 and 5.96 s respectively; Moran, 1994, unpublished data). This is evident in the general speed of the Australian game of Rugby League.

The isokinetic assessment revealed a hamstring to quadriceps peak torque ratio of 63 - 64 % which is within the recommended range according to the literature. Players produced the greatest quadriceps torque at a knee extension angle of 117 degrees while hamstring peak torque occurred at 30 degrees at a speed of 1.05 rad/s. Appen and Duncan (1986) found that sprinters had higher H:Q ratios (66%) at 5.25 rad/s compared to distance runners (53%). This illustrates that strength profiles will vary depending on the activity, with the increased speed of todays Rugby League game, players may require ratios similar to sprinters.

5 Training Implications

The results of this study suggest that training for professional Rugby League is, to some extent, uniform for all positions. Caution should be advocated when analysing these results as currently players are generally required to complete similar training sessions regardless of their playing position. This may have influenced the uniformity of results depicted in this study. With the overall results kept in mind, training must cater for the specific demands of players so that optimal team performance can be achieved.

Strength and power are important for all playing positions. Differences in training programmes will depend on individual strengths and weaknesses and correcting any muscle imbalance. Quadriceps and hamstring strength should be improved with a continued resistance programme. Power to weight ratio needs to increase to optimise speed and acceleration. Appropriate plyometrics and resistance training will help to achieve this goal.

A greater aerobic base would be beneficial, particularly for Hookers and Halves due to their high work rates. Interval running over varying distances and different work: rest ratios are also recommended. Speed-recovery work is important for all positions. Speed is advantageous for all players with longer sprints being required by the Backs.

6 References

Appen, L. and Duncan, P.W. (1986) Strength relationship of the knee musclulative: Effects of gravity and sport. **Journal of Orthopaedic and Sports Physical Therapy**, 7, (5), 232-235.

Bell, W., Cobner, D., Cooper, S.M., Phillips, S.J. (1993) Anaerobic performance and body composition of international Rugby Union players, in **Science and Football** II (eds. T. Reilly, J. Clarys and A. Stibbe), E and F.N. Spon, London, pp. 40- 42.

Douge, B. (1988) Football: the common threads between the games, in **Science and Football** (eds T. Reilly, A. Lees, K Davids and W.J. Murphy), E and F.N. Spon, London, pp. 3-19.

Ekblom, B. (1986) Applied physiology of soccer. **Sports Medicine**, 3, 50-60.

Green, S. (1992) Anthropometric and physiological characteristics of South Australian soccer players. **The Australian Journal of Science and Medicine in Sport,** 24(1), 3-7.

Leger, L.A. and Lambert, J. (1982) A maximal multistage 20m shuttle run test to predict VO_2 max. **European Journal of Applied Physiology, 49**, 1-5.

Maud, P.J. (1983) Physiological and anthropometric parameters that describe a Rugby Union team. **British Journal of Sports Medicine, 17**, 16-23.

Puga, N., Ramos, J., Agostinho, J., Lomba, I., Costa, O and de Freitas, F. (1993) Physical profile of a first division Portuguese professional soccer team, in **Science and Football II** (eds T. Reilly, J. Clarys and A. Stibbe), E. and F.N. Spon, London, pp. 40-42.

Rigg, P. and Reilly, T. (1988) A fitness profile and anthropometric analysis of first and second class Rugby Union players, in **Science and Football** (eds T. Reilly, A. Lees, K. Davids and W.J. Murphy), E. and F.N. Spon, London, pp. 194-200.

A COMPARISON OF UPPER BODY STRENGTH IN COLLEGIATE RUGBY PLAYERS

R.J. TONG and G.L. WOOD

Cardiff Institute of Higher Education, Cyncoed Centre, Cardiff, CF2 6XD. Wales

1 Introduction

Strength is an important component of fitness for Rugby Union players. Rugby forwards who are often described as the ball winners are frequently involved in activities which demand high levels of upper body strength. The front row, second row, and back row forwards all have different physiological characteristics and positional demands. For example in the scrummage the front row players are in contact with the opposition, whereas the second row and back row forwards have to push against the front row players. The physical and physiological characteristics of rugby players have been investigated, but the component of strength has only received limited attention (Maud and Shultz, 1984; Rigg and Reilly, 1988; Holmyard and Hazeldine, 1991; Tong and Mayes, 1996). There are several different methods of assessing strength which are currently being used to test rugby players, many of which are based on the maximum number of repetitions (RM) of an exercise which can be performed before exhaustion (DeLorme and Wilkins, 1951). It is useful to know a player's repetition maximum for a wide range of activities since several strength training programmes use percentages of repetition maximum for prescribing training loads. The aim of the study was to identify if there were any significant differences between the upper body strength amongst rugby forwards and to investigate the relationship between different methods of assessing upper body strength.

2 Methods

Thirty rugby players (10 front row, 10 second row, 10 back row forwards) from the Cardiff Institute Rugby club participated in the study. The stature and body mass of the subjects were recorded and they were assessed by 11 strength related tests over a 2-week period. The tests were all preceded by a standardised warm up and all weight lifting tests used Olympic free weights (Power Sport, Llanelli). One repetition maximum bench press (1RMPress) and three repetition maximum bench press (3RMPress) were measured and the maximum number of repetitions of 80 kg bench press (80kgPress) was also assessed. One repetition maximum bench pull (1RMPull) and three repetition maximum bench pull (3RMPull) were measured and the maximum number of repetitions of 70 kg bench pull (70kgPull) was determined. One repetition maximum arm curl was determined, using a Weider arm blaster to standardise the range of movement. Right and left grip strength were assessed using a handgrip dynamometer (Takei, Japan) and back and leg strength via an adapted stiff leg "dead lift" (O'Shea, 1976). Abdominal endurance was assessed via paced sit ups (National Coaching Foundations, G.B. 1991).

To identify differences between the playing positions One Way Analysis of Variance with post-hoc Tukey tests were performed. The relationship between the strength tests was investigated using Pearson product moment correlation analysis.

3 Results and Discussion

The second row forwards were significantly taller and heavier than both the front row and back row forwards (P<0.01). The physical characteristics of the players were similar to those reported for first and second class English Rugby Union players by Rigg and Reilly (1988). Compared to the Japanese collegiate rugby players tested by Ueno et al. (1991) and previous Welsh college players (Bell, 1979), the forwards were taller and heavier. However, they were shorter and lighter than international rugby players (Bell et al.,1991; Holmyard and Hazeldine, 1991; Carlsen et al., 1994; Tong and Mayes, 1995). Overall the front row players performed better than the back row and second row forwards in nine of the eleven strength tests, although these differences were not significant (P > 0.05). The second row forwards performed better than the front row and back row forwards in the back and leg strength as well as right grip strength tests (P > 0.05). The results of the strength tests are presented in Table 1.

The bench press scores recorded for the three groups (front row, 114.0 ± 15.6 kg; second row, 100.5 ± 15.2 kg; back row, 103.5 ± 8.2 kg) were all higher than those previously recorded for US forwards by Maud (1983). When body weight was taken into account the front row lifted body weight plus 28 kg, compared to body weight plus 0.1 kg for the second row forwards and body weight plus 14.5 kg for the back row forwards. The front row forwards lifted 101.5 ± 1.2 kg, the second row 89.5 ± 11.7 kg and back row 93.5 ± 9.7 kg for the 3RMPress test. The mean value for the 30 players was higher than that reported for Welsh U21 rugby players (83.1 ± 14.4 kg) but less than the Wales senior squad (98.7 ± 13.7 kg) (Mayes and Nuttall, 1995). The front row, second row and back row forwards lifted 90.2, 89.4 and 89.3 % of their 1RMPress during the 3RMPress.The front row also outperformed the second row and back row players in the 80kgPress test. This agreed with the findings of Rigg and Reilly (1988) which showed that front row players performed more press ups than second row or back row forwards. The front row forwards outperformed both the second row and the back row forwards in the 1RM and 3RM bench pull tests, although these differences were not significant (P > 0.05). When expressed relative to body weight the front row forwards lifted body weight plus 4.8 kg, compared to body weight minus 8.2 kg for the second row forwards and body weight minus 2.0 kg for the back row forwards. A comparison of the 3RM to 1RM bench pull showed that the front row, second row and back row forwards lifted 83.7, 85.7 and 85.2 % of their 1RM bench pull score. All players were able to bench press more than they could bench pull for both the 1 RM and the 3 RM tests

Table 1. Mean (SD) physical characteristics and strength results

	Front	row	Second	row	Back	row
	Mean	SD	Mean	SD	Mean	SD
Height (cm)	179.1	5.9	190.1	3.0	183.7	5.2
Body mass (kg)	93.2	8.6	100.5	6.5	89.6	5.6
Arm curl 1RM (kg)	60.5	7.6	55.5	7.6	54.5	4.6
Back strength (kg)	185	21.7	188.5	21.7	174.5	28.3
Sit ups	70	38	70	32	78	23
Grip strength						
Right (N)	657	47	662	35	593	42
Left (N)	624	41	620	24	570	33
Bench Press						
1RM (kg)	114	15.6	100.5	15.7	103.5	8.2
3RM (kg)	101.5	12.5	89.5	11.7	93.5	9.7
80 kg reps	13	5	8	5	10	5
Bench Pull						
1RM (kg)	98	9.8	91	7.8	87.5	9
3RM (kg)	82	8.6	78	5.4	74.5	9
70 kg reps	7	3	5	2	6	4

(Table 1). The players were able to bench pull 86.9% of their 1RMPress score and 82.4% of their 3RMPress (1RMPress, 106 kg; 1RMPull, 92.0 kg; 3RMPress, 94.8 kg; 3RMPull, 78.2 kg). The second row players produced the highest scores in the back and leg strength dead lift lifting 188.5 ($\pm$ 21.7) kg compared to 185 ($\pm$ 21.7) kg for the front row players and 174.5 ($\pm$ 28.3) kg for the back row players. No significant differences existed in either the arm curl or the sit ups tests between the different playing positions and the players in this study completed 72 $\pm$ 31 sit ups, compared to 64 $\pm$ 26 sit ups previously reported for the Wales senior squad (Tong and Mayes, 1995).

For all three groups right hand grip strength was significantly better than the left grip strength ($P < 0.01$), although no significant differences existed between the three groups of players ($P > 0.05$). The grip strength of the players was lower than previously reported values for the Wales senior rugby forwards (Tong and Mayes, 1995). However, significant differences between the right and left grip strength ($P < 0.01$) agreed with the findings of Maud and Shultz (1984) and Tong and Mayes (1995).

Table 2. Correlation matrix for strength tests

	3RM Press	80kg Press	1RM Pull	3RM Pull	70kg Pull	1RM Curl	Back	Situp	Grip left	Grip righ
1RM Pres	0.98**	0.89**	0.78**	0.69**	0.67**	0.78**	0.49*	0.285	0.57**	0.46**
3RM Pres	-	0.93**	0.76**	0.69**	0.69**	0.73**	0.41*	0.17	0.53**	0.42*
80kg Press		-	0.68**	0.62**	0.64**	0.63**	0.33	0.11	0.52**	0.39*
1RM Pull			-	0.93**	0.88**	0.83**	0.58**	0.25	0.57**	0.55**
3RM Pull				-	0.93**	0.74**	0.61**	0.19	0.59**	0.57**
70kg Pull					-	0.68**	0.53**	0.2	0.46**	0.39*
1RM Curl						-	0.61**	0.44*	0.58	0.54**
Back							-	0.53**	0.59**	0.53**
Situp								-	0.2	0.201
Grip left									-	0.93**

** $P < 0.01$; * $P < 0.05$

Significant relationships existed between 1RMPress results and most of the upper body strength tests, with the exception of the sit up test ($P < 0.01$). The correlation matrix in Table 2 shows the relationships between the various strength tests. Significant relationships existed between 1RM and 3RM for both the bench press and the bench pull (r = 0.93 and r = 0.97, $P < 0.01$). Also the relationship between 1RMPress and the 80kgPress test and 1RMPull and the results of the 70kgPull test were significant (r = 0.89 and r = 0.87, $P < 0.01$). This suggests that either the 3RMPress or 3RMPull or the 70kgPull and 80kgPress tests may be used as alternatives for assessing upper body strength. This is useful since these tests are easier and quicker to administer than 1RM testing. Significant relationships also existed between grip strength for both right and left and 1 RM bench press ($P < 0.01$). This again will be useful since the time is not always available to assess rugby players using free weights.

The results of this study failed to provide evidence of significant differences for upper body strength of collegiate front row, second row and back row forwards. Nevertheless, there are relationships between different methods of assessing upper body strength.

5 References

Bell, W. (1979) Body composition of rugby union football players. **British Journal of Sport Medicine**, 13, 19-23.

Carlsen, B. R., Carter, J.E.L., Patterson, P., Petti, P., Orfanos, S.M. and Noffal, G.J. (1994) Physique and motor performance characteristics of US national rugby players. **Journal of Sports Sciences,** 12, 403-412.

DeLorme, T. and Wilkins, A.L. (1951) **Progressive Resistance Exercise**. New York, Appleton-Century-Crofts.

Maud, P.J. and Shultz, B.B. (1984) The US national rugby team: A physiological and anthropometric assessment. **Physician and Sportsmedicine,** 12, 86-99.

Mayes, R. M. and Nuttall, F. M. (1995) A comparison of the physical characteristics of senior and U21 elite rugby union players. **Journal of Sports Sciences,** 13, 13-14.

O'Shea, J.P. (1976) **Scientific Principles and Methods of Strength and Fitness**, Mass, Adison Wesley.

Rigg, P. and Reilly, T. (1988) A fitness profile and anthropometric analysis of first and second class rugby union players, in **Science and Football** (eds T. Reilly, A. Lees, K. Davids and W. J. Murphy), London, E. & F.N. Spon, pp. 194-200.

Tong, R. J. and Mayes, R.M. (1996) The effect of pre-season training on the physiological characteristics of international rugby players, in **Science and Football III**, E. and F.N. Spon, London, (this volume).

Ueno, Y., Watai, E., Ishii, K. (1988) Aerobic power and anaerobic power of Rugby Football players, in **Science and Football** (eds T. Reilly, A. Lees, K. Davids and W.J. Murphy), E. and F.N. Spon, London, pp. 201-205.

'AEROBIC' AND 'ANAEROBIC' FIELD TESTING OF SOCCER PLAYERS

K. ODETOYINBO and R. RAMSBOTTOM
Department of Sport Studies, Roehampton Institute London, West Hill, London SW15 3SN, England.

1 Introduction

During match play in soccer it is very difficult to isolate or evaluate physical performance. During a busy season, where non-professional players may only meet 2-3 times per week, the coach may wish to maximise skills development or tactical appreciation, with little time for the evaluation of physical performance. Nevertheless there needs to be some formalised assessment, for the coach to determine the effectiveness of an intervention programme, such as physical training, on player development. Incorporating sports specific testing and evaluation into an overall soccer programme may aid individualized training regimes and player motivation (Balsom, 1994). With respect to physical performance the coach would be interested in the ability of the player to maintain a high overall work rate during the game ('endurance'), speed-endurance and speed off the mark/sprinting ability. These particular physical attributes reflect the underlying physiological systems which contribute to successful soccer performance and roughly correspond to energy derived from oxidative phosphorylation (aerobic energy pathway), glycogen to lactate and degradation of phosphocreatine (PCr) (anaerobic energy pathways), respectively.

The playing season for English University soccer players runs from approximately October to March with many of the players having commenced pre-season training with outside clubs in August. Generally the pre- and early-season is characterised by predominantly 'steady rate' endurance training with the aim of building a foundation for the specific fitness requirements of the playing season. Once the season is underway (early-season) high intensity training (short sprints/shuttle runs) takes a higher priority as players require these particular fitness components in order to cope with the demands of match play. As the season progresses (mid-season) maintenance of sport specific fitness remains important. As the demands of playing and tactical preparation increase (late-season) the bulk of fitness training is orientated towards sprinting and high intensity exercise.

Rarely at club level does testing and evaluation of players' fitness take place for the purpose monitoring the effectiveness of the training programme(s) over the season. Thus the purpose of the present study was two-fold, i) to assess the effectiveness of a shift in training emphasis on physical performance during the early- and mid-season: ii) to assess indirectly, the underlying physiological energy supply processes in soccer (with particular reference to anaerobic metabolic processes) using simple equipment and field tests which are readily available to club coaches.

2 Methods

Fourteen University soccer players took part in the initial tests. Due to injury only ten completed the second battery of tests (post-training) and the results are reported here for n=10. The players comprised forwards (n=3), defenders (n=4) and midfield players (n=3). In order to control environmental conditions, all testing took place in a gymnasium with a sprung wooden floor. The order of testing was the same on each occasion and all players were well familiarised with the experimental methods used in the present study.

Anthropometric measures (mean $\pm$ SD) included age (19.6 ± 1.4 years), height (1.77 ± 0.06 m) and body mass (73.3 ± 4.7 kg) with subjects attired in athletic shorts (Seca combined stadiometer and weigh scale). Physical performance was assessed during shuttle running (over 20 metres) and sprint activity. Shuttle running consisted of two tests, a progressive shuttle run test (PST) and a high intensity shuttle run test (HIST). The PST was performed first, followed by a minimum of 45 min rest (Doherty et al., 1991), after which the HIST was performed. Performance on both PST and HIST was assessed as total distance attained (m). Heart rate was monitored using a portable telemetry device (PE 4000, Polar Electro; Finland) during both PST and HIST, the highest heart rate recorded during PST was defined as the maximum heart rate. Subjects were given 15 minutes further rest before performing three all-out sprint trials over 10 m. A full recovery (2-3 min) was allowed between sprints and the fastest trial was recorded.

Maximal aerobic power (VO_{2max}) was predicted from performance on PST (Ramsbottom et al., 1988). Values for accumulated oxygen deficit (AOD), which has been suggested as a capacity measure of the anaerobic energy supply processes (Medbo et al., 1988), were estimated from performance in a high intensity shuttle run test (HIST) (Ramsbottom, 1994). Prior to HIST a standardised warm-up was followed which consisted of 3 min jogging, 4 'strides', two 20 m shuttle runs at the subject's appropriate HIST speed and 3 min individualised stretching. A sprint distance of 10 metres was chosen to represent the typical distance a player may move to make an interception or 'close down' an opponent. Sprint times were recorded with hand-held digital stopwatches.

Following the initial testing the soccer players underwent an eight week programme of physical conditioning, after which they repeated the pre-training tests. The training programme was specifically designed to enhance the player's ability to perform high intensity exercise and short sprints.

Training over the first 4 weeks was organised around the two weekly matches, shown in Table 1. The duration of training was approximately 2 hours of which 1 hour was devoted to fitness objectives. Training was orientated around circuits with players performing various exercises with and without a ball in various 'stations' around the circuit. For the purpose of high intensity exercise, set sprints over 10-30 metres were performed with maximal effort. Players maintained an all-out effort for 45 seconds. Exercise to recovery was in the ratio 1:1.

During the last four weeks of training the same exercise stations were used; however, the exercise time decreased to 30 seconds as did the recovery periods. Speed training was also performed with the emphasis on quality of effort with complete recovery. Stations were again used to emphasise speed off the mark and agility over 10-25 m as well as speed over longer distances (25-50 m). Players worked for 4 minutes at each of 5 stations and completed 2 circuits (40 minutes in total). A mixture of exercises was again used involving work with and without a ball. Players also performed low intensity endurance exercise as part of the overall programme, particularly on 'rest days'. Careful consideration was given to the training station

Table 1. Typical weekly schedule employed during the eight week high intensity training programme during the early- and mid-season for University soccer players.

Day	Training
Saturday	Game : Inter-collegiate
Sunday	Low intensity exercise (baseline endurance training,2-3 miles)
Monday	Allocated rest day (no structured training)
Tuesday	High intensity exercise (soccer specific circuits, see methods for details)
Wednesday	Game : British University soccer league.
Thursday	Development of speed endurance and absolute speed using distances of (25-50 m) and (10-25 m) respectively, together with soccer specific circuits, (see methods for details)
Friday	Allocated rest day (no structured training)

design and soccer specific activities were used where possible. The results were analysed using a Students t-test for correlated data with a probability value of $P<0.05$ taken to indicate a significant difference between pre- and post-training values.

3 Results

Running speed on the performance tests showed no significant change during the course of the study (PST, 3.89 ± 0.15; HIST, 4.16 ± 0.19; 10 m sprint, 5.31 ± 0.27 m/s, pre-training vs. PST, 3.90 ± 0.14; HIST, 4.14 ± 0.18; 10 m sprint, 5.44 ± 0.42 m/s; post-training). Performance on the HIST increased from 498 ± 116 to 562 ± 145 m ($P<0.05$). Performance on the PST remained unchanged 2260 ± 271 vs. 2274 ± 256 m, pre- and post-training values respectively.

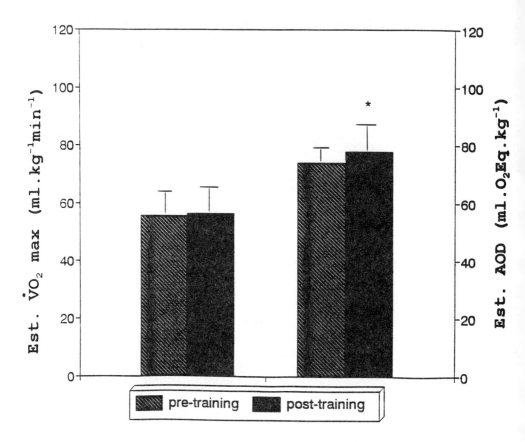

Figure 1. Estimated accumulated oxygen deficit and maximal aerobic power pre- and post-training (* significant difference between pre- and post-training means, P<0.05)

Ten metre sprint times showed no significant change over the period of the present study, 1.89 ± 0.10 s (pre-training) vs. 1.85 ± 0.15 s (post-training; NS). The increase in HIST performance led to significantly higher estimated AOD values post-training (Fig 1). Estimated VO$_2$ max values showed no change over the 8 week period. Maximal heart rates attained at the end of PST were 190±7 and 193±10 beats/min pre- and post-training respectively (NS). Similar values were recorded during HIST, 193±8 and 193±11 beats/min, pre- and post-training respectively (NS).

4 Discussion

The main finding of the present study was that HIST performance ('speed-endurance') was better after the period of training with more high intensity training. Improved HIST performance led to parallel increases in estimated AOD values. The underlying assumption is that metabolic adaptations took place within skeletal muscle during training which provided a greater energy supply from the anaerobic metabolic processes - enabling the improved post-training performance. Initial estimated AOD values were 74±3.0 ml O_2 Eq/kg, and approached similar values (approximately 80 ml O_2 Eq/kg) to those reported by Holmyard and Hazeldine (1993) in international rugby union players (threequarters/backs) after the period of high intensity training. The 12.9% increase in HIST performance and 5.4% increase in estimated AOD values in the present study were far less than those values reported by Ramsbottom et al. (1991) after a similar period of high intensity training in physically active men and women. However, the subjects in the present study were already well-trained, which would lead to a smaller proportional increase in any performance/physiological variable under consideration compared with less highly trained subjects.

There was no significant change in PST performance as a result of training. Therefore estimated maximal aerobic power was unchanged with the high intensity training regime which characterised the present study, and confirms earlier studies where VO_2 max was directly determined under laboratory conditions (e.g. Nevill et al., 1989; Sjodin et al., 1976). Although there was a suggestion that 10 m sprint times were slightly faster, after compared with before training, this difference did not attain statistical significance. The main limitation with respect to 10 m sprint times may well have been the use of a stopwatch, whereby a more sophisticated timing mechanism may be needed to detect any small improvements in short-distance sprint times.

Thus appropriate field tests, judiciously used during the season provide valuable ongoing information for the athlete involved in multiple-sprint sports such as soccer. Future developments may well see field tests which more closely mimic the activity patterns and energy demands in specific sports. Nevertheless the combination of simple field tests used in the present study would seem both valid and sensitive in monitoring any change in 'aerobic' and 'anaerobic' fitness parameters during a competitive soccer season.

5 References

Balsom, P. (1994) Evaluation of physical performance, in **Football (Soccer)** (ed B. Ekblom), Blackwell Scientific Publications, Oxford, pp. 102-123.

Doherty, M., Dunbar, J., Collins, D. J. McInnis, G. and Faulmann, L. K. (1991) Optimal recovery from an endurance task prior to the Wingate anaerobic test. **Journal of Sports Sciences**, 9, 413-414A.

Holmyard, D. J. and Hazeldine, R. J. (1993) Seasonal variations in the anthropometric and physiological characteristics of international rugby union players, in **Science and Football II** (eds T. Reilly, J. Clarys and A. Stibbe), E. and F. N. Spon, London, pp. 21-26.

Medbo, J. I., Mohn, A-C., Tabata, I., Bahr, R., Vaage, O. and Sejersted, O. M. (1988) Anaerobic capacity determined by maximal accumulated O_2 deficit. **Journal of Applied Physiology**, 64, 50-60.

Nevill, M. E., Boobis, L. H., Brooks, S. and Williams, C. (1989) Effect of training on muscle metabolism during treadmill sprinting. **Journal of Applied Physiology**, 67, 2376-2382.

Ramsbottom, R. (1994) Accumulated oxygen deficit and running performance in man. **PhD. Thesis**, Loughborough University of Technology.

Ramsbottom, R., Hazeldine, R., Nevill, A. and Williams, C. (1990) Shuttle run performance and maximal accumulated oxygen deficit. **Journal of Sports Sciences**, 8, 292A.

Ramsbottom, R., Nevill, A. M., Nevill, M. E. and Williams, C. (1991) Effect of training on maximal accumulated O_2 deficit and shuttle run performance. **Journal of Sports Sciences**, 9, 429-430A.

Ramsbottom, R., Brewer, J. and Williams, C. (1988) A progressive shuttle run test to estimate maximal oxygen uptake. **British Journal of Sports Medicine**, 22, 141-144.

Sjodin, B., Thorstensson, A., Frith, K. and Karlsson, J. (1976) Effect of physical training on LDH activity and LDH isozyme pattern in human skeletal muscle. **Acta Physiologica Scandinavica**, 97, 150-157.

FITNESS PROFILES OF ENGLISH PROFESSIONAL AND SEMI-PROFESSIONAL SOCCER PLAYERS USING A BATTERY OF FIELD TESTS

G.M.J. DUNBAR and K. POWER*
Human Performance Lab. St. Mary's University College, Strawberry Hill. TW1 4SX. UK
*Winning Edge (PEC) Ltd. 39 Earlham St, London WC2 9LD. UK

1 Introduction

Assessment of fitness profiles in elite soccer has become common in recent years. Profiles from fitness testing can be used to monitor and evaluate physical performance throughout the year, thus examining training adaptations and the efficacy of training programmes utilised. Individual fitness profiles can also be constructed to help diagnose relative strengths and weaknesses for each player and thus aid training prescription.

Much of the published data regarding fitness profiles of soccer players are laboratory, rather than field based (Reilly et al., 1988; Reilly et al., 1993; Tumilty, 1993). Many teams find that cost, travel and training time are too large a constraint to justify the use of laboratory testing. With a battery of field tests performed in a sportshall, fitness profiles for a squad of at least 15 players can be established comfortably within 90 minutes.

The battery of field tests should examine the fitness requirements of soccer. Thus flexibility, speed, speed endurance and aerobic endurance, should all be analysed in constructing valid, sport specific fitness profiles.

The purpose of this study was to examine fitness profiles of both senior and junior players from a variety of playing standards, using a battery of field tests.

2 Methods

A total of seventy soccer players all performed the battery of fitness tests, during the month of September 1993. The players were:
- (a) senior players (PS) from a Premier League Club   (n=18);
- (b) junior squad players (PJ) from the same club   (n=14);
- (c) senior players (ES) from a Division Three Club   (n=14);
- (d) junior players (EJ) from the same club   (n=12);
- (e) senior players (VS) from a Vauxhall Conference Club (n=12).

2.1 Body composition

Skinfold measurements were taken from biceps, triceps, subscapular and supra-iliac sites. Two measurements were taken from each site and the mean established, provided that there was a difference of no greater than 3 mm between measurements; in this case a third measurement was taken and the median value was used. For consistency, all skinfold measurements were taken by the same investigator. An estimation of body fat was calculated according to the equation used by Durnin and Womersley (1974).

2.2 Flexibility

A simple measure of flexibility was established by use of the sit-and-reach test, which focuses on the hamstring and lumbar regions. After a thorough warm up, subjects were allowed three attempts, holding the stretched position for a minimum of three seconds, before the value was recorded. The best of the three trials was taken as the correct value.

2.3 Speed

Running speed was assessed by electronic timing over a thirty metre distance. This has previously been shown to be an effective distance for such assessment and is suited to examination of maximal running velocity (Förenbach et al., 1986). Each player performed two trials, with the fastest value recorded.

2.4 Speed endurance

A timed 6 x 20 metre shuttle test was used to evaluate speed endurance. The test is an effective and specific means of assessment, due to the requirement of repeated acceleration throughout. Players were graded according to 30 metre sprint times and performed the test in pairs to give an element of competition.

2.5 Aerobic endurance

A progressive shuttle run to exhaustion was used as a performance test to assess aerobic endurance. This also enabled the estimation of maximum oxygen consumption (VO_2max), according to the method validated by Ramsbottom et al (1988). We have previously found this field test to be an effective means of monitoring endurance performance in games players (Dunbar and Doherty, 1991).

2.6 Statistical analysis

Results were analysed using standard descriptive statistics, whilst ANOVA was used to examine differences between subjects from different playing standards, as well as differences between junior and senior player squads. A P value of 0.05 was taken to indicate significance.

3 Results and Discussion

The fitness profiles of each group of English soccer players are summarised in Table 1.

Table 1. Fitness profiles of soccer players using a battery of field tests expressed as group means (±S.D.)

	PS (n=18)	PJ (n=14)	ES (n=14)	EJ (n=12)	VS (n=12)
Age	22.5	16.1	25.8	16.3	24.1
(years)	(3.6)	(0.6)	(4.7)	(0.4)	(3.2)
Body Mass	77.7	69.6	73.8	72.3	73.4
(kg)	(7.6)	(6.8)	(5.8)	(8.4)	(8.0)
Est. Body Fat	12.6	13.1	12.7	13.3	14.4
(%)	(2.9)	(2.6)	(3.2)	(2.9)	(2.9)
Flexibility	12.9	12.7	9.9	11.6	14.8
(cm)	(6.3)	(6.2)	(4.7)	(7.3)	(5.2)
30 m Sprint	3.94 *	4.08	4.15	4.24	3.96 *
(s)	(0.21)	(0.17)	(0.15)	(0.13)	(0.10)
6 x 20 m	22.13 *	22.81	22.86	23.07	22.44 +
Sprint (s)	(0.64)	(0.34)	(0.58)	(0.43)	(0.42)
PSR number	131.9	122.0	124.5	133.1	124.4
of shuttles	(10.8)	(11.1)	(12.1)	(20.8)	(18.9)
Est. VO_2max	60.7	58.1	58.8	61.1	58.7
(ml/kg/min)	(2.9)	(3.1)	(3.2)	(5.6)	(5.2)

* Significantly different from ES and EJ ($P<0.05$)
+ Significantly different from EJ ($P<0.05$)

No significant difference was found between any of the groups for flexibility, estimated body fat or aerobic endurance, expressed either as predicted maximum oxygen uptake, or number of shuttles in the progressive shuttle run test. The flexibility levels found here fall within the range found elsewhere for professional and amateur soccer players (Smith et al., 1994). Lack of difference between groups in the current data may be a result of the fact that flexibility is not usually viewed as an important fitness component by soccer players.

Our percent body fat data contradict findings by Brewer and Davis (1991) who found distinct differences between professional and semi-professional players. They found a body fat percentage of 11% for professional and 15% for semi-professional players. Professional Portuguese players have been shown to have body fat percentages of between 10.0-11.5% (Puga et al., 1993), whilst values of between 9 and 19% have been previously described elsewhere (Reilly, 1990).

The aerobic endurance performance gave predicted maximum oxygen consumption values similar to those seen when collected in a laboratory (Tumilty, 1993). A value of around 60 ml/kg/min seems acceptable for well trained soccer players, although individual variation is expected according to playing position. Our group data contain values for a whole squad, including goalkeepers, who typically have lower aerobic endurance. Our data also produced similar values to those seen in professional and semi-professional soccer players, using similar methodology (Brewer and Davis, 1991).

The 30 metre sprint was completed faster by the PS and VS group than the ES and EJ groups (P <0.05). This partly supports the findings of Kollath and Quade (1993), who reported that significant differences in sprinting speed existed between professional and amateur players. Within both of the professional squads, the senior players were faster than the juniors, although this difference was not significant. The 30 m sprint times for all squads, except for the ES group, were faster than the mean time recorded by a professional German squad.

In the speed endurance shuttle run test, the PS players were significantly faster than both the ES and EJ players, whilst the VS players were faster than the EJ players. This again points towards the trend of senior players being faster than junior players, with the somewhat surprising finding that, the semi-professional players were faster over 30 m than the lower standard professional players. One possible explanation for this is that some players in the VS squad choose to play in the semi-professional league, despite having both the physical and technical ability to play in professional soccer, for financial and career reasons.

4 Conclusions

It is concluded from results of a battery of field tests that professional players from a higher standard were better at the shorter run tests, than those from a lower playing standard. It was observed, however, that there was little difference in the overall fitness profiles of soccer players from a variety of standards. It was also seen that there was little difference between the fitness profiles of senior and junior players within the same club.

5 References

Brewer, J. and Davis, J. (1991) A physiological comparison of English professional and semi-professional players. Communication **to Second World Congress on Science and Football**, Eindhoven, The Netherlands.

Dunbar, G.M.J. and Doherty, M. (1991) An investigation of training effects: Multistage vs OBLA. **Journal of Sports Sciences**, 9, 413-414.

Durnin, J.V.G.A. and Womersley, J. (1974) Body fat assessed from total body density and its estimation from skinfold thickness: measurements on 481 men and women aged 16 to 72 years. **British Journal of Nutrition**, 32, 77-97.

Förenbach, R., Hollmann, W., Mader, A. and Thiele, W. (1986) Testverfahren und metabolisch orientierte Intensitats-steuerung im Sprinttraining mit submaximaler Belatungs-struktur. **Leistungssport**, 5, 15-24.

Kollath, E. and Quade, K. (1993) Measurement of sprinting speed of professional and amateur soccer players, in **Science and Football II** (eds T. Reilly, J. Clarys and A. Stibbe), E. & F.N. Spon, London, pp. 31-36.

Puga, N., Ramos, J., Agostinho, J., Lomba, I. and Costa, O. (1993) Physiological profile of a 1st Division Portuguese professional football team, in **Science and Football II** (eds T. Reilly, J. Clarys and A. Stibbe), E. & F.N. Spon, London, pp. 40-42.

Ramsbottom, R., Brewer, J. and Williams, C. (1988) A progressive shuttle run test to estimate maximal oxygen uptake. **British Journal of Sports Medicine**, 22, 141-144.

Reilly, T. (1990) Football, in **Physiology of Sports** (eds T. Reilly, N. Secher, P. Snell and C. Williams), E. & F.N. Spon, London, pp. 371-425.

Reilly, T., Clarys, J. and Stibbe, A. (1993) **Science and Football II**. E. & F.N. Spon, London.

Reilly, T., Lees, A., Davids, K. and Murphy, W.J. (1988) **Science and Football**. E. & F.N. Spon, London.

Smith, C., Donnelly, A., Brewer, J. and Davis, J. (1994) An investigation of the specific aspects of fitness in professional and amateur footballers. **Journal of Sports Sciences**, 12, 165-166.

Tumilty, D. (1993) Physiological characteristics of elite soccer players. **Sports Medicine**, 16, 80-96.

COMPARISON OF THE PHYSIOLOGICAL CHARACTERISTICS OF THE FIRST, SECOND AND THIRD LEAGUE TURKISH SOCCER PLAYERS

G. TÍRYAKÍ, F. TUNCEL, F. YAMANER, S.A. AGAOGLU, H. GÜMÜÞDAÐ and M.F. ACAR
Middle East Technical University, Faculty of Education, Department of Physical Education and Sports, Ankara, Turkey.

1 Introduction

Success in soccer is dependent upon a variety of factors. These include the physical characteristics and physiological capacities of the players, their level of skill, their degree of motivation, and the tactics employed by them against the opposition. Some of these factors are not easily measured objectively, but others can be tested by using standardized methods and can provide useful information for coaches (Mosher, 1985).

Physical and physiological characteristics of soccer players can be used by coaches to modify training programmes and to help players prepare for the game strategy. The modern game of soccer relies on the ability of all players to attack and defend whenever necessary. Therefore, it is important that all players must achieve a high level of performance in the basic skills of kicking, passing, trapping, dribbling, tackling, and heading. Because of this, it is important to analyze the physical and physiological characteristics and determine the specific requirements for optimal performance.

It may therefore be useful to analyze the physical and physiological components of professional soccer players from the different leagues. Players from the First league (MKE Ankaragücü), from the Second league (Petrolofisi), and from the Third league (Sekerspor) of Turkish professional soccer during 1992-93 were chosen as subjects for this study.

2 Methods

Measurements were performed on 16 professional soccer players from each team. This provided a total of 48 trained healthy professional soccer players (age 18-30 years), from the First, Second, and Third National leagues.

The players performed Cooper's (1978) 12 min run test on a 400 m running track. Maximum oxygen uptake (VO_2 max) was estimated by the equation of Balke (1961); $VO_{2max} = 33.3 + (x - 150) \times 0.178$ ml/kg/min, where x = the distance covered in metres.

The vertical jump test was used to determine leg muscle performance. The subject reached as high as possible with heels kept on the floor and made a mark on a board with his chalked fingers. Then he executed three jumps from a crouched position, making a mark each time on the board. The distance from the top of the highest mark was recorded. Measurement was taken to the nearest 1 cm. In order to determine the subject's leg power, the Lewis Nomogram was used (Fox and Mathews, 1988).

A hand dynamometer (Lafayette Instrument Co., Lafayette, IN, USA) was used to measure the force of the hand's muscular contraction. Maximum running speed was measured in a 50 m sprint. The subject ran 50 m on the running track and time was recorded by means of a hand chronometer. Flexibility was measured using a sit-and-reach flexibility box, the scores were recorded in mm, and were determined by the location of the fingertips. The test was done twice, the better result counting as the score.

Skinfold thicknesses were used to estimate percent body fat of subjects. The measurement was made according to the method suggested by Behnke and Wilmore (1974). The anatomical landmarks for selected skinfold sites were:- chest, subscapula, thigh, triceps, biceps, and suprailiac skinfolds. Percent body fat was determined by the equation of Green (1970). Total percent body fat (%) = (Sum of six skinfolds x 0.097) * 3.64.

All subjects were weighed on a beam balance scale without footwear, and wearing only shorts. Height was measured on a scale fitted with a sliding headpiece that was brought down to touch the top of the head.

Analysis of variance (ANOVA) was used to test for significance of differences among First, Second and Third league professional soccer teams. Differences in physical fitness variables were tested for statistical significance at 0.05 confidence level.

3 Results and Discussion

The purpose of this study was to compare the physiological and physical characteristics of Turkish professional soccer teams in different leagues (Table 1). Therefore a total of 7 physical fitness variables were recorded for the purpose of this study and test results were compared among First, Second, and Third league professional soccer teams.

Table 1. Physiological characteristics of Turkish professional players playing in different leagues

	MKE Ankaragücü First League	Petrolofisi Second League	Sekerspor Third League
Percent body fat (%)	7.6 ± 0.7	7.1 ± 0.4	7.2 ± 0.5
Height (cm)	178.8 ± 3.8	177.7 ± 3.4	178.8 ± 5.9
Body mass (kg)	*74.8 ± 6.6	69.6 ± 4.1	72.7 ± 6.5
Vertical jump (cm)	#*64.8 ± 4.6	54.1 ± 5.7	57.0 ± 7.5
VO$_2$ max (ml/kg/min)	51.6 ± 3.1	51.1 ± 2.0	51.3 ± 2.1
Lewis nomogram (W)	*1268.2 ± 74.6	1098.2 ± 108.3	1176.3 ± 147.4
50 m dash (s)	6.8 ± 0.2	6.9 ± 0.4	6.7 ± 0.2
Flexibility (cm)	28.8 ± 6.2	28.0 ± 4.6	31.1 ± 3.8
Grip strength (N)			
Right hand	499.8 ± 73.0	505.6 ± 49.0	566.4 ± 53.7
Left hand	461.1 ± 74.3	456.6 ± 54.6	516.3 ± 46.3

Mean ± SD are given
* Significant difference (P<0.05) between First and Second League players
#*Significant difference (P<0.05) between First and Third League players

The results of one-way analysis of variance (ANOVA) indicated that significant differences were found in mass, anaerobic power and grip strength of three different league professional soccer teams (P<0.05). No significant differences were found in percent body fat, height, estimated VO_2 max, 50 m dash, and flexibility in the three professional soccer teams.

In this study, the mean percent body fat and height were the same for players in the three leagues (Table 1). There were significant differences among the mean body mass values of the players of the three teams (P<0.05). The mean body mass of the First league team was significantly higher than that of the Second league team. However, there were no differences between the mean body mass of the First league team and that of the Third league team and between the mean of the Second league team and that of the Third league team (Table 1).

There were significant differences in mean vertical jump scores among the three teams (F= 13.31; P<0.05). The mean vertical jump scores of the First league team was significantly higher than those of Second and Third league professional soccer teams (P<0.05; Table 1). There was no significant difference between the means of vertical jump scores of Second and Third league soccer teams.

The vertical jump scores also were evaluated by using the Lewis Nomogram in order to estimate power output of the subjects. There were significant differences in the power production of First league and Third league teams and First league and Second league professional soccer teams (F= 8.88; P<0.05). There was no significant difference between the anaerobic power of the Second and Third league soccer teams.

The mean vertical jump values of the First league team of this study (64.8 cm) was higher than that of Konyaspor (56.7 cm; Ziyagil, 1989). Vertical jump scores of Gaelic football players were found to be 48.6 cm which was much lower than the value found in this study (Kirgan and Reilly, 1993). The Second and Third league soccer teams of this study had approximately the same mean vertical jump scores. The First league soccer team of this study did more plyometric training during the season than the teams in the other leagues, so this type of training programme could have an effect on their higher vertical jump scores.

There were no significant differences among the VO_{2max} values of First, Second and Third league players (Table 1). Mean VO_{2max} max of the Turkish National B-Youth soccer team players (48.8 ml/kg/min.) was lower than those of the three teams of this study (Gündüz, 1990). Ziyagil (1989) found in Konyaspor players similar results for VO_{2max} (51.0 ml/kg/min). Yamaner (1987) tested Gençlerbirliði junior soccer players, and he found the mean VO_{2max} to be 54.6 ml/kg/min. This was higher than those of First, Second and Third league teams of this study. This difference may have been due to the Gençlerbirliði junior soccer team's endurance type of training programme during that season.

This study showed that the VO_{2max} values for Turkish First, Second and Third league professional soccer teams were in the category of high according to Cooper's (1978) classification. The mean values of VO_{2max} found in this study were similar to those reported in the literature (50-52 ml/kg/min) for professional soccer players; however, they were much lower than the VO_{2max} of 65 ml/kg/min which is suggested for top soccer players (Puga et al., 1993; Matkavich et al., 1993; Nagahama et al., 1993 and Reilly, 1993).

One-way ANOVA revealed that there were no significant differences in 50 m dash results among the First, Second and Third league professional soccer teams. Soccer requires frequent sprints at high intensity during 90 minutes of play with short rest periods. As a result, speed as a part of physical fitness of soccer players is important. Yamaner (1987) found that the Gençlerbirliði junior soccer team had a mean 50 m dash of 6.5 s which is better than results of First, Second and Third league soccer teams of this study. Age, state of training, weight, height and body composition could have effects on speed. Sprint training is an important factor for developing speed (ATP-PC system) and muscular strength. It is suggested that the teams of this study should employ more sprint training in their programme since their 50 m dash scores are slower than that of an elite junior team.

No significant differences were obtained among the mean flexibility values of the First, Second and Third league soccer teams (Table 1). Gündüz (1990) and Ziyagil (1989) found similar mean flexibility values of the Turkish National B-Youth soccer team (28.7 cm) and Konyaspor soccer teams (28.2 cm). These results are similar to those of First league and Second league teams, but lower than that of Third league soccer team of this study. Soccer players need to have a good range of motions at the joints. Regularly scheduled programmes involving stretching exercises (2 to 5 days per week, 15 to 60 min per day) can improve flexibility within a few weeks (Fox and Mathews, 1988).

The results of this study confirm the findings obtained with transverse studies demonstrating that the performance of a team depends on factors (e.g. technical and tactical) other than physiological characteristics, because in most of the physiological capacities, there were no significant differences between three different groups of soccer players in this study. Also, it seems that physiological and physical characteristics of Turkish professional soccer players need to be developed to reach the values of world class soccer players.

4 References

Balke, B. (1961) Cardio-pulmonary and Metabolic Effects of Physical Training. **Health and Fitness in the Modern World**, The Athletic Institute and ACSM, Chicago.

Cooper, K.H (1978) The Aerobics Way. Corgi, London.

Behnke, A.R. and Wilmore, J.H. (1974) **Evaluation and Regulation of Body Build and Composition**. Englewood Cliffs, N.J., Prentice-Hall, pp. 385-86.

Fox, E.L. and Mathews, D.K. (1988) **The Physiological Basis of Physical Education and Athletics**. Brown, New York: p. 674, 422-423.

Green, H.J. (1970) **Laboratory Manual on the Principles of Measurement in Human Performance**. University of Waterloo, Canada, pp. 23-24.

Gündüz, H. (1990) Physical and physiological characteristics of 1989 Turkish National 13-Youth soccer team players (**Unpublished master's thesis, METU**).

Kirgan, B. and Reilly, T. (1993) A fitness evaluation of Gaelic football club players, in **Science and Football II** (eds T. Reilly, J. Clarys and A. Stibbe), E & F Spon, London, pp. 59-61.

Matkavich, B.R., Jankovic, S. and Heimer, S. (1993) Physiological profile of top Croatian soccer players, in **Science and Football II** (eds T. Reilly, J. Clarys and A. Stibbe), E. & F.N. Spon, London, pp. 37-39.

Mosher, R.E. (1985) Interval training: The effects of 12- week programme on elite, prepubertal male soccer players. **Journal of Sports Medicine and Physical Fitness**, 25, 84-86.

Nagahama, M., Isokawa, M., Suziki, S. and Ohashi, J. (1993) Physical fitness of soccer players affected by maximal intermittent exercise 'MIE', in **Science and Football II** (eds T. Reilly, J. Clarys and A. Stibbe), E. & F.N. Spon, London, pp. 47-52.

Puga, N., Ramos, J., Agostinho, J., Lamba, I., Costa, O. and Defreitas, F. (1993) Physical profile of a first division Portuguese professional soccer team, in **Science and Football II** (eds T. Reilly, J. Clarys and A. Stibbe), E .& F.N. Spon, London, pp. 40-42.

Reilly, T. (1993) Science and football: an introduction, in **Science and Football II** (eds T. Reilly, J. Clarys and A. Stibbe), E. & F.N. Spon, London, pp. 3-14.

Roberts, D.F. (1977) The changing pattern of adolescence age, in **Growth and Development of Physique**. (ed O.G. Eiben) Budapest, Akademisi Kiade, pp. 167-175.

Yamaner, F. (1987) Gençlerbirliði Ümit Futbol Takýmýnýn Çeþitli Fiziki Kapasitelerinin Ölçümü ve Deðerlendirilmesi". **(Unpublished Master's Thesis, Gazi University)**.

Ziyagil, A. (1989) Physical and physiological characteristics of Konyaspor professional soccer players **(Unpublished Master's Thesis, METU)**.

PHYSIOLOGICAL CHARACTERISTICS OF TURKISH FEMALE SOCCER PLAYERS

K. TAMER[*], M. GÜNAY[*], G. TÍRYAKÍ[*], I. CICIOOLU[*] AND E. EROL[*]

* Gazi University, School of Physical Education and Sports, Ankara, Turkey
** Middle East Technical University, Department of Physical Education and Sports, Ankara, Turkey

1 Introduction

The organization of the first world women's soccer cup held by FIFA in China during November 1991, also increased the popularity of soccer among Turkish women. As in other sports, at the beginning stage the first groups to become interested were female physical education students at universities. The Turkish female soccer league started for the first time in 1994 and now is continuing with growing interest throughout the country. Evaluation of elite athletes is one means of determining characteristics that contribute to performance. Besides structural aspects such as somatotype and body composition, the balance between anaerobic and aerobic power is a primary concern in soccer. Soccer is an aerobic-anaerobic sport requiring players to display great muscular power, together with the capacity to produce energy through aerobic and anaerobic metabolism. Since female soccer in Turkey is quite new, there are no data available on elite Turkish female soccer players. Therefore, the purpose of this study was to describe some structural and functional characteristics of elite Turkish female soccer players and to make comparisons with other data on female soccer players.

2 Methods

Twenty two subjects participated in this study to determine the physiological profiles of Turkish elite female soccer players during the competition season. Percent body fat was estimated from skinfolds using the formula developed by Sloan et al. (1962).

Somatotype was determined by the Heath-Carter method. Aerobic power was estimated using the Multistage 20 m Shuttle Run test and anaerobic power was obtained by using the vertical Jump Test and Lewis Nomogram. Pulmonary functions were measured by using a Vitalograph (Buckingham) spirometer. Means and standard deviations were computed by using statview 512 statistics program.

3 Results and Discussion

Table 1 shows the physiological characteristics of the Turkish elite female soccer players. The players have physical and physiological characteristics similar to those reported by Davis and Brewer (1992), Jensen (1991), Rhodes and Mosher (1991), Evangelista et al. (1992) and Tumilty and Darby (1992) for elite female soccer players. However, there are some differences in physical parameters compared to those observed within average members of the population of a similar age.

Table 1. The physiological characteristics of the female soccer players

Variables	$\bar{x}$	± SD	Range
Resting HR (beats/min)	75.2	7.6	64-80
VO_2 max (ml/kg/min)	43.15	4.06	36.42-45.60
% Body Fat	18.3	1.71	14.9-19.0
Vertical Jump (cm)	35.3	4.7	27.0-44.0
Anaerobic Power (kgm/s)	96.13	7.0	82.4-104.2
Endomorphy	4.0	0.84	2.4-5.25
Mesomorphy	3.9	1.4	1.7-6.6
Ectomorphy	2.5	0.9	1.06-4.9
Vital Capacity (l)	3.45	0.48	2.92-4.21
FVC (l)	3.55	0.43	2.91-4.16
FEV_1 (l)	3.31	0.36	2.27-3.79
MVV (l)	124.2	13.15	102-141

The mean aerobic power of the elite Turkish female soccer players was less than those of previous data of other female soccer players reported in the literature already referred to. The subjects' aerobic power was less than British (48.4 ml/kg/min), Danish (53.3 ml/kg/min), Canadian (47.1 ml/kg/min), Italian (49.75 ml/kg/min) and American (48.3 ml/kg/min) female soccer players. The anaerobic power of these elite female soccer players was intermediate, when compared with the Danish, Italian and Australian female soccer players. None of the players equalled or exceeded the average female % body fat values of 25%. Mean percent body fat of Turkish female soccer players was less than Italian (21.5%), Danish (22.3%) and Canadian (19.7) female soccer players. As in most sports, leanness is rewarded and at least a moderate preponderance of mesomorphy is necessary, but outstanding players are of moderate stature and not exceptional in terms of height or body weight. The spirometric measurements of all players are about the same as population values for the same age as reported in the Bulletin of European Physiopathology Respiration (1983).

In conclusion, the whole group compared well on body composition with other nations' female athletes, though vertical jump and anaerobic power were moderate. However,

In conclusion, the whole group compared well on body composition with other nations' female athletes, though vertical jump and anaerobic power were moderate. However, aerobic fitness was less than the other nations' trained female athletes. The intensity of female soccer competition and club training in Turkey is not yet physiologically demanding, so it seems that enthusiastic players should perform individual conditioning programmes to improve fitness.

4 References

Davis, J.A. and Brewer, J. (1992) Physiological characteristics of an international female soccer squad. **Journal of Sports Sciences**, 10,142.

European Physiopathology Respiration (1983) **Bulletin of European Physiopathology Respiration.**

Evangelista, M., Pandolfi, O., Fanton, F. and Faina, M. (1992) A functional model of female soccer players: analysis of functional characteristics. **Journal of Sports Sciences**, 10, 165.

Jensen, K. (1991) Variations of physical capacity in a period including supplemental training of the Danish national soccer team for women. **Journal of Sports Sciences**, 10,114.

Rhodes, E.C. and Mosher, R.H. (1991) Aerobic and anaerobic characteristics of elite female university soccer players. **Journal of Sports Sciences,** 10,143-4.

Sloan, A.W., Burt, J.J. and Blyth, C.S (1962) Estimation of bodyfat in young women. **Journal of Applied Physiology**, 17, 967-970.

Tumilty, D.Mc A. and Darby, S. (1992) Physiological characteristics of Australian soccer players. **Journal of Sports Sciences**, 10, 45.

PART TWO

Metabolism and Nutrition

THE PHYSIOLOGY OF INTERMITTENT ACTIVITY IN FOOTBALL

JENS BANGSBO
Copenhagen Muscle Research Center, August Krogh Institute,
University of Copenhagen, Denmark.

1 Introduction

In football the players perform many different types of exercise; the intensity can alternate at any time and range from standing still to maximal running. For example, Thomas and Reilly (1976) found that English First Division soccer players had about 1000 changes in playing activities during a match with each activity lasting for a mean duration of 5-6 s. The intermittent nature separates football from sports in which continuous exercise is performed at either a very high or moderate intensity during the entire event, such as a 400 m and a marathon run, respectively. This review will focus on the physiology of intermittent activity in soccer, but many of the aspects brought up will be transferable to other football games.

There is a large variability in the demands imposed on football players, since the activities of an individual during a match are influenced by several factors such as tactics, the importance of the game and quality of the opponent. However, examining top-class players may provide data about the physiological demands in general, as it can be expected that a certain minimum demand is placed on all players. The amount and rate of energy provided from the aerobic and the anaerobic reactions, and further, which substrates are used during a soccer match, will be evaluated in this review. It is clear that physical performance in soccer is influenced by environmental conditions such as high temperatures and high altitude. Physiological demands are also increased due to other conditions, such as playing on a muddy field or when humidity is high. In this review only matches played under "normal" conditions will be considered.

2 Aerobic energy production

There have been several attempts to determine the aerobic contribution to energy expenditure during soccer by measuring oxygen uptake ($\dot{V}O_2$) during match-play (for references see Bangsbo, 1994a). However, the values obtained are probably not representative of $\dot{V}O_2$ during match-play, since the collecting procedure interferes with normal play and only minor parts of a match are analyzed.

Another way to obtain information about the aerobic energy expenditure during soccer is by measuring heart rate (HR) continuously during a match and estimating energy expenditure from the HR-$\dot{V}O_2$ relationship determined in the laboratory. As HR measurements can be performed without any restrictions on the player, they might represent a more exact picture of the contribution of the aerobic system in soccer. Mean values of HR during a match have been observed to be between 157 and 175 beats/min (Reilly, 1986; Van Gool et al., 1988; Bangsbo 1994a).

Based on individual relationships between HR and $\dot{V}O_2$ obtained during standardised exercise in the laboratory, the HR determinations for each player during match-play can be converted to oxygen uptake (Bangsbo, 1994b). By such estimations mean values of about 75% of $\dot{V}O_2$-max have been obtained (Reilly and Thomas, 1979; Ekblom, 1986; Bangsbo 1994a). It has to be emphasized that HR determinations provide an indirect measure of the aerobic energy production and, thus, problems related to the conversion of HR to $\dot{V}O_2$ have to be considered (see Bangsbo, 1994a). It should be noted that large inter-individual differences exist in the aerobic energy production during a match due to the variety of factors influencing the exercise intensity.

3 Anaerobic energy production

3.1 Adenosine triphosphate and creatine phosphate utilisation

For elite male players the total duration of high intensity exercise during a soccer match is about 7 min, including about 19 sprints with a mean duration of 2.0 s (Bangsbo et al., 1991). Degradation of muscle creatine phosphate (CP), and to a lesser extent the stored muscle adenosine triphosphate (ATP), provides a considerable amount of energy during the intense exercise periods. As a result of the intermittent nature of the game, the CP concentration probably alternates continuously (Bangsbo, 1994a). Although the net utilization of CP is quantitatively small during a soccer match, CP has a very important function as an energy buffer, providing phosphate for the resynthesis of ATP through the creatine kinase reaction during rapid elevations in the exercise intensity.

3.2 Lactate production

Almost immediately after the onset of exercise, glycolysis in muscles appears to be activated and lactate is formed (Hultman and Sjöholm, 1983). Lactate is also produced at a high rate during intense exercise. The question is how much energy is delivered from glycolysis that ends in formation of lactate during soccer?

The concentration of lactate in the blood is often used as an indicator of the anaerobic lactacid energy production in soccer. Blood samples for analysis of lactate have mainly been obtained at half-time and after full-time, but in some studies also during match-play. An example of plasma lactate for six players at various time points during a competitive match is shown in Fig. 1 (Bangsbo, 1994a).

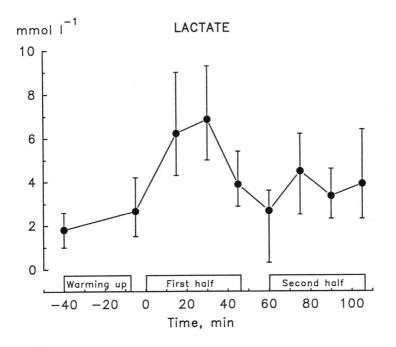

Figure 1. Arm venous plasma lactate concentration for six players before, during and after a competitive soccer match. In order to collect the samples the match was stopped for one minute twice in each half. Data are presented as means and range (from Bangsbo, 1994a).

In most studies where blood lactate has been determined during match- play a large variation in blood lactate levels has been observed, and peak values higher than 10 mmol/l have frequently been noted. In addition, determinations of blood lactate from the same player several times during a match have shown pronounced differences (Ekblom, 1986; Bangsbo et al., 1991). These findings are likely to be a result of differences in the activities before sampling, since it has been demonstrated that blood lactate measurements were related to the incidence of high intensity running prior to blood sampling (Bangsbo et al., 1991).

For various reasons single blood lactate determinations cannot be considered to be representative of lactate production during an entire match (see Bangsbo, 1994a). In general, lactate in the blood taken during match-play may reflect, but underestimate, the lactate production in a short period prior to the sampling. Therefore, based on the finding of high blood lactate concentrations in several studies, it can be concluded that lactate production during a match can at times be very high.

It is difficult to quantify lactate production during a soccer match, but a minimum value may be obtained from estimations of the rate of lactate removal from the blood and the accumulation of lactate in blood. Based on such calculations the total anaerobic energy production related to lactate release from the active muscles corresponded to about 1% of the average aerobic energy production (Bangsbo, 1994a). It has to be emphasized that this is an underestimation of the lactate production, as the lactate metabolized within the active muscles is not included in these calculations. In spite of the small contribution to the total energy turnover during a game, the anaerobic energy production is extremely important, as it provides energy at a very high rate during the periods of intense exercise in a match.

There may be large differences in lactate production between individuals, as the amount of high intensity exercise during a match is dependent on factors such as the player's motivation, the style of play, tactics and team strategy. The latter can also explain major differences between teams and between matches, e.g. higher mean blood lactate values were observed when teams used man-to-man marking compared to "zone-coverage" (Gerisch et al., 1988).

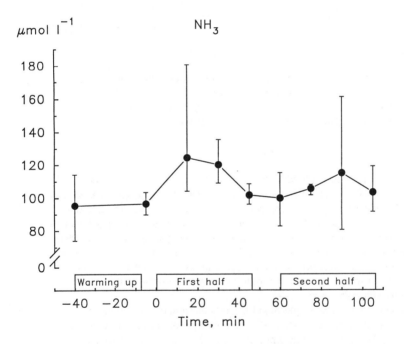

Figure 2. Venous blood ammonia and ammonium (NH_3) concentration for six players before, during and after a competitive soccer match. The players and the match are the same as referred to in Fig. 1. Data are presented as means and range (from Bangsbo, 1994a).

3.3 Ammonia, hypoxanthine and uric acid production in soccer

The concentration of ammonia and ammonium (NH_3 represents the sum of these forms) in blood was elevated during a soccer match (Fig. 2). Thus, both the muscle adenylate kinase (adenosine diphosphate (ADP) + ADP → adenosine monophosphate (AMP) + ATP) and the AMP deaminase reaction (AMP → inosine monophosphate (IMP) + NH_3) appear to be activated in soccer, indicating that the metabolic demands are very high during periods of a game. This is supported by the finding of an elevated hypoxanthine concentration during match-play, indicating that a part of the IMP produced during the intense exercise periods of match-play was dephosphorylated (Fig. 3). In addition, the concentration of uric acid in the blood was higher than at rest, which suggests that a proportion of the hypoxanthine formed is further oxidized to uric acid (Bangsbo, 1994a).

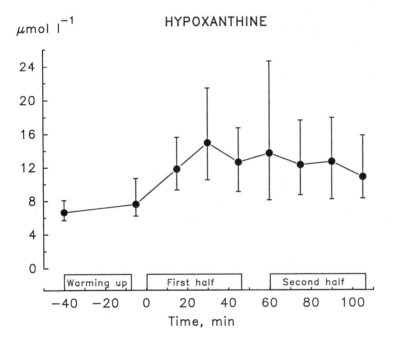

Figure 3. Venous plasma hypoxanthine concentration for six players before, during and after a competitive soccer match. The players and the match are the same as referred to in Fig. 1. Data are presented as means and range (from Bangsbo, 1994a).

4 Substrate utilization

The large aerobic energy production in soccer and the pronounced anaerobic energy turnover during periods of a match are associated with a large consumption of substrates. The dominant substrates are carbohydrate (CHO) and fat either stored within the exercising muscle or delivered via the blood to the muscles. The role of protein in metabolism in soccer is unclear, but studies with continuous exercise at a mean work-rate and duration similar to soccer play have shown that oxidation of proteins may contribute less than 10% of the total energy production (Wagenmakers et al., 1990).

4.1 Carbohydrate metabolism

The carbohydrate used during a soccer match is mainly the glycogen stored within the exercising muscles, but glucose extracted from the blood may also be utilized by the muscles.   During a competitive match the blood glucose concentrations were higher than at rest and no player had values below 4 mmol/l (Fig. 4). In addition, mean values for Swedish and Danish elite players after a match were 3.8 and 4.5 mmol/l, respectively, with a few measurements below 3 mmol/l (Ekblom, 1986; Bangsbo, 1994a). Higher values (6-7 mmol/l) were reported by Smaros (1980). Thus, it appears that the liver releases enough glucose to maintain and even elevate the blood glucose concentration during a match, and that hypoglycaemia occurs only in very rare cases.

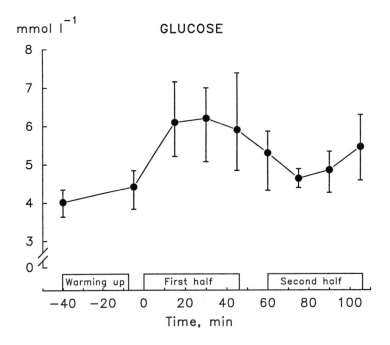

Figure 4. Venous blood glucose concentration for six players before, during and after a competitive soccer match. The players and the match are the same as referred to in Fig. 1. Data are presented as means and range (from Bangsbo, 1994a).

Information about the utilisation of muscle glycogen during a soccer match can be obtained from determinations of glycogen in muscle samples taken before and after the match. In a Swedish study the average glycogen concentrations in thigh muscles of five players were 96, 32 and 9 mmol/kg w.w. before, at half-time and after a non-competitive match, respectively (Saltin, 1973). Four other players started the same match with low muscle glycogen levels (45 mmol/kg w.w.) as a result of extensive physical exercise the day prior to the game. For these players the muscle glycogen storage was almost depleted by half-time. In a Finnish study muscle glycogen was observed to be 84 mmol/kg w.w. before a match, and it was reduced to 63 and 43 mmol/kg w.w. at half-time and after the match, respectively (Smaros, 1980). Similarly, for 15 Swedish players the glycogen concentration in the quadriceps muscle was found to be 46 mmol/kg w.w. at the end of a match (Jacobs et al., 1982). Thus, the muscle glycogen stores are not always totally emptied during a soccer match.

4.2 Fat oxidation

It has been observed that the free fatty acid (FFA) concentration in the blood increased during competitive soccer, and more so towards the end of the match (Bangsbo, 1994a). The higher FFA concentrations were associated with more frequent rest and low intensity exercise periods during the second half of the match which probably elevated the blood flow to the major adipose tissues and promoted a higher release of FFA (Bülow and Tøndevold, 1981). This, together with hormonal changes, may explain why the FFA concentration was elevated in the second half.

Despite the significant increase in the plasma FFA concentration, only a minor rise in the glycerol levels was found during a match (Bangsbo, 1994a). This suggests a high uptake of glycerol in various tissues. The most important tissue is likely to be the liver, which presumably has a larger uptake of glycerol during a match than observed during continuous exercise, due to a high blood flow to the liver in the rest periods within a game (Ahlborg and Felig, 1982). Thus, glycerol might represent a significant gluconeogenic precursor during soccer play.

The uptake of FFA and the amount of fat oxidized during a soccer match cannot be determined from the blood FFA and glycerol concentrations, as they reflect the balance between release to and removal from the blood. Furthermore, studies of repeated intense exercise bouts suggest that intramuscular triglyceride (TG) is a major source of the fat oxidized in the recovery periods in between the exercises, and thus probably also during soccer (Essen, 1978). This further complicates the determination of fat metabolism. Instead fat oxidation may be evaluated in an indirect way. The respiratory exchange ratio (R) can be determined during standardized intermittent exercise simulating the activity pattern of soccer. Under steady state conditions the R-value during the intermittent exercise may represent the non-protein respiratory quotient. Based on such determinations and HR measurements during a soccer match, the contributions from CHO and fat were estimated to be 60% and 40%, respectively, of the total oxidation. By using these numbers in combination with assumed values which seem reasonable in soccer, the total oxidation of CHO and fat during a match can be calculated. For a player with a body mass of 75 kg and a $\dot{V}O_2$-max of 60 ml/kg/min, the total oxidation of CHO and fat would be about 1140 (205 g) and 230 (56 g) mmol, respectively. It has to be emphasized that these calculations are based on several assumptions and that mean values are used, although there are likely to be large inter-individual differences.

4.3 Hormones

Various hormones have been measured in blood samples taken before and during a competitive soccer match (Bangsbo, 1994a). The insulin concentration remained at the pre-match level during the first half of the match, while it was significantly lowered in the second half. The catecholamines were elevated in the first half and they increased further in the second half, but neither the adrenaline or noradrenaline concentrations were close to values observed during maximal exercise (Kjær, 1989). Nevertheless, these hormones are likely to have had a pronounced influence on metabolism during the soccer match.

The elevated adrenaline and noradrenaline probably increased lipolysis in the adipose tissue, and thus, the release of fatty acids into the circulation (Galbo, 1983). In the first half this effect was probably counteracted by the unchanged insulin concentration and the high blood lactate concentrations (Fig. 1), which suppresses mobilization of fatty acids from the adipose tissue (Galbo, 1983). It might explain the modest increases in the FFA concentration in the first part of the match. Correspondingly, the lowered insulin and lactate concentrations in the second half (Fig. 1) and the progressively enhanced catecholamine concentrations have probably increased the FFA concentrations towards the end of the match. Also, growth hormone has a stimulating effect on lipolysis and appears to be elevated during a soccer match (Carli et al., 1984). Therefore, it is likely that the increased FFA concentration towards the end of the match was also caused by an elevated concentration of growth hormone.

The progressively increased FFA concentration during a match is probably associated with a higher uptake and oxidation of FFA by the exercising muscles (Hagenfeldt, 1979) and also with a lowered uptake of glucose. In addition, a higher utilization of muscle TG might have occurred towards the end of the match, partly as a result of the elevated catecholamine concentrations (Galbo, 1992). The lipids possibly provided an alternative fuel to blood glucose and muscle glycogen, and probably contributed to elevated blood glucose levels throughout the match (Fig. 4). In addition, a higher adrenaline level may have raised the relative rate of glycogenolysis in the muscles and, thus, limited the uptake of glucose (Chasiotis, 1983). The elevated blood glucose was probably also the result of an elevated hepatic glucose production and a decreased uptake of glucose by most tissues due to the decline in circulating insulin in the second half (Wasserman et al., 1989a). Also, a lower mean work rate in the second half may have attenuated a progressive increase in glucose uptake by exercising muscles as has been observed during long-term intermittent exercise (Essén,

1978). Other hormones might also have influenced the blood glucose level. Cortisol appears to be elevated during a soccer match, and it stimulates hepatic gluconeogenesis with amino acids as a precursor (Carli et al., 1984; Wasserman et al., 1989b). On the other hand, it is unlikely that major changes in glucagon occurred during the soccer match, as the blood glucose concentrations were high during match-play (Sotsky et al., 1989).

5 Summary

The aerobic energy cost during a soccer match can be estimated from measurements performed during or immediately after the game. Based on heart rate determinations the aerobic energy production for elite players has been estimated to be about 75% of maximum oxygen uptake. The anaerobic energy production only accounts for a minor part of the total energy production but it is very important during the intense exercise periods during a match. Muscle glycogen appears to be the most important substrate, but glucose taken up from the blood and fat, particularly towards end of a match, are also used by the exercising muscles.

6 Acknowledgements

The original data presented in this review were obtained in studies supported by grants from Idrættens Forskningsråd, Team Danmark and Danish Natural Science Foundation (11-0082).

7 References

Ahlborg, G. & Felig, P. (1982) Lactate and glucose exchange across the forearm,legs, and splanchnic bed during and after prolonged leg exercise. **Journal of Clinical Investigation,** 69, 45-54.

Bangsbo, J. (1994a) The physiology of soccer with special reference to intense intermittent exercise. **Acta Physiologica Scandinavica,** 151, Suppl. 619, 1-156.

Bangsbo, J. (1994b) The physiological demands of playing football, in **Football (Soccer)** (ed B. Ekblom), IOC/Blackwell, London, pp. 43-58.

Bangsbo J., Nørregaard L., & Thorsøe F (1991) Activity profile of competition soccer. **Canadian Journal of Sport Science,** 16, 110-116.

Bülow, J. & Tøndevold, E. (1981) Blood flow in different adipose tissue depots during prolonged exercise in dogs. **Pflügers Archives,** 392, 235-238.

Carli, G., Baldi, L., Lodi, L., Prisco, C.L., Martelli, G. & Viti, A. (1984) Hormonal and metabolic changes following a football match. Napoli, Idelson. **Estratto dal LX**, 78-79.

Chasiotis, D. (1983) The regulation of glycogen phosphorylase and glycogen breakdown in human skeletal muscle. **Acta Physiologica Scandinavica**, Suppl. 518, 1-68.

Ekblom, B. (1986) Applied physiology of soccer. **Sports Medicine**, 3, 50-60.

Essén, B. (1978) Studies on the regulation of metabolism in human skeletal muscle using intermittent exercise as an experimental model. **Acta Physiologica Scandinavica,** Suppl. 454, 1-32.

Galbo, H. (1983) Hormonal and metabolic adaptation to exercise. Thieme-Stratton, New York.

Galbo H. (1992) Exercise physiology: humoral function. **Sport Science Review**, 1, 65-93.

Gerisch, G., Rutemöller, E. & Weber, K. (1988) Sportsmedical measurements of performance in soccer, in **Science and Football** (eds T. Reilly, A. Lees, K. Davids and W.J. Murphy), E & F N Spon, London/New York, pp. 60-67.

Hagenfeldt, L. (1979) Metabolism of free fatty acids and ketone bodies during exercise in normal and diabetic man. **Diabetes**, 28, 66-70.

Hultman, E. & Sjöholm, H. (1983) Energy metabolism and contraction force of human skeletal muscle in situ during electrical stimulation. **Journal of Physiology**, 345, 525-532.

Jacobs, I., Westlin, N., Karlsson, J., Rasmusson, M. & Houghton, B. (1982) Muscle glycogen and diet in elite soccer players. **European Journal of Applied Physiology**, 48, 297-302.

Kjær, M. (1989) Epinephrine and some other hormonal responses to exercise in man: with special reference to physical training. **International Journal of Sports Medicine**, 10, 2-15.

Reilly, T. (1986) Fundamental studies on soccer, in **Sportwissenschaft und Sportpraxis** (ed R. Andresen), Ingrid Czwalina Verlag, Hamburg, pp. 114-121.

Reilly, T. & Thomas, V. (1979) Estimated daily energy expenditures of professional association for footballers. **Ergonomics,** 22, 541-548.

Saltin, B. (1973) Metabolic fundamentals in exercise. **Medicine and Science in Sports and Exercise**, 5, 137-146.

Smaros, G. (1980) Energy usage during football match, in **Proceedings 1st International Congress on Sports Medicine Applied to Football** (ed L Vecchiet), D. Guanello, Rome 11, pp. 795-801.

Sotsky, M.J., Shilo, S. & Shamoon, H. (1989) Regulation of counter-regulatory hormone secretion in man during exercise and hypoglycemia. **Journal of Clinical Endocrinology and Metabolism**, 68, 9-16.

Thomas, V. & Reilly, T. (1976) Application of motion analysis to assess performance in competitive football. **Ergonomics**, 19, 530.

Van Gool, D., Van Gerven, D. and Boutmans, J. (1988) The physiological load imposed on soccer players during real match-play, in **Science and Football** (eds T. Reilly, A. Lees, K. Davids, and W.J. Murphy), E. & F.N. Spon, London/New York, pp. 51-59.

Wagenmakers, A.J.M., Coakley, J.H. & Edwards, R.H.T. (1990) Metabolism of branched-chain amino acids and ammonia during exercise: clues from McArdle's disease. **International Journal of Sports Medicine**, 11, 101-113.

Wasserman, D.H., Spalding, J.A., Lacy, D.B., Colburn, C.A., Goldstein, R.E. & Cherrington, A.D. (1989a) Glucagon is a primary controller of hepatic glycogenolysis and gluconeogenesis during muscular work. **American Journal of Physiology**, 257, E108-E117.

Wasserman, D.H., Williams, P.E., Lacy, D.B., Goldstein, R.E. & Cherrington, A.D. (1989b) Exercise-induced fall in insulin and hepatic carbohydrate metabolism during muscular work. **American Journal of Physiology**, 256, E500- E509.

FLUID LOSS AND REPLACEMENT IN ENGLISH PREMIER LEAGUE SOCCER PLAYERS

P. D. DAVIES[1], C. B. COOKE[1] AND R. F. G. J. KING[2]

[1] Carnegie P.E. and Sports Science, Leeds Metropolitan
University. Leeds LS6 3QS, UK
[2] Division of Surgery, Leeds General Infirmary. Leeds LS1 3EX, UK

1 Introduction

It is well established that both sprint and endurance performance are limited by dehydration (Saltin *et al.*, 1988; Nielsen, 1982 and Armstrong *et al.*, 1985). It has been shown that fluid losses, totalling only a 2% reduction in body mass (i.e. 3% of body water) can reduce performance in continuous aerobic activity by as much as 20% (Saltin and Costill, 1988).

Studies that directly address the effects of dehydration upon exercise involving the patterns of intermittent high intensity effort seen in soccer, are limited. It has been concluded from studies of both sprint and endurance cycling and running, that performance of footballers will suffer from the effects of dehydration in a similar manner (Maughan and Leiper, 1994).

In addition to observations of deterioration in work output, there is also evidence to suggest that a body mass loss totalling 2% or more, can cause reductions in cognitive function (Gopinathan, 1988). Given that the ability to maintain both work output and cognitive function is paramount to optimal performance in, an observed 2% reduction in body mass can be hypothesised to cause a reduction in a footballer's competitive ability.

Measurements of fluid losses encountered during 90 minutes of soccer currently appear focused upon games played in temperate or hot conditions. Controlled research studying losses in cool (<10°C) environments is absent, as is research focusing specifically on the English game. Whilst an indication of fluid losses may be gained by reference to studies completed in Europe, the differences in both playing style and environmental conditions may significantly reduce the relevance of such data to the English player.

The aim of this study was to observe an English Premier League soccer team over a period of one month, in order to assess the fluid demands of high standard soccer played under winter conditions.

2 Methods

Subjects
Ten players from an English Premier League soccer team were studied for four matches, over a period of four weeks (1st - 28th January 1995). All subjects were members of the first team squad and were all regular first team players. Individual subject characteristics are given in Table 1.

Table 1. Player characteristics

Player	Age (Years)	Body Mass (kg)
A	20	67.1
B	29	79.6
C	23	88.1
D	26	90.9
E	30	81.1
F	25	82.0
G	33	81.3
H	20	76.3
I	30	81.1
J	27	86.6
n = 10	Mean = 26.3	Mean = 81.4
	SD = 4.4	SD = 6.6

Experimental trials
Prior to each game fluid replacement drinks (2.5% hexose plus sodium, potassium and magnesium) were prepared for each individual player. The formulation of the drink (marginally hypotonic) was such that rapid gastric emptying and rapid intestinal absorption were expected (Maughan and Noakes, 1991). The drink was supplied in plastic sports drinking bottles, after being weighed to assess volume. The quantity of fluid provided (1000-1500 ml) was in excess of that likely to be consumed. The drinking habits of each player had been determined by prior observation.

On match day each player was weighed, after voiding, in underwear one hour prior to the start of the game. After being weighed, the players were given the known quantity of fluid replacement beverage, which they were allowed to drink *ad libitum* both before the game and during the half time interval. Due to the access restrictions imposed, it was not possible to assess the volume or frequency of fluid consumption at each interval.

Upon completion of each game the players were towel-dried to remove surface sweat and then weighed in underwear. The bottles were then collected from each player and the quantity of fluid remaining was assessed by weighing. After each game the players were asked to assess the drink by the use of a short questionnaire. They were questioned about the palatability of the drink, any discomfort they may have experienced and were asked to report their feelings about the volume of drink consumed. An opportunity was also given for players to pass comment on any other aspect of their experience with the drink.

From the player and bottle weighings, calculations of body mass lost, percentage body mass lost (%BM) and fluid consumed were possible. Total body mass losses were also derived (mass lost adjusted for fluid intake) by adding fluid consumed to the difference between pre- and post-match weights.

Measurements of body mass were corrected for the wearing of underwear if appropriate. Only data for players completing a full 90 minutes were used in the subsequent analysis. This resulted in a total of seven sets of data being obtained for each match studied.

3 Results

The observations for each player for each match, match times, temperature and relative humidity (RH), can be found in Tables 2 to 5. A summary of data compiled for all four matches can be found in Table 6.

Table 2. Weights recorded 14th January (16:00 hours, 9.1° C, 93% RH)

Player	Body Mass Pre-match (kg)	Body Mass Post-match (kg)	Loss (kg)	% Body Mass Loss	Fluid Consumed (ml)	Fluid Lost Corrected (l)	% Body Mass Corrected
A	66.7	66.0	0.7	1.0	1005	1.7	2.6
B	79.2	78.3	0.9	1.1	1013	1.9	2.4
C	87.7	86.3	1.4	1.6	897	2.3	2.6
D	91.2	89.0	2.2	2.4	1012	3.2	3.5
E	81.2	79.5	1.7	2.1	1002	2.7	3.3
F	81.0	79.0	2.0	2.5	627	2.6	3.2
G	80.7	78.8	1.9	2.4	604	2.5	3.1
MEAN	81.1	79.6	1.5	1.9	880	2.4	3.0
SD	7.1	6.8	0.5	0.6	172	0.5	0.4

Table 3. Weights recorded 17th January (21:00 hours, 6.6° C, 72% RH)

Player	Body Mass Pre-game (kg)	Body Mass Post-game (kg)	Loss (kg)	% Body Mass Loss	Fluid Consumed (ml)	Fluid Lost Corrected (l)	% Body Mass Corrected
A	67.5	66.3	1.2	1.8	298	1.5	2.2
C	88.7	86.6	2.1	2.4	1009	3.1	3.5
D	91.2	89.2	2.0	2.2	941	2.9	3.2
E	81.3	79.2	2.1	2.6	927	3.0	3.7
F	82.6	80.4	2.2	2.7	803	3.0	3.6
G	81.5	79.1	2.4	2.9	549	3.0	3.6
H	76.3	74.3	2.0	2.6	966	3.0	3.9
MEAN	81.3	79.3	2.0	2.5	785	2.8	3.4
SD	7.3	7.0	0.4	0.3	245	0.5	0.5

Table 4. Weights recorded 23rd January (21:00 hours, 5.7°C, 77% RH)

Player	Body Mass Pre-game (kg)	Body Mass Post-game (kg)	Loss (kg)	% Body Mass Loss	Fluid Consumed (ml)	Fluid Lost Corrected (l)	% Body Mass Corrected
B	79.6	78.8	0.8	1.0	905	1.7	2.1
C	88.1	86.3	1.8	2.0	994	2.8	3.2
D	91.1	89.4	1.7	1.9	1469	3.2	3.5
E	81.4	79.4	2.0	2.5	812	2.8	3.5
F	83.1	81.3	1.8	2.2	482	2.3	2.7
J	86.8	85.6	1.2	1.4	1014	2.2	2.5
G	81.6	79.8	1.8	2.2	502	2.3	2.8
MEAN	85.4	82.9	1.6	1.9	883	2.5	2.9
SD	3.9	3.8	0.4	0.5	313	0.5	0.5

Table 5. Weights recorded 28th January (16:00 hours, 6.1°C, 81% RH)

Player	Body Mass Pre-game (kg)	Body Mass Post-game (kg)	Loss (kg)	% Body Mass Loss	Fluid Consumed (ml)	Fluid Lost Corrected (l)	% Body Mass Corrected
B	80.1	79.1	1.0	1.2	789	1.8	2.2
C	88.0	85.9	2.1	2.4	324	2.4	2.8
D	89.9	89.0	0.9	1.0	1374	2.3	2.5
E	80.6	79.3	1.3	1.6	998	2.3	2.9
F	81.2	79.5	1.7	2.1	546	2.3	2.8
I	81.1	80.5	0.6	0.7	256	0.9	1.1
J	86.3	85.5	0.8	0.9	961	1.8	2.0
MEAN	83.9	82.7	1.2	1.4	750	2.0	2.4
SD	3.8	3.7	0.5	0.6	371	0.5	0.6

Table 6. Mean data for all four games observed

Player	Body Mass Pre-game (kg)	Post-game (kg)	Mass Lost (kg)	(% BM)	Fluid Consumed (ml)	Fluid Lost Corrected (l)	Mass Lost Corrected (% BM)
MEAN	**82.7**	**81.1**	**1.6**	**1.9**	**824**	**2.4**	**2.9**
SD	**6.1**	**5.9**	**0.5**	**0.6**	**296**	**0.6**	**0.6**
RANGE	**24.5**	**23.4**	**1.8**	**2.2**	**1213**	**2.4**	**2.8**
(min-max.)	66.7-91.2	66.0-89.4	0.6-2.4	0.7-2.9	256-1469	0.9-3.2	1.1-3.9

A Pearson product moment correlation coefficient was used to determine if any relationship existed between fluid consumption and weight loss. No correlation was found between the amount of fluid consumed and the body weight lost or % body weight lost (r = 0.20, r = 0.15).

Responses from the post-match questionnaire revealed that no player had experienced any problem with either the palatability or the volume of the drink consumed. There were no reported instances of gastro-intestinal disturbances with the current drink, with more players commenting positively on the lack of problems associated with the specific beverage consumed.

4 Discussion

It can be seen from observation of the adjusted fluid losses in Tables 2 to 5, that with one exception (player I game 4) all values show that significant dehydration (>2% body mass loss) would have occurred had some form of fluid replacement not been implemented. However, reference to the unadjusted losses shows that in 43% of individual cases % body mass lost is less than 2%.

If it is accepted that a 2% loss in body mass will reduce performance in soccer, it can be seen that despite consuming fluid for rehydration, the performance of half of all the players may be compromised. This may not be so serious if the situation is well controlled. However, if the use of rehydration fluid is arbitrary and the attitude for replacement is laissez faire, then many of these players will be in situations, at least during some games, where their performance will suffer.

In the present study 43% of the cases that showed significant dehydration (>2% BM loss) were successfully offset by the consumption *ad libitum* of a formulated fluid replacement beverage. This group of players could be considered to be at low risk. Reduction of the risk for dehydration in all players may not be exactly predicted, but a reasonable assessment could be made from their body weight measurements and expected game conditions. In this way risk could be minimised.

If the range of both fluids consumed and % body mass lost are observed it can be seen that there is considerable inter-individual variance in both the amount of fluid consumed and mass lost. The rate at which individuals sweat is influenced by factors that include exercise intensity, ambient conditions, body mass and thermoregulatory efficiency. Because of the large variation in body mass losses seen in this study, it is suggested that any recommendations for fluid consumption be based upon the assessment of individual responses to both ambient conditions and match difficulty. The upper limit for volume of fluid replacement will also be subject to individual differences; it is therefore recommended that this should also be based upon individual observation.

5 Limitations

The study was constrained by various limitations imposed both by the nature of the subject group and the environment in which the study occurred. The ability to weigh the players any closer to the kick-off time would have been beneficial, but under the circumstances was impractical. This limitation may have had the effect of increasing the fluid loss values reported if significant voiding occurred between the weighing times and the start of the match. Players were questioned about their toilet habits prior to the game and at half time. It was reported that after the initial voiding prior to weighing, urination was attempted prior to the start of the match but not at half time. These volumes, whilst not recorded, were reported by the players to be only slight, due more to nervousness or habit than need.

6 Conclusion

When playing professional soccer in the Premier League, even in English winter condtions, there is a real danger of dehydration if fluid replacement is not implemented. Fluid losses can be offset by the consumption of fluid *ad libitum* in the majority of cases. Individual weighing and assessment of drinking habits are recommended to ensure dehydration does not reach levels where performance will be limited.

7 References

Armstrong, L.E., Costill, D.L. and Fink, W.J. (1985) Influence of diuretic-induced dehydration on competitive performance. **Medicine and Science in Sports and Exercise,** 17, 456-461.

Bangsbo, J. (1994) The physiology of soccer - with special reference to intense intermittent exercise. **Acta Physiologica Scandinavica,** 151, suppl., 619.

Ekblom, B. (1986) Applied physiology of soccer. **Sports Medicine,** 3, 50-60.

Gopinathan, P.M., Pichan, G. and Sharma, V.N. (1988) Role of dehydration in heat stress induced variations in mental performance. **Archives of Environmental Health,** 43, 15-17.

Kirkendall, D.T. (1993) Effects of nutrition on performance in soccer. **Medicine and Science in Sports and Exercise,** 25, 1370-1374.

Maughan, R.J. and Noakes, T.D. (1991) Fluid replacement and exercise stress: a brief review of studies on fluid replacement and some guidelines for the athlete. **Sports Medicine,** 12, 16-31.

Maughan, R.J. (1994) Fluid and electrolyte loss and replacement in exercise. **Sportorvosi Szemle/Hungarian Review of Sports Medicine,** 35, 83-93.

Maughan, R.J. and Leiper, J.B. (1994) Fluid replacement requirements in soccer. **Journal of Sports Sciences,** 12, S29-S34.

Murray, R. (1992) Nutrition for the marathon and other endurance sports: environmental stress and dehydration. **Medicine and Science in Sports and Exercise,** 24, S319-S323 .

Nielsen, B., Kubica, R., Bonnesen, A., Rasmussen, I.B., Stoklosa, J. and Wilk, B. (1982) Physical work capacity after dehydration and hyperthermia. **Scandinavian Journal of Sports Sciences,** 3, 2-10.

Saltin, B. and Costill, D.L. (1988) **Fluid and Electrolyte Balance during Prolonged Exercise**. Macmillan, New York.

THE INFLUENCE OF WATER INGESTION ON REPEATED SPRINT PERFORMANCE DURING A SIMULATED SOCCER MATCH

J.L. FALLOWFIELD, A.G. JACKSON, D.M. WILKINSON and J.J.H. HARRISON
Centre for Sports Sciences, Chichester Institute of Higher Education, College Lane, Chichester, West Sussex, PO19 4PE, UK

1 Introduction

Soccer is a 'multi-effort' sport where periods of moderate intensity activity or rest are punctuated by brief periods of maximum sprinting (Ekblom, 1986). The ability to maintain exercise capacity over 90 min is limited by carbohydrate availability (Ahlborg et al., 1967), and dehydration (Armstrong et al., 1985).

Losses in body mass during a soccer match, mainly through evaporation of sweat, range between 1.0 and 3.5 kg (Ekblom, 1986; Mustafa and Mahmoud, 1979). A fluid loss equivalent to ~2.0% reduction in body mass has been associated with impaired submaximal exercise performance (Armstrong et al., 1985). A high rate of fluid loss may reduce blood volume and compromise cardiovascular functioning. Maintenance of central blood pressure is prioritised over peripheral circulation, such that the capacity to dissipate heat becomes impaired and core temperature rapidly increases (Gisolfi & Copping, 1974). An increase in core temperature has been associated with elevated carbohydrate oxidation and muscle glycogenolysis (Febbraio et al., 1994). Fluid ingestion during exercise may attenuate this temperature rise (Costill et al., 1970).

In contrast to submaximal exercise performance, dehydration does not appear to reduce the ability of muscle to contract maximally (Saltin, 1964). Nerve impulse propagation (Saltin, 1964) and muscle cell membrane excitability (Costill et al., 1976) do not appear to be impaired. However, total maximal work time and blood lactate concentrations are reduced (Saltin, 1964). Thus, a dehydratory limitation to maximal exercise capacity appears to lie within the muscle cell (Saltin, 1964).

The present study examined the influence of water ingestion during a simulated soccer match on repeated maximum sprint performance.

2 Methods

Eight college soccer players (mean±SE; age 20.9±0.5 years; body mass 73.1±2.5 kg; height 177.2±3.4 cm) performed two simulated soccer matches on a non-motorised treadmill (Woodway), interfaced with an Archimedes computer. Subjects were initially familiarised with treadmill sprinting, after which the trials were performed, 7-days apart, in a counter-balanced design.

initially familiarised with treadmill sprinting, after which the trials were performed, 7-days apart, in a counter-balanced design.

On the morning of each trial subjects arrived at the laboratory after an over-night fast of 10-h and emptied their bladders before pre-test measurements were made. Nude dry body mass was measured before and after each match simulation. Subjects completed a standardised 5 min warm-up of stretching, jogging and striding, and a maximal 6 s calibration sprint on the treadmill. The simulation comprised 30 maximal 6 s sprints, each contained within a 3 min repeating cycle. Each sprint was preceded by 45 s walking, 30 s jogging, and 15 s running at percentages of pre-determined maximum sprint speed (i.e. walk 17%, jog 30%, and run 55%), and was followed by a further 30 s jogging, 45 s walking, and 9 s rest (adapted from Yamanaka et al., 1988).

Duplicate 25 µl capillary blood samples were drawn pre-match, at 15 min intervals during the match, and 5 min post-match, for determining blood glucose and blood lactate concentrations (2300 StatPlus, Yellow Springs Instruments Co. Inc.). In one trial, no fluid was ingested during the match (NW-trial). Whilst during a water ingestion (WI) trial a water bolus equivalent to 8.0 ml/kg body mass was ingested prior to the warm-up and again at half-time, with further serial feedings each equivalent to 2.0 ml/kg body mass being ingested at 15 min intervals during the match. The total volume of water ingested was recorded at the end of the WI-trial and accounted for in post-match changes in body mass. Ratings of perceived thirst were determined at 15 min intervals during both trials using a 10-point scale (1-'Very, very thirsty'; 5-'Comfortable '; 10-'Very bloated'). Heart rate was continuously recorded by short range telemetry (PE3000 Polar Sports Tester). Subjects maintained a constant training regime during the study, and refrained from heavy exercise 48-h prior to each trial. Dietary intake was also controlled over this period. Subjects itemised the foods consumed and approximate portion sizes prior to the first trial, and followed the same diet over the 48-h prior to the second trial.

Data were analysed by two-way ANOVA with repeated measures on both factors (time and treatment). A Tukey post hoc test was used to examine any differences. Significance was accepted at the $P \leq 0.05$ level.

3 Results

Maximum sprint speed was equally maintained during both trials (WI-trial: 6.86±0.11 m/s; NW-trial: 6.77±0.08 m/s), though notably, mean sprint speed was higher during the second-half in the WI-trial in comparison with the NW-trial (Figure 1). This was associated with a greater total distance covered during the 6 s sprint phases in the second-half of the WI-trial (WI-trial: 560.6±6.4 m; NW-trial: 547.1±7.1 m, $P \leq 0.01$). Total distance covered during the first and second halves of the simulation were 4418 ±58 m and 4426±56 m in the WI-trial, and 4414±56 m and 4412±56 m in the NW-trial. There was no difference between the trials in total distance covered.

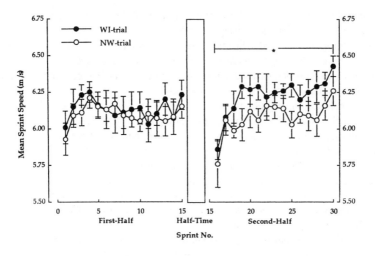

Figure 1.   Mean sprint speed (m/s) during the 6 s sprint phases of each cycle
during the water ingestion (WI) and no water ingestion (NW) trials
(mean±SE) (* denotes P≤0.05).

Body mass was maintained during the WI-trial (pre- vs post-test:72.9±2.6 kg vs 72.7±
2.6 kg). In contrast, body mass decreased by 2.3 (±0.2)% in the NW-trial (pre- vs
post-test:73.4±2.7 kg vs 71.6±2.6 kg, P≤0.01). Nevertheless, heart rate was similar
during both trials, ranging from 130±2 beats/min at the end of the stand phase to 181±
2 beats/min post-sprint in the WI-trial and from 136±2 beats/min at the end of the
stand phase to 185±2 beats min post-sprint in the NW-trial.

Blood lactate concentrations increased following the onset of exercise, and were
maintained at ~8.0 mmol/l throughout the simulation in both trials (Table 1). Blood
glucose concentrations were equally maintained during the two trials (Figure 2).
Concentrations increased through-out the first-half, but remained relatively stable
during the second-half of the simulation.

Table 1.   Blood lactate concentrations (mmol/l) during the water ingestion (WI)
and no water (NW) trials (mean±SE)

| | | First-Half (min) | | | | Second-Half (min) | | |
	Pre-	15	30	45	Pre-	60	75	90	End+5
WI	0.83	8.20	8.33	8.66	4.76	7.50	8.35	8.79	7.14
	0.06	0.76	0.72	0.67	0.34	0.52	0.75	0.66	0.67
NW	0.86	7.80	8.47	8.65	4.52	8.03	7.92	8.19	6.23
	0.06	0.60	0.90	0.76	0.40	0.85	0.76	0.72	0.90

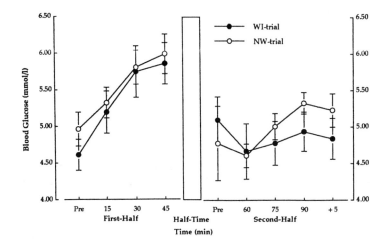

Figure 2.   Blood glucose concentrations (mmol/l) during the water ingestion (WI)
and no water (NW) trials (mean±SE).

Ratings of perceived thirst indicated that subjects were more thirsty during the NW-
trial after 30 min of the first-half (NW-trial vs WI-trial 3.3±0.3 vs 5.8±0.4, $P \leq 0.01$),
and throughout the second-half of the match simulation (90 min: NW-trial vs WI-trial
1.2±0.1 vs 5.4±0.3, $P \leq 0.01$).

Table 2.   Time spent in each movement mode during the match simulation

	Stand	Walk	Jog	Run	Sprint
Total time (s)	270	2700	1800	450	180
Percentage of total time (%)	5	50	34	8	3

4 Discussion

The main finding of the present study was that water ingestion during a simulated
soccer match did not influ-ence maximum sprint performance, but was associated
with improved sprint capacity during the second-half. The total distance covered in
the match simulations were consistent with distances estimated in the field during
match-play (Reilly & Thomas, 1976). The time spent in each movement mode as a
percentage of total match time (Table 2) is also in agreement with match-play data
(Tumilty, 1993). Furthermore, the physiological demands of the simulation, as
reflected in heart rate and blood lactate profiles, is consistent with data measured in
the field (Smith et al., 1993).

WI-trial, with greater distance covered 'at speed' in comparison with the NW-trial. This was associated with the maintenance of pre-match body mass in the WI-trial. Whereas the 2.3% reduction in body mass observed during the NW-trial has previously been associated with impaired athletic performance (Armstrong et al., 1985). Nevertheless, there were no differences in heart-rate between the trials, suggesting that cardiovascular integrity was not compromised. The maintenance of performance in the WI-trial might be due to more favourable physio-logical conditions at a muscle cell level (Saltin, 1964).

Fallowfield et al. (1995) reported elevated blood lactate concentrations at the same relative exercise intensity during a NW-trial in comparison with a WI-trial. In the present study, blood lactate concentrations were similar during the two trials. This was despite more work being done during the sprint phases in the WI-trial. Febbraio et al. (1994) reported elevated carbohydrate oxidation and muscle glycogenolysis, (i.e. enhanced glycolytic flux), when temperature regulation is compromised, as is potentially the case in a NW-trial.

In conclusion, water ingestion during a simulated soccer match maintained body mass and improved sprinting capacity in the second-half.

5 References

Ahlborg, B., Bergstrom, J., Ekelund, L-G. and Hultman, E. (1967) Muscle, glycogen and muscle electrolytes during prolonged physical exercise. **Acta Physiologica Scandinavica,** 70, 129-142.

Armstrong, L.E., Costill, D.L. and Fink, W.J. (1985) Influence of diuretic-induced dehydration on competitive running performance. **Medicine and Science in Sports and Exercise,** 17, 456-461.

Costill, D.L., Cote, R. and Fink, W.J. (1976) Muscle water and electrolytes following varied levels of dehydration in man. **Journal of Applied Physiology,** 40, 6-11.

Ekblom, B. (1985) Applied physiology of soccer. **Sports Medicine,** 3, 50-60.

Fallowfield, J.L., Williams, C., Wilson, W.M., Booth, J., Growns, S. and Choo, B.H. (1985) Effect of water ingestion on endurance capacity during prolonged constant pace running. **Journal of Sports Sciences,** 13, 26-27.

Febbraio, M.A., Snow, R.J., Hargreaves, M., Stathis, C.G., Martin, I.K. and Carey, M.F. (1994) Muscle metabolism during exercise and heat stress in trained men: effect of acclimatisation. **Journal of Applied Physiology,** 76, 589-597.

Gisolfi, C.V. and Copping, J.R. (1974) Thermal effects of prolonged treadmill exercise in the heat. **Medicine and Science in Sports and Exercise,** 6, 108-113.

Mustafa, K.Y. and El-Din Ahmed Mahmoud, N. (1979) Evaporative water loss in African soccer players. **Journal of Sports Medicine and Physical Fitness,** 19, 181-183.

Reilly, T. and Thomas, V. (1976) A motion analysis of work rate in different positional roles in professional football match-play. **Journal of Human Movement Studies,** 2, 87-97

Saltin, B. (1964) Aerobic and anaerobic work capacity after dehydration. **Journal of Applied Physiology,** 19, 114-118.

Saltin, B. (1964) Aerobic and anaerobic work capacity after dehydration. **Journal of Applied Physiology,** 19, 114-118.

Smith, M.S., Clarke, G., Hale, T. and McMorris, T. (1993) Blood lactate levels in college soccer players during match-play, in **Science and Football** (eds T Reilly, A. Lees, K. Davids and W.J. Murphy), E. & F.N. Spon, London, pp. 129-134

Tumilty, D. (1993) Physiological characteristics of elite soccer players. **Sports Medicine,** 16, 80-96.

Yamanaka, K., Haga, S., Shindo, M., Narita, J., Koseki, S. and Matsuura, Y. (1988) Time and motion analysis in top class soccer games, in **Science and Football** (eds T Reilly, A. Lees, K. Davids and W.J. Murphy), E. & F.N. Spon, London, pp. 334-340.

THE INFLUENCE OF CARBOHYDRATE INGESTION ON REPEATED SPRINT PERFORMANCE DURING A SIMULATED SOCCER MATCH

D.M. WILKINSON, J. GARNER, J.L. FALLOWFIELD and J.J.H. HARRISON
Centre for Sports Sciences, Chichester Institute of Higher Education, College Lane, Chichester, West Sussex, PO19 4PE, England

1 Introduction

Soccer involves 90 minutes of high intensity, intermittent activity (Ekblom, 1986). Distances covered range from 8 to 12 km, of which 15% may be covered sprinting (Tumilty, 1993). The average work rate during a game is estimated to be around 70% of maximum oxygen uptake (Bangsbo, 1994).

Muscle glycogen concentration may be reduced by 21-90% during the course of a game (Karlsson, 1969, cited in Ekblom, 1986; Currie et al., 1981). This may be one factor contributing to fatigue and the lower work rates reported during the second half of some games (Reilly and Thomas, 1976). This is supported by Karlsson (1969, cited in Ekblom, 1986) who found reduced work rates in those players with the lowest intramuscular glycogen levels. Furthermore, Bangsbo (1992) provided indirect evidence to support a link between pre-exercise muscle glycogen concentration and fatigue, observing that two days on a high carbohydrate diet improved intermittent running performance.

Carbohydrate (CHO) supplementation during exercise has also been shown to improve endurance running capacity by sparing muscle glycogen (Tsintzas, 1993). However, few studies have examined the influence of CHO ingestion on soccer specific performance (Kirkendall, 1988; Leatt and Jacobs, 1989), especially in a well controlled laboratory environment.

The purpose of this study was 1) to devise and validate a laboratory based simulation of the physical demands of a soccer game and 2) to investigate the influence of CHO ingestion on repeated sprint performance.

2 Methods

Eight college soccer players (mean±SE: age 20.8±0.6 years, body mass 74.5±7.3 kg, height 177.8±8.9 cm) participated in the study. After familiarisation, each player performed two simulated soccer matches on a non-motorised Woodway treadmill in a double-blind counter-balanced design.

The simulations were performed at the same time of day approximately one week apart. The treadmill was interfaced with an Archimedes computer running software that displayed the subject's current running speed and the target running speed for the simulation.

The simulation was based on the time and motion analysis of Yamanaka et al. (1988). It consisted of two 45 minute halves separated by a 15 minute rest period. Each half comprised 15 maximal 6 s sprints, contained within a 3 minute repeating cycle. Each sprint was preceded by 45 s walking, 30 s jogging and 15 s running (set at 17, 30 and 55 % respectively of maximal 6 s sprint speed which was determined after a 5 minute warm-up period) and was followed by a further 30 s jogging, 45 s walking and 9 s stand.

Prior to the first trial, subjects recorded their food intake for 3 days. The same diet was then followed for the 3 day prior to the second trial. The simulation tests were both performed after at least one day of complete rest and 3 hours after a light CHO meal.

Ten minutes before a test, and during the first 10 minutes of the 15 minute rest period, subjects ingested either 8 ml/kg body mass of an 8% glucose-polymer solution (CHO-trial) or an equal volume of a placebo solution (P-trial). The glucose-polymer consisted of 91% glucose polymer, 7% maltose and 2% dextrose (Maxim, AMS Ltd) and the placebo only water. Both drinks were flavoured with a non-caloric orange drink.

A 25 ml fingertip blood sample was taken pre-ingestion and at 15, 30, 45, 60, 75, 90 and 5 minutes post-game for analysis of blood glucose and lactate concentration using a YSI 2300 StatPlus (Y.S.I. Co. Inc.) Heart rate was recorded via short range telemetry (Polar PE3000 Sports Tester) throughout the game at the end of each 6 s sprint and 9 s stand.

The results were analysed using 2-way ANOVA with repeated measures on both factors (time and treatment). A Tukey post-hoc test was used to examine any differences and significance was accepted as $P < 0.05$.

3 Results

Table 1 shows the results of the breakdown of each movement mode for the game simulation.

Performance of the repeated 6 s sprints in the two trials is shown in Fig 1. Both maximum sprint speed (CHO-trial 6.93 ± 0.12 m/s, P-trial 6.86 ± 0.12 m/s) and mean 6 s sprint speed (CHO-trial 6.24 ± 0.11 m/s, P-trial 6.14 ± 0.12 m/s) did not differ between conditions. Also maximum and mean 6 s sprint speed did not differ between the first half (max. 6.87 ± 0.10 m/s, mean 6.16 ± 0.11 m/s)

Table 1.   Time and distance in each movement mode during the test as a percentage of the total 90 minutes

	Stand	Walk	Jog	Run	Sprint
Time (%)	5.0	50.0	33.3	8.3	3.3
Distance (%)	0.0	32.0	38.0	17.0	13.0

and the second half (max. 6.92 ± 0.14 m/s, mean 6.22 ± 0.14 m/s) of the simulation.

Blood glucose concentration was above resting concentration ($P < 0.01$) for the entire CHO-trial (Fig 2). In contrast the glucose concentration in the P-trial was only elevated above resting levels at 30 and 45 min ($P < 0.05$) and was similar to the resting level for the rest of the simulation.

Blood lactate concentration (Fig 3), mean post-sprint heart rate (CHO-trial 170 ± 2 b/min, P-trail 173 ± 4 beats/min) and mean post-stand heart rate (CHO-trial 143 ± 6 beats/min, P-trail 141 ± 5 beats/min) did not differ between conditions.

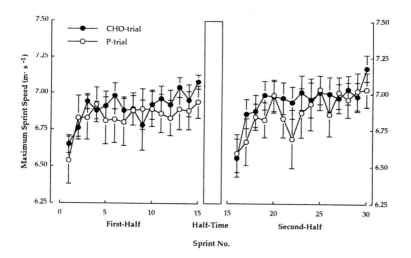

Figure 1.   Maximum 6 s sprint speed during the carbohydrate (CHO) and placebo (P) trials (mean$\pm$SE).

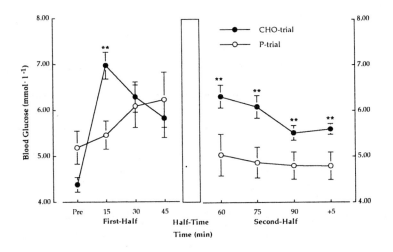

Figure 2.   Blood glucose concentrations during the carbohydrate (CHO) and placebo (P) trials (mean±SE). **P<0.01

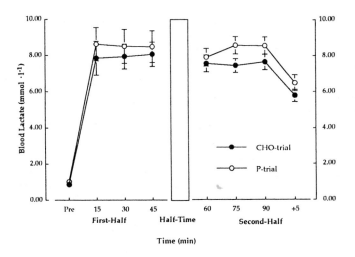

Figure 3.   Blood lactate concentrations during the carbohydrate (CHO) and placebo (P) trials (mean±SE).

4 Discussion

The first part of this study aimed to develop and validate a laboratory test simulating the physical demands of a soccer game. Table 1 shows the time and distance covered in each movement mode, which is consistent with the previous studies reported by Tumilty (1993). The total distance covered during the simulation of 9 to 10 km is also in agreement with distances reported by Ekblom (1986). The physiological responses to the simulation were similar in nature and magnitude to those reported during match-play for heart rate, blood lactate and blood glucose concentrations (Smith et al., 1993; Leatt and Jacobs, 1989).

The simulation was limited by an inability to take account of the physical demands imposed by activities such as changing direction, heading and tackling, as well as tactical considerations and competitive stress. This may partly explain the maintenance of sprint performance during the whole simulation. This is in contrast to the decrements in performance observed during the later stages of an actual game (Reilly and Thomas, 1976). Therefore the simulation should be viewed as a preliminary model for examining the physiological responses of soccer players during match-play.

The results of the study show that carbohydrate ingestion before and at half time of a simulated soccer match elevated blood glucose concentrations but did not improve repeated sprint performance. This may be a result of the maintenance of performance during the simulation, even in the P-trial, as Kirkendall (1988) has reported a 30% increase in "running distance at speed" during the second half of a game following ingestion of a 23% CHO solution. The lower CHO dosage used in this study is unlikely to explain the failure to improve repeated sprint performance. Leatt and Jacobs (1989) observed that a 7% glucose polymer solution spared muscle glycogen utilisation by 31% during a game. This would have an impact on performance when glycogen concentrations reach low levels. This does not always occur during a single game (Leatt and Jacobs, 1989), and may support the maintenance of sprint performance in both trials in the present study.

The higher post-game blood glucose concentrations in the CHO-trial will promote muscle glycogen resynthesis (Jacobs et al., 1982) and improve post-match recovery. This may prove beneficial in extra-time or during a demanding season when regular matches limit the time available for restoration of glycogen stores.

In conclusion, carbohydrate ingestion before and at half-time of a simulated soccer match elevated blood glucose concentrations but was not associated with improved repeated sprint performance.

5 References

Bangsbo, J., Norregaard, L. and Thorsoe, F. (1992) The effect of carbohydrate diet on intermittent exercise performance. **International Journal of Sports Medicine**, 13, 152-157.

Bangsbo, J. (1994) Energy demands in competitive soccer. **Journal of Sports Sciences,** 12, S5-S12.

Currie, D., Bonen, A., Belcastro , A.N., Kirby, R.L. and Sopper, M. (1981) Glycogen utilisation and circulating substrate responses during match play soccer. (Abstract) **International Journal of Sports Medicine**, 2, 217.

Ekblom, B. (1986) Applied physiology of soccer. **Sports Medicine**, 3, 50-60.

Jacobs, I., Westlin, N., Karlsson, J., Rasmusson, M. and Houghton, B. (1982) Muscle glycogen and diet in elite soccer players. **European Journal of Applied Physiology**, 48, 297-302.

Kirkendall, D.T., Foster, C., Dean, J.A., Grogan, J. and Thompson, N. (1988) Effect of glucose polymer supplementation on performance of soccer players,in **Science and Football** (eds T. Reilly, A. Lees, K. Davids and W.J. Murphy), E.& F.N. Spon, London, pp. 33-41.

Leatt, P.B. and Jacobs, I. (1989) Effect of glucose polymer ingestion on glycogen depletion during a soccer match. **Canadian Journal of Sports Sciences,** 14(2), 112-116.

Reilly, T. and Thomas, V. (1976) A motion analysis of work rate in different positional roles in professional football match-play. **Journal of Human Movement Studies**, 2, 87-97.

Smith, M., Clarke, J., Hale, T. and McMorris, T. (1993) Blood lactate levels in college soccer players during match-play, in **Science and Football II** (eds T. Reilly, J. Clarys and A. Stibbe), E.&F.N. Spon, London, pp. 129-134.

Tumilty, D. (1993) Physiological characteristics of elite soccer players. **Sports Medicine**, 16(2), 80-96.

Tsintzas, O.K. (1993) Influence of carbohydrate-electrolyte drinks on muscle metabolism and endurance running performance in man. **Unpublished PhD Thesis**, Loughborough University of Technology.

Yamanaka, K., Haga, S., Shindo, M., Narita, J., Koseki, S., Matsuura, Y. and Eda, M. (1988) Time and motion analysis in top class soccer games, in **Science and Football** (eds T. Reilly, A. Lees, K. Davids and W.J. Murphy), E.& F.N. Spon, London, pp. 334-340.

THE LIPID PROFILE OF A RUGBY UNION FOOTBALL SQUAD

C.P.O'BRIEN AND J.F.FIELDING
The Royal College of Surgeons in Ireland Department of Medicine , Beaumont Hospital, Dublin, Ireland

1 Introduction

Life expectancy rates have risen only marginally in Ireland (2.7 years) and in the U.S.A. (3.8 years) over the past 28 years (OECD, 1991). Coronary heart disease (CHD) is one of the major causes of mortality in these western societies. The Republic of Ireland has the 6th highest incidence of mortality from CHD (Shelly et al., 1991). The health benefit of exercise on risk factors for heart disease has been observed for many years (Morris and Crawford, 1958). Aerobic exercise, in particular, modifies risk factors such as high fasting blood cholesterol and abnormal lipoproteins (Wood, 1988). A prospective study of 13,000 men and women with an 8-year follow-up has shown that higher levels of exercise and physical fitness appear to delay all causes of mortality, primarily due to lower rates of cardiovascular disease and cancer (Blair et al., 1989).

Many groups of athletes have been studied to observe the benefit that their particular type of sport and exercise has on serum lipids. These have included long distance runners (Hartung 1980) cross-country skiers (Carlson, 1969) soccer players (Lehtonen and Viikari, 1974) and Australian rugby football players (Burke and Read, 1988).

Rugby union football is one of the most popular European and Antipodean field sports. The purpose of this study was to observe the cholesterol and lipid profiles of the squad (N=30) of senior Irish rugby union players.

2 Methods

Thirty rugby players who comprised the rugby squad of a Dublin Rugby Union club were evaluated during the competitive rugby season. The subjects had a mean age of 27 years with an age range of 18 to 38 years. These players were further divided into playing positions. These were: "Front Five Forwards" (N=10), playing position number 1 - 5; "Back Row Forwards and Half Backs" (N=10), playing positions number 7 - 10; and "Three-Quarters and Full Backs" (N =10), playing positions number 11 - 15.

A matched control group (N=12) was also evaluated. These control subjects were not exercising and were not involved in manual labour. Their mean age was 29 with an age range of 18 to 24 years. Signed informed consent was obtained from each of the 42 participants.

Twelve hour fasting blood samples were drawn in November of 1989. This was at the competitive period of the rugby season. Serum cholesterol was estimated by the enzymatic colorometric precipitation method. A Boehringer Mannheim kit was used. High density lipoprotein and its subfractions were determined by a standard manganese phosphate tungstic acid method following precipitation of the low density lipoprotein (LDL) and the very low density lipoprotein (VLDL) from the serum. The LDL was subsequently calculated from the Friedwald formula (Godfrey, 1989).

Aerobic fitness was estimated and body fat percent were calculated on the day the blood examples were drawn. The method of assessing aerobic fitness was the shuttle run test (Ramsbottom et al., 1988). Body fat was calculated from skinfold thicknesses (Durnin and Womersley, 1974) determined by means of Harpenden calipers.

The "frequency" of exercise was recorded as was the number of "years involved" in training and playing competitive rugby by interviewing the players.

The duration of exercise was recorded by noting the actual time in training. Rugby union training sessions are "stop start". In the main, the training involved running and practising unopposed plays. These were punctuated by coach intervention and team talks. The training sessions were timed and the actual time in exercise was noted and taken to be the "training exercise duration." The games were also observed, the actual time the ball was "in play" was timed by a stop watch - this was taken to be the "game exercise duration". Ten games and ten training sessions were observed.

The student t-test was the method used to evaluate the cholesterol and lipoprotein data.

3 Results

The results of the study showed that the mean fasting cholesterol level of the rugby players was 4.4 ± 0.53 mmol/l. The mean fasting cholesterol level of the control group was 4.75 ± 0.70 mmol/l (Table 1). Both these cholesterol levels were within the normal range.

The mean HDL level of the rugby players was 1.47 ± 0.44 mmol/l. The mean HDL level for the control group was 1.07 ± 0.23 mmol/l. The mean HDL of the rugby players was greater than the normal range and greater than the control group ($P < 0.005$)

The "risk ratio" (which is the ratio of HDL to total cholesterol) was calculated. The normal range for this ratio is 3.8 - 5.9 Values below this are considered to be "favourable" and above this range are considered to be "unfavourable". The mean rugby player "risk ratio" was "favourable" at 2.99 ± 0.91. The control group had a "standard" risk ratio at 4.44 ± 1.40. When the rugby players were considered by playing positions, the mean values also placed each playing position group in the "favourable" range.

The mean HDL2 level of the rugby players was 0.30 ± 0.19 mmol/l. This is in the upper range of the normal value which is 0.13 to 0.59 mmol/l and was greater than the control group 0.22 ± 0.08 mmol/l (see Table 1).

Table 1. Cholesterol and lipoprotein profiles of Rugby player and control groups

	Cholesterol mmol / l	HDL mmol / l	C/HDL ratio mmol / l	HDL2
Players	4.4 ±0.53	1.47 ± 0.44	2.99 ± 0.91	0.30 ± 0.19
Control	4.75± 0.70	1.07 ±0.23	4.44 ±1.4	0.22 ± 0.08
Normal range	3.5 -5.9	0.9 -1.4	3.8 -5.9	0.13 -0.39

The physiological characteristics of the 30 rugby players showed that they had a mean estimated maximun oxygen uptake (VO$_2$ max) of 45.3 ml/kg/min. The "Front Five Forwards" had a mean of 42.2 ± 4.5 ml/kg/min. The "Back Row Forwards and Half Backs" had a mean value of 45.8 ± 5.9 ml/kg/min; and the "Three-Quarters and Full Backs" had a value of 47.7 ± 4.7 ml/kg/min (see Table 2).

The estimated body fat percentage values for the three player subgroups were 21% ± 3; 19% ± 3 and 16% ± 3, respectively,with a mean of 18.7% (see Table 2). The frequency of exercise participation was three sessions a week. All trained with the rugby club on Tuesday and Thursday evenings and played one match on the weekend.

The duration of exercise was 27 minutes for game duration and 25 minutes for training duration. The apparent short duration is due to the "stop start" nature of rugby football. The game duration data concur with previous studies, Reilly (1990) noting that the ball was actually in play for less than 30 minutes of the 80 minute play period. In a similar way, training also had a "stop start" pattern due to re-formation after ruck and maul break-down.

The mean participation period in Rugby Union Football was eight years with a range of fifteen years to four years (see Table 2).

Table 2. Exercise characteristics of the rugby players

VO$_2$ max (ml/kg/min)	Body fat %	Frequency	Duration (min)
45.3	18.7%	3 sessions weekly	25-27

3 Discussion

The value of exercise in modifying cardiac risk factors is well established. Vigorous habitual exercise is known to reduce body weight, percent body fat and results in elevation of the protective HDL and HDL2 lipoprotein subfraction (Wood, 1988). The effect of exercise on fasting cholesterol levels is less significant.

The rugby playing population showed a beneficial cholesterol and lipoprotein profile. This was similar to other field athletes such as the Australian Rules Football players (Burke and Read, 1988) and soccer players (Lehtonen and Viikari, 1978).

The serum cholesterol level was 4.6 - 0.51, which is below the critical level of 5.2 mmol/l, defined by Pekkanen (1990). Individuals with fasting levels below this value are deemed to have a more favourable cardiac risk profile. The control group had a similar result. The rugby players' cholesterol results were similar to the Australian Rules Football players' 4.8 mmol/l (Burke and Read, 1988).

High HDL levels has been shown to have an inverse relationship with coronary heart disease (Hubert et al., 1983). The rugby players had a mean HDL value of 1.47 ± 0.4 mmol/l. This was greater than the normal range and was significantly greater than the control group, 1.07 ± 0.2 mmol/l (P < 0.005). This finding has been previously observed in a group of endurance trained athletes who consistently had higher HDL concentrations than matched controls (Haskell, 1984). Elevated HDL has also been reported in long distance runners

(Hartung, 1980), cross-country skiers (Carlson, 1964), soccer players (Lehtonen and Viikari, 1978)and tennis players (Vodac, 1980).

The high density lipoprotein subfraction 2 (HDL2) is the lipoprotein subfraction which has the most powerfully inverse relationship with the presence and severity of coronary artery disease (Northcote, 1994). Elevated HDL2 levels have been observed in various sporting groups including retired endurance runners (Nortecote et al., 1988), athletes (Haskell 1984), and sedentary men who commenced an exercise programme (Wood, 1988). The rugby players showed a mean HDL2 level of 0.30 ± 0.19 mmol/l, which was in the high normal range, and was elevated when compared to the control group, 0.22 ± 0.08 mmol/l, highlighting the benefit of this particular type of exercise programme.

The rugby players had an abnormally high body fat percentage of $18.7 \pm 3\%$. The normal range for males in this age group is 13-14% (Wilmore and Costill,1994). Favourable lipoproteins have been observed in athletic groups who have lower body fat percentage such as Australian Rules Football players (Burke and Read, 1988). The subjects in this group had favourable lipoprotein profiles despite a high mean estimated body fat percentage.

The lipoprotein profile appears to be related to the training regime. Players engaged in 25-27 minutes of "stop start" competitive aerobic exercise three days a week for an eight year period. The season starts in July and ends in March and is continuous for 39 weeks. The rugby players appear to have derived their beneficial profile from the prolonged period involved in formal exercise , thus the "volume" of exercise was high. High volumes of exercise have been suggested as a more critical element in health promoting fitness programmes, and as a means of improving lipoprotein profiles (Gaesser and Rich ,1984).

This exercise regime which is common to all European rugby teams delivers a mode, frequency and duration of exercise which has been recommended for health benefit. While the fitness profiles of the rugby players were not of an extremely high level, it was sufficient to produce a healthy lipid profile and lessen the risk of coronary artery disease.

4 References

Blair, S.N., Kohl, H.W., Parffenburger R.S., Clarke D.G., Cooper K.H. and Gibbons, L.W. (1989) Physical fitness and the cause of mortality. Prospective study of healthy men and women. **Journal of the American Medical Association,** 262, 2395-2401.

Burke, L.M., and Read, R.S.D. (1988) A study of dietary patterns of elite Australian Football players. **Canadian Journal of Sports Science,** 13, 15-19.

Carlson, J. (1969) Acute effects of prolonged exercise on the concentration of lipid lipoproteins in man. **Acta Physiologica Scandinavica,** 62, 51-59.

Durnin, J.V.G.A. and Womersley, J. (1974) Body fat assessed from total body density and its estimation from skinfold thickness. Measurement on 481 men and women aged from 16-27 years. **British Journal of Nutrition,** 32, 77-97.

Gaesser, G.A. and Rich, R.G. (1984) Effects of high and low intensity exercise training on aerobic capacity and blood lipids. **Medicine and Science in Sports and Exercise,** 16, 269-274.

Godfrey, M. (1989) Focus on lipids. **Mimms Magazine,** July p 3-6.

Hartung, G.H. (1980) Relationship of diet to high density lipoprotein in middle-aged marathon runners, joggers and inactive men. **New England Journal of Medicine,** 303, 357-361.

Haskell W.L. (1984) Exercise induced changes in plasma lipids and lipoproteins. **Preventative Medicine** 13, 23-26.

Hubert, H.B., Feinleib, M., McNamara, P.M. and Casteli, W.P. (1983) Obesity as an independent risk factor for cardiovascular disease; a 26 year follow up of participants in the Framingham Heart Study. **Circulation,** 67, 968-977.

Lehtonen, A. and Viikari, J. (1978) Serum triglycerides and cholesterol and HDL in highly physically active men. **Acta Medica Scaninavica** 204, 111-114.

Morris, J. and Crawford F. (1958) Coronary heart disease and physical activity of work; evidence of a national necropsy study. **British Medical Journal,** 259(10).

Northcote R.J. (1994) Heart and exercise: Clinical aspects, in **Oxford Textbook of Sports Medicine** (eds M.Harries, C.Williams, W.D. Stanish and L.J.Micheli), Oxford University Press, Oxford, pp. 282-289.

Northcote, R.J., Canning, G.C., Todd, I.C. and Ballanytne, D. (1988) Lipoprotein profiles of elite veteran endurance athletes. **American Journal of Cardiology,** 81, 934-936.

O.E.C.D. (1991) Major demographic trends in the member states of the Council of Europe. O.E.C.D., Brussels.

Pekkanen J.H. (1990) Hazard risk of coronary heart disease. **Modern Medicine of Ireland,** April p. 16.

Ramsbottom, R., Brewer, J., and Williams, C. (1988) A progressive shuttle run test to estimate maximum oxygen uptake. **British Journal of Sports Medicine**, 22, 141-144.

Reilly, T. (1990) Football, in **Physiology of Sports** (eds T.Reilly, N.Secher, P.Snell and C.Williams), E. and F.N. Spon, London, pp. 371-425.

Shelly, E., O'Reilly, O., Mulcahy, R. and Graham, I. (1991) Trends in mortality from cardiovascular disease in Ireland. **Irish Journal of Medical Science,** 160(9), 5-9.

Vodac, P.A., Wood, P.D., Haskell, W.L. and Williams, P.T.(1980) HDL cholesterol and other plasma lipids and lipoproteins concentrations in middle aged male and female tennis players. **Metabolism**, 29, 745-752.

Wilmore, J.H. and Costill, D.L. (1994) **Physiology of Sport and Exercise**. Human Kinetics, Champaign, IL.

Wood, P.W. (1988) Changes in lipids and lipoproteins in overweight men during weight loss through dieting as compared with exercising. **New England Journal of Medicine,** 319, 1173-1179.

PATTERN OF ALCOHOL USE IN RUGBY PLAYERS AND RUGBY REFEREES

C.P. O'BRIEN AND J.F. FIELDING
The Royal College of Surgeons in Ireland, Department of Medicine, Beaumont Hospital, Beaumont, Dublin, Ireland.

1 Introduction

Alcohol is a commonly encountered beverage at social gatherings .It is regularly drunk after sporting events, particularly traditional sports such as rugby union football (O'Brien, 1991). Alcohol misuse is a cause of both short term and long term morbidity and occasional mortality.Whilst the acute use of alcohol may not affect the factors that influence physiological performance (American College of Sports Medicine, 1982), the delayed or " hang-over " effect of alcohol does influence physiological performance, in particular reducing aerobic performance (O'Brien, 1992a). Club rugby players have moderate to low aerobic capacities (Maud, 1983). International players'only approach VO_2 max levels of 60 - 65 ml/kg/min (Power, 1989) which are modest when compared to other elite sportsmen (McArdle et al., 1991). This study evaluates the pattern of alcohol use in this group of traditional field athletes to establish if it could potentially affect their sport participation.

2 Methods

Senior rugby players (n=197) from 5 rugby clubs and 39 rugby referees were interviewed during the 1994-1995 rugby season. The mean age of the players was 24.4 years,and 38.9 years for the referees. They completed a questionnaire relating to their use of alcohol.The areas considered were the incidence of use of alcohol the pattern of consumption. The weekly quantity consumed by the players was calculated in standard units of alcohol (i.e. 1 unit = 330 ml of beer,250 ml of wine or a standard small measure of spirits). The beverage of choice was also recorded.

One senior club squad (n = 40) had its aerobic fitness assessed by the 20 m shuttle run test (Ramsbottom et al., 1988). Skinfolds measured at four sites by means of Harpenden calipers were applied to standard body fat percentage tables (Durnin and Womersley, 1974).

3 Results

The results of the survey showed that 94.4% of the rugby players and 96% of the referees drank alcohol; 48% of the players and 80% of the referees drank alcohol on the evening prior to engaging in a rugby match (Table 1). All the players drank alcohol after a Rugby match but none of the subjects interviewed drank alcohol on the morning of a match.

Table 1. Pattern of alcohol use in Rugby Union players and rugby referees

	Rugby players	Rugby referees
Alcohol use	94.4%	96%
Friday night alcohol use	48%	80%
Beer drinkers	96%	94%

The mean weekly alcohol intake in the rugby players who drank alcohol (n = 186) was 23.8 units.Those players who drank alcohol on the evening prior to activity consumed a mean of 26.9 units a week ,and the non- drinkers prior to activity consumed a mean of 20.3 units a week (see Table 2).

Table 2. Units of alcohol consummed by rugby players

Weekly alcohol consumption	23.8 units
Weekly alcohol consumption (Friday night drinkers)	26.9 units
Weekly alcohol consumption (Non-Friday night drinkers)	20.3 units

The beverage of choice for the majority was beer with 96% of the players and 94% of the referee reporting it as their beverage of choice. Only 2% of players and referees named wine as their beverage of choice ,and 2% of the players and 4% of the referees preferred spirits (see Table 1).

The mean estimated VO_2 max for the Rugby player was 51.3 ml/kg/min. The mean body fat percentage of the players was 16.6%

4 Discussion

Alcohol and the athlete have been linked since ancient times. It has been reported to be the most used legal drug in an athletic population up to 88% of the athletes in this large study from Michigan State consumed alcohol (Anderson and McKeag, 1985). The majority of the players (94.4 %)and referees (96%) in this study drank alcohol. The traditional link between sport and alcohol places athletes at potentially greater risk of alcohol related problems (O'Brien, 1993). In particular athletes who have to retire early from competitive sport may run the risk of alcohol related problems (Reilly, 1988). Rugby Union is a high speed contact sport with a significant injury incidence. A frequency of one injury per 31 playing appearances has been reported (O'Brien, 1992b). Rugby players who have to retire early due to injury may be particularly vulnerable to alcohol related problems.

The mean weekly alcohol intake of the rugby players was high at 23.8 units a week, with the players who drank on the evening before a match consuming 26.9 units a week. The World Health Organisation recommends that males should not exceed 20 units in any given week; chronic intake above this level is associated with disease development.

The majority of players do not drink alcohol on the day of a competitive event. This is also the case in the group of rugby referees.A large proportion of the players (48%) and referees (80%) drank on the evening prior to a match. The delayed or " hang - over" effect of alcohol has been reported to reduces aerobic performance by a mean of 11.4% (O'Brien, 1993). This is due to the very slow breakdown of alcohol in the liver by the enzyme alcohol dehydrogenase. The resulting byproducts of alcohol metabolism decrease aerobic performance many hours later by affecting available carbohydrate, the lactate:pyruvate ratio and the level of hydration.

Rugby union is a mixed aerobic and anaerobic sport, with an emphasis on short bursts of intensive anaerobic activity (O'Brien, 1993; McLean, 1992). The players all require a base-line of aerobic fitness to ensure continuous play throughout the 80 minutes of a game.This is particularly important for the back-row players and for the referees who are almost in continuous motion during a match.These individuals should be especially careful regarding drinking alcohol on the evening prior to activity.

Beer was the drink of choice for the majority of the players and referees in this study,and all confirmed they consumed an alcoholic beverage after a game.Beer is a complex solution which contains water, fat, protein, carbohydrate, electrolytes and minerals.It has a low carbohydrate content (approximately 200 kJ in the 6280 kJ of a standard 375 ml can of beer) and is a poor source of sodium (25 mg per 375 ml can). Beer also has the added disadvantage of causing diuresis,which will increase post-exercise dehydration and is therefore a poor replacement fluid. Rugby players and referees should be encouraged to rehydrate and take an appropriate carbohydrate food following exercise, before they drink any alcohol.The practice of drinking beer in the dressing room immediately post-match should be actively discouraged.

The club Rugby Union players in this survey had a modest aerobic capacity and body fat percentage values in the high normal range. These findings concur with other similar surveys on rugby players (Maud, 1983). The elite New Zealand squad of 1988/1989 who were successful in the inaugural World Cup had a low mean body fat percentage of 13% (Power, 1989). Alcohol is a high calorie containing foodstuff with low nutritional value. Its chronic use is associated with obesity, and in turn may be a factor in a reduced aerobic capacity as well as the high to normal skinfold thicknesses. Therefore, serious rugby players should avoid this beverage .

5 Conclusions

Alcohol use in this group of plyers was very high. A significant number drank on the evening prior to activity, thus potentially compromising their physiological function on match-day. Chronic alcohol use is associated with disease development; it may also be a factor in poor aerobic capacity by altering body composition. Traditional sports like Rugby Union should encourage a careful approach to the use of this beverage.

6 References

American College of Sports Medicine (1982) Position Statement on the use of alcohol and Sports Medicine. **Medicine and Science in Sports and Exercise,** 14, XI-X.

Anderson, W.A. and McKeag, D.B. (1985) Substitutes and abuse habits of College student athletes. **Mission Kansas National Collegiate Athletic Association.**

Durnin, J.V.G.A. and Womersley, J. (1974) Body fat assessment from total body density and its estimation from skinfold thickness. Measurement on 481 men and women aged from 16 to 27 years. **British Journal of Nutrition,** 32,77-97.

Maud, P.J. (1983) Physiological and anthropometric parameters that occur in a Rugby Union team **British Journal of Sports Medicine,** 17, 16-23.

McArdle, W.D. ,Katch, F.I. and Katch, V.L. (1991) **Exercise Physiology (3rd edition).** Lea and Febiger, Philadelphia.

McLean, D.A. (1992) Analysis of the physical demands of international Rugby Union. **Journal of Sports Sciences,** 10, 285-296.

O'Brien, C.P. (1992) The hangover effect of alcohol on aerobic and anaerobic performance on a rugby population. **Journal of Sports Sciences,** 10, 139.

O'Brien, C.P. (1992b) Retrospective survey of Rugby injuries in the Leinster Province of Ireland 1987-1989. **British Journal of Sports Medicine,** 26, 243-244.

O'Brien, C.P. (1993) Alcohol and sport. Impact of social drinking on recreational and competitive sports performance. **Sports Medicine,** 10 (2), 71-77.

Power, K. (1989) Fitness. **Rugby World**, 36-40

Ramsbottom, R., Brewer, J. and Williams, C. (1988) A progressive shuttle run test for the prediction of maximal oxygen uptake. **National Coaching Foundation, Leeds.**

Reilly, T. (1988) Alcohol, anti-anxiety drugs and exercise, in **Drugs in Sport** (ed D.R. Mottram), E. and F.N. Spon, London, pp.127-156.

IRON SUPPLEMENTS ARE NOT REQUIRED FOR RUGBY UNION FOOTBALL

C.P. O'BRIEN AND J.F. FIELDING
The Royal College of Surgeons in Ireland Department of Medicine Beaumont Hospital, Dublin, Ireland

1 Introduction

Iron deficiency is the most common identifiable nutritional deficiency in developed countries (Risser and Risser, 1990). The term "sports anaemia" is frequently used to describe a reduction in haemoglobin and haematocrit which approaches clinical anaemia associated with intensive training (McArdle et al., 1991). This is a misleading term which merely describes the normal physiological adaptation to endurance exercise. In these cases the lowered haemoglobin and haematocrit values are caused by an expanding intravascular volume. High intensity exercise causes an increased release of the hormone renin, which ultimately results in an increase in aldosterone secretion and sodium resorption from the kidney. The intravascular volume is therefore expanded (O'Brien, 1994).

Mild anaemia may impair sports performance (Risser and Risser, 1990). In addition, animal studies have shown improved treadmill times in non-anaemic rats who were supplemented with oral iron (Finch et al., 1976). However, iron supplementation in non-anaemic humans has failed to produce an improved physical performance despite an improvement in haematological status (Dressendorder et al., 1991).

It has been suggested that intensive exercise creates an added demand for iron which can outstrip intake (Clement and Asmundsun, 1982). Endurance runners and in particular, female runners are susceptible to exercise related haematological changes (Nickerson et al., 1983). The haematological changes associated with many field sports is unknown. The present aim is to evaluate a group of senior Irish rugby players, to consider the haematological status and nutritional intake in iron of this group of field sport athletes.

2 Methods

Sixteen males who were members of an Irish Senior Rugby Club squad were evaluated. There were 10 forwards and 6 backs in the group. Their mean age was 24.8 with an age range of 20 to 33 years. All were non-smokers and ate a mixed cavernous diet.

Blood samples were drawn in July of 1994, four weeks after pre-season training had commenced. The players had finished the previous season in May of 1994. The blood was analysed by a Keri Coomb automatic device. Haemoglobin, haematocrit and blood indices were quantified.

The subjects also completed a three-day nutritional inventory (Fehilly et al., 1984). This took place over a Thursday, Friday and Saturday. All food and beverages (and their brand names) consumed over the three days were entered into a nutritional diary. Each food item was weighed, using a Hanson weighing scales which had been supplied to each subject. Beverages were also entered by weight. Alcoholic beverages were recorded as bar measures, e.g. ½ pint of Guinness stout. The nutritional diaries were returned following the three days and the results were programmed into the Diet Pro Nutritional Software Package (Smith, 1991) From this the daily iron intake was calculated.

Skinfold thicknesses were recorded on each of the sixteen subjects using a Harpenden caliper. Four site readings were taken in centimetres from the triceps, biceps, anterior superior iliac spine and from the infrascapular region. These were added together to yield a body fat percentage value (McArdle et al., 1991) for each subject.

Aerobic fitness was estimated by performing a 20 m shuttle run test (Ramsbottom et al., 1988).

3 Results

All the rugby players (N=16) had normal haemoglobin levels with a mean of 14.9 ± 1.4 (±SD) g/dl. The haematocrits were also normal with a mean value of 0.413 ± 0.02 (see Table 1). Cell morphology showed a normochromic, normocytic picture in each case.

Table 1. Haemoglobin(Hb), haematocrit(Hct), iron intake, maximum oxygen uptake and body fat percentage in a group (N=16) of rugby players. F = Forward Players; B = Back Players.

POSITION	HAEMOGLOBIN g/dl	HAEMATOCRIT	IRON INTAKE (mg)	Estimated Maximum Oxygen Uptake ml/kg/min	BODY FAT %
F	14.8	0.446	21.0	47.4	20.5
F	14.6	0.439	12.6	45.8	20.2
F	15.7	0.471	18.0	51.4	9.8
F	13.9	0.401	12.4	40.0	19.0
F	15.7	0..457	23.5	49.0	22.4
F	15.3	0.442	11.5	43.3	31.0
F	16.2	0.475	13.9	45.2	12.4
F	15.5	0.463	18.9	45.2	18.6
F	16.6	0.493	18.0	44.5	14.2
F	14.8	0.436	12.6	41.0	23.0
B	13.3	0.392	13.2	44.0	10.2
B	14.6	0.438	22.6	45.0	17.4
B	14.2	0.411	13.5	55.1	15.0
B	13.7	0.406	12.8	54.1	15.2
B	13.4	0.409	14.5	48.2	26.2
B	15.5	0.454	25.0	53.0	17.0
MEAN	14.9	0.413	16.5	47.0	18.3
SD	0.3	0.025	4.4	3.6	5.5

The dietary inventory revealed that the mean daily iron intake was 16.5 ± 4.4 mg/day, with a range of 11.5 to 25 mg/day. The mean body fat percentage of the rugby players was 18.3% ± 5.5, with a range of 9.2 to 24% (Table 1).The forwards had a mean body fat percentage of 19.1% and the backs had a mean body fat percentage of 16.8%.

The mean estimated maximum oxygen uptake (VO$_2$ max) was 47.0 ± 3.6 ml/kg/min, with a range of 39.9 to 57.5 ml/kg/min (Table 1). The mean VO$_2$ max for the forward and back players was 45.3 and 49.3 ml/kg/min, respectively.

4 Discussion

Athletes are constantly trying to improve their physiological performance. Nutritional supplementation is often seen as a means of gaining a legal "edge". American athletic coaches routinely recommend iron supplementation for their athletes (Dressendorfer et al., 1991) and over 91% of female athletes comply and take nutritional supplements (Clarke, 1990). Much of the rationale behind this advise is based on an animal study which showed improved treadmill times in non-anaemic rats supplemented with iron (Finch et al., 1976) and a study which observed an improvement in aerobic performance in anaemic subjects who were treated with iron (Ekblom et al., 1982). No conclusive evidence exists to show that iron supplementation in the non-anaemic state will improve physiological performance (Smith, 1991).

Endurance exercise such as marathon running may entail a risk of iron deficiency anaemia due to increased erythrocyte dysfunction and turnover (McArdle et al., 1991). Other sports such as gymnastics and wrestling are associated with iron deficiency anaemia from inadequate dietary intake. Only certain athletic groups are susceptible to exercise related haematological change. Tennis is a mix of aerobic and anaerobic requirements but there was no evidence of either physiological anaemia or iron deficiency anaemia due to exercise, in international class tennis players (O'Brien, 1995).

The present study evaluating senior rugby players shows a similar pattern. There was no evidence of iron deficiency anaemia in any of the sixteen subjects. Moreover, iron intake from their diet was more than adequate, with a mean intake of 16.5 ± 4.4 mg/dl. The World Health Organisation recommends a daily intake of 10 mg/day. This is also the amount recommended for the exercising athlete (Grandjean, 1990).

The normal haematological status of the rugby players may be explained by their adequate nutritional intake of iron, their fitness levels and the type of sport they play. The aerobic fitness level of the rugby players was modest at 47.0 ± 3.6 ml/kg/min when compared with other athletes i.e. elite rowers 62 ml/kg/min and elite distance runners 80 ml/kg/min (McArdle et al., 1991).

This is further confirmed by observing the estimated percent body fat profile of the rugby players who had a mean of $18.3 \pm 3\%$ This was greater than the normal range for males in this age group which is 10 - 14% (McArdle et al., 1991) and was also high when compared to other athletic groups - wrestlers 9.8%; distance runners 10%, gymnasts 4.6% (Fox, 1983).

Rugby football is a field sport with a high skill level. It is "stop start" in nature, with average play sequences lasting 12 seconds (Reilly, 1990). It has a significant draw on the anaerobic energy system (McLean, 1992) rather than reliant on aerobic energy. Therefore, the stress of training and playing does not mirror the intensive endurance exercise which has been associated with gastrointestinal ischaemia (O'Brien, 1994), local urological trauma (Blacklock, 1977) and foot trauma which results in erythrocyte dysfunction and iron losses (Weight et al., 1991). Nor is the mode, duration and intensity of exercise sufficient to cause the hormonal adaptation which causes the intra-vascular volume to expand.

Non-prescribed iron supplementations is a potentially hazardous undertaking. Nausea, vomiting, rash and cardiac arrythmics have all been reported with oral iron ingestion (Soohami and Moxham, 1990). Perventeral iron is potentially fatal due to anaphalaxis (Formulary, 1993). Drug abuse and blood doping are arguably part of competitive sport. A drug and supplement culture now exists in competitive sport. Education of coaches and athletes is important in highlighting the futility of iron supplementation in the non-anaemic state and the potential hazards of this practice. In field sports such as Rugby Union Football, the use of iron supplements should be actively discouraged as they are unnecessary when there is an adequate nutritional iron intake.

5 References

Blacklock, N.J., (1977) Bladder Trauma in the long distance runner in 10,000 Haematuria. **British Medical Journal of Urology,** 49, 129 - 132.

Clarke, N. 1990 **Sports Nutrition Guide Book.** Leisure Press Campaign, Illinois, U.S.A

Clement, D.B. and Asmundsun, R.C., (1982) Nutritional intake haematological parameters in endurance runners. **The Physician and Sportsmedicine,** 10, 37-43.

Dressendorfer, R.H., Keen, C.L., Wade, C.E., Claybaugh, J.R. and Timmons G.C. (1991) Development of runners' anaemia during a 20 day road race: Effect of iron supplements. **International Journal of Sports Medicine,** 12, 332-336.

Ekblom, B., Goldberg, A.N. and Gullbring, B. (1982) Responses to exercise after blood loss and reinfusion. **Journal of Applied Physiology,** 33, 175-1080.

Fehilley, A.M., Philips, K.M. and Sweetman, P.M. (1984) A weighted dietary survey of men in Caerphilly, South Wales. **Human Nutrition,** 38A, 270 - 276.

Finch, C.A., Miller, L.R. and Inamdar, A.R. (1976) Iron deficiency in the rat: Physiological and biochemical studies in muscle dysfunction. **Journal of Clinical Investigation,** 58, 447 - 453.

Formularly, B.N. (1993) No. 25, March.

Fox, E.L. (1984) **Sports Physiology** (2nd Edition) Sanders College Publishing, Ohio.

Grandjean, A.C. (1990) **Sports Nutrition: The Team Physician's Hand Book**. Hanley & Belfus, pp. 78-91.

Halvorsen, P.A., Lyng, J. and Rithland, S. (1986) Gastro-intestinal bleeding in marathon runners. **Scandinavian Journal of Gastroenterology,** 21, 493-497.

McArdle, W.D., Katch, F.L. and Katch, V.L. (1991) **Exercise Physiology**. Third Edition, Lea & Febiger, Philadelphia/London.

McLean, D.A. (1992) Analysis of the physical demands of international Rugby Union. **Journal of Sports Sciences,** 10, 285 - 296.

Moorcroft, D. (1994) Today's shame was born from the sins of the past. **The Sunday Times -** 28th August; 2.5 London.

Nickerson H.J. and Tripp H.J. (1983) Iron deficiency in adolescent cross-country runners. **The Physician and Sportsmedicine,** 11, 60.

O'Brien C.P. (1994) Runners diarrhoea. **Gastroenterology in Practice** - Feb/Mar 9 (No.1).

O'Brien C.P. (1995) Incidence of anaemia among the Irish Tennis Squad, in **Science and Racket Sports** (eds T.Reilly, M. Hughes and A.Lees), E. and F.N. Spon, London, pp. 190-198.

Porter, A.M.W. (1983) Do marathon runners bleed into the gut. **British Medical Journal,** 287L: 1427-1983.

Ramsbottom, R., Brewer, J. and Williams, C. (1988) A Progressive Shuttle Run Test for Prediction of Maximum Oxygen Uptake. National Coaching Foundation, Leeds.

Reilly, T. (1990) Football, in **Physiology of Sports** (eds T. Reilly, N. Secher, P.Snell and C. Williams), E & F.N. Spon, London, pp. 371 - 426.

Risser, W.L. and Risser, M.H. (1990) Iron deficiency in adolescents and young adults. **The Physician and Sportsmedicine,** 18 (12), 87-101.

Smith, J.S. (1991) **Dietpro for Windows** (Version 1.2). Concept Development Associates Inc. Lifestyle Software Group- St Augustine Florida.

Soohami, R.L. and Moxham, J. (1990) **Textbook of Medicine**. Churchill Livingstone, Edinburgh.

Weight, L.M. (1993) 'Sports anaemia - Does it exist? **Sports Medicine,** 16, 1-4.

Weight, L.M., Byrne, M.J. and Jacobs, P. (1991) The haemolytic effect of exercise. **Clinical Science**, 81, 147-152.

PART THREE

Football Training

RESISTANCE TRAINING BY SENIOR RUGBY UNION PLAYERS - JUST WHAT DO COACHES THINK THEY'RE DOING?

JIM McKENNA
Exercise and Health Research Unit, University of Bristol, 34, West Park, BRISTOL, UK. BS8 2LU.

1 Introduction

The adaptations associated with resistance training, particularly weight training, offer considerable benefits for Rugby Union players (Hazeldene and Holmyard 1993). Indeed, following the trend of specialisation in sports, individual players, in different positions demand a differentiated and sophisticated approach towards this mode of training (King, 1993). Such an approach may serve to enhance performance and recuperation, while lengthening playing life (Garraway, 1993), particularly when concerns to maximise adherence are fully addressed. While numerous training regimens are available for Rugby Union players, e.g. Greenwood (1978) and Frenzelli and Leighton (1989), there is little information concerning players' levels of adherence, associated periodisation practices and the level of monitoring in resistance-training.

The "Diffusion of Innovations" model (Rogers 1982) offers a scheme to describe the rate of adoption of any innovation, like using resistance-training. The model recognises that the adoption of an 'innovation' is a function of the operations of the 'focus' community and the agents of influence (such as change agents) that operate therein. 'Diffusion' is the process by which an innovation (an idea, or practice that's promoted as 'new') is communicated through certain channels, over time, among the members of a social system. Considerations about an innovation serve to locate decision-units on the continuum shown in Figure 1.

Change agents are those individuals who change their normal roles to implement an innovation. The likely influence of change agents is predictable. The closer, or more homophilous, the agent is to the deciders, the greater the likelihood of successful adoption of the innovation.

The model reflects the rate of adoption by members of the decision unit; normally a distorted 's-shaped' curve reflects normal distribution. The categories of adoption are partitioned by standard deviations away from the mean time of adoption: innovators, for example, represent the first 2.5% of any group (Haines and Jones, 1994). The rate of adoption allows classification as 'innovators' (change readily), 'early adopters'(13.5%), 'early majority' (34%), 'late majority' (34%), 'late adopters' (13.5%) and 'laggards' (the last group to change - 2.5%).

Knowledge⇨Persuasion⇨Decision⇨Implementation⇨Confirmation

Figure 1. The Process of Diffusion of Innovations.

This study describes perceptions of first XV squad players' resistance-training, by the 'closest' coach in four resistance-innovation categories; (1) Adoption, (2) Periodisation, (3) Rehabilitation, and (4) Monitoring. It is focused on the 30 senior English clubs, those in National Divisions 1, 2 and 3.

2 Methods

A postal questionnaire was devised, piloted and sent to each club (n=30) in National Divisions 1, 2 and 3. It was directed to the person with the closest connection to players' resistance-training. Responses for both the Pre-season (the entire preparation period preceding the first competitive game of the season) and the In-season (the period between the first and last competitive games) periods were requested. Items concerning the level of club requirement for resistance-training, provision of direct support for it, player uptake of resistance-training were included. Resistance-training practices were recorded using a Likert format of vague qualifiers to encourage responses(1 = No players, 5 = All players).

3 Results

Of the thirty clubs, 17 (56.6%) returned their forms, but only 16 were completed fully. Table 1 shows the size of the first XV squads and the breakdowns by position (forwards and backs). Six (35.2%) of the 17 clubs had no reported resistance-training requirement for any players. In these 6 clubs there was no resistance-training specialist coach. In all clubs resistance-training was undertaken by both forwards and backs.

Table 1. Size of First XV squads

	Mean	S.D.	Range
Whole squad	34.86	8.87	24-51
Forwards[1]	18.64	5.44	12-31
Backs[2]	16.21	3.91	12-26
1 v 2 P<0.01			

3.1 Adoption

The mean number of players who were required to train using resistance methods (Table 2) and who adhered to those requirements (Table 3) declined over the course of the season.

Ten clubs provided both resistance-training facilities at the club site. In all cases, this was associated with the presence of a resistance-training specialist coach, suggesting strong, but localised institutional support for resistance-training. In seven clubs, the resistance-training specialist was the main source for players to learn resistance-training skills.

Table 2. Players required by clubs to weight train - Forwards vs Backs, $P<0.05$

	Mean	S.D.	Range
Forwards	10.29	9.67	0-25
Backs	8.50	8.06	0-20

Forwards' pre-season adherence to club requirements was higher in the presence of a resistance-training specialist (Mean=15.37 ±4.87, vs Mean=9.50 ±0.70, $t(3.26)$, $P<0.01$). No other adherence characteristics differed.

In the pre-season 3-4 sessions per week were the reported club-required doses. This declined to 2 sessions per week for the in-season. For the backs the declining pattern was similar, with 1 or 2 sessions per week required in-season (Table 4).

3.2 Periodisation

The frequency of club-required resistance-training declined pre-season *vs* in-season ($P<0.05$), as did the numbers of forwards plus backs who regularly trained using resistance methods (1+ session per week); 19.65(6.35) *vs* 13.85(4.35), $t(4.00)$, $P<0.001$. The frequency of club-required training (see Table 4) declined from Pre- to In-season in both forwards and backs ($P<0.001$). The actual execution of resistance-training was not reported differently for forwards vs backs.

Table 3. The numbers of players who trained regularly (one or more sessions per week)

		Range	Mean	S.D.
Forwards	Pre-season	0-12	14.20	4.98
	In-season	5-10	10.90	5.00
Backs	Pre-season	0-10	10.20	2.74
	In-season	0- 8	7.30	4.19

Table 4. Club-required resistance-training - sessions per week

		Mean	S.D.
Forwards Pre-season[1]		3.00	0.91
	In-season[2]	1.85	0.69
Backs	Pre-season[3]	2.85	0.90
	In-season[4]	1.54	0.66
Only 1v3 was non-significant			

3.3 Rehabilitation
In 9 of the clubs' players will 'Mostly', or 'All' use resistance-training to aid recovery (where appropriate). This is a high adoption rate when the size of the first XV squads is considered (Table 1) and contrasts with the numbers who normally regularly use resistance-training (Table 3).

3.4 Monitoring
Twelve of the clubs' (n=16) reported monitoring resistance-training progress. Monitoring was reportedly identical for forwards and backs, though the frequency and form of this innovation demonstrated no discernible pattern. The monitoring appeared to reflect local initiative and perceived need.

4 Discussion

These results provide the first evidence concerning the place of resistance-training in senior English Rugby Union clubs since the advent of the national leagues. However, there are some limitations to the study. First, the relatively low response rate (17 of 30) raises questions about the generalisability of these results. Further, the reports reflect the beliefs and perceptions of one individual, not even, necessarily, an individual directly managing players' resistance-training. The actual status and level, of involvement of the respondent with players' resistance-training was not identified. It is with these provisos that the study should be considered.

The results suggest the importance of localised responses to resistance-training by, and within senior clubs. Relatively high levels of adoption characterise the use of resistance-training as a rehabilitative tool (diffusion label 'late majority'), as does the level of support for resistance-training as evidenced by specialist staff and on-site facilities (same diffusion label). However, low numbers of players regularly use resistance-training (50% of those required by clubs - pre-season, and 40% in-season) and a number of clubs have no requirement. Existing communication channels have limited sustained motivational effects on players' use of resistance-training, therefore. It would appear that there are issues relating to adoption of resistance-training for club requirements and issues relating to adherence for players' actual execution of it.

This study suggests that the action of change agents declines over the course of the season and proposes a need to review the motivational strategies of these agents. The presence of a resistance-training specialist, with on-site facilities, is associated with more players controlling the volume of resistance-training over the course of the training year. It is not clear why this variable is controlled differently, over any other periodisation variable. Again, the existing communication channels of the resistance-training specialists may be influential here.

Regular resistance trainers (those who regularly train one or more times per week) are reported to do longer sessions than required by their clubs. Yet, relatively few appear to have suffered from overtraining attributable to this mode. This suggests that these players have a working understanding of short-term approaches to effective use of resistance-training. The explanation for this is not clear from these data. The use of monitoring in the clubs is not well developed and perhaps this will provide a means to promote resistance-training as a regular feature of players' training.

5 Conclusion

Overall, the adoption profile of the various elements of resistance-training is between 'Innovation' and 'Early majority' in this sample. Institutionalised support for resistance-training is not matched by the level of adoption by players and more can be done to maximise the resources provided in these clubs. The communication channels of existing change agents, and perhaps the recruitment of new types of change agents, may require examination. The presence of a resistance-training specialist, with on-site facilities, is associated with reports of higher numbers of players who regularly use resistance-training. However, the number of such players is not high and subject to substantial local variability.

6 References

Frenzelli, R. and Leighton, R.D. (1989) A kinesiological description of the rugby spin pass and a rugby training program. **National Strength and Conditioning Association Journal,** 11, 3, 6-13.

Garraway W. (1993) Epidemiology of rugby injuries, in **Intermittent High Intensity Exercise: Preparation, Stresses and Damage Limitation** (eds D.A.D. MacLeod, R.J. Maughan, C. Williams, C.R. Madeley, J.C.M. Sharp and R.W. Nutton), E. and F. N. Spon, London. pp. 407-418.

Greenwood, J. (1978) **Total Rugby.** London, A. and C. Black.

Hazeldene, R. and Holmyard, D.J. (1993) Preparation for performance, in **Intermittent High Intensity Exercise: Preparation, Stresses and Damage Limitation** (eds D.A.D. MacLeod, R.J. Maughan, C. Williams, C.R. Madeley, J.C.M. Sharp and R.W. Nutton), E. and F. N. Spon, London. pp. 71-77.

Haines, A. and Jones, R. (1994) Implementing findings of research. **British Medical Journal,** 308, 1488-1492.

King, I. (1993) Strength training for rugby. **New Zealand Journal of Sports Medicine.** 21, 4, 62-65.

Rogers, E.M. (1982) **Diffusion of Innovations. Third Edition.** The Free Press, New York.

RUGBY UNION PLAYERS' RESISTANCE TRAINING - AN APPLICATION OF THE TRANSTHEORETICAL MODEL.

JIM McKENNA and ALAN MUCKLE
Exercise and Health Research Unit, University of Bristol, 34 West Park, Bristol, UK.
BS8 2LU.

1 Introduction

The Transtheoretical Model (Prochaska and DiClemente, 1992) describes 'stages' of intentional behaviour change. The model is an 'umbrella theory' beneath which other aspects of 'self' (attribution, attitudes, intentions, etc.) operate (Courneya, 1994; Marcus and Owen, 1992). There are five stages of change; Precontemplation (no intention to change), Contemplation (thinking of change), Preparation (infrequent levels of change), Action (involved in change) and Maintenance (sustained change). Relapse is seen as a phase, not a discrete stage, that can occur between any stages.

As progression through the stages relates to the systematic use of *processes* of change, stage-matched interventions have been proposed (Prochaska and DiClemente, 1992 and DiClemente, 1993). Such interventions are effective in achieving changed exercise behaviour (Cardinal and Sachs, 1994). Stage of change on entering a programme relates to programme outcomes, so the TM is capable of predicting future exercise behaviour, including vigorous exercise (Armstrong et al., 1993). Self-reports of behaviour are accurate and reliable representations of stage and they relate to intensity (Armstrong et al., 1993) and mode preferences (Naylor and McKenna, 1995).

There is a growing need to generate interventions based on existing models of behaviour change to maximise adherence levels. At present only limited data on the current practices of senior Rugby Union players are available. It follows that for junior standard players even less information is available. Since the use of resistance training is an intentional act, the application of the model is appropriate. This study describes the stages of change for resistance training for adult, junior-standard Rugby Union players and examines stage-associated practices.

2 Methods

A questionnaire was developed based on that of Marcus et al. (1992). This device included a measure of stage of change for resistance training, and 12 items reflecting periodisation practices (1 = Always, 5 = Never). Questions focused on the deliberate modification of volume, intensity and frequency of resistance training over the course of the training year (Pre-season 'all preparation preceding the first competitive game' and In-season 'from the first to the last competitive game'). The questionnaire achieved a Flesch Grade Level of 8.1 years. It was distributed to players in April of 1993. At this time, it was felt, players would be able to represent accurately their In-season and Pre-season resistance training practices.

4 Results

A response rate of 90.5% was achieved (200 distributed, 181 returned). All subjects (n=181) were male volunteers (mean age = 28.18 ±5.37 years) from 15 clubs, who played for their first XV in competitive leagues. The mean playing years was 12.94 ±7.10 years. The distribution by stage is shown in Table 1; 119 subjects (65.7%) actively employed resistance training (Preparation + Action + Maintenance). Only 49 (27.1%) respondents had attended a course on the use of resistance training for Rugby Union and this was not associated with a significantly different stage profile. The stage profile did not differ by individual player positions, e.g. props, fly-half, nor by player grouping (forwards vs backs). Players in only two clubs reported a 'club requirement' to use resistance training. However, this was not associated with significant stage differences.

The twelve questions relating to training practices were significantly different (Friedman, 2-way ANOVA χ^2=276.84, df=11, P<0.0001). All training practice items, e.g. 'deliberately varying sets', 'deliberately varying volume', and 'deliberately varying intensity' differed by stage (P<0.05). Significant differences (P<0.05) were rarely found between Action and Maintenance responses, but were consistently evident between all other stages. These results are important as they demonstrate a 'working knowledge' of how to implement resistance training in the Pre- and In-season periods. Further, the use of record-keeping differed by stage(χ^2=14.41, df=5, P<0.01) and being tested for progress in resistance training were each associated with greater levels of Action and Maintenance (χ^2=22.88, df=5, P<0.001). These results suggest the existence of process differences as described in the literature.

Table 1. Number and percentage of respondents by resistance training stage of change (n=181)

Stage of change	n	%
Precontemplation	19	10.5
Contemplation	14	7.7
Preparation	59	32.6
Action	12	6.6
Maintenance	48	26.5
Relapse	28	15.5

5 Discussion

These findings demonstrate distinct stages of change for resistance training in this population. The most frequent stage report was Preparation (only 60 subjects - Action + Maintenance - were routinely using resistance training), suggesting that the majority of men in junior-level competitive Rugby Union are prepared to incorporate it into their training, albeit, in an infrequent way. However, to use an eating analogy, since 'snacking' characterises this stage, it is unlikely that they will achieve the potential offered by more regular resistance. A *process of change* approach is suggested to help move these individuals into the Action stage (and subsequently into Maintenance). More resistance training specialists in local clubs would serve to help in this regard. This raises issues concerning the preparation of coaches. The first issue relates to the generation of more resistance training specialist coaches in junior rugby. Secondly, how will these specialists be trained to generate maximum adoption of resistance training. The literature proposes that stage-matched approaches are most likely to achieve high rates of change.

The role of specific resistance training courses is not associated with more levels of Action or Maintenance, but may relate to increased intention to use resistance training. Further, the results suggest that to assess the effect of resistance training courses, measurement of stage at programme outset is required. This will help identify which stages are most and least affected, and in what ways, by the existing programmes.

5 Conclusion

This is the first study of the use of resistance training by men in competitive junior-level Rugby Union. It is also the first to examine the issues from this theoretical base and the, as yet, undemonstrated relationships between self-reported stage for resistance training and actual use of resistance training. The results confirm the internal consistency of this methodology and are concordant with the existing stage-based literature. However, caution should be exercised in generalising from these results as it is likely that the stage profiles depicted here reflect local conditions.

Despite these problems, the results confirm those found in UK-wide senior players. More can be done to increase the levels of adopting resistance training by Rugby Union players. On the basis of these findings and those relating to changed exercise behaviour, stage-matched interventions may increase the levels of its adoption in competitive junior-level Rugby Union players.

8 References

Armstrong, C.A., Sallis, J.F., Hovell, M.F. and Hofstetter, C.F. (1993) Stages of change, self-efficacy and the adoption of vigorous exercise: A prospective study. **Journal of Sport and Exercise Psychology,** 15, 390-402.

Cardinal, B.J. and Sachs, M.L. (1994) Increasing physical activity using the stages of change model and mail-delivered exercise programs. **Research Quarterly for Exercise and Sports**, 65,1 (Suppl), A45.

Courneya, K.S. (1994) Understanding readiness for regular physical activity in older individuals: an application of the theory of planned behaviour. **Health Psychology**, 14,1, 80-87.

DiClemente, C.C. (1993) Changing addictive behaviours: a process perspective. **Current Directions in Psychological Science,** 2 (4), 101-106.

Marcus, B.H. and Owen, N. (1992) Motivational readiness, self-efficacy and decision-making for exercise. **Journal of Applied Social Psychology.** 22, 3-16.

Marcus, B.H., Rossi, J., Selby, V., Naiura, R.S. and Abrams, D.B. (1992) The stages and processes of exercise adoption and maintenance in a worksite sample. **Health Psychology.** 11, 386-395.

Naylor, P-J. and McKenna, J. (1995) Stages of change, self-efficacy and behavioural preferences for exercise among British University students. **Journal of Sports Sciences,** 13, 68.

Prochaska, J. and DiClemente, C.C. (1992) In search of how people change. **American Psychologist,** 47, 1102-1114.

THE EFFECT OF PRE-SEASON TRAINING ON THE PHYSIOLOGICAL CHARACTERISTICS OF INTERNATIONAL RUGBY PLAYERS

R.J. TONG [1] and R. MAYES [2]
Cardiff Institute of Higher Education, Cyncoed, Cardiff, CF2 6XD, Wales [1]
Sports Council for Wales, Sophia Gardens, Cardiff, CF1 9SW, Wales [2]

1 Introduction

Rugby Union football places high physical and physiological demands on international players, with some players playing approximately 35 matches a season. In addition to these match demands players will normally be expected to attend two organised club training sessions per week and during the Home Nations Championships will be involved in international squad weekends and evening training sessions. It is well documented that fitness levels of sportsmen can be improved following systematic training programmes (Bangsbo and Mizuno, 1988) but these training programmes need to be strictly adhered to in order to gain the desired training effects. This is not always possible during the playing season since match and team training commitments severely restrict the time available for players to complete their individual training. Despite this, seasonal changes in the fitness levels of English international rugby players have been demonstrated (Holmyard and Hazeldine, 1991). Findings included variations in body composition, aerobic power and speed during a playing season. These findings are further supported for 1st division soccer players who also showed seasonal variations in fitness levels (Brewer, 1990). Although it is possible to improve fitness levels during the playing season, it would appear that the largest improvements are made during the pre-season training period (Holmyard and Hazeldine, 1991). Islegen et al. (1988) also reported improvements in physical fitness in soccer players following pre-season training.

Differences in physical and physiological variables including stature, body mass, body composition, speed and aerobic power have been reported between different playing positions (Maud and Shultz, 1984; Rigg and Reilly, 1988; Holmyard and Hazeldine, 1991). The main purposes of this study were to determine the effects of pre-season training of the anthropometric and physiological characteristics of international rugby players and to examine any differences between backs and forwards.

2 Methods

Thirty nine players (18 backs, aged 24.6 ± 2.7 years and 21 forwards, aged, 25.6 ± 3.3 years) participated in the study. The players were all members of Wales senior squads and were assessed at the end of the 1991-92 season and the start of the 1992-93 season. The sample consisted of 12 full-backs and three-quarter backs, 6 half-backs, 8 front row, 6 second row and 7 back row forwards. Stature, body mass and sum of four skinfold thicknesses (biceps, triceps, suprailiac and subscapula) were measured. Maximum oxygen uptake was predicted from the 20 m stage shuttle running test (Ramsbottom et al.,1988). Grip strength was measured using a hand grip dynamometer (Takei, Japan) and "explosive leg strength" assessed by performance in a vertical jump test using a jump meter (Takei, Japan). Flexibility was assessed by a standard sit and reach test and abdominal endurance using paced sit-ups (National Coaching Foundation, G.B. 1991).

Following the initial testing session in June 1992, the players were prescribed individual training programmes related to their positional demands and levels of fitness. All programmes included strength, endurance, flexibility and speed training sessions. Following the twelve week training programme the players were reassessed in September 1992 using the same test battery. Dependent t-tests were used to examine the effects of the training programme and independent t-tests used to compare data for forwards and backs.

3 Results and Discussion

The results of the two assessment sessions are shown in Table 1. To enable the comparison of the current data with previous studies it is important to consider the number of players in each position (full and three-quarter backs (TQ), half-backs (HB), front row (FR), second row (SR) and back row (BR) forwards) and the playing level (international, 1st or 2nd class, collegiate). The results of this study suggest that the Welsh squad rugby forwards were taller and heavier than U.S. national rugby players and their English counterparts, at both international and club level (Rigg and Reilly, 1988; Holmyard and Hazeldine,1991; Carlson et al., 1994). The physical characteristics of the backs were similar to those reported in previous studies (Rigg and Reilly,1988; Holmyard and Hazeldine,1991). The forwards in this study were both taller and heavier than Welsh collegiate players (Bell, 1979), but similar to the players in the previous Welsh squads (Bell et al., 1991). The forwards in this study were significantly taller than the backs, with the second row players being taller than the front and back row players (P < 0.01). The front row forwards were shorter (P < 0.05) than the back row and second row forwards but no differences existed between the backs (P > 0.05).

Table 1. Mean (SD) physical and physiological results

	Backs June	Backs Sept.	Forwards June	Forwards Sept.
Age (years)	24.6 (2.7)	24.9 (2.7)	25.6 (3.3)	25.9 (3.3)
Height (m)	1.76 (0.03)	1.77 (0.04)	1.87 (0.09)	1.88 (0.09)
Body mass (kg)	82.6 (6.6)	81.5 (5.9)	105.1 (9.3)	105.6 (8.1)
Sum of skinfolds(mm)	35.8 (8.0)	32.6 (7.6)**	49.6 (11.6)	46.0(11.4)**
Shuttle run (level)	13:2	13:8**	11:12	12:2
VO_2max (ml/kg/min)	57.5 (2.7)	59.1 (2.8)**	53.8 (3.5)	54.3 (3.1)
Sit-ups	102 (33)	92 (34)	61 (21)	68 (32)
Right Grip Strength (N)	583 (53)	623 (54)**	611 (65)	656 (60)**
Left Grip Strength (N)	554 (51)	580 (57)**	598 (78)	628 (64)**
Flexibility (cm)	13.3 (4.3)	15.2 (3.9)*	11.1 (5.4)	13.5 (4.8)**
Vertical Jump (cm)	60.5 (3.7)	59.6 (3.5)	60.6 (7.7)	57.9 (7.6)

Significant differences between June 1992 and Sept. 1992
* $P < 0.05$; ** $P < 0.01$

The forwards had significantly larger sums of skinfold thicknesses than the backs in both June and September and both groups reduced their sum of skinfold thicknesses following pre-season training ($P < 0.01$). Similar improvements were demonstrated by English international players as a result of pre-season training (Holmyard and Hazeldine, 1991). Using the estimation of percentage body fat from the skinfold thicknesses (Durnin and Womersley, 1974) the forwards in this study had 18 ($\pm$ 3.0) % body fat in September compared to 13.7 ($\pm$ 2.4) % body fat for the backs. These values were similar to those reported for English international players at the same time of the season (Holmyard and Hazeldine, 1991).

The backs demonstrated significant improvements in estimated VO_2max following pre-season training ($P < 0.01$), whereas the forwards showed no significant improvement in estimated VO_2max. Estimated VO_2max for the forwards was significantly lower than the backs in both June and September ($P < 0.01$). The Welsh forwards had lower aerobic fitness levels than their English counterparts, at the same time during the season. The estimated VO_2max for the backs compare favourably with the values reported by Holmyard and Hazeldine (1991), but were considerably higher than values estimated by Bell (1980).

Neither the backs nor the forwards showed any improvement in their abdominal endurance and the backs actually performed less sit-ups post-training compared to pre-training. The forwards produced significantly lower scores ($P < 0.01$) than the backs both pre- and post- training. The better scores of the backs followed the trend suggested by Rigg and Reilly (1988). Following training both the forwards and the backs produced significantly higher scores on the hand grip test for both the left and the right side of the body ($P < 0.01$). The forwards were also significantly stronger ($P < 0.01$) than the backs in both test sessions (Table 1). Right hand grip strength was significantly higher than the left hand grip strength for the whole squad at both test sessions, although no account was taken for dominant/non-dominant arms ($P < 0.01$).

Significant improvements in performance for the sit and reach test were demonstrated by both the forwards ($P < 0.01$) and backs ($P < 0.05$) following pre-season training (Table 1). No differences in the jumping performance existed between the backs and forwards but the squad's results were higher than those previously reported for first and second class players of similar playing positions (Reilly and Rigg, 1988). Carlson et al. (1994) reported similar performances for the U.S. rugby squad. Following the pre-season training phase the squad as a whole showed a slight reduction in "explosive leg strength" which was not suprising since the training programmes were not designed to improve "explosive leg strength". This aspect of fitness was concentrated on nearer to the Home Nations Championship.

4 Conclusion

The results of this study suggest that during pre-season training players can improve their strength and flexibility, and reduce their mass of body fat. Additionally the backs in this study improved their aerobic fitness whilst the forwards failed to improve their estimated VO_2max following pre-season training. Therefore the results suggest that pre-season training is beneficial for both forwards and backs although forwards may need to place greater emphasis on aerobic training during pre-season training.

5 References

Bangsbo, J. and Mizuno, M. (1988) Morphological and metabolic alterations in soccer players with detraining and their relation to performance, in **Science and Football** (eds T. Reilly, A. Lees, K. Davids and W J Murphy), E. & F.N. Spon, London, pp.114-124.

Bell, W. (1979) Body composition of rugby union football players. **British Journal of Sports Medicine**, 13, 19-23.

Bell, W. (1980) Body composition and maximal aerobic power of rugby union forwards. **Journal of Sports Medicine and Physical Fitness,** 20, 447.451.

Brewer, J. (1990) Changes in selected physiological characteristics of an English first division soccer squad during a league season. **Journal of Sports Sciences,** 8, 76-77.

Carlson, B. R., Carter, J.E.L., Patterson, P., Petti, P., Orfanos, S.M., and Noffal, G.J. (1994) Physique and motor performance characteristics of US national rugby players. **Journal of Sports Sciences,** 12, 403-412.

Durnin, J.V.G.A. and Womersley, J. (1974) Body fat assessment from total-body density and its estimation from skinfold thickness measurements on 481 men and women aged 16 to 72 years. **British Journal of Nutrition,** 32, 169-179.

Islegen, C. and Akgun, N. (1988) Effects of 6 weeks pre-seasonal training on physical fitness among soccer players, in **Science and Football** (eds T. Reilly, A. Lees, K. Davids and W. J. Murphy), E. & F.N.Spon, London, pp. 125-129.

Maud, P.J. and Shultz, B.B. (1984) The US national rugby team: A physiological and anthropometric assessment. **The Physician and Sportsmedicine,** 12, 86-99.

Ramsbottom, R., Brewer, J. and Williams, C. (1988) A progressive shuttle run test to estimate maximal oxygen uptake. **British Journal of Sports Medicine,** 22, 141-144.

Rigg, P and Reilly, T. (1988) A fitness profile and anthropometric analysis of first and second class rugby union players, in **Science and Football** (eds T. Reilly, A. Lees, K. Davids and W. J. Murphy), E & F N Spon, London, pp 194-200.

EFFECTS OF DIFFERENT PRE-SEASON PREPARATIONS ON LACTATE KINETICS IN PROFESSIONAL SOCCER PLAYERS

Ç. ISLEGEN[*], M.F. ACAR[**], A. ÇEÇEN[***], T. ERDINÇ[*],
R. VAROL[**], G. TIRYAKI[****] and O. KARAMIZRAK[*]

[*]   Department of Sports Medicine, Ege University /Izmir/TURKEY
[**]   School of Physical Education and Sports, Ege University/ Izmir/TURKEY
[***]   Ministry of Youth and Sports Health Center, /Izmir/TURKEY
[****] Physical Education and Sports, M.E.T.U. /Ankara/TURKEY

1 Introduction

Blood lactate determinations are widely used in the assessment of soccer players. To determine the effects of different pre-season preparation programmes, lactate responses to a "modified shuttle run" test were recorded in two Second League soocer teams.

2 Materials and Methods

Players of two Second League teams (Team A: n=13, age 22.2 ± 3.4 (means ± SD) years, height 177.5 ± 5.3 cm, body mass 73.3 ± 3.3 kg; Team B: n=16, age 22.2 ± 3.4 years, height 178.8 ± 6.2 cm, body mass 73.2 ± 5.3 kg) participated in the study. They performed (on a grass football field) a modified shuttle run test consisting of three stages of running at speeds of 10, 12 and 14 km/h between two marks 20 m apart; the speed was adjusted by means of an acoustic signal. Fingertip capillary blood samples were taken during the one-minute interval between the stages, to determine plasma lactate concentrations using a YSI 23L (Yellow Springs Instruments Inc., Ohio, USA) blood lactate analyser. Heart rates were monitored using short range radio telemetry (Sporttester PE 3000, Polar Electro, Kempele, Finland) during the runs. The tests were repeated at the end of a six week pre-season preparation. The training programme for team A placed emphasis on sessions aiming to increase aerobic capacity. Team B, which appeared to have a better aerobic capacity at the first test, gave priority to workouts on strength, anaerobic capacity, technique and tactics. Statistical analysis included calculations of means and standard deviations. Comparisons between means employed the student t-test.

3 Results

Significantly lower plasma lactate concentrations and heart rates were observed at each running speed for Team A during the second evaluation (Table 1). The effect was more pronounced at the lower speeds, suggesting beneficial effects especially in aerobic capacity. No significant decrease in plasma lactate concentrations at the 10 km/h stage was observed for Team B, following the 6-week period, whereas a decrease was observed at the higher running speeds (Table 1). Heart rates decreased at each speed for Team B during the second visit.

Table 1. Plasma lactate concentrations and heart rates obtained during two tests six weeks apart for Team A. Figures are as means ± SD

Team A	10 km/h		12 km/h		14 km/h	
n=13	Lactate mmol/l	Heart rate beats/min	Lactate mmol/l	Heart rate beats/min	Lactate mmol/l	Heart rate beats/min
First test	7.6±1.7	158±9.2	10.9±1.5	178±10	20.4±2.2	187±11
Second test	4.9±1.1	136±12.5	7.6±1.5	163±10	16.4±3.5	177±9
t-test	$P<0.001$	$P<0.001$	$P<0.001$	$P<0.001$	$P<0.01$	$P<0.05$

Table 2. Plasma lactate concentrations and heart rates obtained during two tests six weeks apart for Team B. Figures are as means ± SD.

Team B	10 km/h		12 km/h		14 km/h	
n=16	Lactate mmol/l	Heart rate beats/min	Lactate mmol/l	Heart rate beats/min	Lactate mmol/l	Heart rate beats/min
First test	4.7±1.3	162±7	8.8±2.0	178±7	17.8±3.2	191±5
Second test	4.1±1.0	148±7	6.6±2.0	166±7	15.0±3.3	180±5
t-test	$P>0.05$	$P<0.001$	$P<0.01$	$P<0.001$	$P<0.05$	$P<0.001$

4 Discussion

The shuttle run test is specific to soccer in that it involves directional changes of motion and acceleration. Plasma lactate concentrations and heart rates during the test were higher when compared with previous results (Kinderman et al., 1993; Schnabel et al., 1981) obtained on continuous treadmill or field running tests. The relatively high lactate concentrations in the present study may be partly explained by the use of plasma values which are higher than whole blood lactate (Buono and Yeager, 1986) Team B appeared to start the preparation programme in a more favourable state than Team A, in terms of plasma lactates, which were significantly lower for Team B ($P<0.01$) at all speeds. This is not surprising as Team B participated in a play-off league 5 weeks before the first test, whereas Team A had detrained for 8 weeks. No significant differences existed between the two teams after the second test. Thus the changes in plasma lactate concentrations suggest a more pronounced improvement of aerobic capacity in Team A. This finding parallels the observation that aerobic capacity improves more, if starting at a lower level of fitness (Fox and Mathews, 1981) Whereas changes in plasma lactate and heart rate levels proceeded in parallel for Team A, no such trend was observed for Team B. This may be due to the nature of the training (anaerobic threshold training), where dissimilar changes may be seen in blood lactates and heart rates.

5 Conclusions

i) The "modified shuttle run test" is especially in evaluating the changes in aerobic capacity of soccer players.
i) The differences observed between two teams at the start of the preparation period necessitate the modification of training plans. In this study, it was obvious that team B could lower the emphasis on general aerobic capacity training within the soccer season.

6 References

Buono, M.J. and Yeager, J.E. (1986) Intraerythrocyte and plasma lactate concentrations during exercise in humans. **European Journal of Applied Physiology,** 55, 326-329.
Fox, E.L. and Matthews, D.K. (1981) Physiological Effects of Physical Training. **The Physiological Basis of Physical Education and Athletics,** CBS College Publishing, pp. 293-393.
Kinderman, W., Gabriel, H., Coen, B. and Urnhausen, A. (1993) Sportmedizinishe Leistungsdiagnostik im fußball. **Deutsche Zeitschrift für Sportmedizin,** 44, 232-244.
Schnabel von, A., Kindermann, W. and Schmit, W.M. (1981) Aerobe Kapazität von Fußballspielern unterschiedlicher Spielstärke. **Deutsche Zeitschrift für Sportmedizin,** 5, 120-127.

ENDURANCE CAPACITY OF SOCCER PLAYERS PRE-SEASON AND DURING THE PLAYING SEASON

A. N. REBELO and J.M.C. SOARES
Faculty of Physical Education and Sport Sciences
University of Porto, Portugal

1 Introduction

Soccer calls for intermittent prolonged efforts combined with short periods of high intensity and long periods of low intensity exercise. The distance covered in high intensity activities decreases in the second half of matches (Bangsbo et al., 1991; Rebelo and Soares, 1992). It was demonstrated that glycogen depletion is correlated with fatigue in endurance exercise (Gollnick, 1982; Sahlin et al., 1990); this has also been shown to occur in soccer (Karlsson, 1969; Jacobs et al., 1982). This has been confirmed by other studies (Rebelo and Soares, 1993; Bangsbo, 1993; Wilmore and Costill, 1994). Bangsbo (1993) found a decrease in lactate and an increase in free fatty acid concentrations during the second half of soccer games.

Apparently, the soccer player needs a good aerobic capacity to maintain the intensity of exercise in matches and to recover from the more highly demanding activities. Endurance training has a "glycogen sparing" effect (Henriksson, 1977). An increased utilization of fat as a metabolic fuel during exercise reduces the rate of glycogen utilization as an energetic source, and this phenomenon might be of special importance for improving endurance capacity (Karlsson et al., 1974). With a good aerobic capacity, the players can reduce their glycogen consumption, using more lipids in the low intensity activities, saving glycogen for more intensive demands (Gollnick et al., 1974). Moreover, endurance training also effectively improves the rate of clearance of lactate produced during anaerobic efforts (Donovan and Brooks, 1983; Donovan and Pagliassotti; 1990).

The aerobic capacity of soccer players needs to be evaluated in a specific way, i.e., by specific intermittent tests. The pre-season in soccer is usually described as the main period of annual training to improve the physical capacity of players. The physiological demands of matches also have some impact on the players' fitness. The aim of this study was to compare the level of fitness of soccer players before and after the pre-season period as well as in the middle of the playing season.

2 Methods

The main characteristics of the type of training during pre-season and during the playing season are presented in Table 1.

Table 1. Characteristics of the training during pre-season and during the playing season

		Pre-season	Season
Number of training sessions per week		8.2	8
Number of training weeks		6	20
Training time per week		561 min (9h 20min)	503 (8h 18min)
Time per training session		67 min	62.7 min
Aerobic training		16.3 %	10.8 %
Anaerobic training:	Alactacid	1.5 %	2.3 %
	Lactacid	12.6 %	1.2 %
Strength training:	Endurance	7.7 %	0.7 %
	Power	3.0 %	0.4 %
Training match		5 %	23.1 %
Gaming drills		34.7 %	42.6 %
Match		18.4 %	18.2 %
Number of matches		5	23

Eleven male professional soccer players belonging to a first-league team in Portugal were studied. The players carried out a field test (intermittent field test, IFT) designed by Bangsbo and Lindquist (1992). The activity changed between high- and low-intensity exercise for 15 and 10 s, respectively. The duration of the test was 16.5 min and the result was the distance covered during the 10 min high intensity running. Heart rate of the players was monitored with a short range radio telemeter (Sport-tester PE-4000) during all tests and was sampled at 15 s intervals.

The players were evaluated three times: at the begining (July) and at the end (August) of the pre-season and in the middle (January) of the playing season.

3 Results

The distance covered in August was longer than in July and the distance covered in January was longer than in August (Fig. 1).

Table 2. Distance covered (m) during the IFT

	July	August	January	Global sample
Mean	1821	1904*	1992**	1906
Range	1693-1930	1818-1990	1841-2155	1693-2155

* Higher values (P<0.01) than in July ** Higher values (P<0.05) than in August

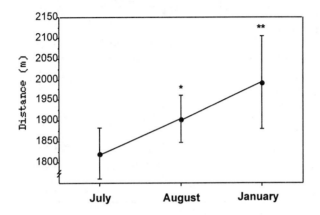

Figure 1. Distance covered (m) during the IFT
* Higher values (P<0.01) than in July ** Higher values
(P<0.05) than in August

Mean HR during IFT was lower in August than in July (Table 3; Fig. 2).

Table 3. Heart-rate (beats/min) during the IFT

	July	August	January
Mean±SD	170±17	165±13*	167±12
Range	130-189	130-181	128-182

* Lower values (P=0.012) than in July

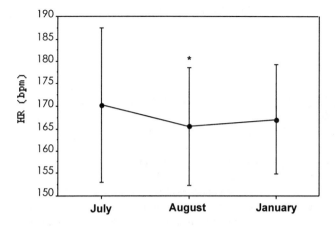

Figure 2. Heart-rate (beats/min) during the IFT
* Lower values (P=0.012) than in July

4 Discussion

The IFT is employed to evaluate the soccer-specific endurance capacity (Bangsbo and Lindquist, 1992). In this study, the mean distance covered in the three tests periods (1906 m) appeared a little lower than that found by Bangsbo (1994) in Danish top level soccer players (1926 m).The distance covered in the IFT in August was higher than in July. These results speak in favour of an efficient pre-seasonal training, because in the beginning of the pre-season, soccer players usually show a lower physical fitness level when compared with the level noted in the playing season. The performance in the IFT in January was even higher than in August, which could be explained by the small number of training weeks during pre-season (6 weeks). Another reason could be the number of matches played before the seasonal test. During pre-season, the athletes played only 5 matches and in some of these they did not play the whole game. Bangsbo (1994) showed that the endurance of Brøndby players was higher in the middle than at the begining of the playing season. Ekblom (1989) evaluated the performance of Swedish First Division soccer players with a field test; this test included specific activities of the game (e.g. jump, running backwards, changing of direction,and so on.). The performance showed a progressive increase during the competitive period.

   Heart rate during the IFT was 168±14 beats/min or 86% of maximum HR. Smodlaka (1978) found that the HR during a match was 85% of HR-max for 57% of the playing time, which corresponds to an oxygen consumption close to 80% of VO_2 max (Ekblom, 1986). Ali and Farrally (1991) reported a mean HR of 171 beats/min in semi-professional players during the match. Bangsbo (1992) found a mean HR of 164 beats/min during the first half and 154 beats/min during the second half for players in a Danish League match. So, the exercise intensity during the IFT was sligthly higher than during those matches. This can be explained by the differences in the "time motion" characteristics of the game (Bangsbo et al., 1991; Rebelo, 1993) and of the IFT. The IFT consists of high-intensity exercise periods of 15 s and recovery periods of 10 s. During a match, the mean duration of high-intensity exercise periods is shorter and the duration of low-intensity longer exercise periods. However, the distance covered during the IFT is correlated with the performance in an intermittent endurance test designed with reference to the "time motion" characteristics of soccer (Bangsbo and Lindquist, 1992).

When comparing the distances covered in the three tests, higher values were obtained in August than in July, as well as in January compared to August. However, HR values were lower in August than in July. This could reflect a training effect on submaximal exercise heart-rate, i.e., training and matches seem to improve the endurance of the players in a way that they can inprove their performance in the IFT with decreased physiological costs. This effect might represent a certain benefit during match performance.

The present data suggest that (i) the pre-season period was probably not long enough to prepare the players for the first matches of the season and (ii) the match practice is of special importance for an improvement in the capacity of soccer players for intermittent endurance exercise.

5 References

Ali, A. and Farrally, M. (1991) Recording soccer players` heart rates during matches. **Journal of Sports Sciences**, 9, 183-189.

Bangsbo, J. (1992) Metabolism in soccer. Abstract from the **European Congress on Football Medicine**, Stockholm.

Bangsbo, J. (1993) **The Physiology of Soccer - With Special Reference to Intense Intermittent Exercise**. Ho+Storm, Copenhagen.

Bangsbo, J. (1994) **Fitness Training in Football - a Scientific Approach**. HO+Storm, Copenhagen.

Bangsbo, J and Lindquist, F. (1992) Comparison of various exercise tests with endurance performance during soccer in professional players. **International Journal of Sports Medicine,** 13 (2), 125-132.

Bangsbo, J. Norregaard, L. and Thorso, F. (1991) Activity profile of competition soccer. **Canadian Journal of Sport Sciences,** 16 , 110-116.

Donovan, C. and Brooks, G. (1983) Endurance training affects lactate clearance, not lactate production. **American Journal of Physiology**, 244, E83-E92.

Donovan, C. and Pagliassotti, M. (1990) Enhanced efficiency of lactate removal after endurance training. **Journal of Applied Physiology**, 68 (3), 1053-1058.

Ekblom, B. (1986) Applied physiology of soccer. **Sports Medicine**, 3,   50-50.

Ekblom, B. (1989) A field test for soccer players. **Science and Football**, 1, 13-15.

Gollnick, P.D. (1982) Peripheral factors as limitations to exercise capacity. **Canadian Journal of Applied Sport Sciences**, 7, 14-21.

Gollnick, P.D., Piehl, K. and Saltin, B. (1974) Selective glycogen depletion patterns in human skeletal muscle fibres after exercises of varying intensity and at varying pedalling rates. **Journal of Physiology**, 241, 45-57.

Henriksson, J. (1977) Training induced adaptations of skeletal muscle and metabolism during submaximal exercise. **Journal of Physiology**, 270, 661-675.

Jacobs, I., Westlin, N., Karlsson, N. and Rasmusson (1982) Muscle glycogen and diet in elite soccer players. **European Journal of Applied Physiology**, 48, 297-302.

Karlsson, H. (1969) Kolhydratomsartning under en fotbollsmatch. **Report Department of Physiology III**, reference 6, Karolinska Institute, Stockolm.

Karlsson, J. Nordesco, L.O. and Saltin, B. (1974) Muscle glycogen utilization during exercise after physical training. **Acta Physiologica Scandinavica**, 90, 210-217.

Rebelo, A. N. (1993) Time-motion analysis of soccer players during matches. **Masters Thesis**. Faculty of Physical Education and Sport Sciences. University of Porto (in Portuguese).

Rebelo, A. N. and Soares, J.M.C. (1992) A comparative study of time-motion analysis during the two halves of a soccer game. Abstract from the **First World Congress of Notational Analysis of Sport,** Liverpool, November 22nd-25th.

Rebelo, A. N. and Soares, J.M.C. (1993) Is the blood lactate concentration an objective method for intensity evaluation during soccer games? Abstract from the **FIMS 7th European Sports Medecine Congress,** Nicosia, Cyprus.

Sahlin, K., Katz, A.and Broberg, S. (1990) Tricarboxylic acid cycle intermediates in human muscle during prolonged exercise. **American Journal of Physiology**, 259, C834-C841.

Smodlaka, V. J. (1978) Cardiovascular aspects of soccer. **The Physician and Sportsmedicine**, 18, 66-70.

Wilmore, J.H. and Costill, D.L. (1994) **Physiology of Sport and Exercise**. Human Kinetics, Champaign, Illinois.

FITNESS PROFILES OF PROFESSIONAL SOCCER PLAYERS BEFORE AND AFTER PRE-SEASON CONDITIONING

T.H. MERCER, N.P. GLEESON, and J. MITCHELL
Division of Sport, Health and Exercise, Staffordshire University, Stoke-on-Trent, ST4 2DF, U.K.

1 Introduction

The physical preparation of the professional soccer player in England has principally been based upon an intense 5-7 week period of pre-season training (Reilly, 1990). On this basis, players are expected to acquire a foundation level of physical conditioning to enable them to perform successfully over a competitive season of around nine months duration and often involving more than 50 matches.
English professional players enter the pre-season period in a poor state of physical fitness (Reilly and Thomas, 1977; White et al., 1988). However, Davis et al. (1992) have also reported English professional players (n=135) as exhibiting good performance for selected physical fitness attributes, immediately prior to the commencement of a competitive season. It is noteworthy that relatively little research (Reilly and Thomas, 1977) has examined the effect of conventional English pre-season conditioning programmes upon physical fitness. The aim of this study was to investigate the influence of a pre-season conditioning programme upon the fitness profiles of professional soccer players.

2 Methods

2.1 Subjects
The subjects for this study were 15 members of the first-team squad of an Endsleigh Football League First Division club. The sample (Mean±SD; 24.7±3.8 years; 1.79± 0.08 metres; 78.1±9.16 kg) comprised 2 goalkeepers, 4 defenders, 5 midfield players, and 4 forwards. This represented 75% of the complete first team squad and included only those players in the club who were able to complete all pre- and post-conditioning assessments.

2.2 Pre-season conditioning programme
Pre-season conditioning at this club followed a well-established programme (4 years) which consisted of 21 training days, 7 "friendly" (warm-up) matches and 7 rest days. The organisation of this conditioning schedule is summarised in Table 1.

Table 1. Organisation of pre-season conditioning

	MON	TUES	WED	THUR	FRI	SAT	SUN
WEEK 1	-	-	-	RTC	PRE	T	OFF
WEEK 2	T	T	T	T		T	OFF	Game
WEEK 3	T	Game	T	T		T	Game	OFF
WEEK 4	T	Game	T	T		T	Game	OFF
WEEK 5	T	Game	T	T		T	T	OFF
WEEK 6	T	Game	T	POST	T	OFF	FLG

RTC = Return to Club; T = Training; OFF = Rest Day;
Game = "Friendly" match; FLG = First League match;
PRE & POST = Pre- & Post-conditioning fitness assessments.

Training consisted of two sessions per day, each of approximately 90-120 minutes duration. The conditioning emphasis of sessions in weeks 1-3 (n=26) was 85% aerobic/endurance conditioning and 15% game-related activity. The aerobic conditioning was based almost exclusively on variants of distance running (cross-country running, fartlek-running, aerobic interval running, hill-running). The game-related activity was based around small-sided games (3 v 3, 5 v 5). The conditioning emphasis in weeks 4-5 (16 sessions) was 60% aerobic conditioning, 20% functional training/high-intensity shuttle-running, and 20% tactical training/set-plays (re-starts).

2.3 Fitness assessment
A battery of fitness assessments was administered to all players one day prior to and one day before the end of pre-season training. These assessments and their scheduling are outlined in Table 2, below. All subjects completed standardised warm-ups prior to specific assessments. All running tests were carried out in an indoor sports hall and all other tests in an exercise science laboratory.

Table 2. Phasing of assessment

Schedule	Content
09.25-11.50:	Body Composition
	Isokinetic Leg Strength (1.05 rad/s)
	Sit and Reach Flexibility
	Explosive Leg Strength (vertical jump)
	Illinois Agility Run
11.55-12.40:	Group warm-ups
	20 m Maximal Multi-stage Shuttle Run
12.25-14.00:	Snack break & questionnaire completion
14.05-15.00:	Group warm-ups
	Repeated Sprint runs
	Warm-down

Anthropometric measures included height, body mass and percent body fat estimated from skinfold thickness (Durnin and Womersley, 1974). Isokinetic leg strength (peak knee extension and flexion torques and peak torque ratio at 1.05 rad/s) was assessed using a Lido isokinetic dynamometer (Loredan Inc., Ca USA) according to the protocol of Gleeson and Mercer (1992). Vertical jump (with counter movement and arm-swing) was used as index of "explosive" leg muscle performance (Balsom, 1994). Sit-and-Reach flexibility (hip forward flexion) was assessed according to the method of Corbin and Lindsey (1988). An index of motor coordination was determined from Illinois Agility Run performance (Adams et al., 1968). Following test familiarisation and practice all performance tests (flexibility, explosive leg muscle performance and agility) were assessed as the best score of three trial attempts.

Maximal aerobic power was estimated from performance on the 20 m Maximal Multistage shuttle run (U.K. National Coaching Foundation, Leeds, 1988). After a period of recovery the players performed 8 x 50 m sprints in the form of a shuttle run with a turn at 25 m. All sprints started and finished at the same point and were hand-timed (0.01 s). A recovery period of 30 seconds duration separated each sprint. Fastest, slowest and mean sprint times were recorded.

2.4 Statistical analyses
Statistical differences between pre- and post-conditioning fitness profiles were analysed using ANOVA repeated measures design (MANOVA). Statistical significance was accepted at P<0.05. All statistical analyses were programmed using SPSS/PC+ (V3.1).

3 Results

No significant differences were observed between pre- and post-conditioning isokinetic leg strength (Table 3).

Table 3. Isokinetic leg strength performance: pre-and post-conditioning [n=15; Mean (SD)]

(1.05 rad/s)	Pre-	Post-	P
Peak Torque Ext-L (Nm)	222 (21)	218 (32)	NSD
Peak Torque Ext-R (Nm)	226 (28)	223 (23)	NSD
Peak Torque Flex-L (Nm)	145 (35)	139 (32)	NSD
Peak Torque Flex-R (Nm)	139 (26)	139 (24)	NSD
Flex/Ext-L ratio (%)	65 (13)	63 (09)	NSD
Flex/Ext-R ratio (%)	61 (08)	62 (10)	NSD
L-R Ext ratio (%)	98 (09)	97 (10)	NSD
L-R Flex ratio (%)	104 (28)	100 (18)	NSD

Ext = knee extension; Flex = knee flexion; L = left leg;
R = right leg; NSD = no significant difference.

Analysis of anthropometric measures revealed no significant differences in body mass following the conditioning period. Sum of skinfolds and associated estimation of percent body fat were observed to be reduced significantly at the end of the conditioning programme. Estimated VO_2 max (ml/kg/min) was significantly increased at the end of the conditioning period.

Table 4. Body composition and estimated VO_2 max: pre-and post-conditioning [n=15; Mean (SD)]

	Pre-	Post-	P
Body Mass (kg)	78.1 (9.2)	77.6 (8.7)	NSD
Sum of Skinfolds (mm)	44.1 (12)	40.3 (9.7)	F= 9.2; P<0.01
Body Fat (%)	17.3 (3.7)	16.2 (3.4)	F=10.7; P<0.01
Estimated VO_2 max (ml/kg/min)	56.8 (4.9)	62.6 (3.8)	F= 109; P<0.001

Table 5 illustrates the magnitude of change(s) in Illinois Agility Run time and Vertical Jump (counter movement and arm-swing) performance observed over the investigative period.

Table 5. Sit & Reach flexibility, Vertical Jump, Illinois Agility Run, and Repeated Sprint Run performance: pre-and post-conditioning [n=15; Mean (SD)]

	Pre-	Post-	P
Sit & Reach flexibility (cm)	43.1 (4.5)	41.8 (4.7)	NSD
Vertical Jump (cm) (no arm-swing)	44.1 (7.4)	44.8 (6.8)	NSD
Vertical Jump (cm) (arm-swing)	54.6 (8.5)	52.7 (8.2)	F=15.4; P<0.01
Illinois Agility Run (s)	16.5 (0.4)	16.0 (0.4)	F=53.3; P<0.001
Repeated Sprint [FAST] (s)	8.60 (0.25)	8.61 (0.27)	NSD
Repeated Sprint [SLOW] (s)	9.27 (0.33)	9.13 (0.34)	NSD
Repeated Sprint [MEAN] (s)	8.93 (0.29)	8.88 (0.27)	NSD

4 Discussion

The physical characteristics of the players observed in this study are very similar to other groups of English Football League professionals of comparable training status. The estimated percent body fat values of our subjects compare favourably with the 19.3±0.6% reported by White et al. (1988) for First Division professionals (n=17), but less well with the 10.5±1.8% reported by Davis et al. (1992) for a sample of 122 First and Second Division outfield players.

Vertical jump performance of the present sample falls within the range of performances reported for comparable subjects by Reilly (1990). Similar performance levels were achieved for the Illinois Agility Run time in comparison with the subjects of White and colleagues (1988) (16.5 s and 16.4 s respectively).

The pre-conditioning estimated aerobic power of players in the current study (56.8 ± 4.9 ml/kg/min) compares very favourably with values reported by White et al. (1988) (46.6 ± 1.2 ml/kg/min) for players returning to pre-season training. The post-conditioning values of this study (62.6 ± 3.8 ml/kg/min) also compare favourably with data reported by Davis et al. (1992) for players near the end of the pre-season conditioning phase (60.4 ± 3.0 ml/kg/min).   Given the nature and volume of conditioning undertaken it is not surprising that both a significant reduction in percent body fat and a significant improvement in estimated VO_2 max should have occurred. This pattern of adaptation confirms the earlier work of Reilly and Thomas (1977) who also noted a significant improvement in cardiovascular fitness during the pre-season period. Moreover, the improvement in VO2 max of the players in the current study places them above the level of 60 ml/kg/min recommended, as desirable by Reilly (1994), for elite outfield players.

The improvement in agility run performance might plausibly be attributed to game-related training. Mercer (1988) has observed that changes of direction and/or speed occur approximately every 3 s in 5 v 5 game play. This type of activity therefore appears to provide sufficient stimulus for the development of agility.

It is also noteworthy that isokinetic leg strength was not altered and explosive leg muscular performance was significantly decreased after the period of pre-season conditioning. These results confirm the earlier findings of Reilly and Thomas (1977) with regard to the impairment of muscle strength consequent to an over-concentration on endurance training. Whilst these results are unsurprising they are a cause for some concern as Reilly and Thomas (1980) have reported that stronger individuals were the most successful in avoiding injuries throughout a season. Since none of the pre-season conditioning period is conventionally focused on strength development, it seems reasonable to surmise that potential deficiencies in leg strength performance are likely to be carried into the competitive season.

5 Conclusion

This study confirms the effectiveness of a conventional pre-season conditioning programme in favourably altering maximal aerobic power, skinfold thickness and agility run performance of English professional soccer players. It is recommended, however, that a more comprehensive periodisation of preparatory conditioning is undertaken to offset any potential deficiencies in strength performance.

6 References

Adams, W.C., Haskill, W.L., Leigh, R.D., Razor, J.E., and McCristal, K.J. (1968) **Foundations of Physical Activity.** Stipes and Co. Champaign, IL, pp. 111.
Balsom, P. (1994) Evaluation of physical performance, in **Football (Soccer): Handbook of Sports Medicine and Science** (ed B.Ekblom), Blackwell Scientific Publications, Oxford, pp. 113-115.
Corbin, C. and Lindsey, R. (1988) **Concepts of Physical Fitness.** W.C.Brown, Dubuque, Iowa, pp. 105.
Davis, J.A., Brewer, J. and Atkin, D. (1992) Pre-season physiological characteristics of English first and second division soccer players. **Journal of Sports Sciences**, 10, 541-547.
Gleeson,N.P. and Mercer,T.H.(1992) Reproducibility of isokinetic leg strength and endurance characteristics of adult men and women. **European Journal of Applied Physiology**, 65, 221-228.
Mercer, T.H. (1988) Movement pattern characteristics and heart-rate responses during indoor soccer play. **Journal of Sports Sciences**, 6, 250 - 251.

National Coaching Foundation. (1988) **Multistage Fitness Test**. White Line Press, Leeds.

Reilly, T. (1990) Football, in **Physiology of Sports** (eds T. Reilly, N. Secher, P.Snell and C.Williams), E. & F.N. Spon, London, pp. 372-401.

Reilly, T. (1994) Physiological profile of the player, in **Football (Soccer): Handbook of Sports Medicine and Science** (ed. B.Ekblom), Blackwell Scientific Publications, Oxford, pp. 78-94.

Reilly, T. and Thomas, V. (1977) Effects of a programme of pre-season training on the fitness of soccer players. **Journal of Sports Medicine and Physical Fitness**, 17, 401-412.

Reilly, T. and Thomas, V. (1980) The stability of fitness factors over a season of professional soccer as indicated by serial factor analyses, in **Kinanthropometry 11** (eds M. Ostyn, G. Beunen, and J. Simons), Baltimore, University Park Press, pp. 245-257.

White, J.E., Emery, T.M., Kane, J.L., Groves, R. and Risman, A.B. (1988) Pre-season fitness profiles of professional soccer players, in **Science and Football** (eds T. Reilly, A. Lees, K.Davids and W.J.Murphy, London, E. & F.N. Spon, pp. 164-171.

AN INVESTIGATION INTO THE FITNESS OF PROFESSIONAL SOCCER PLAYERS OVER TWO SEASONS

K. BRADY*, A. MAILE and B. EWING
Moray House Institute of Education, Heriot-Watt University, Cramond Campus, Edinburgh, Scotland.

* Present address: Centre for Sport and Exercise Sciences, Liverpool John Moores University, Byrom street, Liverpool, L3 3AF, England.

1 Introduction

As the soccer season extends over 10 months of the year, it is essential that training is designed both to enable players to cope with the physiological demands and technical excellence required in a single game, and to maintain an optimal level of fitness over the season. Whilst the anaerobic energy systems play an essential role in soccer, the aerobic system supplies the greatest amount of energy, accounting for up to 90% of the total consumption. Thus, the improvement and maintenance of the aerobic system, together with a high tolerance to lactate is essential in professional soccer.

To date, few studies have focused on changes in fitness levels over a competitive season. Of these, the findings are equivocal with Bangsbo (1994) and Reilly and Thomas, (1980) indicating fitness levels are maintained over the season, whilst Heller et al. (1992) suggested optimal fitness may not be maintained over the season.

The present study therefore had two purposes: firstly, to monitor the aerobic capacity of a group of professional soccer players throughout two competitive seasons, and secondly, to assess the effects of a close season training programme on pre-season levels of fitness.

2 Methods

A total of twenty-four professional soccer players comprising the playing squad of a Scottish Premier Division soccer club were tested over two seasons. Tests were conducted in June 1992, December 1992, April 1993 (pre, middle and end of playing season for season 1), and June 1993, July 1993, December 1993 and March 1994 (beginning of pre-season, end of pre-season, mid-season and end of season for season 2).

At each test, players performed an incremental exercise test at intensities starting at 10 km/h and finishing at 17 km/h, with the intensity increasing by 1 km/h every 4 min. Fingertip blood was collected during the last 15-30 s of each work intensity. Blood lactate was determined by way of an Analox micro-stat GM7 analyser (London), and the lactate values plotted against work intensity. In order to obtain a specific threshold, a straight line was drawn between the two points corresponding to 10 and 17 km/h from which the lactate value furthest from the line was identified.

Two lines of regression were then calculated and drawn, the first comprising all lactate values from 10 km/h up to and including the point furthest from the line, and the second comprising the remaining lactate values. A specific "lactate threshold" was identified as the point of intersection of the two regression lines. Differences in the work intensity and the lactate values corresponding to the lactate threshold were analysed over time (two competitive seasons) using one-way ANOVA.

With the use of short range radio telemeters (Polar Sport Tester, Kemple, Finland), resting heart rates (RHR) were recorded 5 minutes prior to exercise and sub-maximal heart rates collected every 15 s throughout the exercise period. These sub-maximal heart rate data were then plotted against work intensity, and a specific work intensity corresponding to a sub-maximal heart rate of 170 identified. Differences in work intensity and resting heart rate were analysed (using one-way ANOVA) for effects of time.

Lactate and heart rate data from April 1993 were used to design closed season training programmes for each player. From the lactate graphs, a specific threshold was identified and this point, together with the previous lactate data point on the graph was used to identify a 'band' of work intensity. When transferred to the heart rate graphs, a heart rate 'band' was then identified, the centre of which was found, and a heart rate range of 10 beats/min (5 beats/min either side of the centre) recorded. Each player was given a training programme highlighting the distance to run, time to completion and an estimated heart rate 'band' in which to exercise.

3 Results

Table 1 shows resting heart rates (RHR), work intensity at a heart rate of 170 beats/min, plus the lactate and work intensity values corresponding to the lactate threshold (Tlac) for the squad over both seasons.

Table 1. Mean resting heart rates, work intensity at a heart rate of 170, plus lactate and work intensity at the lactate threshold

Test date	Number of players	RHR (beats/min)	Work intensity at 170(km/h)	Lactate values at Tlac (mM)	Work intensity at Tlac (km/h)
June 92	18	75	12.8	2.06	13.4
Dec 92	17	70	14.1*	1.63	13.7*
April 93	21	71	13.9	1.86	13.4
June 93	18	77	12.6	1.87	12.8
July 93	13	66*	14.8*#	1.53	13.6*
Dec 93	12	67	14.7*#	1.41	14.1*
March 94	13	69	14.2*	1.69	13.8*

* Significantly different from June 1993.
# Significantly different from June 1992.

In comparison to June 1993, the work intensity corresponding to a heart rate of 170 was significantly higher in December 1992, July 1993, December 1993 and March 1994, whilst in comparison to June 1992, significantly higher work intensities were found only for July and December 1993. Only at July 1993 (end of pre-season) and December 1993 (mid-season) were players found to have significantly higher work intensities in comparison to early pre-season for both season 1 (June 1992)and season 2 (June 1993). No significant differences were noted between the start of pre-season in season 1 and the start of pre-season in season 2, or between the end of season 1 (April 1993)and the start of season 2 (June 1993). The resting heart rates measured at the end of pre-season in season 2 (July 1993) were significantly higher than those recorded only eight weeks previously at the beginning of pre-season training (June 1993).

Whilst no significant differences were seen between the lactate values corresponding to the lactate threshold, the work intensities corresponding to the lactate threshold were found to be significantly higher in December 1992, July 1993, December 1993 and March 1994 in comparison to June 1993. No significant difference was observed between the start of pre-season in season 1 (June 1992) and the start of pre-season in season 2 (June 1993). No significant difference was observed between the end of season 1 and the start of season 2.

4 Discussion

While the physiological preparation of professional players aims to maintain an optimal level of fitness over the course of a season, fluctuations in both volume and intensity of training occur which may have obvious consequences, not only on fitness levels, but also on performance. Results from this study appear to highlight this fact, showing fitness levels of players may change significantly at various points of the season.

In season 1, the work intensity corresponding to a sub-maximal heart rate of 170 beats/min had improved by the middle of the season, and whilst in decline towards the end of the season was not found to be significantly different. However, results for season 2 indicate that this increased work intensity may well have reached its peak by the end of pre-season. It may be the case that players achieve peak aerobic fitness levels prior to the season, maintain this level during the first half of the season and although not found to be significant, may start to lose some of their aerobic fitness during the second half of the season.

Following consultations with the coaching staff it appears that the pre-season preparation period was typically identified by a high volume of training. The intensity, whilst never reaching very high levels, rose steadily over this time.

Similarly, the work intensity at which the lactate threshold occurred was higher by the middle of the season and in decline during the remainder of the season in season 1, although again, these results were not significant. Significant results were found in season 2, whereby the work intensity corresponding to the lactate threshold increased sharply during the pre-season period, but did not peak until around the middle of the season. The work intensities had declined slightly by the end of the season.

As previously mentioned, the volume of training is high during pre-season with the intensity increasing slowly during this period. Once the season starts, the emphasis changes to a slightly lower volume of training and an increased intensity. Most players have to play two games each week during the early part of the season and so training volume is reduced and speed emphasised. It is presumed therefore, that such an exercise regimen accounts for the peak work intensities (heart rate of 170 beats/min) found at the end of pre-season, and the peak work intensities (lactate threshold) found in the middle of season 2.

In both cases, however, the work intensity was declining by the end of the season and whilst not significant, must be noted. This may be a consequence of a reduced level of fitness training, in both volume and intensity, in an attempt to keep the players fresh for the remaining games.

The closed season training programme given to all of the players was an attempt to help them maintain a degree of fitness during this period, and whilst the lack of any significant difference between April 1993 and June 1993 suggests the programme may have been effective, subjective responses tended to suggest otherwise. Verbal feedback from the players on return to pre-season training indicated the programmes were too light in intensity and therefore, may not have delivered the stimulus required to maintain the degree of fitness previously acquired. It must also be noted that players were not supervised during the closed season.

In comparison to season 1, all of the results for season 2 suggest the players achieved a higher level of fitness during the course of the second season. This may be a consequence of informative discussions between the coaching staff and the physiologists whereby, in relation to the club's fixtures and the results from the first season, a planned and progressive programme of preparation was implemented over the pre-season and early competitive season period. As the season progressed, less emphasis was placed on physiological information.

Finally, as previously noted by Reilly and Thomas (1977), fitness levels are significantly improved during the pre-season due to the fitness of the players being at its lowest point at the beginning of pre-season training. With the fitness levels in June 1993 returning to the levels witnessed in June 1992, it may be that the fitness of professional soccer players is lost during the closed season and does not improve from year to year.

Whilst it is acknowledged that players require a break following a long playing season, it is advisable that players avoid the large decreases in fitness that occur through inactivity. The 'race' back to full fitness for some players during pre-season may predispose them to injury and undue stress.

5 Conclusions

The present data show that variations in fitness occur throughout the competitive season and that fitness levels may not be maintained throughout the course of a complete season. This is due to the fluctuations in both volume and intensity of training with respect to the timetable of games to play.

It is suggested that coaches endeavour to assess both the volume and the intensity of training in an attempt to ensure fitness levels are maintained throughout the season. This is particularly relevant towards the end of the season. Preparation therefore, must be a continual year round process whereby, inclusive of rest and recuperational factors, physical training, through attention to established physiological information, must be systematic, planned and progressive in nature, in order that players achieve an optimal level of performance throughout the season.

6 References

Bangsbo, J. (1994) The physiology of soccer - with special reference to intense intermittent exercise. **Acta Physiologica Scandinavica,** 151, Suppl. 619.

Heller, J., Prochazka, L., Bunc, V., Dlouha, R. and Novotny, J. (1992) Functional capacity in top league football players during the competitive period. **Journal of Sports Sciences**, 10, 150.

Reilly, T. and Thomas, V. (1977) Effects of a programme of pre-season training on the fitness of soccer players. **Journal of Sports Medicine and Physical Fitness**, 17, 401-411.

Reilly, T. and Thomas, V. (1980) The stability of fitness factors over a season of professional soccer as indicated by serial factor analysis, in **Kinanthropometry 11** (eds M. Ostyn, G. Beunen and J. Simons), University Park Press, Baltimore, pp. 247-257.

PART FOUR

Medical Aspects of Football

FOOTBALLERS' BODY CLOCKS

T. REILLY
Centre for Sport and Exercise Sciences, School of Human Sciences, Liverpool John Moores University, Mountford Building, Byrom Street, Liverpool L3 3AF.

1 Introduction

Many biological processes are influenced by timing mechanisms and as a consequence display rhythmic fluctuations. Human circadian rhythms refer to cycles or regular fluctuations that occur within a period of about 24 hours. The circadian body clock refers to those biological mechanisms that have habituated to the solar day. In this review the relevance of the body clock to exercise in general and to football in particular is considered.

Circadian rhythms in the human are characterized as endogenous or exogenous depending on the degree to which they are affected by factors extraneous to the individual. An endogenous rhythm presupposes an innate cluster of cells that acts as a timekeeper. Timekeeping functions have been attributed to the suprachiasmatic nucleus cells of the hypothalamus and to the pineal gland (Minors and Waterhouse, 1981). Local timekeepers have been isolated in heart and skeletal muscles. Exogenous rhythms, on the other hand, are easily altered with changes in the environment. The main environmental factors that provide time cues are light, temperature, physical and social activity (Reilly, 1990).

There is probably a family of clocks organised hierarchically and two major rhythms that have relevance for exercise and sports performance. These are the rhythms in body temperature, regarded as the fundamental variable, and the sleep-wake cycle, by means of which humans order their rest-work schedules. Both of these cycles enter into consideration when rhythms in football performance are examined.

Those rhythms in performance that have relevance to the football codes are first highlighted. This has consequences for the time of day in which training is optimised. Sleep and sleep disturbances are considered in terms of interactions with circadian effects. The influences of travel fatigue and body clock disturbances are discussed before outlining the procedures that have potential for reducing effects of jet-lag.

2 Rhythms in Exercise Performance

The components of football performance vary between the different codes, although all football codes have requirements for muscle strength, muscle power output, flexibility, agility, aerobic power and endurance. Football makes demands on neuromotor functions including reaction time, information processing and decision making, game-related skills and timing of actions. Football performance is generally assessed by the game result which is insensitive to individual players' contributions to the total team effort or unique components of each player's performance. Nevertheless any detraction from players' potential to produce maximal effort is likely to affect the team's functioning most effectively as a playing unit.

Many components of human performance show cycles closely in phase with the circadian curve in body temperature (Table 1). Such performance measures include jumping ability and running, speed of limb movement and muscle strength (Reilly, 1990). The variation in jumping ability is attributable to a circadian rhythm in muscular power output which has been reported for arm exercise as well as leg exercise (Reilly and Down, 1992). A rhythm in isometric leg strength of the knee extensors incorporates an amplitude (mean to peak difference) of 7% (Taylor et al., 1994), similar to that observed in other muscle groups. Dynamic muscle performance as reflected in peak torque on an isokinetic dynamometer varies by about the same extent for back and for leg muscles (Coldwells et al., 1994). These observations have an impact in a clinical context when muscle strength is being assessed. They have relevance also in a conditioning context where the highest weight training loads can be handled at the time that body temperature at rest is at its peak (Wilby et al., 1987)
As maximal voluntary contractions are greatest at the time that body temperature is at its high point, it is likely that this is the best time for training muscle strength.

Joint stiffness is greatest after getting up in the morning, decreases during the day as joint temperature rises until stiffness starts to increase again in the evening. Flexibility measures follow a similar but inverse pattern, being poorest in the morning and best in the afternoon or early evening. The perception of exertion also varies during the day and is most easily confirmed by the exercise intensity at which athletes choose to train. Metabolic responses to steady-rate exercise also vary with time of day (Reilly and Brooks, 1982, 1990): a further discomfort associated with training early in the morning is due to the low VE/VO_2 ratio at that time (Reilly, 1982). Indications are that a graded warm-up is especially important for morning training sessions. Provision of a strength training stimulus is best effected in the afternoon or evening: this applies irrespective of whether the variation in muscle performance is due to a central component reflected in motivation to perform or a peripheral component, expressed as an endogenous circadian rhythm in muscle function.

The practice in many professional soccer clubs is to have training sessions in the morning. This applies even though matches are usually scheduled for afternoon or evening times. The main reason for this asynchrony is related to lifestyle organisation in the profession. The practice is different among amateur players and in other codes (for example, Gaelic football) where training is invariably in the evening, after normal working hours.

Table 1. The amplitude and acrophase (time of day at at which the peak is observed) of circadian rhythms reported in the literature

Variable	Amplitude (% of mean)	Acrophase	Reference
Rectal temperature	1.1%	18:00	Taylor et al. (1994)
	1.2%	17:46	Reilly and Brooks (1990)
Oxygen consumption	6.2%	17:23	Reilly and Brooks (1990)
Maximal isometric strength	7.1%	17:48	Taylor et al. (1994)
Leg strength	8.9%	18:20	Coldwells et al. (1994)
Back strength	10.5%	16:53	Coldwells et al. (1994)
Jump performance	3.4%	17:45	Reilly and Down (1986)
Anaerobic power	2.1%	18:11	Reilly and Down (1992)

Activities that are highly dependent on central nervous system operations tend to peak around mid-day or early afternoon. This is due to rhythms in arousal which tend to lead those associated with body temperature by about 4 hours. The time for peak exercise performance with multivariate components extends over a window of 4-6 hours rather than coincides with a particular time of day. Nevertheless, for football teams with a facility for training twice a day, chronobiological theory would designate skills training for the first session and the more strenuous conditioning work for the later session.

3 Sleep and Sleep Loss

Sleep is an enigma in the sense that it has never been conclusively demonstrated why it is needed. The predominant theory is that the major need for sleep resides in nerve cells and related substances in the brain. Sleep is also linked with maintenance of the immune system. Football players, like other athletes, are convinced that good quality sleep is important as a pre-requisite for optimum preparation for both training and competing.

There is a large variation between individuals in the duration of sleep taken. Professional soccer players spend longer in bed than does the adult population and also a large amount of time during the working day in resting or recumbent postures (Reilly and Thomas, 1979). The distribution of their sleeping patterns during the week is also varied: it is likely that the time spent sleeping on some days exceeds that which is required for purposes of `restitution' (Horne, 1988).

The need for sleep becomes evident when effects of sleep loss on performance are examined. It is possible to continue to play soccer without sleeping for up to 3 to 4 days at a low intensity: this has been demonstrated in studies of 5-a-side indoor soccer played for 91 hours for charity fund raising. After the second consecutive night of complete sleep loss a majority of the players experienced temporary visual hallucinations (Reilly and Walsh, 1981). The activity level of the players varied systematically during the day according to the normal body temperature curve. The circadian rhythm in muscle (grip) strength was retained without a fall from day to day whereas neuromotor and cognitive functions (unprepared reaction time, decision making) showed a deteriorating trend. That circadian variation in gross motor function, such as muscle strength, is greater than the effects of sleep loss has been demonstrated in females as well as in males (Reilly and Hales, 1988).

Clearly the effects of sleep loss are influenced by the nature of the task. Complex and challenging activities are less affected than are monotonous and boring ones, and so players are less likely to be influenced by disturbed sleep prior to match-play than they might believe. Strong motivation can often override the effects of sleep loss. Sleep loss and environmental factors interact but not in an additive or predictable manner. Heat, for example, compounds the effects of loss of sleep whilst noise tends to offset them partly. Individual expectations and previous experience of sleep deprivation may also be relevant, so that it is not easy to ascertain the interplay of all the factors influencing football performance after sleep loss.

Partial sleep loss is a more common problem for footballers than is sleep deprivation for a full night. Disturbed sleep can promote anxiety in those who believe that good quality sleep is essential. Nevertheless behaviourial rather than pharmacological means of treating sleeplessness related to competition stress are recommended in view of potential hang-over effects of sleeping tablets (Reilly et al., 1997). This might include an afternoon nap (or rest in bed to relax) prior to an evening kick-off.

Partial sleep loss has potential to influence the effectiveness of training practices. A regimen of three consecutive nights of sleeping 3 hours only each night was reported to have no influence on performance of weight-training exercises (Reilly and Piercy, 1994). This maintenance of performance was restricted to the exercises completed in the early part of the training session. As the session progressed, performance began to deteriorate, an effect observed by the third day (i.e. after 3 nights of disturbed sleep).

This has consequences for the safety of such regimens and the increased risk of injury with protracted sleep disturbances.

4 Travel `Fatigue' and Jet-Lag

Travel fatigue refers to feelings of tiredness and inertia following a journey whether it be by road, rail or air. It may be linked with boredom during the journey, or stiffness due to restricted postures whilst travelling. To safeguard against adverse effects of `travel fatigue', professional football teams may undertake to travel to the competitive venue the evening before. This strategy has to be balanced against any discomfort due to players sleeping in unfamiliar environments. Effects of long journeys are quickly relieved by light stretching and the refreshment of a shower. These do not apply when circadian rhythms are desynchronized as a result of airflight across multiple time-zones.

Rhythms are desynchronized in conditions of nocturnal work or crossing time zones. Young individuals seem to have better tolerance of shift work due to better regulated rhythms. Fitness also seems to play a role, physically active subjects demonstrating higher amplitudes in resting rhythms indicative of better control.

Athletes travelling across time zones to compete are prone to jet lag that results from desynchronoses. Symptoms include nausea, disorientation, difficulties sleeping and so on. These are worse when travelling eastwards than going westwards and performance tends to be affected for some days. The extent of the deterioration depends, among other things, on the number of time zones crossed.

The body temperature adapts at a rate of about 60 min per day for each time zone crossed. In long haul flights between Britain and Australia/New Zealand, the direction of travel doesn't seem to make much difference. In a study of Rugby League players, the rate of adaptation of grip strength was only a little faster than this `one hour per time zone' rule. The grip strength was better in the morning than in the evening at first, returning to equality by Day 4 in Australia after which the normal circadian rhythm was soon reasserted. In such circumstances it was recommended that training practices should be held in the morning until jet lag symptoms abated (Reilly and Mellor, 1988).

Performance of footballers can be adversely affected even when flights are within one country, coast to coast in U.S.A. and Australia for example. American football teams are at a disadvantage after travelling between eastern and western coastal zones if the game is scheduled for a time of day incompatible with chronobiological criteria (Jehue et al., 1993). For day games, west coast teams were found to be at a disadvantage when playing on the opposite coast (a 3-hour phase advance). In contrast, they were advantaged by night games against East and Central teams. Normal training times can be adapted in advance of trips coast-to-coast to take the scheduled game time into consideration.

Various strategies may be adopted to cope with jet lag. These include diet, drugs, light, and most used by athletes are phase adjustment and exercise strategies.

In one experiment athletes adjusted their sleeping patterns in 3 groups (3, 4 and 5 hour phase shifts), alternating phase delays and phase advances. Otherwise they lived their normal lifestyle. Rhythms were determined at baseline, and 3 and 7 days after the shifts; the rhythms were readjusted by these manoeuvres but incompletely so. Performance deteriorated in the process. It was concluded that this kind of adjustment has little benefit to the athlete in preparation for competing overseas, except for 1-2 time-zone changes (Reilly and Maskell, 1989).

Napping is the traveller's usual recourse when strong jet lag feelings are experienced. This is counter-productive since it anchors rhythms at the zone of departure and retards resynchronization. Exercise is more useful as it helps to re-tune rhythms to the new local conditions. Experience with footballers returning to England from the Far East is that light training, on the day of arrival if time permits, helps accelerate readjustment and relieves jet lag symptoms (Reilly, 1993).

5 Summary

In summary, circadian rhythms are shown to affect performance both in gross motor performance measures and in co-ordination skills. Athletes are mostly unaware of their effects until rhythms are desynchronized as occurs in jet-lag syndrome. These self-sustaining rhythms in exercise performance should be recognised by practitioners concerned with the preparation of footballers and their travel plans.

6 References

Coldwells, A., Atkinson, G. and Reilly, T. (1994) Sources of variation in back and leg dynamometry. **Ergonomics**, 37, 79-86.

Horne, J.A. (1988) **Why We Sleep: the Function of Sleep in Humans and Other Mammals**. Oxford University Press, Oxford.

Jehue, R., Street, D. and Huizenga, R. (1993) Effect of time zone and game time changes on team performance : National Football League. **Medicine and Science in Sports and Exercise**, 25, 127-131.

Minors, D.S. and Waterhouse, J.M. (1981) **Circadian Rhythms and the Human**. John Wright, Bristol.

Reilly, T. (1982) Circadian variations in ventilation and metabolic responses to submaximal exercise. **British Journal of Sports Medicine**, 16, 115-117.

Reilly, T. (1990) Human circadian rhythms and exercise. Critical Reviews in **Biomedical Engineering**, 18, 165-180.

Reilly, T. (1993) Science and football: an introduction, in **Science and Football II** (eds T. Reilly, J. Clarys and A. Stibbe), E. and F.N. Spon, London, pp. 3-11.

Reilly, T. and Brooks, G.A. (1982) Investigation of circadian rhythms in metabolic responses to exercise. **Ergonomics**, 25, 1093-1107.

Reilly, T. and Brooks, G.A. (1990) Selective persistence of circadian rhythms in physiological responses to exercise. **Chronobiology International**, 7, 59-67.

Reilly, T. and Down, A. (1986) Circadian variation in the standing broad jump. **Perceptual and Motor Skills**, 62, 830.

Reilly, T. and Down, A. (1992) Investigation of circadian rhythms in anaerobic power and capacity of the legs. **Journal of Sports Medicine and Physical Fitness**, 32, 342-347.

Reilly, T. and Hales, A.J. (1988) Effects of partial sleep deprivation on performance measures in females, in **Contemporary Ergonomics** 1988 (ed E.D. Megaw), Taylor and Francis, London, pp. 509-515.

Reilly, T. and Maskell, P. (1989) Effects of altering the sleep-wake cycle in human circadian rhythms and motor performance. in Proceedings **First IOC Congress on Sport Science**, Colorado Springs, 1989, 106-107.

Reilly, T. and Mellor, S. (1988) Jet lag in student Rugby League players following a near-maximal time-zone shift, in **Science and Football** (eds T. Reilly, A. Lees, K. Davids, and W.J. Murphy). E. and F.N. Spon, London, pp. 249-256.

Reilly, T. and Piercy, M. (1994) The effect of partial sleep deprivation on weight-lifting performance. **Ergonomics**, 37, 107-115.

Reilly, T. and Thomas, V. (1979) Estimated daily energy expenditures in professional association footballers. **Ergonomics**, 22, 541-548.

Reilly, T. and Walsh T. (1981) Physiological, psychological and performance measures during an endurance record for 5-a-side soccer play. **British Journal of Sports Medicine**, 15, 122-128.

Reilly, T., Atkinson, G. and Waterhouse, J. (1997) **Biological Rhythms and Exercise**. Oxford University Press, Oxford.

Taylor, D., Gibson, H., Edwards, R.H.T. and Reilly, T. (1994) Correction of isometric leg strength tests for time of day. **European Journal of Experimental Musculoskeletal Research**, 3, 25-27.

Wilby, J., Linge, K., Reilly, T. and Troup, J.D.G. (1987) Circadian variation and the effects of circuit weight-training. **Ergonomics**, 30, 47-54.

INJURIES IN AMERICAN FOOTBALL

DONALD T. KIRKENDALL, KEVIN P. SPEER and WILLIAM E. GARRETT, JR
Section of Sports Medicine, Duke University Medical Center, Durham, NC USA
27710

1 Introduction

Professional American football (hereafter referred to as football) was born in 1892 when "Pudge" Hefflefinger was paid $500 to play a game of football against the Pittsburgh Athletic Club. In 1919, the American Professional Football League began operation. This league was the predecessor to the National Football League (NFL) which was formed in 1922. The game is the most popular collision sport in the country and interest in the game has spread beyond the borders of the United States of America. The Canadian Football League operates teams in Canada and the USA. The NFL holds preseason exhibition games in Europe and the Far East and the World Football League, a developmental league for the NFL, has had teams throughout Europe.

There is an intimate relationship between television and football. The intermittent nature of the game allows for instant replays, commentator and fan analysis, commercials and so on. Over 130 million people in the USA alone watch the championship game, the Super Bowl. In comparison, the World Cup has over 1.5 billion people worldwide watching the final match. The growth and interest in football closely parallels the improvement in technology and growth of television.

Football presented a unique opportunity to physicians. The game became the early laboratory for the diagnosis and treatment of athletic injuries. Football injuries could be seen at the time of the injury and replayed numerous times. The mechanism of injury could be studied and the communcation media followed the progress of the player as he attempted to return to play. It may not be a coincidence that the growth of football, televised sport and sports medicine parallel each other. This review concentrates on orthopaedic injuries sustained during practice and games to the exclusion of other potential problems such as dehydration and temperature regulation.

2 Epidemiology of Football Injuries

The 22 players on the field at any one time have specific assignments that involve direct contact, deception and surprise. This can match players of widely divergent sizes coming into contact or collision at varying rates of speed, leading to the potential for injury.

It is estimated that there are 1.3 million High School and 75,000 College players who participate in American Football each year. The estimates are around 600,000 injuries (Adkison et al., 1974; DeLee and Farney, 1992) each year resulting in an injury rate of 11-81%. In the NFL, there are 1.5 injuries/player/year (Irrgang et al., 1994) while in high school the rate is 0.5 injuries/player/year (DeLee and Farney, 1992). High school football players are twice as likely as their non-playing peers to have a severe injury and 6 times as likely to require knee surgery (DeLee and Farney, 1992). Although the majority of time is spent in practice, over half the injuries occur during games resulting in a 3-20 greater risk of injury in a game vs. practice (Olson, 1979) and catastrophic injuries are most likely to happen during a game. Half the injuries occur to the leg and 30% to the arm. Overall, the knee sustains 20% of all injuries closely followed by the ankle (DeLee and Farney, 1992). Sprains and strains account for 40% of all injuries followed by contusions (25%), fractures (10%), concussions (5%) and dislocations (5%) with other injuries accounting for the remaining 15% (Irrgang et al., 1994). Running backs sustain the most injuries and centers the least (Prager et al., 1989; Andresen et al., 1989). There is no difference between injuries suffered by members of the offense and defense. Injuries occur during tackling (32%), blocking (26%), running with the ball (19%) and being blocked (10%, Andresen et al., 1989). Most of the injuries occur in the 2nd and 3rd quarter and the least occur in the 1st quarter. The peak injury rate is mid-season and the lowest rate is at the end of the season.

3 Risk Factors and Injuries

The first of four risk factors is the field surface. The number of knee and ankle injuries can be reduced significantly with maintenance of the fields. Further reductions can be achieved if the soccer style moulded sole is used instead of the long screw-in shoe cleats (Mueller and Blyth, 1974). The injury rate is also reduced when the game is played on a wet surface, whether the surface is natural or artificial (Andresen et al., 1989). There does appear to be an increase in injuries on artificial turf, but definitive data are still unavailable.

The typical football shoe had 7 cleats of 0.5-0.75 inches (1.3-1.9 cm) in length which can fix the foot to the ground. Changing to a soccer style shoe with a moulded sole reduced the number of ankle injuries, but increased the number of "turf toe" injuries. Current shoes have cleats 0.5 inches (1.3 cm) long and 0.375 inches (0.9 cm) in diameter. The use of high-top shoes, to protect the ankle, by the interior linemen has increased.

Practice activities also affect the risk of injuries. Practice factors include the length of practice, the amount of contact allowed, time of year and the experience of the coaches. There is a high risk of injury during a long practice with a lot of contact conducted by an inexperienced coach in the preseason.

The fourth risk is within the rules of the game. Changes in rules have led to reductions in one type of injury and increases in others. Catastrophic neck injuries have decreased dramatically since spearing (using the head as a battering ram when tackling) was outlawed, but shoulder labral tears increased when the blocking rules were changed.

4 Football Injuries

Most football injuries are routine orthopaedic trauma (from player-to-player, player-to-ground, overuse, strains-sprains and so on). There are some injuries that are peculiar to football and specific to certain positions. We assume that the reader is familiar with the names and responsibilities of the individual football positions.

4.1 Head and neck injuries
Concussion. Despite the protection afforded by the helmet, it is estimated that there are more concussions in football than in any other sport in the USA. There has been a great deal of publicity about the number and severity of concussions suffered by quarterbacks and receivers that have necessitated early retirement rather than risk further injury. The lack of firm guidelines on grading of a concussion and return to play add to the debate.
Facial injuries. The improvement in the face mask has led to a dramatic reduction in facial lacerations and fractures (Irrgang et al., 1994). Nonetheless, nasal fractures and septal injuries still occur.
Cervical sprains and sprains. Neck strains are the most common neck injury and involve the sternocleidomastoid, trapezius, rhomboid, levator scapulae, erector spinae, and scalenes. The initial pain usually subsides and the player returns to play only to have pain and limited motion in the hours to days after a game. Cervical sprains typically involve the capsule of the facet joints of the vertebra. This is usually caused by a compression impact. Local tenderness or neurologic symptoms are rare. Thirty-three to 50% of college football players show radiographic changes in the cervical spine after 4 years of competition (Speer and Kelly, unpublished observations).
Cervical fractures and dislocations. These injuries are rare, but catastrophic, resulting in paraplegia or quadriplegia. Data on neck injuries from 1959-1963 were compared with 1971-1975. While the rate of neck injuries declined, the number of cervical spine fractures increased by 204% and the number of cases of quadriplegia increased by 116%. Rules changes prohibiting spearing were implemented in 1976 resulting in a dramatic decrease in cases of quadriplegia (Figure 1).

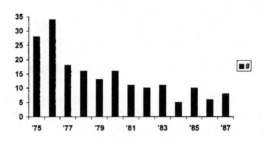

Figure 1. Number of cases of quadreplegia from football per year.

4.2 Shoulder

Brachial plexus. During blocking, tackling or collision with the ground, a forced lateral deviation of the neck can result in pain or numbness in the ipsilateral arm. These are referred to as "stingers" or "burners" and have happened to half the college players at some time in their career (Robertson et al., 1979); unfortunately, many of these go unreported to the medical staff (Sallis et al., 1992). These can be associated with cervical spine injuries and require spine and neurological evaluation.

Acromioclavicular injuries. Football can account for over 40% of the acromioclavicular injuries seen in athletes (Cox, 1981). The mechanism of injury is from a direct blow due to a fall on the point of the shoulder. A player's arms may be held during tackling and in the resultant fall may contact the ground first on the point of the shoulder.

Glenohumeral instability. Improper tackling techniques are blamed for shoulder instability. An "arm tackle" in football involves attempting to tackle with one arm, usually abducted and externally rotated, when force is applied to the arm. Posterior instability can occur from a direct blow to the anterior aspect of the shoulder or from a fall on an internally rotated and adducted arm.

Rotator cuff. Injuries to the rotator cuff are seen in activities that entail overhead throwing. In football, this is usually limited to the quarterbacks. However, the throwing motion in quarterbacks is different than pitching in baseball. As a result, rotator cuff injuries are not as common as in other overhead sports.

Glenoid labral tears. This injury is peculiar to football. The diagnosis of the injury did not occur until after the blocking rules were changed in 1984 allowing the linemen to block with extended arms. If a forceful posterior shear force is applied to the arms when glenohumeral compression forces already exist, the posterior labrum can tear (Speer, personal communication).

Tackler's exostosis. This injury occurs mostly in linebackers who sustain repeated blows to the insertion of the deltoid muscle. These can result in periosteal tearing and formation of new bone.

4.3 Elbow, forearm, wrist and hand

Elbow instability. Quarterbacks are particularly vulnerable to elbow instability. If an opponent hits the quarterback's arm while throwing, the sudden deceleration can cause the elbow to become unstable. Falling on a hyperextended arm may result in an elbow dislocation.

Forearm, wrist and hand. The lower arm and hand are relatively unprotected for most players. Interior linemen may have the forearms padded and hands protected. For them, minor injuries can be overcome while injuries to the hands in running backs, receivers and quarterbacks can be devastating. Forearm fractures can occur from landing on an outstretched arm or from arm tackling. Most injuries to the hand and wrist (contusion, fractures, dislocations) occur from a direct blow to or from rigid protective equipment, the pile-up of players following a tackle or from being stepped on.

4.4 Spine injuries

Lumbar injuries. Injuries to the lumbar spine are common in football players, especially interior linemen. The repetitive flexion, extension and torsional forces place a heavy stress on the lumbar vertebra. Between 12 and 30% of players lose playing time to lumbar injuries. These injuries are mostly sprains, and strains from general trauma of blocking and weight-lifting. Fifty percent of interior linemen have lumbar problems (Speer and Murray, 1995). Other lumbar injuries include disc herniation and spondylolisthesis. Over a 4-year period of college football, 50% of linemen show radiographic changes to their lumbar spine (Speer et al., 1995).

4.5 Hip injuries

Fractures and dislocations of the hip make up less than 3% of all football injuries (Hal and Mitchell, 1981; Culpepper and Niemann, 1983). The most common injury is a contusion to the iliac crest frequently call a "hip pointer." Groin contusions, while not common, can have serious consequences like traumatic phlebitis or femoral neuropathy (Renstrom, 1992). Osteonecrosis of the femoral head from a subluxation may be more common than thought (Cooper et al., 1991).

4.6 Leg injuries

Thigh injuries. Even though the thigh is padded, a direct blow to the muscles can lead to myositis ossificans. Up to 2-3 weeks training may be lost and the injury can lead to a thigh compartment syndrome. Muscle strains are predictable according to position. While all players are susceptible to groin strains, kickers are particularly vulnerable to strains of the rectus femoris while speed players have a high incidence of hamstring strains (Irrgang et al., 1994).

Knee injuries. The nature of the game makes the knee particularly vulnerable to injury and knee injuries account for a quarter to a third of all football injuries (Adkison et al., 1974; DeLee and Farney, 1992; Olson, 1979). The medial collateral ligament is injured when a valgus force is exerted on the leg. While efforts have been made to prevent the injury with prophylactic knee bracing, the effectiveness of such braces is still in question. Interior linemen are particularly vulnerable to medial collateral ligament sprains. Wide receivers who change direction by suddenly decelerating and rotating their upper leg can injure their anterior cruciate ligament. Running backs who receive a direct blow to the proximal tibia while being tackled can have their posterior cruciate ligament injured. Internal/external rotation over a fixed leg can result in meniscal tears and can happen to any player.

Patellofemoral problems. A patellar dislocation is a non-contact injury that can occur when the leg is rotated and the quadriceps contracts to extend the knee. Patellar tendinitis, or jumper's knee, is an inflammatory tendinitis of the patellar tendon as it comes off the inferior pole of the patella. Defensive backs and receivers are the most vulnerable to jumper's knee.

Ankle injuries. In football as in other sports, lateral ankle sprains are the most common type of sprain. A substantial number of medial and syndemosis sprains can occur when the foot supinates with internal rotation of the talus on the tibia (Irrgang et al., 1994). These can occur from a change of direction or in the pile-up following a tackle.

Turf toe. Artificial surfaces and lighter more flexible shoes have led to the so-called "turf toe" injury. This is a sprain of the plantar capsular ligament of the first metatarsophalangeal joint. When tackled, this joint can be forcibly dorsiflexed, spraining the ligament. Most of the injuries occur from forced dorsiflexion although forced plantar flexion, on being tackled from behind, can also lead to turf toe. Pain is felt during the push-off phase of running.

5 Summary

It is obvious that football has served as a useful laboratory for the study of injuries that can occur in sports. While many of the injuries are routine trauma, selected injuries are specific to football. Rules changes have led to decreases in catastrophic injuries while increasing other injuries.

6 References

Adkison, J.W. Requa, R.K. and Garrick, J.G. (1974) Injury rates in high school football. A comparison of synthetic and grass fields. **Clinical Orthopaedics**, 99, 131-136.

Andresen, B.L. Hoffman, M.D. and Barton, L.W. (1989) High school football injuries: field conditions and other factors. **Wisconsin Medical Journal**, 88(10), 28-31.

Cooper, D.E. Warren, R.F. and Barnes, R. (1991) Traumatic subluxation of the hip resulting in aseptic necrosis and condrylolysis in a professional football player. **American Journal of Sports Medicine,** 19, 322-324.

Cox, J.S. (1981) The fate of the acromioclavicular joint in athletic injuries. **American Journal of Sports Medicine,** 9, 50-59.

Culpepper, M.I. and Niemann, K.M.W. (1983) High school football injuries in Birmingham, Alabama. **Southern Medical Journal,** 76, 873-878.

DeLee, J.C. and Farney, W.C. (1992) Incidence of injury in Texas high school football. **American Journal of Sports Medicine,** 20, 575-580.

Hal, R.W. and Mitchell, W. (1981) Football injuries in Hawaii in 1979. **Hawaii Medical Journal,** 40, 180-182.

Irrgang, J.J. Miller, M.D. and Johnson, D.L. (1994) Football, in **Sports Injuries: Mechanisms, Prevention, Treatment** (eds F. Fu and D.A. Stone), Williams & Wilkins, Baltimore, MD, pp. 349-374.

Levy, A.S. Speer, K.P. and Lintner, S. (1995) Pulmonary barotrauma in American football players. Communication to 3rd World Congress on Science and Football, Cardiff, Wales.

Mueller, F.O. and Blyth, C.S. (1974) North Carolina high school football injury study: equipment and prevention. **Journal of Sports Medicine,** 2, 1-10.

Olson, O.C. (1979) The Spokane study: high school football injuries. **The Physician and Sportsmedicine**, 7(12), 75-82.

Prager, B.I. Fitton, W.L. Cahill, B.R. and Olson, G.H. (1989) High school football injuries: a prospective study and pitfalls of data collection. **American Journal of Sports Medicine**, 17, 681-682.

Renstrom, P.A.H.F. (1992) Tendon and muscle injuries in the groin area. **Clinics in Sports Medicine,** 11, 815-833.

Robertson, W.C. Eichman, E.L. and Clancy, W.D. (1979) Upper trunk brachial plexopathy in football players. **Journal of the American Medical Association**, 241, 1480-1482.

Sallis, R.E. Jones, K. and Knopp, W. (1992) Burners: offensive strategy for an underreported injury. **The Physician and Sportsmedicine,** 20, 47-55.

Speer, K.P. and Murray, J. (1995) Injuries to the low back in football. Communication to **3rd World Congress on Science and Football**, Cardiff, Wales.

Speer, K.P., Pavlov, H. Warren, R.F. Moorman, C.T. and Barnes, R. (1995) Lumbar spine abnormalities in elite football linemen. Communication to **3rd World Congress on Science and Football**, Cardiff, Wales.

LUMBAR SPINE ABNORMALITIES IN AMERICAN FOOTBALL LINEMEN

KEVIN P. SPEER, HELENE PAVLOV and RUSSELL F. WARREN
Duke University Medical Center, Box 3371, Durham, North Carolina 27710, U.S.A.

1 Introduction

It is possible that chronic participation in American Football places the spine at risk of trauma. The purpose of this study is to present prevalence data on lumbar spine radiographic abnormalities in elite football linemen.

2 Materials and Methods

This study is an assessment of lumbar spine radiographic abnormalities in 238 elite football linemen. These football players were present at the 1992 and 1993 National Football League (NFL) Combine held in Indianapolis, Indiana. The NFL Combine is an annual pre-draft camp where the top 300 collegiate football players eligible for the draft are comprehensively assessed by physicians and other medical personnel representing all NFL member teams.

The linemen in this study included the offensive centre, offensive guard, offensive tackle, tight end, defensive nosetackle (noseguard), defensive tackle, and defensive end. A thorough history and physical evaluation were obtained and the results for all players in these positions were available for this study. The players were also queried as to whether they had had any prior history of lower-back problems. If so, they were asked if they had lost any time (game or practice) due to low-back injury.

During the 1992 and 1993 NFL Combines, 96% of all football linemen present (total number = 248) had at least a lateral lumbar spine radiograph obtained. Of the 238 linemen with a lateral lumbar radiograph, 107 had additional lumbar spine radiographs. These included an anteroposterior, right and left obliques, and coned-down lumbosacral antero-posterior views. The additional spine radiographs were ordered by one or more of the NFL teams' medical staff. Any NFL head team physician had the authority to order additional radiographs on any player. Thus, many of the additional lumbar films were not necessarily based on actual history of any low-back problems.

The lumbar spine radiographs were reviewed by an orthopaedic radiologist. The interpretive criteria for the various diagnoses were, thus, kept constant. The radiographic abnormalities assessed were:
  i)   Hypolordosis
  ii)   Spondylolysis (Level and Grade)

iii)   Disc space narrowing
iv)   Limbus vertebrae
v)   Schmorl's nodes
vi)   Degenerative disc disease (mild, moderate, or severe)

3 Results

Thirty-nine of the players affirmed a history of a low-back problem. The most common diagnosis was strain. None had had surgery on the lower back. Only five of the athletes acknowledged missing either a game or a practice session due to a low-back disorder. There was no statistical correlation between the affirmation of a history of low-back problem or pain and any of the radiographic lumbar spine abnormalities.

Twenty-six players had radiographic lumbar hypolordosis. None of these players had any increased incidence of other radiographic abnormalities or an increased incidence of a positive response to a history of low-back symptoms.

Spondylolysis was found in 24 players (10.1%). Three players had an L3 spondylolysis (all were Grade 0). Four players had an L4 spondylolysis (2 were Grade 0, 2 were Grade 1). Fifteen players had an L5 spondylolysis (8 were Grade 0, 4 were Grade 1, 2 were Grade 2). Two players had an S1 spondylolysis (1 was Grade 0, 1 was Grade 2). There was no association of the spondylolysis and the reported history of low-back symptoms.

Disc space narrowing was found in 75 players (31.5%). The levels of narrowing are as follows: 2 at T11-T12, 1 at T12-L1, 4 at L1-L2, 4 at L2-L3, 11 at L3-L4, 50 at L4-L5, 2 at L5-S1, 1 at S1-S2. Overall, two players had disc space narrowing at more than one level. There was no association of the disc space narrowing and the reported history of low-back symptoms.

Limbus vertebrae were diagnosed in 33 players (13.9%). Five players had limbus vertebrae at T12, 8 at L1, 5 at L2, 4 at L3, 6 at L4, and 5 at L5. There was no association of the limbus vertebrae and the reported history of low-back symptoms.

Schmorl's nodes were seen in 29 players (12.2%). Four had nodes at L1, 2 at L2, 7 at L3, 6 at L4, and 10 at L5. There was no association of the Schmorl's nodes and the reported history of low-back symptoms.

Mild degenerative disc disease (DDD) was diagnosed in 23 players (9.7%). The involved levels were as follows: 3 at T11-T12, 2 at L1-L2, 3 at L2-L3, 3 at L3-L4, 11 at L4-L5, 2 at L5-S1. Three players had mild DDD at more than one level. There was no association of the mild DDD and the reported history of low-back symptoms.

Moderate degenerative disc disease was diagnosed in 11 players (4.6%). The involved levels were as follows: 1 at T11-T12, 2 at T12-L1, 2 at L1-L2, 3 at L2-L3, 1 at L3-L4, 2 at L4-L5. Two players had moderate DDD at more than one level. There was no association of the moderate DDD and the reported history of low-back symptoms.

Severe degenerative disc disease was seen in only one player. The involved level was T11-T12. This player reported no history of low or mid-back pain.

The interior offensive line positions were defined as offensive centre, offensive guard, and offensive tackle. There were in total 131 players in this study whose position was the interior offensive line. The interior defensive line positions were defined as defensive noseguard (nosetackle) and defensive tackle. Many of the players at the Combine designated as defensive tackles also played defensive end for their college teams. There were altogether 82 players whose position was designated as interior defensive line.

The prevalence of spondylolysis in the offensive line was 10.7% as compared to 8.5% in the defensive line. The overall level distribution was similar with the majority at L5.

The prevalence of disc space narrowing in the offensive line was 39.7% as compared to 14.6% in the defensive line. The overall level distribution was similar with the majority at L4-L5.

The prevalence of mild degenerative disc disease in the offensive line was 11.5% as compared to 7.3% in the defensive line. The prevalence of moderate degenerative disc disease in the offensive line was 6.1% as compared to 3.6% in the defensive line.

4 Conclusions

Lumbar spine radiographic abnormalities are common in elite American Football linemen. This reflects both the nature of the position, the sport and the years these athletes have played football. The low number of players who admit to a history of low-back problems or symptoms reflects the perception of these athletes that this information may denote their draft status and is true for professional athletes in general.

Although these radiographic abnormalities may be the harbinger of future low-back problems, their presence alone should not exclude the athlete from participation.

THE DIAGNOSIS AND TREATMENT OF PULMONARY PNEUMOTHORAX IN GRID-IRON FOOTBALL

ANDREW S. LEVY, KEVIN SPEER, FRANK BASSETT & SCOTT LINTNER
Duke University Medical Center, Division of Orthopaedic Surgery, Sports Medicine Section, Box 3435, Durham, North Carolina 27710, U.S.A.

1 Introduction

While many authors have discussed injuries to the extremities, spine and head in American (grid-iron) football, little has been written regarding pulmonary and thoracic trauma in this sport (Kelly and Nichols, 1991; Watkins, 1986). The hard plastic shoulder pads provide substantial protection to the upper thoracic cavity anteriorly and posteriorly, but do little to defend the lower rib cage and lateral chest wall. While the diagnosis of bruised ribs is often linked with contact sports, small pneumothoraces may be difficult to diagnose on the sidelines. Furthermore, shortness of breath at rest may not be present in a well conditioned athlete. Since 1957, there have been six football related pneumothoraces diagnosed at a single university. The authors report their experience with football-induced pneumothoraces and consider the difficulties in diagnosing and treating this injury.

2 Methods and Materials

Six collegiate grid-iron football players that were initially diagnosed as having a chest contusion were subsequently found to have a pneumothorax. These players' records were retrospectively reviewed and the most recent three players were interviewed regarding their injury, its treatment and their clinical result.

There were four receivers and two running backs involved. Five incidents occurred as the result of a tackle and one occurred on contact with the ground. Four of the six players returned to play immediately after the initial injury and were not diagnosed until after the game. Difficulties with diagnosis included the presence of excessive noise in the vicinity of attempted auscultation and lack of dyspnea at rest. All patients required tube thoracostomy for their initial treatment. The most recent three players all returned to play two weeks post-injury. Rib taping was subjectively beneficial in alleviating chest wall discomfort in all cases.

3 Results and Discussion

A pneumothorax is the accumulation of extrapleural intrathoracic air due to a break in either the visceral or parietal pleura (Kirby and Ginsberg, 1992). It may be introduced directly following traumatic disruption of cutaneous or mucosal barriers or indirectly when the pressure gradient between the alveoli and their surrounding interstitial space is sufficient to cause alveolar rupture (Getz and Beasley, 1983; Jantz and Pierson, 1994). There is only a single case report in the literature on a pneumothorax in a football player. Little information is given on peculiarities of diagnosis, the nature of the mechanism, nor guidelines for treatment and rehabilitation (Moore, 1984).

The diagnosis of this injury on the football field is difficult. The majority of knowledge on pneumothoraces arises from experience in hospital settings. Classically, the predominant clinical signs of a pneumothorax include chest pain and dyspnea (O'Neil, 1987). These may resolve spontaneously within 24 - 72 hours despite persistence of the pneumothorax. The physical examination in a patient with a simple pneumothorax includes decreased breath sounds, loss of tactile vocal fremitus and auscultatory hyper-resonance. In tension pneumothorax, cyanosis, tachycardia, dyspnea and tracheal shift are the hallmark signs (Kirby and Ginsberg, 1992). Rib soreness and temporary windedness are not infrequent with contact sports. Additionally the physical condition of these young athletes probably would require larger ventilatory loss in order to develop dyspnea at rest. All of the classic findings on physical examination require auditory involvement. The excessive noise from the crowd and the band on the field makes this evaluation near impossible. One must also take into account that the auscultative detection of small pneumothoraces may be difficult in even ideal surroundings. In order to help differentiate chest contusions from pneumothoraces the clinical findings of splinting away from the injured side, and dyspnea with exertion should receive additional attention. We therefore require a "winded" player to run along the sideline under observation prior to returning to the game.

Unlike classically described pneumothoraces, the treatment of these injuries in athletes requires not only prevention of a tension pneumothorax and re-expansion of the lung, but also an expedient return to competition. Small pneumothoraces in minimally symptomatic healthy individuals can be observed for progression with serial radiographs (Jantz and Pierson, 1994). If they do not progress, one should expect a two-week time frame for a small pneumothorax to reabsorb completely. Pneumothoraces that are symptomatic, increasing in size or >25% should be evacuated. Percutaneous aspiration is considered successful if immediate cxr and serial cxr demonstrate >90% re-expansion. The problem is that partial collapse of the lung often seals the small breaks in the visceral pleura, but re-expansion breaks this seal and may allow another pneumothorax to occur. Consequently, simple aspiration is associated with a 20-50% recurrence rate (Serementis, 1970 and Swierenga et al., 1974). Another option in smaller symptomatic pneumothoraces is the use of a percutaneous 10-gauge catheter attached to a one-way valve. The use of this Heimlich valve with or without underwater suction has been reported to have an 80% success rate (Perlmutt et al., 1987). The remaining 20% required chest tube drainage. All of the cases presented here eventually required large bore chest tube insertion. Despite this, all were able to play within two weeks of the injury.

After the pneumothorax has been treated and the chest tube removed, a gradual return to play should be instituted. The three factors that must be taken into account are maintaining the player's conditioning, minimizing pain and protecting the injured chest wall. We prefer a goal orientated return to activity, rather than a time based one. Rib taping is very effective in decreasing pain and a flack jacket is utilized to protect the chest wall from impact. Pain, not shortness of breath, poses the greatest hurdle in the return to pre-injury competitive level.

4 References

Getz, S.B. & Beasley, W.E. (1983) Spontaneus pneumothorax. **American Journal of Surgery**, 145, 823-827.

Jantz, M.A. & Pierson, D.J. (1994) Pneumothorax and barotrauma. **Clinics In Chest Medicine**, 15, 75-91.

Kelly, J.P. & Nichols, J.S. (1991) Conclusion in sports. **Journal of the American Medical Association**, 266, 2867-2869.

Kirby, T.J. & Ginsberg, R.J. (1992) Management of the pneumothorax and barotrauma. **Clinics In Chest Medicine,** 13, 97-112.

Moore, S. (1984) Management of a pneumothorax, in a football player: a case report. **Athletic Training**, 19 (2), 129-130.

O'Neil, S. (1987) Spontaneus pneumothorax: Aetiology, management and complications. **Irish Medical Journal**, 80, 306-311.

Perlmutt, L.M., Braun, S.D. & Newmann, G.E. (1987) Transthoracic needle aspiration: use of a small chest tube to treat pneumothorax. **American Journal Roentology** 148, 849-851.

Serementis, M.G. (1970) The management of spontaneus pneumothorax. **Chest**, 57, 65-68.

Swierenga, J., Wagennar, J.P. & Bergstein, P.G. (1974) The value of thoracoscopy in the diagnosis and treatment of diseases affecting the pleura and lung. **Pneumonologie**, 151, 11.

Watkins, R.G. (1986) Neck injuries in football players. **Clinical Sports Medicine**, 5, 215-246.

CERVICAL SPINES OF MIDDLE-AGED SOCCER PLAYERS: RADIOGRAPHIC FINDINGS AND COMPUTER SIMULATION

HIDEKI KUROSAWA and TAKAHIRO YAMANOI
Sapporo Seikeigeka-junkankika Hospital,Kitano 1-2, Toyohiraku, Sapporo 040, Japan

1 Introduction

Soccer is undoubtedly the most popular and favoured sport in the world. It is relatively safe and the injury level in soccer is quite low compared with other team sports (McMaster and Walter,1978; Sullivan et al.,1980). Nevertheless soccer players receive numerous blows to the head and loads to the neck chiefly as a result of heading and occasionally due to other situations during match-play or in training.

Few reports have dealt with the chronic signs or symptoms of the neck resulting from the sport (Kurosawa et al.,1991). Sortland et al.(1982) reported that in examination of former players for the National Football Team of Norway the onset of degeneration was 10-20 years earlier and the frequency of degeneration was significantly higher compared with men of the same age groups.

The purpose of this study was to find out the early degenerative radiographic shadows of the neck of middle-aged soccer players and to analyze the stress distribution in heading using a finite element method (FEM), and to discuss the cause of the degenerative findings.

2 Materials and Methods

Cervical radiographies of twelve amateur veteran soccer players, aged 28 to 53 (average 40.1 ± 5.4) years were examined and the abnormal shadows were classified. The radiographic examination included: anterior-posterior view, lateral view of neutral, flexion and extension positions, and oblique views. They started the sport at an average ageof 14.8 ± 1.9 (9 to 18) years. The average period as active players was 15.0 ± 6.1(3 to 23) years. The bony spur was defined as positive(+) when the protrusion on the X-ray film was measured more than 2 mm.

In FEM analysis, a three-dimensional model was prepared from the radiogram of the lateral cervial spine which was taken at the position in which a ball hit the forehead in heading. The model consisted of the vertebrae, the intervertebral bodies, and the anterior longitudinal, the posterior longitudinal, and the supraspinous ligaments. The atlas and the axis were assumed as one united bony mass and the lower end of the 7th vertebra was assumed to be fixed and immovable. The model head(3.75 kgf) was also affixed to the upper end of the axis and a force from the anterior direction of 15.0 kgf was applied horizontally upon it. The material constants of Young's modulus and Poisson ratio were 1.428 kgf/mm^2 and 0.42 in the intervertebral body, 1.610 x 103 kgf/mm^2 and 0.25 in the vertebrae, and 2.490 x 10 kgf/mm^2 and 0.42 in the ligament.

3 Results

Abnormal radiographic shadows were: calcification of the anterior longitudinal ligament, anterior and posterior vertebral spur, ossicle between the spinous process possibly ligamentous, calcification of the nuchal ligament (Barsony), ossicle on the spinous process, and bony spur of the Luschka joint. Degenerative findings of each player and the incidences of them are shown in Table 1. One of the players(No.12) underwent an operation for the extirpation of the ossification of the nuchal ligament. The radiographs of a short stature payer(160 cm) (No.8), who claimed he was not at all a "header", showed nearly normal findings except for an ossicle in the interspinous ligament of C5 and C6. In one case limbus vertebra was found, which resembled calcification of annulus fibrosus which might be secondary to subclinical or chronic stress on the involved intervertebral disc (Kerns et al.,1986). In four cases a developmental spur was found but was also not regarded as a degenerative change because of the absence of reactive sclerosis beneath the spur (Keats,1988). In von Mises' stress distribution in three dimensional FEM analysis, the stress in heading was exhibited mainly in the lower part of the cervical spine (Fig.1).

Table 1. The degenerative X-ray shadows of each player and respective incidence of them. ALL: anterior longitudinal ligament, pro.: process

CASE	AGE (years)	Active period	Starting age	Barsony	Ossicle C5/6	Ossicle C6/7	Luschka's joint spur	Anterior vertebral spur	Posterior vertebral spur	Ossification of ALL	Ossicle on C7 spinous pr.
1. K.H.	41	20	15	+	+	-	+	+	+	-	+
2. K.T.	41	10	15	-	+	+	±	±	±	-	-
3. K.H.	41	15	15	+	+	-	+	+	+	-	-
4. H.S.	36	21	15	-	-	-	+	±	±	-	-
5. S.C.	53	20	15	+	-	+	+	+	+	-	-
6. T.N.	42	23	18	-	+	+	+	+	+	+	-
7. U.J.	41	3	15	+	-	+	+	+	+	+	-
8. M.Y.	42	15	15	-	+	-	±	±	±	-	-
9. M.M.	28	7	9	+	-	-	+	+	+	-	-
10.Y.T.	40	10	15	-	+	-	+	+	+	-	-
11.Y.H.	37	21	15	+	-	-	+	+	+	-	-
12.A.K.	41	15	15	+	+	+	+	+	+	+	+
	40.1 ±5.4	15.0 ±6.1	14.8 ±1.9	7/12 (58 %)	9/12 (75%)		10/12 (83 %)	9/12 (75 %)	9/12 (75 %)	3/12 (25 %)	3/12 (25 %)

4 Discussion

The finite element method is generally utilized in engineering analysis to overcome the difficulty of the variational methods, because it provides a systematic numerical procedure for the deviation of the approximation functions by dividing the object into finite elements (Reddy,1985; Yamanoi et al.,1991). Although the cervical model of FEM was comprised only of vertebral bodies, intervertebral discs, and two ligaments, the chronic stress which was shown in the FEM analysis of heading may be the cause of the development of the bony spurs or the calcification observed in this study. The calcification in the anterior longitudinal ligament may occur months after an acute hyperextension injury as part of the healing process (Robson,1956).

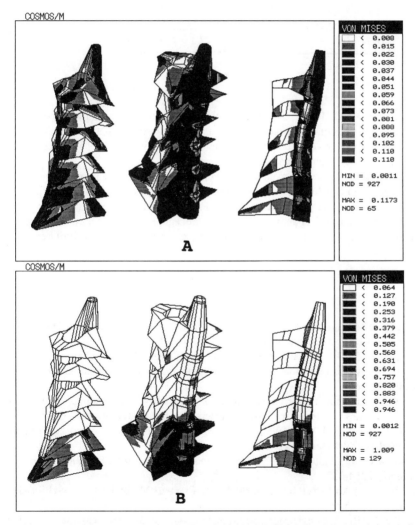

Figure 1. Result of finite element method analysis (von Mises stress) (A) Before heading (B) On heading. Note that the scale of each figure is different.

The incidence of the calcification of the nuchal ligament (Barsony) in our study was 58.33%. on the other hand, an incidence of 5.33% has been reported in 150 normal Japanese male samples under 50 years old (Sasaki, 1980), which we took as a control group. Here, we tested the hypotheses (HO) that the percentage of the morbidity of veteran soccer players group (p_2) is the same as that of normal Japanese males of the corresponding age group (P_2). The alternative hypothesis (H_1) is that the former is greater than the latter, that is H_0: $P_1 = P_2$ H_1: $P_1 > P_2$ - This is a right-tailed test to see if P_1 is significantly greater than P_2. The Z distribution is applicable (Sanders et al.,1985). The rejection region was bounded by Z=2.58 at the 0.001 level of probability. The critical ratio (CR) of this case is computed as follows:

$$CR = \frac{(P_1 - P_2)}{\sqrt{\dfrac{P_1(100 - P_1)}{n_1 - 1}} + \sqrt{\dfrac{P_2(100 - P_2)}{n_2 - 1}}} = 3.538 > 2.58$$

where, $n_1 = 12$, $n_2 = 150$. Hence, the CR fell within the rejection region, so we accepted the H_1.

Although slight radiographic degenerative changes are not regarded as important (Keats,1988) and have no correlation with symptoms (Lestini and Wiesel,1989) cervical spondylosis proceeds naturally with the ageing process.

Additionally,some of the senescent and the pathological changes are morphologically indistiguishable. In conclusion, early degenerative changes observed in the radiographs of the neck of veteran soccer players seemed, therefore, to be the result of acute or chronic trauma in conjunction with spondylosis of senescent degeneration. We may also have to take preventive measures to protect the neck from injury, especially for younger children and females.

5 References

Keats,T.E. (1988) **Atlas of Normal Roentogen Variants that May Simulate Disease.** 4th edition. Year Book Medical Pubishers, Chicago.

Kerns, S., Pope, T.L.Jr., de Lange, E.E., Fechner, R.E., Keats, T.E. and Cimmino, C.(1986) Annulus fibrosus calcification in the cervical spine: radiologic - pathologic correlation. **Skeletal Radiology,** 15,605-609.

Kurosawa, H., Yamanoi, T. and Yamakoshi, K.(1991) Radiographic findings of degeneration in cervical spines of middle-aged soccer players.**Skeletal Radiology,** 20,437 440.

Lestini, W.F. and Wiesel, S.W.(1989) The pathogenesis of cervical spondylosis. **Clinical Orthopedics and Related Research,** 239,69-93.

McMaster, W.C. and Walter, M.(1978) Injuries in soccer. **American Journal of Sports Medicine,** 6,354-357.

Reddy, J.N.(1985) **An Introduction to the Finite Element Method.** McGraw-Hill Book Company, New York.

Robson, P.N.(1956) Hyperextension and heamatomyelia. **British Medical Journal,** 2,848-852.

Sanders, D.H., Eng, R.J. and Murph, A.F.(1985) Chapt 9: Testing hypotheses and making decisions; two-sample procedures.:256, in **Statistics (3rd ed): A Fresh Approach.** McGraw-Hill Book Company, New York.

Sasaki,A.(1980) Radiology of normal cervical spine. **Journal of Japanese Orthopedic Association** 54 (in Japanese), 615-631.

Sortland, O., Tysvaer, A.T, and Storli, O.V. (1982) Changes in the cervical spine in association football players. **British Journal of Sports Medicine,** 16,80-84.

Sullivan, A.J., Gross, R.H., Grana,W.A. and Gracia-moral, C.A.(1980) Evaluation of injuries in youth soccer. **American Journal of Sports Medicine,** 8,325-327.

Yamanoi, T., Kurosawa, H., Okihara,T. and Yamakoshi,K. (1991) An evaluation system for artificial knee joints operations by the use of CAE, in **Computer Applications in Production and Engineering: Integration Aspecto** (eds G. Doumeings, J. Browne and M.Tomljanovich), Elsevier Science Publishers B.V., Amsterdam, pp. 167-173.

KNEE LIGAMENT INJURIES IN SOCCER PLAYERS

JAN EKSTRAND
Sports Clinic, Linköping medical Centre, Klostergatan 68 S-582 70 Linköping, Sweden.

1 Introduction

Soccer is a sport with more than 60 million licensed players in 150 countries associated with the international federation, FIFA. Knee injuries consistently represent 10-20 % of soccer injuries (Ekstrand, 1982; Keller et al., 1987). Lindenfeld et al. (1994) found 3.5 knee ligament injuries per 1000 hours of exposure when studying indoor soccer in the USA. The rate of serious knee injuries for female players was 5.7 times that of male players.

The purpose of this paper is i) to present the mechanisms, symptoms, treatment and rehabilitation of injuries to the knee ligaments in soccer and ii) to present the results of reconstruction of the anterior cruciate ligament (ACL) in soccer players by using the fascia lata as a graft.

2 Medial Collateral Ligament (MCL) Injuries

The mechanism of injury to the MCL is most commonly an impact to the lateral side of the knee, which forces the joint into valgus.There are three types of sprains: Grade I, Grade II and Grade III.

In Grade I injury, there is stretching but not disruption of the MCL. There is tenderness at the site of injury and pain but no laxity at valgus stress testing. Treatment is conservative and soccer can be resumed when pain has disappeared, usually within a few weeks.

In Grade II injury, there is a partial rupture of the MCL. In valgus stress testing there is a mild or moderate laxity (up to 5 mm of excess, compared to the non-injured leg) with a firm end-point. The treatment is conservative and rehabilitation usually takes 3-6 weeks.

In Grade III injury, there is complete rupture of the MCL. Valgus stress testing shows more than 5 mm laxity without a distinct end-point. If the medial joint opens up more than 10 mm, a cruciate ligament is usually also injured.

The treatment of Grade III sprains is debatable, but the recent trend has also been to treat Grade III injuries conservatively. An arthroscopy is recommended to rule out concomitant injuries. Shelbourne and Porter (1992) reported that the non-operative management of MCL injuries in conjunction with adequate reconstruction of the ACL is a reasonable and possibly advantageous management approach for the patient with a combined ACL-MCL injury. Any mild residual medial laxity appears to be asymptomatic and, if the ACL graft is stable, there will be a low risk for subsequent meniscal damage after return to full activity.

3 Posterior Cruciate Ligament (PCL) Injuries

Injuries to the PCL are relatively uncommon in soccer and their treatment is controversial. The PCL is a 38 mm long, strong ligament which is responsible for 90% of the resistance to posterior displacement of the tibia (Fowler and Messieh, 1987). Hyperflexion of the knee, with or without pretibial trauma, is the most common mechanism of PCL-injury in soccer.

Diagnosis should be based on the history of injury, the presence of a posterior sag, and a posterior drawer test. An X-ray should be performed to rule out bony avulsions from the tibia, and MRI or arthroscopy is recommnded to confirm the diagnosis and to rule out other pathology.

Soccer players with an isolated PCL-injury generally function well without surgery. As a rule, they can return to soccer and other contact sports without any significant functional problems (Parolie and Bergfeld, 1986). At clinical examination they often show a significant posterior drawer but they show good results in functional tests.

In order to maintain the high degree of knee function required in soccer, a player with PCL-deficiency must strive to attain and maintain at least 100% quadriceps strength equality. Acute injuries should be treated with a programme consisting of early exercise within the limits of pain, and intensive progressive resistance exercises for quadriceps and hamstrings. As with the rehabilitation of ACL-injuries, stationary cycling, water jogging, and co-ordination exercises are important in the rehabilitation programme.

Long-term follow-ups of conservatively-treated PCL injuries have not shown any deterioration with time (Fowler and Messieh, 1987). Indication for surgery exists in selected cases: in isolated PCL-injuries with a bony avulsion from the tibia, in acute PCL-injuries with associated pathology, and in chronic PCL-injuries with combined instability.

4 Anterior Cruciate Ligament (ACL) Injuries

Injuries to the ACL are fairly common in football. Hewson et al.(1986) reported an incidence of 2.4 ACL injuries per year in an American college football team. The incidence in soccer has been estimated to be 1 injury/100 players/year amongst senior players (Ekstrand et al., 1990).

Injuries to the ACL can occur in contact (60%) as well as in non-contact (40%) situations (Ekstrand and Gillquist, 1983). The mechanism in a contact injury is either hyperextension of the knee or a valgus-outward rotation. The non-contact injuries usually occur in dribbling, cutting or quick changes of direction. It has been shown that knee-injuries occurring in non-contact situations often happen to players with previous knee injury and persistent instability (Ekstrand and Gillquist, 1983).

Another important factor is the shoe-surface relationship. The relationship between knee injuries and the fixation of the foot to the ground is not yet fully evaluated in soccer. In American football, the severity and incidence of knee and ankle injuries were reported to be significantly lower when using shoes with lower friction properties (Torg and Quedenfeld, 1971). In American football, severe injuries typically occur in collision situations independent of the surface. Soccer is characterised by sprinting, cutting and pivoting movements, where shoe-surface relationships are essential and frictional forces must be within an optimal range. High friction between shoe and surface may produce excessive forces on the knees with a risk of ACL injuries. However, too little friction may be the reason for slipping, which affects performance negatively, and may cause other injuries (Ekstrand and Nigg, 1989). Future research should address this compromise between performance and protection. The symptoms of an acute ACL-injury are sudden pain, a sense of giving-way and severe swelling of the knee within 1-2 hours. The severe swelling is pathognomonic of haemarthrosis. More than 70% of all athletes with haemarthrosis following acute knee trauma have a torn ACL.

A soccer player with an adequate trauma and a swelling of the knee within 6 hours should be considered to have an ACL-injury and the diagnosis should be confirmed by an arthroscopy and a stability test under anaesthesia. During arthroscopy it is important to diagnose associated joint pathology such as meniscus tears and chondral lesions. Magnetic resonance imaging is also valuable; Speer and co-authors (1992) have identified a high incidence of MRI-detectable bone and soft tissue injuries in the lateral compartment following ACL disruption. The questions as to how these lesions correlate to the mechanism of injury, and what the prognostic significance for these lesions is, have yet to be answered.

5 Treatment of ACL Injuries

The treatment of an ACL-injury in a soccer player should as a rule be surgical. The ACL is the key ligament of the knee and tear of the ACL with resulting instability is a major cause of disability and is not readily tolerated by soccer players. Several studies have pointed out that soccer players with untreated ACL-injuries who try to continue playing soccer show a high incidence of reinjury, loss of function and as a rule have to discontinue the sport (Lysholm, 1981; Ekstrand, 1982; Balkfors, 1982).

The acute ACL tear should receive a primary repair and an augmentation of the repair or a primary reconstruction (Shelbourne et al., 1990). Suture of the ACL alone, leads to re-elongation in 50% of cases (Odensten, 1984).

The satisfactory surgical reconstruction of the chronic ACL-insufficient knee is a challenge. Replacement of the injured ACL using autologous tissues surrounding the knee joint, as well as a variety of synthetic material, has been described. A successful result after ACL-reconstruction depends, however, on several factors such as selection of patient, selection of graft, operative technique and rehabilitation.

The selection of patients in the case of soccer players is obvious, since players with an ACL- insufficiency either need an operation or have to abandon soccer since conservative treatment is unsuccessful. The selection of appropriate graft material for ACL reconstruction is also important. The use of the patellar tendon is probably the "gold standard" autologous graft in ACL reconstructions but other autologous tissues such as the semitendinosus tendon and the fascia lata are also commnly used. It has been suggested that tissues in top athletes are in excellent condition, allowing high quality reconstruction(Higgins and Steadman, 1987). The tissue response to exercise is consistent with our knowledge of connective tissue response to exercise according to Wolff's law, stating that collagenous tissue is trainable, but adequate time is required after any disuse state to return the tissue to normal strength levels (Noyes et al.,1983; Ekstrand, 1989 a).

A correct surgical technique is another important factor for the success of ACL-reconstruction. The use of a miniarthrotomy or an arthroscopical technique leaves the extensor mechanism undisturbed, thus permitting faster rehabilitation (Zarins and Rowe, 1988). A proper anatomical positioning of the graft and the use of a notchplasty (removal of osteophytes from the lateral femoral condyle in order to prevent impingement of the graft in the intercondylar notch) and a secure fixation of the graft are other important technical factors (Shelbourne and Nitz, 1990; Fu et al., 1992).

Optimal rehabilitation is without doubt a prominent factor in surgical success and it has been stressed that postoperative rehabilitation is just as important as the details of the surgery (Paulos et al., 1981). Rehabilitation after ACL-reconstruction begins immediately after operation. It has been demonstrated that postoperative pain inhibits muscle function and the use of continuous epidural analgesia may prevent catabolism in the muscles and increase the ability to institute early rehabilitation, thus possibly preventing early atrophy (Eriksson, 1981). Continuous passive motion (CPM) seems to be advantageous in that it maintains nutrition to and the physical characteristics of cartilage, ligament and muscle, as well as avoiding contracture problems (Eriksson, 1981; Paulos et al., 1981; Higgins and Steadman, 1987; Zarins and Rowe, 1988). Immediate movement under very strict protective conditions is beneficial for the joint. The graft needs to be stressed if it is to remodel in the lines of functional demands.

According to Wolff's law, the early healing period is governed by the principle requiring absolute control of forces so as to prevent disruption or elongation of the graft. Closed kinetic exercises should be emphasised, and open kinetic quadriceps exercises should be avoided (Shelbourne and Nitz, 1990; Fu et al., 1992). During closed chain exercises for the lower extremity, there is cocontraction of the quadriceps and hamstring muscles. The hamstring cocontraction minimizes the anterior tibial displacement produced by the quadriceps and minimizes stress on the ACL (Fu et al., 1992). In closed chain exercises, the distal segment of the extremity is fixed (Fu et al., 1992). Closed kinetic exercises are performed with the foot placed on a surface (floor, step, pedal etc.) with the entire limb bearing a load. This causes all of the joints in the extremity to be compressed by the load. In open kinetic exercises (i.e. leg extension) where the foot is free, a relatively larger shear stress is applied to the joint with less joint compression. In addition, closed kinetic chain activities place functional stresses (anatomical kinesiological loading) on the joint and extremity in ways that are similar to normal weight-bearing activities (Shelbourne et al., 1990; Fu et al., 1992). Stationary cycling seems to be advantageous in that it increases the range of movements as well as providing exercise for the thigh muscles without putting stress on the ACL. A soccer-specific rehabilitation phase is equally important since the goal for the soccer player is to return to pre-injury activity level. This period is designed to achieve maximum strength and restore neuromuscular coordination and endurance (Wojtys and Huston, 1994). In optimal cases the player can return to soccer participation within 5-6 months of ACL surgery (Ekstrand, 1989 b).

6 Results of Reconstruction of the ACL in Soccer Players

This prospective study describes results for treatment of chronic ACL instability in competitive soccer players. One-hundred and thirty competitive soccer players (age 17-32 years) with a symptomatic chronic ACL-deficient knee and unable to participate in soccer, underwent intraarticular reconstruction of the ACL. A 4.5 cm wide and 16 cm long, distally attached strip of fascia lata was used as a graft. The operative technique included notchplasty, as well as anatomical positioning and secure fixation of the graft. The extensor mechanism was not compromised. Postoperative rehabilitation included continuous epidural analgesia, immediate exercise and protected, gradually increasing stress of the graft according to Wolff's law. The goal of rehabilitation was to return to pre-injury level and the final stage of the rehabilitation programme was soccer oriented.

Subjective and objective evaluation preoperatively and postoperatively at 6,8,10 and 12 months and then annually included the Tegner activity level for activity grading, the Lysholm

(1981) score for the patient's subjective evaluation of the disability after knee ligament surgery (Tegner and Lysholm, 1985), measurement of range of movements and muscle strength and function tests such as one-leg-hop and instrumental measurement of sagittal stability. The follow-up period was between 4 and 10 years.

Stability measurements showed a mean decrease in joint laxity from 6.5 mm preoperatively to 1.0 mm at 6 months and between 1.0 and 1.2 mm at subsequent follow-up. All tests were improved as well as the subjective knee-score. Muscle strength and jumping ability returned to pre-injury levels within 6 months but further improvements were noticed up to 24 months postoperatively. Seventy-five per cent of the players returned to training at a mean of 6.7 months. Sixty-seven per cent of the patients returned to playing in matches at a mean of 8.2 months postoperatively. It is concluded that this concept provides the possibility of a rapid return to soccer after reconstruction of the ACL.

7 Summary

- The non-operative treatment of MCL injuries and PCL injuries can give good to excellent functional outcomes in soccer players.
- The treatment of an ACL-injury in a soccer player should as a rule be surgical.
- A successful result after ACL-reconstruction depends on several factors such as selection of graft, operative technique and rehabilitation.
- The use of closed kinetic chain exercises and a soccer-specific rehabilitation phase are important factors in an optimal rehabilitation programme.
- In optimal cases the player can return to soccer participation within 5-6 months of ACL surgery.

8 References

Balkfors, B. (1982) The course of knee ligament injuries. **Medical Dissertation**, University of Lund, Sweden.

Ekstrand, J.(1989 a) Reconstruction of the anterior cruciate ligament in athletes, using a fascia lata graft. **International Journal of Sports Medicine**, 10, 225-232

Ekstrand, J.(1989 b) Reconstruction of the anterior cruciate ligament in soccer players. **Science and Football**, 2, 19-27.

Ekstrand, J.(1982) Soccer injuries and their prevention. Linköping University Medical Dissertations No 130, Linköping, Sweden.

Ekstrand, J. and Gillquist, J. (1983) Soccer injuries and their mechanisms: a prospective study. **Medicine and Science in Sports and Exercise**, 15, 267-270.

Ekstrand, J. and Nigg, B.(1989) Surface-related injuries in soccer. **Sports Medicine,** 8, 56-62.

Ekstrand, J., Roos, H. and Tropp, H.(1990) Normal course of events amongst Swedish soccer players: an 8-year follow-up study. **British Journal of Sports Medicine**, 24, 117-119.

Eriksson, E. (1981) Rehabilitation of muscle function after sport-injury. A major problem in sports medicine. **International Journal of Sports Medicine**, 2, 1-6.

Fowler, P.J. and Messieh, S.S. (1987) Isolated posterior cruciate ligament injuries in athletes. **American Journal of Sports Medicine**, 15, 553-557.

Fu, F.H., Woo, S.L.Y. and Irrgang, J.J. (1992) Current concepts for rehabilitation following anterior cruciate ligament reconstruction. **Journal of Sport and Physical Therapy**, 15, 270-278.

Hewson, G.F., Mendini, R.A. and Wang, J.B. (1986) Prophylactic knee bracing in college football. **American Journal of Sports Medicine**, 14, 262-266.

Higgins, R.W. and Steadman, J.R. (1987) Anterior cruciate ligament repairs in world class skiers. **American Journal of Sports Medicine**, 15, 439-447

Keller,C.S., Noyes, F.R. and Buncher, R. (1987) The medical aspects of soccer injury epidemiology. **American Journal of Sports Medicine**, 15, 230-237.

Lindenfeld, T.N., Schmitt, MS., Hendy, M.P., Mangine, R.E. and Noyes, F. (1994) Incidence of injury in indoor soccer. **American Journal of Sports Medicine**, 22, 364-371.

Lysholm, J. (1981) Arthroscopy in surgery of the knee. Linköping University **Medical Dissertations** No 106,Linköping, Sweden 1981.

Noyes, F.R. Butler, D.L., Paulos, L.E. and Grood, E.S. (1983) Intra-articular cruciate reconstruction. **Clinical Orthopedics and Related Research**, 172, 71-77.

Odensten, M. (1984) Treatment of the torn anterior cruciate ligament. Linköping University **Medical Dissertations** No 177, Linköping, Sweden.

Parolie, J.M. and Bergfeld, J.A. (1986) Long-term results of non-operative treatment of isolated posterior cruciate ligament injuries in the athlete. **American Journal of Sports Medicine**, 14, 35-38.

Paulos, L., Noyes, F.R., Grood, E. and Butler, D.L. (1981) Knee rehabilitation after anterior cruciate ligament reconstruction and repair. **American Journal of Sports Medicine,** 9, 140-149

Shelbourne,K.D. and Nitz, P. (1990) Accelerated rehabilitation after anterior cruciate ligament reconstruction. **American Journal of Sports Medicine,** 18, 51-57

Shelbourne, K.D. and Porter, D.A. (1992) Anterior cruciate ligament-medial collateral ligament injury: Nonoperative management of medial collateral ligament tears with anterior cruciate ligament reconstruction. **American Journal of Sports Medicine**, 20, 283-286.

Shelbourne, K.D., Whitaker, H.J., McCarroll, J.R. Rettig, A.C. and Hirschman, L.D. (1990) Anterior cruciate ligament injury: Evaluation of intraarticular reconstruction of acute tears without repair. **American Journal of Sports Medicine,** 18, 484-489.

Speer, K.P. Spritzer, C.E., Bassett, F.H. Feagin, J.F. and Garrett, W.E. (1992) Osseous injury associated with acute tears of the anterior cruciate ligament. **American Journal of Sports Medicine**, 20, 382-389.

Tegner, Y. and Lysholm, J. (1985) Rating systems in the evaluation of knee ligament injuries. **Clinical Orthopedics and Related Research**, 198, 43-49.

Torg, J.S. and Quedenfeld, T.(1971) Effect of shoe type and cleat length on incidence and severity of knee injuries among high school football players. **Research Quarterly**, 42, 203-211.

Wojtys, E.M. and Huston, L.J. (1994) Neuromuscular performance in normal and anterior cruciate ligament deficient lower extremities. **American Journal of Sports Medicine**, 22, 89-104.

Zarins, B. and Rowe, C.R. (1988) Combined anterior cruciate ligament reconstruction using semitendinosus tendon and iliotibial tract. **Journal of Bone and Joint Surgery**, 68A, 160-177.

INJURIES IN RUGBY FOOTBALL

D.A.D. MACLEOD
Scottish Rugby Union, Murrayfield, Edinburgh, U.K.

1 Introduction

Injury and illness patterns related to any individual sport have been identified in the past on the basis of clinical experience and published reports. These patterns of injury and illness have rarely, if ever, been subjected to critical scientific review. Most of our knowledge is therefore anecdotal, as well as retrospective and fails to meet the requirements of a prospective cohort study.

Sports medicine is developing as a recognised speciality with a solid foundation in the basic sciences. This development must ensure that the principles of the Public Health sciences and Epidemiology are included in all future research projects if progress is to be maintained.

The Joint Scottish Royal Colleges Board in Sports Medicine, established in 1989, agreed a definition for the speciality, based on the International Olympic Committee regulations. Establishing the definition of sports medicine was an essential preliminary before the Board could develop a Diploma examination for registered medical practitioners. This definition, which emphasises the importance of the basic sciences as well as appropriate data recording, states that -

> "Sports medicine is a discipline which includes theoretical and practical branches of the relevant basic sciences in medicine which investigate, document and measure the influence of lifestyle, exercise, training and sport - or lack of these - on both healthy and physically or psychologically ill or handicapped people in order to produce useful results of the prevention of disease or injury, treatment, rehabilitation and improvement of the education, health and overall performance of the individual and society at large."

2 Definition of Injury

One of the major problems facing all sport is that there is no universally applicable definition as to what constitutes a sports injury or illness. Many different definitions have been utilised in the extensive literature on rugby football. It is difficult to interpret these findings because of different criteria used for the definition of an injury and injury ascertainment is invariably incomplete. In addition, the appropriate denominators have not been identified and game analysis has not been carried out.

Definitions of a sports injury vary widely but usually include the effects of the illness or injury on the individual's performance, i.e. the time that the individual is unable to participate in sport. This view of injury is widely accepted but is of little clinical relevance as it does not record the lesion.

Table 1. Defining a sports injury

* The player is unable to complete the event (competition or training)
transient
permanent

* The player is unable to participate in a subsequent event
1 week +   minor injury
4 weeks +   moderate injury
12 weeks +   severe injury

A player may choose to retire from sport following a transient, minor moderate or severe injury. Also a player may experience delayed effects from his injury, such as osteoarthitis affecting weight-bearing or injured joints, or the "punch drunk syndrome" developing following cumulative minor head injuries.

A sports injury definition used in many studies relates to the mechanism of injury. In rugby football the most frequently reported injuries relate to direct contact. As players at top level become taller, heavier , stronger and fitter, the forces applied to their limbs as a result of their momentum in conjunction with a change in direction can often lead to injury following even the most apparently trivial force. Such injuries include a spinal fracture of the fibula, a rupture of the medial collateral ligament of the knee and damage to the meniscus.

All participants in sport, including rugby football nowadays, train to improve both their fitness and technical abilities. This can lead to over-use injuries as a result of repetitive stress and failure of synergistic action of muscle group function compounded by poor technique, poor equipment and fatigue. Another parameter commonly incorporated in the definitions of a sports injury or illness is consideration of the result and demands made on medical services. The player may receive treatment because it is available at an event or seek treatment from the appropriate individual or primary care facility. The player may also require the services of more specialist facilities such as the Accident & Emergency Department of a hospital, access to investigative and laboratory medicine or in-patient hospital care. Many of these latter requirements may not be identified until days, weeks or even months after the original injury occurs. Players may also require the services of a rehabilitation facility.

The social effects of injury or illness may be relevant such as time off education or work. Another measurement of the effects of a sports injury or illness would be to ascertain whether or not an insurance claim was made for either treatment or as a result of a disability which may be temporary or permanent. In addition, the player may die.

Under-performance or loss of form is one aspect of the definition of injury or illness in sport which is of considerable concern to both athletes and coaches. This has been increasingly recognised as having an immunological and biochemical basis. Detailed assessment of this common complaint in sport can make enormous demands on medical services.

Ideally a definition of an injury or illness should also incorporate a clinical description of the disease process or lesion which should be identified in anatomical terms as well as the associated loss of normal function in the appropriate tissues. The development of nuclear magnetic resonance imaging and increased access to laboratory medicine has improved this aspect of sports medicine. It is now possible to identify clearly the damaged tissue and the effects on function rather than giving a best guess as to the nature of a "hamstring pull" or "dead leg".

It is therefore apparent that a sport such as rugby has a major problem in identifying the appropriate definition which would be the basis of prospective cohort studies.

3 Injury Analysis

Injuries in rugby are inevitable because it is an intermittent, high intensity collision sport requiring considerable skill and fitness. The risk of injury can be reduced by ensuring that rugby players are physically and psychologically suited to participate in the game and this is particularly important with regard to the young, the old and women. It is important that, wherever possible, teams are composed of individuals who are appropriately matched for age, sex and maturity. Players' physique should be reviewed to include assessment of joint mobility as hypermobility is believed to carry an increased risk or injury. An individual's personality may also be of relevance as well as his or her general state of health. The choice of an appropriate training programme reviewing intensity, duration, frequency and content to ensure an appropriate work-rest ratio is also essential.

The risk of injury in rugby is minimised by ensuring that the laws by which the game is regulated are soundly formulated and properly supervised by the referee. The game must also be played on a good surface and in a safe environment.

The Scottish Rugby Union, through its Medical Advisory Committee, has undertaken a series of studies over the years on rugby injuries. After a series of pilot studies, the Scottish Rugby Union would encourage all rugby clubs to report injuries that resulted in a player's admission to hospital or in the death of a player. This system is based on the co-operation of clubs and is inevitably associated with under-reporting. Various information has, however, been identified which has proved of considerable interest. Between 1979 and 1994, six deaths have occurred in Scottish rugby from which only one was directly related to the game in that a player died following a high cervical spinal cord injury resulting in quadriplegia. Five other deaths have taken place due to coincidental medical conditions including three myocardial infarcts, one player with hypertrophic cardiomyopathy and one spontaneous cerebral haemorrhage. Three other players in the same period have suffered a quadriplegia as a result of scrummaging and one tackling injury. In addition we have recorded a series of other life threatening injuries including one player who developed tetanus, two players with ruptured spleens, one player who required a nephrectomy and two players with haemopneumothorax. There have also been two players with serious head injuries which required craniotomy.

The most common injury requiring hospital admission is concussion, accounting for 17% of all reported serious injuries. Injuries to the ligaments of the knee and fractures of the cheek bone and leg make up the bulk of all remaining injury reports. These injuries are attributed to the tackle in 70 % of occasions with 60 % of the most seriously injured players being the individual who has been tackled. The frequency of replacements increases as the game progresses, 43 % of replacements taking place in the fourth quarter. The most commonly injured players are the flanker, prop-forward, No 8 and lock (Sharp et al., 1992).

The Accident & Emergency Department of the Borders General Hospital in Scotland recorded all injured players who presented during the season 1990-91. Altogether 292 players were seen in the Accident & Emergency Department on the basis of 17,865 player appearances in rugby. This gave an incidence of rugby injuries per hundred player appearances as 1.29 in Division 1 rugby, 1.72 in all other club rugby and 0.64 injuries per 100 appearances in school rugby (Bremner, D., Borders General Hospital, personal communication).

The Rugby World Cup was initiated in 1987 and was subsequently held for the second occasion in 1991. The Medical Advisory Team supporting the Scottish effort in the Rugby World Cup used standard definitions and documentation. The agreed definition of an illness or injury was one which prevented the player being able to complete or participate fully in an event, such as training or playing. In 1987, Scotland played in four World Cup matches and the average duration of training sessions was 2 hours 10 minutes, giving rise to an injury incidence of one every 52 minutes in a match and one injury every 29 hours while training. This resulted in a 20% loss of available playing days for the squad. In 1991, Scotland participated in seven matches and finished fourth in the overall competition. The average duration of training in this competition was 1 hour 25 minutes, giving an injury rate of one for every 70 minutes during matches and one injury every 40 hours while training. This resulted in a percentage loss of available playing days during matches but the increased availability of playing days from a pool of 26 players is quite dramatic when reviewing the incidence of injuries which occur during training.

Data collected in Scotland confirm that the tackle is the most dangerous aspect of rugby football but no information is available as to the relative risk of a tackle to either the tackler or the individual being tackled. Detailed analysis has not been undertaken to identify the frequency of tackles, the technique of tackling and injuries that occur in relationship to the tackle. This type of analysis is essential if player safety is to be enhanced.

It is possible from the published literature to identify various key indicator injuries that occur in rugby as a result of contact or non-contact forces and over-use stresses. The key indicator injuries as a result of contact would include lacerations causing a transient injury, concussion and acromio-clavicular sub-luxation causing minor injury lasting one to four weeks, facial fractures for moderately severe injury lasting four to eleven weeks and serious injuries such as anterior cruciate ligament and cervical spine injury which cause incapacity for over twelve weeks. Typical key indicator injuries reviewing non-contact over-use would include groin strains and hamstring tears.

Dalley et al. (1992) from New Zealand and Williams (1984) from Wales have both presented a large series of rugby injuries in which 19% of their injuries were lacerations. Of these lacerations, 75% affected the head and face (Williams P. Five Nations Committee Report on the Epidemiology of Rugby injuries. Personal communication 1984).

Concussion is accepted as a common problem in rugby football but it is one of the most difficult areas with which to achieve co-operation with players, coaches and club officials because of the requirement in rugby that any concussed player must rest for three weeks. Accordingly documentation of concussion is considered to be widely under-reported. This is an area of grave concern because of the effects of trauma on damaged nerve cells which die and recovery requires recruitment of alternative pathways. Recruitment is impaired by previous concussion, a second impact, alcohol or age.

Rugby football is associated with a small but regrettable risk of quadriplegia which can occur at the tackle, in the scrum or ruck and maul. Detailed studies undertaken in New Zealand (Calcinai, 1992) have helped reduce the incidence of quadriplegia by modification of the scrummaging and tackling technique. This success has not been emulated in South Africa where detailed investigations undertaken by Sher (1993) identified poor technique, misguided aggression and careless or illegal play as being significant factors in the causes of quadriplegia in the 117 patients they reviewed.

4 Conclusion

In this paper, I have highlighted some of my concerns with regard to the definition of injuries and illness as a result of sport, and reviewed some studies undertaken in Scotland. I have also suggested that there are key indicator injuries which can give a reasonable review of what is occurring in rugby football. However, none of these parameters have identified and met the requirements of a scientifically based prospective cohort study with agreed definitions of injury, accurate documentation of exposure to training and playing, complete injury ascertainment and accurate identification of relevant denominators. In addition, studies should review the loss of time from education and work as well as sport and document ongoing morbidity. These studies should be related to a more detailed analysis of the game of rugby football and identification of those injuries which are clearly related to specific aspects of the game. This would require the establishment of activity based injury case registers (Garraway et al., 1994) and as well as improved documentation and ascertainment of key indicator injury reports.

Attempts of this type of study are presently underway in New Zealand and Scotland. In New Zealand, the rugby injury and performance review project (Simpson et al., 1994) has attempted to review a prospective cohort of players utilising professional data collecting principles on the basis of a pre-season questionnaire and examination, weekly telephone contacts with the players and their prospective coaches during the season and their post-season questionnaire. A detailed study has recently been completed in the south of Scotland which utilised a prospective cohort of 1196 players in an analysis of prevalence rates for injuries (Garraway and Macleod, 1995).

The future of sports medicine and player safety in Rugby Football requires the involvement of epidemiologists in all studies designed to look into illness and injury patterns which are related to exercise and sport.

5 References

Calcinai, C. (1992) Cervical spinal injuries. **New Zealand Journal of Sports Medicine**, 20, 14-15.

Dalley, Lang, D.R. and McCartin, P.G. (1992) Injuries in Rugby Football. Christchurch 1989. **New Zealand Journal of Sports Medicine**, 20, 205.

Garraway, W.M. and Macleod, D.A.D. (1995) The epidemiology of Rugby. **The Lancet** (in press).

Garraway, W.M., Macleod, D.A.D. and Sharp, J.C.M. (1994) Rugby injuries. **British Medical Journal** (Leading article), 303, 1082-1083.

Sharp, J.C.M. (1993) Scottish Rugby Union data collection systems, in **Intermittent, High Intensity Exercise** (eds D.A.D Macleod, R.J. Maughan, C. Williams, C.R. Madeley, J.C.M. Sharp and R.W. Nutton), London: E. and F.N. Spon, pp. 427-435.

Sher, A.T. (1993) The consequences of injuries to the spinal cord in contact sport: South African experience of Rugby injuries, in **Intermittent, High Intensity Exercise** (eds D.A.D Macleod, R.J. Maughan, C. Williams, C.R. Madeley, J.C.M. Sharp and R.W. Nutton), London: E. and F.N. Spon, pp. 543-569.

Simpson, J., Chalmers, D., Waller. A., Bird, Y., Quarry, K., Gerard, D., Hancock, P. and Marshall. S. (1994) Tackling Rugby Injuries - Recommendations for reducing injuries to Rugby Union players in New Zealand. A report prepared on behalf of the **Rugby Injury and Performance** Project for the Accident, Rehabilitation and Compensation Corporation and the New Zealand Rugby Football Union.

EFFECT OF A FATIGUE TASK ON ABSOLUTE AND RELATIVISED INDICES OF ISOKINETIC LEG STRENGTH IN FEMALE COLLEGIATE SOCCER PLAYERS

N. GLEESON[1], T. MERCER[1] and I. CAMPBELL[2]

[1]Division of Sport, Health & Exercise, School of Sciences, Staffordshire University, Leek Road, Stoke-on Trent ST4 2DF, U.K..
[2]Division of Sport Science, Crewe and Alsager Faculty, Manchester Metropolitan University, Hassall Road, Alsager, ST7 2HL, UK..

1 Introduction

An increasing orthopaedic interest has focussed on the incidence and severity of anterior cruciate knee ligament injury in female team-sport athletes (Weesner et al., 1986). The anterior cruciate ligament (ACL) is the principal ligamentous restraint to anterior tibio-femoral displacement (Butler et al., 1980). A model which defines the limits of normal knee movement comprises primary ligamentous restraints interacting with the other static stabilisers (osseous geometry, capsular structures, and menisci) and with the dynamic muscle stabilisers (Fu, 1993). Compared to males, smaller ACL size, decreased femoral notch to width ratio and an unfavourable notch shape may predispose female team-sport athletes to increased threat of ACL injury (Hutchinson and Ireland, 1995).

The dynamic stabilisation of the knee joint provided by the knee flexor musculature may be compromised by limited strength capacity and by excessive agonist strength (Grace, 1985). Furthermore, such limitations may be exacerbated by muscle fatigue. The knee flexor muscle group promotes dynamic knee joint stability via regulation of anterior tibial translation and tibio-femoral rotation, while the knee extensor muscle group provokes an anterior tibial force and threat to ACL integrity (Fu, 1993). The aetiology of ACL disruption during participation in dynamic sports activity such as soccer remains unclear. It is common to have an ACL injury history suggestive of a sudden deceleration of body or limb momentum with the femur undergoing external rotation or the tibia internal rotation (Rees, 1994). Thus it may be important to evaluate specifically the strength capacity of the dynamic muscle stabilisers near to the extremes of the joint range of motion where the ACL is placed under the greatest mechanical strain (Fu, 1993).

Angle-specific torque indices of isokinetic leg strength are appealing physiologically since strength capacity appraisal is undertaken theoretically at constant fibre length. However, such indices at the extremes of the joint range of motion appear to offer limited measurement utility compared to the accepted index of peak torque (PT) (Gleeson and Mercer, 1994). The latter finding may be due to mechanical restraint artifacts of the dynamometer. Angle-relativised torque (ART) indices of isokinetic knee extension and flexion strength which are relativised to the maximal voluntary range of motion (ROM), demonstrate measurement utility and sensitivity at the extremes of the joint range of motion approximating to that of PT indices. Provided that constant angular velocity of movement is indicated at the extremes of the joint range of motion, ART indices should be preferred as potentially important discriminators of thigh muscle weakness and dysfunction on this basis (Gleeson and Mercer, 1995).

The aim of this study was to investigate the effects of a fatigue task on PT and ART indices of isokinetic knee extension and flexion strength in female collegiate soccer players.

2 Methods

Eleven female collegiate soccer players (age 21.0 ± 2.4 years; height 1.65 ± 0.06 m; body mass 61.7 ± 6.6 kg [mean ± SD]) gave their informed consent to participate in this study. Each subject completed one familiarisation session and three test sessions at the same time of day (± 1 hour) separated by three days. The same test administrator performed all measurements. Within each session the subjects completed a standardised warm-up followed by control and fatigue exercise tasks separated by 3 min passive recovery. The control exercise task comprised of two sets of three reciprocal maximal voluntary actions of the knee extensors and flexors of the preferred limb (defined as the leg chosen to kick a ball) using an isokinetic Dynamometer (Lido 2.1, Loredan Inc., Davis, California).

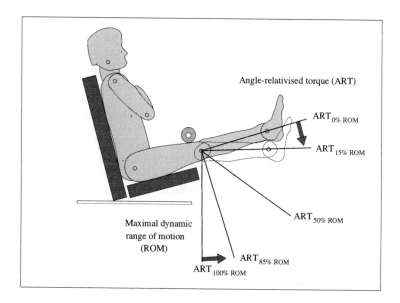

Fig.1. Subject and dynamometer orientation: angle-relativised torques.

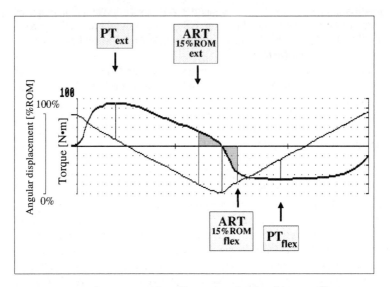

Fig. 2. Exemplary data from one subject illustrating the time history of knee extension PT and ART (15%), knee flexion PT and ART (15%) and knee joint angle relative to ROM during a single reciprocal muscle action.

Muscle actions were performed through a maximal voluntary ROM at an angular velocity of 3.14 rad/s (180°/s). Sets were separated by a 40 s rest period. The fatigue task comprised 30 reciprocal maximal voluntary actions of the knee extensors and flexors of the preferred limb. The apparatus and subject orientation during assessment is shown schematically in Figure 1.

   Pre- and post-intervention gravity corrected indices of knee extension and flexion PT and ART at 15% and 85% of ROM (100% = full knee flexion) (Figure 2) were estimated as the mean of 3 inter-day trials via interrogation of reciprocal actions 2 and 29, respectively, using data-reduction software . In addition, composite indices of PT ratio (PTR) ([flexion PT / extension PT] x 100%) and ART ratio (ARTR) ([flexion ART / extension ART] x 100%) at 15% and 85% ROM were calculated. The reproducibility of indices of isokinetic leg strength and endurance characteristics have been reported elsewhere (Gleeson and Mercer, 1992; 1995).

   The selected indices were described using ordinary statistical procedures (mean ± SD). Scores for PT, ART (15%) and ART (85%) were compared using a 2 (knee motion [extension, flexion]) x 2 (time [pre-, post-intervention]) x 2 (condition [fatigue intervention, control]) factorial repeated measures ANOVA. Composite indices of PTR and ARTR were compared using a 2 (time [pre-, post-intervention]) x 2 (condition [fatigue intervention, control]) multivariate factorial repeated measures ANOVA. An a priori alpha level of 0.05 was applied in all statistical procedures. All statistical analyses were programmed using SPSS/PC+ (V3.1) software (SPSS Inc., 1989).

Table 1. The mean (SD) peak torque (PT), angle-relativised torque (ART,15% and 85% ROM) of knee extensor and flexor muscles for female collegiate soccer players (n=11) across three inter-day trials of pre- and post-fatigue and control exercise tasks

			FATIGUE		**CONTROL**	
			Pre-	Post-	Pre-	Post-
PT	ext	[N•m]	84.1 (16.0)	56.0 (8.1)	90.6 (15.4)	86.8 (12.5)
	flex	[N•m]	58.1 (14.0)	46.3 (9.0)	54.9 (12.5)	53.9 (13.2)
ART (15%)	ext	[N•m]	57.5 (13.8)	37.6 (7.9)	42.9 (10.5)	39.9 (9.8)
	flex	[N•m]	12.8 (9.1)	5.0 (3.4)	16.0 (8.6)	12.3 (6.0)
ART (85%)	ext	[N•m]	33.8 (11.9)	20.7 (3.1)	36.6 (6.8)	35.5 (6.9)
	flex	[N•m]	45.3 (14.0)	31.3 (11.1)	33.0 (9.2)	31.8 (11.7)

3 Results

Table 1 shows group mean (SD) PT, ART(15%) and ART(85%) of the selected knee extensor and flexor muscle groups. Table 2 shows group mean (SD) PTR, ARTR(15%) and ARTR(85%) of the selected knee extensor and flexor muscle groups.

Repeated measures ANOVA of PT, ART(15%) and ART(85%) scores revealed significant fatigue/control task by pre- and post-intervention interactions ($F_{1,10}$=44.8, $F_{1,10}$=41.2 and $F_{1,10}$=32.3, respectively: P<0.0005). These results suggest that while indices remained relatively constant during the control task, scores were reduced (range 20% to 60%) following the fatigue intervention.

Multivariate repeated measures ANOVA of composite indices of PTR, ARTR(15%) and ARTR(85%) revealed an overall non-significant fatigue/control task by pre- and post-intervention interaction. The latter finding suggests that the ratio of isokinetic knee flexor to extensor strength remains constant following a fatigue task intervention.

Table 2. The mean (SD) peak torque ratio (PTR) ([flexion PT / extension PT] x 100%) and angle-relativised torque ratio (ARTR) ([flexion ART / extension ART] x 100%, 15% and 85% ROM) of knee extensor and flexor muscles for female collegiate soccer players (n=11) across three inter-day trials of pre- and post-fatigue and control exercise tasks.

		FATIGUE		**CONTROL**	
		Pre-	Post-	Pre-	Post-
PTR	[%]	68.7 (7.4)	82.4 (9.1)	60.2 (7.2)	61.8 (11.4)
ARTR (15%)	[%]	21.7(13.4)	13.2 (7.8)	37.8 (18.2)	33.0 (19.4)
ARTR (85%)	[%]	139.7 (43.0)	150.6 (48.2)	90.7 (23.3)	92.2 (44.3)

4 Discussion

The present findings suggest that a fatigue task reduces the capacity of the knee extensors and flexors to generate force by 20% to 60% during concentric muscle actions. The reduction in strength is evidenced by the index of peak torque and indices of angle-relativised torque near to the extremes of the range of motion. Such a loss of force-generating capacity in the knee flexor musculature due to fatigue may be commensurate with compromised joint stabilising capacity during concentric muscle action and so potentially, an increased risk of injury. Under conditions of fatigue, any protective concentric actions of the hamstring muscle group, for example restraint of anterior tibial translation and rotation, may not occur with sufficient force to offset any threat to knee stability posed by unfavourable game-related mechanical stressors on ligamentous restraints. Equivalent loss of force-generating capacity in the knee extensor musculature due to fatigue suggests that the threat of anterior tibial translation posed by forceful concentric actions of the knee extensor musculature may be attenuated. Statistical similarity in concentric knee flexor strength expressed relative to concentric extensor strength (PTR, ARTR at 15% and 85% ROM) prior to and following the fatigue task underscore an equivalence of loss of force-generating capacity.

Heavy-resistance strength conditioning may represent an optimal intervention in soccer players since it would be expected to increase directly the maximal joint stabilising capacity of the knee flexor muscle groups and improve concomitantly the capacity for muscular endurance (Colliander and Tesch, 1990). The latter would be expected to permit adequate force generation by the knee flexors and thus stabilising capacity to prevail for a longer duration during passages of fatigue-provoking soccer play.

The potential increased threat to knee stability posed by agonist-antagonist muscle group concentric action imbalance is not exacerbated by the mode of fatigue-task employed in this study. The threat to knee stability posed by soccer performance-related improvements to knee extensor muscle group strength or fatigue-related decreases in knee flexor muscle group strength was alluded to earlier. It may be appealing intuitively to focus attention from an ACL injury prevention perspective on the conditioning of the knee flexor muscle group which would be expected to alter the knee flexor-extensor muscle group balance in favour of the former muscle group. However, conditioning outcomes of improved absolute strength and especially endurance capacity in the knee extensor muscle group would be expected also to permit a more 'flexed-knee' playing position to be maintained for the duration of the soccer match. This process would facilitate a favourable position mechanically for the dynamic stabilising function of the hamstrings (Moore and Wade, 1989).

The present study represents a preliminary examination of a conceptual model for selected aspects of knee joint dynamic stability. Further research is needed to verify this study's findings using a soccer-specific fatigue task.

5 References

Butler, D.L., Noyes, F.R. and Grood, E.S. (1980) Ligamentous restraints to anterior-posterior drawer in the human knee; A biomechanical study. **Journal of Bone and Joint Surgery**, 62A, 259-270.

Colliander, E.B. and Tesch, P.A. (1990) Effects of eccentric and concentric muscle actions in resistance training. **Acta Physiologica Scandinavica**, 140, 31-39.

Fu, F.H. (1993) Biomechanics of knee ligaments. **Journal of Bone and Joint Surgery**, 75A, 1716-1727.

Gleeson, N.P. and Mercer, T.H. (1992) Reproducibility of isokinetic leg strength and endurance characteristics of adult men and women. **European Journal of Applied Physiology and Occupational Physiology**, 65, 221-228.

Gleeson, N.P. and Mercer, T.H. (1994) An examination of the reproducibility and utility of isokinetic leg strength assessment in women. Access to Active Living: **Proceedings of the 10th Commonwealth and International Scientific Congress** (eds F.I. Bell and G.H. Van Gyn) Victoria BC: University of Victoria, 323-327.

Gleeson, N.P. and Mercer, T.H. (1995) Reliability of relativised angle torque and angle-specific torque indices of isokinetic leg strength in women. **Medicine and Science in Sports and Exercise**, 27, 5, S209.

Grace, T.G. (1985) Muscle imbalance and extremity injury: A perplexing relationship. **Sports Medicine**, 2, 77-82.

Hutchinson, M.R. and Ireland, M.L. (1995) Knee injuries in female athletes. **Sports Medicine**, 19, 288-302.

Moore, J.R. and Wade, G. (1989) Prevention of anterior cruciate ligament injuries. **National Strength and Conditioning Association Journal**, 14, 35-40.

Rees, D. (1994). ACL reconstructions: Possible modes of failure. **Proceedings of the Royal College of Surgeons, Edinburgh** - Football Association, Sixth Joint Conference on Sports Injury, Lilleshall, 2nd-3rd July.

Weesner, C.L., Albohn, M.J. and Ritter, M.A. (1986) A comparison of anterior and posterior cruciate ligament laxity between female and male basketball players. **The Physician and Sportsmedicine**, 14 (5) 149-154.

TRAINING AND RE-TRAINING MUSCLE STRENGTH

J.P. CLARYS, E. ZINZEN, D. CABOOR and P. VAN ROY
Experimental Anatomy, Vrije Universiteit Brussel

1 Introduction

The world of training (and re-training) of muscular strength is both full of surprises and subject to commercial concerns. Strength training is carried out for purposes of improving, restoring and/or developing force. This increase in strength can be obtained in a static or a dynamic mode (Fig. 1). One could assume that it is only a matter of "the better choice of training". It is important to point out that all static and all dynamic strength training methods, techniques and approaches can improve, restore and develop force, and thereby can increase strength.

The dynamic (isotonic) methods of strength training can be placed into three categories : i) constant, ii) variable, and iii) accommodating resistance (Pipes, 1978). Numerous strength training machines have been developed as alternatives to the traditional free weights, providing a more compact, convenient, and safer form of external loading.

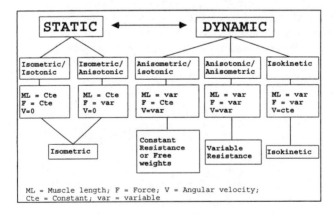

Figure 1. The terminology of static and dynamic forces.

The increasing application of strength-training machines in the top professional soccer clubs and medical fitness centres has raised the inevitable question of which machine is superior with respect to strength gain, and in what respect for each of the categories. In constant resistance machines, the load is always the same, i.e.the resistance is the same through the total range of motion. Therefore, loading occurs at the weakest point in the system, while the rest of the system is working at a lower capacity. To overcome this shortcoming, the variable resistance devices use pulley and cam systems in an attempt to vary the resistance as the muscle changes length. Variable resistance devices produce position-dependent increases which point to a training effect at the specific joint angle at which peak loading is induced by the device. A valuable feature of isokinetic exercise (testing, training, therapy, assessment) is that the moment produced by the athlete (or patient) is given in a unit of measure (foot-pounds or Newton-metre). This feature makes it possible to obtain a measure of the "functional" capability of a muscle group at a certain joint.The moment produced represents the interaction between the lever arm of the motion and the expression of the muscular moments as they act around a joint.

The trainer and therapist now have a tool with which strength can be expressed as a value at any point angle they want. This allows comparison of muscle groups on one side of the body with their heterolateral counterparts, and comparison of agonists with antagonist. It is possible also to evaluate progression during a given training or therapeutic programme. The objective quantitative features of the dynamometer can also be used to provide normative data for assessment of a group of subjects/athletes/patients and can be used as a reference for the individual. A requirement is that the subject belongs to that group which must be normalised to age, gender, type of training, sport and daily activities of the subject and the type of dynamometer used for testing.

Isokinetic equipment was first designed in the late 1960's. Many investigations have focused on the agonist-antagonist relationships and left-right imbalances, in order to present data for the assessment of musculoskeletal injuries. Furthermore, the isokinetic principle has been applied in rehabilitation to minimise rehabilitation time, because it is thought that it may give a near optimal training stimulus to the musculoskeletal system.

With all this new information of the last two decades including the late acknowledgement of eccentric versus concentric work, the better choice of strength training in football is not only a health matter but also a socio-economic matter. The aims in this report are to: (i) compare the results of a constant resistance training regime (CR) with a variable resistance training regime (VR); (ii) summarize a number of beneficial characteristics of eccentric training; and (iii) illustrate the advantages of isokinetically controlled strength rehabilitation of two case studies of severely traumatized professional soccer players.

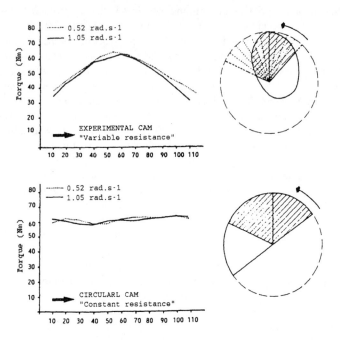

Figure 2. Cam form and corresponding torque pattern.

2 A Constant versus a Variable Resistance Training Regime

Informed consent was obtained from 22 female and 26 male medical students who volunteered to participate in the experiment(Claesen et al., 1990). The ages ranged from 19.9 to 28.5 (mean 22.7) years. None of the individuals was participating in training or sport activities. This choice of young healthy individuals with no training experience was made to avoid the influences of daily training on the results. Within each sex group, subjects were randomly selected into three groups: 1) a control group with no training; 2) a group working with variable resistance apparatus (VR) ; and 3) a group using constant resistance apparatus (CR). The two groups in training exercised on the same "Knee extension machine" (FYSIOCAM, Antwerp, Belgium). For the VR group we used a cam form validated for its variable resistance execution : an experimental cam (De Witte et al., 1988), while the CR group trained with a circular cam system (Fig. 2). The training programme lasted for six weeks with both groups training three days per week. The strength training regime used was the sub maximal contraction repetition method with constant load (Schmidtbleicher, 1986).

Before and after training, all groups were tested for isotonic 1RM strength and for isokinetic strength. The isokinetic pre- and post training measurements were taken with an isokinetic computer-controlled dynamometer (KIN/COM, Chattecx, Chattenooga, USA). Each subject performed (after a standard warming-up) five reciprocal repetitions of maximal voluntary concentric and eccentric exercises at 30° and 60°/s (0.52 and 1.05 rad/s), with the knee extensor muscle groups.

Speed settings on the isokinetic device were based upon the average movement speeds achieved during the training exercise (Lander et al., 1985). This was chosen as a practical means of equating performance for the two different regimes. The subjects were allowed at least five minutes recovery between each velocity, so fatigue could not become an influencing factor. Stabilisation of the pelvis, trunk, thigh and arm was done by means of straps and belts. Pre- and post-maximal forces (defined as the average of five repetitions) were calculated at 10° interval, to obtain force-angle curves for each exercise.

The influences of training on the selected parameters were statistically analysed using a t-test. Post-test differences between experimental conditions vary differently at each angle point in both training groups. The observed percentage force changes for the three experimental groups and the comparison of these force changes between the VR and CR groups over the entire ROM are presented in Figure 3. These results clearly indicate that the VR group overall had the greatest strength gains both in males and females which were significantly different from the CR groups. The results showed significant improvement in eccentric muscle activity also, again to the advantage of the variable resistance training regime group.

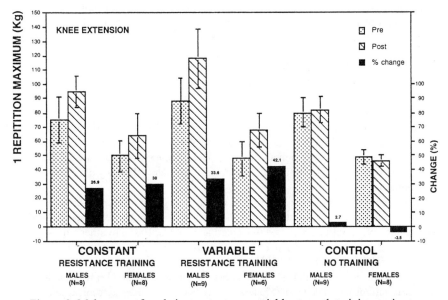

Figure 3. Male versus female in constant vs. variable strength training regimes.

The six-weeks-training period is just adequate to cause significant force gains, as compared to the pre- training period. This is in agreement with the findings of Schmidtbleicher (1986) who suggested that this training period is a practical situation to avoid external influences. At the same time it might be an economy factor for the professional daily practice and/or for rehabilitation. Within the scope of the present study, these data suggest that the VR training creates the better loading conditions over the whole ROM and therefore VR training is the better choice!

3 Concentric versus Eccentric Training

For a long time there has been an explosion of information on muscle training with concentric actions (both in exercise and in isokinetics). Partly because our knowledge in the area of eccentric muscle training, using isotonics, isokinetics and other forms of exercise had to be expanded and also because commercial and manufacturers such as Cybex brought devices on the market that were not able to measure and quantify eccentric force,to the point that comparies with advice from notorious physicians described eccentrics as dangerous. Fortunately the recent introduction of better computerised eccentric instrumentation (including the new Cybex, Kin-Com, Biodex, Lido, and so on) led to an increase in quality and diversity of research on the effects of eccentric training.

Eccentric actions can be defined as muscle loading that involves an external force application which results in increased tension as the musculo-tendinous unit is lengthened(Albert, 1991). It is well known that this type of muscle loading creates the highest tension possible within an "eccentric-->isometric-->concentric" hierarchy. In comparison and as a guideline we know that eccentric forces ranges from 1.1 times (for elbow flexors - Griffin, 1987) to 3.0 times (for quadriceps - Seliger et al., 1980) the concentric force. An example is given for the knee flexion - extension, concentric and eccentric in two different test positions (Fig. 4).

3.1 The better choice...?
Albert (1991) devoted a full chapter of his book "Eccentric muscle training in sports and orthopaedics" in describing the potential advantages and benefits of eccentric exercise. They fit perfectly into professional football (soccer) because it deals with economy... associated with electrophysiological, thermoregulatory and efficiency of energy consumption.

Many authors have reported lower EMG activity at a given resistance for eccentric work in comparison to concentric work (Asmussen, 1953; Bigland & Lippold, 1954; Basmajian, 1979; Seliger et al., 1990; Rouard and Clarys, 1995). In other words given an assumed equal torque (Nm), the EMG intensity of concentric contractions can exceed the eccentric action by about 30% (Fig. 5).

In addition Knuttgen et al. (1982) found that for equal (comparable) workloads, eccentric actions requires up to 75% less energy (VO_2max) than concentric actions. Many studies have pointed out that even up to exhaustion, eccentric activity remained

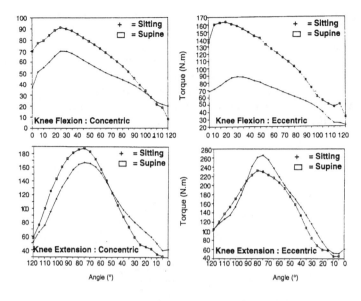

Angular velocity = 1.57 rad.s-1 (90°/s); Kin/Com

Figure 4. Different positions, different muscle action, different torque.

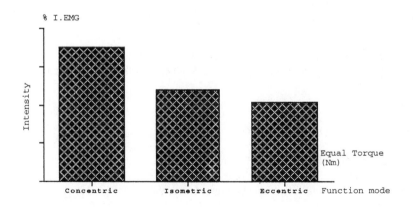

Figure 5. Isometric and eccentric actions demand lower EMG levels then concentric actions.

the most economic loading regime(Albert, 1991). As for thermoregulation, Nielsen et al.(1972) reported a threefold greater heat production during eccentric actions than during concentric actions for an equal level of exercise (Fig.6).

Other features related to eccentric exercise have been described extensively by Albert (1991). They are summarized in a simplified way in Table 1.

The role of eccentric muscle loading, its positive and economic relations in addition to the fact that its strength level dominates in the force hierarchy, make eccentric exercise an important element in the management of strength training.

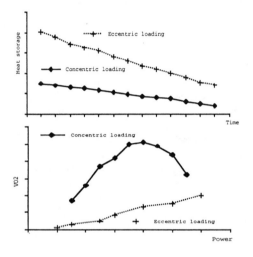

Figure 6. The relation (schematic) of concentric and eccentric loading with heat production and energy expenditure (adapted from Palud et al., 1980 and Knuttgen et al., 1982).

4 Isokinetic re-training in rehabilitation

4.1 Case study 1 : Medical resection of patellar tendon.
A 32-year old professional soccer player (goal keeper) suffering from a partial rupture of the patellar tendon, was surgically treated by resection of the medial (necrotic) part of the injured ligamentar tissue.

Table 1. Eccentric and concentric responses

Feature	Eccentric action	concentric contraction
EMG	↘	↗
VO2	↘	↗
Temperature	↗	↘
Sweat production	↗	↘
Blood pressure	↗	↘
Perceived exertion (Borg scale)	↘	↗
Fatigue resistance	↗	↘
Protective function (Bone)	↗↗	↗

The mean maximal strength of the injured leg was dramatically reduced, in comparison with the healthy knee. At rapid movement velocities, no strength measurements were possible because of pain.

After 15 weeks of immobilisation, a progressive but intensive variable isokinetic rehabilitation and training regime was started (in conjuction with functional exercises at a later stage of the programme). After 8 weeks of rehabilitation (three times per week, 30 to 45 minutes per session including isometric and variable exercises) the strength of the quadriceps muscle was significantly increased. In the end it became significantly greater than the strength of the healthy leg.

4.2 Case study 2 : Tibial and fibular fracture
This patient was a 33-year professional player who was injured in the right tibia and fibula during a soccer game. Repositioning of the fractures was carried out by means of an external fixator. After full consolidation of the fracture, the patient was treated for general muscle weakness. Therefore, normal walking and running were incorporated as proprioceptive exercises into the rehabilitation programme. After 12 weeks of strength training, satisfactory gains could be demonstrated. However, at higher angular velocity both concentric and eccentric strength did not totally recover, although the differences found were not of any practical significance.

5 Conclusion

Training and re-training strength in soccer players is an important part of both performance & health management. Amongst the better choices are variable resistance training and eccentric loading regimes. They are safe, healthy, efficient and economical.

6 References

Albert, M. (1991) **Eccentric Muscle Training in Sports and Othopaedics.** Churchill Livingstone, New York.

Asmussen, E. (1953) Positive and negative work. **Acta Physiologica Scandinavica**, 28, 364 - 382.

Basmajian, J.V. (1979) **Muscles Alive. Their Functions Revealed by Electromyography.** 4th ed. Williams & Wilkins, Baltimore.

Bigland, B. and Lippold, O.C.J. (1954) The relation between force, velocity and integrated electrical activity in human muscles. **Journal of Physiology**, 123, 214 - 219.

Claesen, L., Clarys, J.P., Cabri, J.and De Witte, B. (1990) Strength training in soccer : the effect of constant versus variable resistance training. **Science and Football**, 3, 13-17.

De Witte, B., Claessen, L.and Clarys, J.P. (1988) An evaluation of a variable resistance exercise device, in **Biomechanics XI** (International Series on Biomechanics) (eds P. Hollander, G. De Groot, P. Huying, and G.J. van Ingen Schenau), Human Kinetics, Champaign, pp. 1010-1015.

Griffin, J.W. (1987) Differences in elbow flexion torque measured concentrically, eccentrically and isometrically. **Physical Therapy**, 67, 1205 - 1209.

Knuttgen, H.G., Patton, J.F.and Vogel, J.A. (1982) An ergometer for concentric and eccentric muscular exercise. **Journal of Applied Physiology**, 53, 784 - 789.

Lander, J.E., Bates, B.T., Sawhill, J.A.and Hamill, J. (1985) A comparison between free-weight and isokinetic bench pressing. **Medicine in Science and Sports and Exercise**, 17, 344-353.

Nielsen, B., Nielsen, S.L.and Bonde-Peterson, F. (1972) Thermoregulation during positive and negative work at different environment temperatures. **Acta Physioligica Scandinavica**,85, 249 - 257.

Palud, P., Ravussin, K.J., Acheson, J.and Jequiuer, E. (1980) Energy expenditure during oxygen deficit of submaximal concentric and eccentric exercise. **Journal of Applied Physiology**, 49, 16 - 21.

Pipes, T.V. (1978) Variable resistance versus constant resistance training in adult males. **European Journal of Applied Physiology**, 39, 27-35.

Rouard, A. and Clarys, J.P. (1995) Co-contraction in the elbow and shoulder muscles in rapid cyclic movements in an aquatic environment. **Journal of Electromyography and Kinesiology**, 6, (in press).

Schmidtbleicher, D. (1986) Neuromuscular control and adaptations using different strength training methods. **Geneeskunde en Sport**, 1, 6-12.

Seliger, V., Dolejs, L.and Karas, V. (1980) A dynamometric comparison of maximum eccentric, concentric and isometric contractions using EMG and energy expenditure measurements.**European Journal of Applied Physiology**,45,235 - 244.

ISOKINETIC ASSESSMENT OF RUGBY LEAGUE PLAYERS WITH GROIN PROBLEMS

DONNA O'CONNOR
Human Movement and Health Education, University of Sydney, 2006, Sydney, Australia.

1 Introduction

An area of concern to Rugby League coaches today is the increased incidence of groin injuries amongst players. In a three year prospective study of a professional Australian Rugby League club, Gibbs (1993) found that a groin musculotendinous tear (n=15) was the most common specific injury within this period. Groin strain sustained by Rugby League players involves damage to the adductor longus in 95% of cases (Halpin, University of Sydney, personal communication, 1993). Groin pain may also include osteitis pubis, conjoint tendon tear, inguinal hernia, adductor tendinitis or nerve entrapment.

Isokinetic assessment may be utilised to reveal specific deficiencies in strength or power in professional Rugby League players. These deficiencies may predispose a player to injury. Estwanik, Sloane and Rosenberg (1990) stated that groin injuries frequently occur in sports involving quick acceleration and sudden changes of direction due to the abnormal lengthening of the muscle components surrounding the hip. Hughes and Fricker (1994) found that injuries were more likely to occur towards the conclusion of a game and during early season games. This trend suggests that fatigue and fitness level are important etiological factors in the incidence of injuries. Further analyses of groin injuries by Smodlaka (1980), Kulund (1982) and Renstrom (1994) suggest that sudden, powerful over-stretching of the leg and thigh in abduction and external rotation is the cause of such injuries. This view supports Merrifield and Cowan (1973) who stated that it is the strain of the adductor muscles caused by a sudden violent external rotation of the thigh while the leg is widely abducted and the foot firmly planted as occurs during a side-step, which leads to groin pain.

The aim of this investigation was to determine the characteristics of Rugby League players with groin injuries and identify any trends that may help in developing strategies to reduce the number of groin injuries in future.

2 Methods

2.1 Sample

Eleven professional Rugby League players participating in the Australian Rugby League Competition volunteered to participate in this study. All players had been diagnosed with chronic adductor enthesopathy by the same physician. Groin pain was experienced for a minimum of three months.

2.2 Procedure

Informed consent was received from all players prior to testing. Testing occurred during the week prior to surgery and all players received an injection of 0.2 ml lignocaine administered to the injured site by their physician at the time of testing. Consequently, the testing was under 'pain free' conditions to determine a more accurate profile.

The Cybex 340 isokinetic dynamometer was utilised to determine concentric peak torque, work, power and peak torque ratios of the hip abductors and adductors at 0.57, 2.1 and 3.72 rad/s. Calibration of the dynamometer was done prior to testing. The players were positioned on their side on the UBXT with the axis of the dynamometer aligned with the greater trochanter. The thigh pad was attached proximally to the knee. The torso, pelvis and contralateral leg were stabilised using Velcro straps. Correction for gravity was then conducted. Warm up and familiarisation consisted of two submaximal and two maximal repetitions at each angular velocity. Testing involved 5 maximal repetitions at 0.57 and 2.1 rad/s and 20 repetitions at 3.72 rad/s. The procedure was then repeated for the opposite limb.

3 Results

Demographic data are shown in Table 1. It was revealed that eight 'backs' and three forwards had sustained a chronic groin injury. Further analysis suggests that the site of injury (left or right) is not influenced by the dominant leg as 10 players were right dominant yet four left, five right and two bilateral injuries were diagnosed.

Table 1. Demographic results

	Mean	SD
Age (years)	25.2	3.2
Height (cm)	181.6	5.7
Mass (kg)	90.9	7.5
Experience (years)	4.5	2.5

Analysis of the isokinetic data revealed a large imbalance between the dominant and non-dominant leg for peak torque, power and work in abduction and adduction (Table 2). Values range from 16-37.4 % for adduction deficits and 21-53 % for abduction deficits.

The absolute values for these variables are depicted in Table 3. Due to the large differences in scores for each leg the results for both legs have been collated and the average is listed in the table. In comparison to adduction readings there is less force and power generated in hip abduction. An increase in angular velocity resulted in a decrease in peak torque. The abduction to adduction strength ratio was 102 % at 0.57 rad/s.

Table 2. Adduction and abduction deficits (%). (Mean values are given, standard deviation in parentheses)

	rad/s	Adduction	Abduction
Peak torque(Nm)	0.57	16 (13.1)	34 (15.3)
	1.05	28 (23.8)	21 (15.4)
	3.72	33 (21.2)	43 (25.8)
Power (watts)	0.57	19 (17.2)	40 (37.2)
	1.05	26 (17.6)	38 (21.2)
	3.72	37 (20.6)	49 (22.9)
Total Work (J)	3.72	33 (16.5)	52.7 (23.2)

Table 3. Peak torque, power and work for adduction and abduction (Mean, with standard deviation in parentheses)

Variable	rad/s	Adduction	Abduction
Peak Torque	0.57	127.4 (38.3)	126.2 (27.4)
(Nm)	1.05	109.3 (31.4)	102.5 (26.2)
	3.72	67.1 (29.4)	56.2 (22.8)
Power	0.57	36.4 (17.4)	35.0 (12.1)
(Watts)	1.05	102.3 (21.4)	94.5 (25.6)
	3.72	114.2 (29.7)	115.2 (19.1)
Total Work (J)	3.72	685.6	654.2

4 Discussion

Despite the fact that a small sample was investigated, there are many noteworthy trends which emerge from this study. There were predominantly more backs who had sustained a chronic groin injury requiring surgery. This supports Garrett (1990) who suggested that speed athletes would be more susceptible to muscle strain injuries.

Results in Table 2 indicate that large deficits were evident when comparing limbs for both abduction and adduction. This may be an influencing factor leading to groin strain. Merrifield and Cowan (1973) found ice hockey players sustaining adductor strains had a peak torque and power imbalance of at least 25% between the injured and non-injured leg. All the injured players except one recorded a force-power imbalance of more than 45%. Only five of the 45 non-injured recorded an imbalance of that magnitude. The deficits recorded in the present study were also extremely high. Table 3 illustrated that the adductors generated more force than the abductors when assessed at high angular velocities. This supports the work of Calahan et al.(1989) who recorded peak torque values for males at 121 Nm (adduction) and 103 Nm (abduction). Kushner et al.(1992) noted that the abductors were 20% weaker than the adductors at 1.05 rad/s and this increased to 40% at 3.14 rad/s. This increased sensitivity of the abductors at higher velocities has also been reported in studies of soccer players (Poulmedis, 1985) and baseball pitchers (Tippett, 1986). The soccer players described by Poulmedis (1985) were assessed under the same protocol as utilised in this study. Players recorded 160 Nm and 119 Nm (0.57 rad/s) for hip adduction and abduction respectively. This is in contrast to the injured sample (Table 3) where there is little difference between the force generated by the two muscle groups. It is the force produced during adduction that is considerably weaker than that documented in the literature. Abduction and adduction peak torque values are also lower than that recorded by players who had previously sustained a groin injury (192.4 v 127.4 Nm; 147.4 v 126.2 Nm for adduction and abduction respectively, O'Connor and Heazlewood, 1994). The previously injured players had all participated in some form of rehabilitation to increase the strength of the hip adductors.

A further disparity from the literature is revealed when abduction to adduction ratios are inspected. Kushner et al.(1992) found that the strength values of the hip abductors were 80% of the adductors in a group of male professional ballet dancers while soccer players recorded a 74% ratio (Poulmedis, 1985).

5 Conclusion

Several characteristics have emerged from this study which may be unique to the player with a chronic groin injured athlete:
(a) Backs appear to be more susceptible than forwards to groin injury.
(b) Limb dominance does not influence site of the injury.
(c) The ratio of abduction to adduction was nearly identical compared to that in previous studies on "healthy" populations where the adductors were significantly the stronger muscle group.
(d) The absolute strength values of the adductors are lower than those recorded in previous studies.
(e) Larger deficits between left and right limbs were recorded for injured players in both abduction and adduction.

These results suggest that pre-season testing should involve the assessment of hip abductors and adductors. Specific rehabilitation exercises need to be prescribed to increase the strength of these muscles and diminish the imbalance between the left and right limb. Generally the hip abductors and adductors are largely ignored when resistance training programmes are being devised as the emphasis is on increasing the strength and power of the quadriceps and hamstrings. Due to the large amount of lateral movement and use of the hip abductors and adductors in the game of Rugby League, a more balanced resistance programme is required.

6 References

Calahan, T.D., Johnston, M.E., Liu, S. and Chao, E.Y. (1989) Quantitative measurements of hip strength in different age groups. **Clinical Orthopaedics**, 246(Sept), 136-145.

Estwanik, J.J., Sloane, B. and Rosenberg, M. (1990) Causes of groin strain. **The Physician and Sportsmedicine**, 18, 55-60,65.

Garrett, W.E. (1990) Muscle strain injuries:clinical and basic aspects. **Medicine and Science in Sports and Exercise**, 22, 436-443

Gibbs, N. (1993) Injuries in professional rugby league: a three year prospective study of the South Sydney professional Rugby League football club. **American Journal of Sports Medicine,** 21, 696-700.

Hughes, D. C. and Fricker, P. A. (1994) A prospective survey of injuries to first-grade rugby union players. **Clinical Journal of Sports Medicine,** 4 (4), 249 - 256.

Kulund, D.N. (1982) **The Injured Athlete**, J.B. Lipponcott, Philadelphia, 358-359.

Kushner, S., Reid, D., Saboe. L and Penrose, T (1992) Isokinetic torque values of the hip in professional ballet dancers. **Clinical Journal of Sports Medicine,** 2, 114-120.

Merrifield, H.H. and Cowan, R. (1973) Groin strain injuries in ice hockey. **Journal of Sports Medicine and Physical Fitness**, 13, 41-42.

O'Connor, D. and Heazlewood, I. (1994) The differences in force, work, power and flexibility between groin injured and non groin injured professional rugby league players. (Abstract)**Access to Living**. 10th Commonwealth and International Scientific Congress, 10-14 August.Victoria, Canada.

Poulmedis, P. (1985) Isokinetic maximum torque power of Greek elite soccer players. **Journal of Orthopaedic and Sports Physical Therapy**, 6, 293-295.

Renstrom, P. (1994) Groin and hip injuries, in **Clinical Practice of Sports Injury Prevention and Care** (ed P. Renstrom), Blackwell Scientific, Oxford, pp. 97-114.

Smodlaka, V.N. (1980) Groin pain in soccer players. **The Physician and Sportsmedicine,** 8, 57-61.

Tippett, S.R. (1986) Lower extremity strength and active range of motion in college baseball pitches: a comparison between stance and kick leg. **Journal of Orthopaedic and Sports Physical Therapy**, 8, 10-14.

PART FIVE

Paediatric Science and Football

SPORTS INJURIES AND PHYSICAL FITNESS IN ADOLESCENT SOCCER PLAYERS

T. KOHNO, N. O'HATA, M. OHARA, T. SHIRAHATA,
Y. ENDO, M. SATOH, Y.KIMURA and Y. NAKAJIMA
Department of Sports Medicine,
Jikei University School of Medicine, TOKYO, JAPAN

1 Introduction

It ia thought that there may be a relationship between physical fitness and injuries in soccer. Therefore we have conducted a study examining the physical fitness of adolescent soccer players and their injuries.

2 Methods

The subjects were 56 male players between the ages of 12 and 18 years (3 twelve year-olds, 13 thirteen year-olds, 10 fourteen year-olds, 7 fifteen year-olds, 8 sixteen year-olds, 11 seventeen year-olds, 11 seventeen year-olds, 4 eighteen year-olds). They belonged to a soccer school run by a sports club in Tokyo.

Data were collected through a history interview focused on previous injuries, an orthopaedic examination (42 subjects only), and the following measures of physical fitness: maximum oxygen uptake, isokinetic muscle strength and speed of joint movement. In addition each subject's sports history and current training practices were studied.

To measure maximum oxygen uptake, an incremental exercise test was employed and the oxygen used during exercise was measured with an auto-metabolic analyzing machine (System 5, AIC, Japan). To measure knee extension and flexion muscle strength at 60 deg/s (1.05 rad/s) and 180 deg/s (3.14 rad/s), an isokinetic machine (Cybex II) was used. For the measurement of knee extension and flexion speed, an Ariel machine was used; when 5 kg and 20 kg loads were presented during isotonic exercise, knee extension and flexion speed was measured in rad/s.

The ground used for training purposes was artificial grass. Practices were held for two hours at a time for junior high school players (between 12 and 15 years old) and for senior school players (between 16 and 18 years old). For the group of junior high school players the frequency was 4.5 hours/week and for the senior high school players group the frequency was 5.4 hours/week.

3 Results

Table 1 depicts the subjects' injury history. It includes injuries that caused at least a 2-week recovery period, during which they did not attend the regular exercise sessions. In terms of the different types of injuries, fractures occurred in each group. The high school group had more cases of ligament injury. Osgood-Schlatter's disease and stress fractures were seen more among the junior high school group. Low back pain occurred in both groups. There was a similar incidence of injury, with as many injuries per year of playing, in both the junior high school and senior high school groups.

The location of current complaints is indicated in Table 2. Sites of complaints were lower legs, especially knee joints and ankles. The number of complaints is almost the same in both groups.

Table 1. Type of past sports injuries

Type of injury	Number of injuries	
	age 12-15 years*	age 16-18 years**
Fracture	7	6
Ligament injury	3	5
Contusion	1	3
Menisucus injury	0	1
Dislocation	0	1
Low back pain	3	3
Ligament overuse	0	2
Osgood-Schlatter's disease	4	0
Stress fracture	3	0
Total	21	21
Injury occurrence per year of playing	0.34	0.35

*N=27 **N=15

The high school group had twice as many complaints per player as the junior high school group. As shown in these data, current complaints were higher among high school players.

Fig. 1 shows the differences in maximum oxygen uptake, which was higher in the 16-year old compared to 15-year old boys ($P<0.05$). Fig. 2 shows the differences in knee extension muscle strength. Significant differences were found between 13 and 14 years old ($P<0.01$), and between 17 and 18 years old boys ($P<0.05$). Knee extension muscle strength gradually increase from the age of 14 to 17 and for the 18 year old boys it was close to that of adult soccer players (Kohno et al., 1991). Given a 5 kg (light) load the speed of knee joint extension differed significantly ($P<0.05$) between 13 and 14 years old and between 15 and 16 years old boys (Fig. 3). At a 20 kg (heavy) loading a significant difference was found between 15 and 16 year-olds ($P<0.01$) (Fig. 4).

Table 2. Location of current complaints

Location	Number of current complaints	
	age 12-15 years*	age 16-18 years**
Low back	2	2
Hip	1	2
Knee	5	6
Ankle	3	4
Foot	3	2
Total	14	15
Complaints per player	0.52	1.0

*N=27 **N=15

The average number of injuries mentioned in the past histories of those subjects between 12 and 15 years old was 0.34 per year of playing. For those between 16 and 18 years old it was 0.35 per year of playing. Thus there was no difference in the average number of injuries. The average number of current complaints were 0.52 per subject for those between 12 and 15 years of age, while for those between ages 16 and 18 it was 1.0. Again the average number of current complaints doubled for this increase in age.

By physical fitness category the biggest changes in knee extension muscle strength were between ages 13 and 14; between ages 13 and 14 year-olds and 15 and 16 year-olds in knee extension speed under a light load; between ages 15 and 16 in maximum oxygen uptake and in knee extension speed with the heavy load.

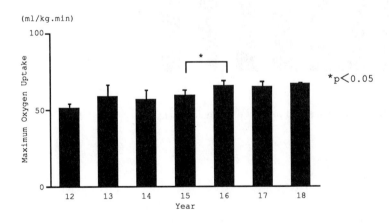

Figure 1. Maximum oxygen uptake in adolescent male soccer players (n=56).

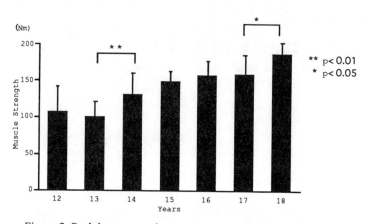

Figure 2. Peak knee extension strength in adolescent male soccer players (Cybex II⁺, 60 deg/s; n=56).

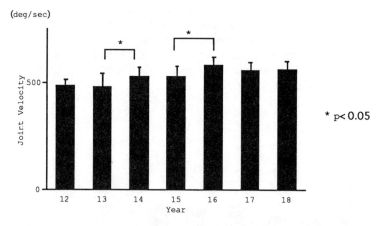

Figure 3. Peak extension speed in adolescent male soccer players (Ariel, 5 kg; n=56).

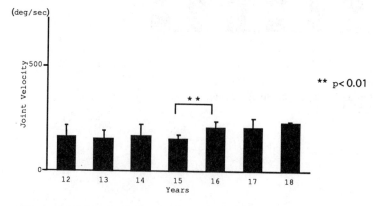

Figure 4. Peak extension speed in adolescent male soccer players (Ariel, 20 kg; n=56).

4 Discussion

The high school group had twice as many current complaints per player as the junior high school group. In our sports clinic statistics of sports injuries, 16 year-olds have the most injuries, next are seventeen year-olds, followed by 18 year-olds (O'Hata, 1992). In Japan pupils up to 15 years old belong to junior high school teams. At 16 they change to high school teams. There are changes in their practice environment, an increase in practice hours, and an increase in the severity of training in this age group.

These results suggest that between the ages of 13 and 14 when knee extension muscle strength increases greatly, it would be best to avoid kicking exercises which put pressure on knee joints and instead focus exercise around short distance passing, dribbling, and mini-games. Then muscle training may start with appropriate loads from the age of 14 years, because knee extension muscle strength increases gradually from the age of 14 to 17. Also at age 14, when the increase in joint movement speed is highest, sprint training should be performed. At age 16, when the maximum oxygen uptake gets closer to that of adult soccer players (Kohno et al., 1991), endurance training may be started.

Considering adolescent soccer players' fitness level, it would be best to organize teams by ages: 12-13, 14-15, 16-17, and 18 year-olds and older together. In Japan the teams are made up of 13 to 15 year-old boys (junior high school) and 16 to 18 year-old boys (high school). Therefore, children in different developmental stages of fitness level practice together which may result in an excessive burden on some of them.

Adolescent soccer should be played with enjoyment but safely. It is necessary to create an environment which prevents injuries so that injuries will not cause players to discontinue playing soccer and adolescent players can grow up to become adult players. Changes in fitness levels need to be understood and soccer training should be considered according to age.

It was found that current complaints increase above the age of 16 years. Injuries may be decreased by taking changes in fitness level of adolescent players into consideration when designing training programmes.

5 Conclusion

In conclusion, from the age of 12 to 13 it is best first to conduct technical exercises that will not be too much for knee joints, and then, at the age of 14, progess to improving muscle power (with appropriate loads) and sprint training. At age 16 years, endurance training may be started. Sports injuries increased in the players above the age of 16. By performing training adjusted to the different levels of fitness and according to age, these injuries may be decreased.

6 References

Kohno, T., O'Hata, N. et al. (1991) Sports injuries and fitness level of the company soccer team for 3 soccer seasons. **Japanese Journal of Orthopaedic Sports Medicine**, 10, 469-72, 1991

O'Hata, N. (1992) Sports injury on children. **Pediatric Internal Medicine**, 24, 551-557.

HIGH-SCHOOL SOCCER SUMMER TOURNAMENTS IN JAPAN - COMPARISON OF LABORATORY DATA OF THE PLAYERS IN SUMMER AND WINTER -

M. KOBAYASHI, H. AOKI, S. IKEDA, T. KATSUMATA, T. KOHNO,
K. SHIONO, J. SEKI, T. TAKAGI, T. TAKEI, J. TANAKA,
K. NABESHIMA, K. NOMURA, S. FUKAYA, T. FUKUBAYASHI,
S. MIYAKAWA, T. MURAKAMI, T. MORIKAWA, T. MORIMOTO
F. YAMASHITA, M. WAKAYAMA and N. O'HATA
Sports Medical Committee, Football Association of Japan,
Dept. of Sports Medicine, Jikei Univ. School of Medicine,
3-25-8, Nishishinbashi, Minato-ku, Tokyo, 105 JAPAN

1 Introduction

Soccer played in a hot and humid environment may pose a potential problem for the players' health, but few studies have focused on this problem.

In this report we examined blood chemistry of the players in high-school soccer tournaments in mid-summer and compared them to those in mid-winter.

2 Methods

Twenty four soccer players, 6 persons per team, were randomly selected from 4 teams who entered the semi-final matches (35 minutes half) in the tournaments of summer and winter. The composition of each team was different in the summer and winter tournaments. Players were allowed to have fluid intake during matches.

Body mass was determined and venous blood and urine samples were collected from the same individuals in a medical office immediately after and the morning after a soccer match. Blood analysis included complete blood count, aspartate aminotransferase (AST), alanine amino-transferase (ALT), lactic acid dehydrogenase (LDH), serum creatinine, serum total protein (TP), electrolytes, serum osmolality (Osm), serum ferritin (Fe), creatine kinase (CK), myoglobin, anti-diuretic hormone (ADH), plasma renin activity (PRA), and plasma angiotensin II (Ang II).

Data are presented as mean ± standard deviation (SD). The significance of difference between groups was calculated using Student's paired and/or unpaired t-test.

3 Results

Average temperature of the days of matches was 27°C in the summer and 8°C in the winter. Body mass decreased from 65.7 ± 5.4 kg to 63.7 ± 6.1 kg in the summer and from 64.6 ± 5.7 kg to 63.5 ± 5.7 kg in the winter.

Blood data of the 24 players in the soccer tournaments in the summer and the winter are shown in Table 1.

Blood TP used as index of dehydration was observed to be elevated after matches in the summer. On the other hand, the TP levels after matches in the winter were not elevated, and lower than after matches in summer (P<0.001, Fig. 1).

Similarly, serum Na and Osm levels were significantly increased after matches in the summer compared to those in the winter (P<0.001, Fig. 2, Table 1).

The ADH, PRA and Ang II values were higher after matches in the summer compared to those in the winter (Fig. 3, Table 1). In these, ADH levels in the morning after matches remained over the normal range in eight summer players.

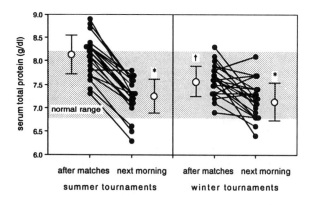

Figure 1. Individual (filled circles) and mean (open circles) serum total protein levels of the high-school players after and the morning after the soccer matches in summer and winter tournaments. *, P<0.001 compared with levels after matches. †, P<0.001 compared with levels of summer tournaments.

In this situation, creatinine levels used as index of renal function were also higher than the normal range in 3/4 of the players in the summer matches (P<0.001, Fig. 4).

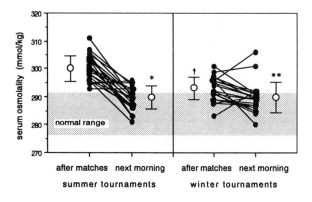

Figure 2. Individual (filled circles) and mean (open circles) serum osmolarity levels of the high-school players immediately after and the morning after the soccer matches in summer and winter tournaments. *, P<0.001 ; **,P<0.02 compared with levels after matches. †, P<0.001 compared with levels of summer tournaments. Data are mean ± SD (n=24).

Table 1. Blood data of 24 high-school players in the summer and winter soccer tournaments

Items of blood analysis		summer tournaments		winter tournaments	
		after matches	next morning	after matches	next morning
RBC	(x10⁶/μl)	5.01±0.26	4.82±0.29*	4.92±0.32	4.92±0.31
Hb	(mg/dl)	15.39±0.86	14.69±0.96*	15.38±0.86	14.61±1.15
AST	(IU/l)	36.2±5.6	27.1±4.3*	42.0±14.5	38.9±15.2*†
ALT	(IU/l)	21.3±6.4	19.8±5.8*	28.4±8.3†	25.4±8.3*†
LDH	(IU/l)	614.2±94.6	460.1±67.5*	572.4±102.6††	485.7±105.8*
Creatinine	(mg/dl)	1.35±0.14	0.96±0.09*	1.21±0.16†	0.96±0.11*
Total Protein	(g/dl)	8.14±0.41	7.28±0.39*	7.60±0.33†	7.16±0.40*
Na	(mmol/l)	148.0±2.0	143.2±1.3*	139.6±1.6†	139.3±2.0†
Cl	(mmol/l)	106.4±2.6	104.8±1.9*	100.9±1.9†	102.1±1.5*†
Serum Osmolality	(mmol/kg)	300.5±4.5	289.6±4.1*	292.9±4.2†	289.7±5.3*†
Serum Fe	(μg/dl)	162.4±34.2	89.3±39.9*	100.4±39.2†	69.8±23.2*††
CK	(IU/l)	621.9±334.6	442.7±229.7*	717.1±551.6	771.3±630.5††
Myoglobin	(ng/ml)	138.3±56.5	41.9±12.7*	282.9±127.1†	76.0±36.6*†
ADH	(pg/ml)	8.81±6.01	2.99±2.54*	6.06±4.57	3.3±2.48**
PRA	(ng/ml/hr)	10.86±6.77	1.25±0.89*	6.65±3.15†	1.89±0.96*††
Angiotensin II	(pg/ml)	230.6±332.9	17.9±13.5*	42.3±45.3†	10.9±7.2*

*, $p < 0.01$, **, $p < 0.05$ compared with the value after matches.
†, $p < 0.01$, ††, $p < 0.05$ compared with the value of summer tournaments.

The LDH and serum Fe levels significantly increased after matches in the summer ($P<0.05$, Fig. 5 A and B). Conversely MG as index of muscle damage after matches was observed to have higher levels in the winter compared to those in the summer ($P<0.01$, Table 1).

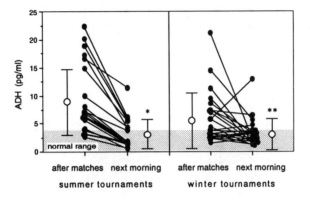

Figure 3. Individual (filled circles) and mean (open circles) plasma anti-diuretic hormone (ADH) levels of the high-school players after and the morning after the soccer matches in summer and winter tournaments. *, $P<0.001$; **, $P<0.02$ compared with levels after matches. †, $p<0.01$ compared with levels of summer tournaments. Data are mean ± SD (n=24).

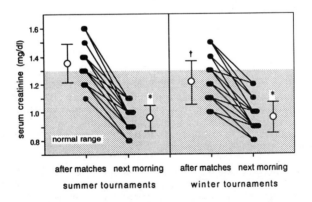

Figure 4. Individual (filled circles) and mean (open circles) serum creatinine levels of the high-school players after and the morning after the soccer matches in summer and winter tournaments. * $P<0.001$ compared with levels after matches. †, $P<0.003$ compared with levels of summer tournaments. Data are mean ± SD (n=24).

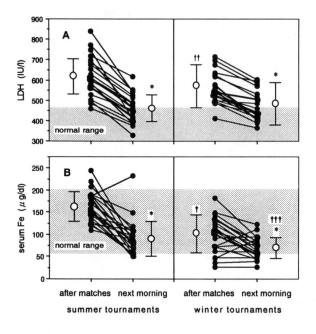

Figure 5. Individual (filled circles) and mean (open circles) LDH levels (A), and serum Fe levels (B) of the high-school players after and the morning after the soccer matches in summer and winter tournaments. *, P<0.001 compared with levels after matches. †, P<0.001; ††, P<0.03; †††, P<0.05 compared with levels of summer tournaments. Data are mean ± SD (n=24).

4 Discussion

The greatest potential problem for the players' health in the summer soccer tournaments is dehydration caused by high temperatures. In the present study, the high-school players in the summer tournaments had taken water during matches, but the serum TP, Na and Osm levels, used as index of dehydration, were significantly higher after matches in the summer compared to those in the winter. In some players the concentrations had not returned to resting revels in the morning after matches. These results suggest that the players dehydrated considerably during the games in the summer.

It is well known that dehydration leads to increments of plasma ADH, PRA and Ang II levels (Rowell, 1990). Mean ADH, PRA and Ang II after matches in the summer were observed to have higher concentrations compared to those in the winter. These increments probably caused a decline of renal blood flow, and creatine levels used as index of renal function were increased over the normal range in 3/4 of the summer players.

The MG levels, used as index of muscle damage, were significantly elevated immediately after and the morning after the matches in the winter. Furthermore, creatine kinase levels were significantly higher in the morning after matches in the winter compared to those after matches in the summer. These increments may result from severity in movements of the players in the winter matches compared with the summer. On the other hand, LDH concentrations were higher after matches in the summer compared to those in the winter. Additionally, serum Fe levels were higher after matches in the summer players compared to those in the winter. Previous studies have demonstrated intravascular haemolysis in athletes, namely "runner's anaemia" or "athlete's anaemia", but the mechanism inducing the anaemia remains unclear (Eichner, 1985, Selby, 1986,). The high levels of LDH and serum Fe may represent intravascular haemolysis due to dehydration and footstrike in summer tournaments.

5 Conclusion

The present study suggests that the soccer players of summer tournaments in Japan, since it is hot and humid, have a potential risk of acute renal failure due to severe dehydration, decline of renal blood flow and intravascular haemolysis based on increments in LDH and serum Fe levels.

6 References

Eichner, E.R. (1985) Runner's macrocytosis: a clue to footstrike hemolysis. **The American Journal of Medicine**, 78, 321-325.

Rowell, L.B. (1990) Exercise physiology, in **Principles of Physiology** (eds R.M. Byrne and M.N. Levy), Mosby, St.Louis, pp. 618-645.

Selby, G.B. et al. (1986) Endurance swimming, intravascular hemolysis, anemia, and iron depletion. **The American Journal of Medicine**, 81, 791-794.

HEART RATE RESPONSES OF CHILDREN DURING SOCCER PLAY

B. DRUST and T. REILLY
Centre for Sport and Exercise Sciences, Liverpool John Moores University,
Byrom Street, Liverpool, L3 3AF, England

1 Introduction

Participation in soccer is not restricted to the elite male performer as participants also include females, the old and the young. Scientific literature regarding the sport relates almost exclusively to adult male players with little information being available on other groups, particularly young soccer players.

Soccer entails high intensity, intermittent exercise. Quantification of the physiological load placed on adult players has been achieved by means of a variety of methods ranging from use of model games to the implementation of non-invasive indices of physiological strain (Reilly, 1990). Heart rate responses to match-play have been employed to indicate physiological loading (Rohde and Espersen, 1988). Monitoring of heart rate permits a realistic assessment of the circulatory strain placed on players in match situations (Ali and Farrally, 1991). Heart rate responses to game play have been reported for university players (Van Gool et al., 1988) and top class Danish players (Bangsbo, 1994). One study which focused on the young player (Klimt et al., 1992) did not include continuous monitoring and consequently could not provide a comprehensive view of physiological responses.

Small-sided games are popular with all soccer playing populations. Such games, as well as their recreational prevalence, are an important component of competitive teams' training and fitness schedules (MacLaren et al., 1988). In many countries such participation is the only form undertaken by children. It is therefore important to assess physiological demands placed on players in relation to the stimulus of small-sided games.The aim of this study was therefore to determine the physiological load in terms of the heart rate responses of boys and girls to short duration small-sided soccer games.

2 Methods

Eighteen children (11 males, 7 females, age range 7-13 years), mean characteristics shown in Table 1, were examined. Heart rate responses to 10 min 8-a-side outdoor soccer games were recorded using a short-range radio telemeter (Sports Tester, Polar Electro, Kempele, Finland). Heart rate was recorded continuously (5 s samples). This equipment has the benefit of being extremely light and is unrestrictive to the subject when exercising . Each individual's heart rate responses were recorded in separate games. Pitch size was 60 x 40 m. No positional differences were examined as small-sided games do not adhere to the conventional positions seen in 11-a-side games.

Table 1. Mean ± S.D anthropometric characteristics of the subjects

	Age	Height	Body Mass	Playing experience	BMI
	(years)	(m)	(kg)	(years)	
boys	10	140.1	36.5	5	18.2
	± 1.6	± 9.1	± 8.0	± 1.5	± 2.4
girls	10	140.4	32.7	4	16.2
	± 1.5	± 11.6	± 13.8	± 1.5	± 4.2

Mean heart rates (HR) for game play were calculated for both sexes and analysed using a two sample t-test. As activity levels, and hence heart rate responses, can be influenced by body composition, mean values were correlated with body mass index (BMI) and playing experience using Pearson's product moment method. A heart rate range (HR max during game period - minimum heart rate during game period) was also calculated for each individual. Five of the eighteen subjects (4 boys, 1 girl) completed a further 10 min period of play immediately after the first phase to explore fatigue effects in the second session. Paired sample t-tests were performed on the data.

3 Results

Mean ($\pm$ S.D) heart rate for the games was 169$\pm$6 beats/min. No significant difference ($P > 0.05$) was observed between sexes (boys 170$\pm$18, girls 167$\pm$20 beats/min). Figure 1 shows the mean heart rate response to the 10 min game for male and female players.

Mean heart rate range was found to be 36$\pm$18 beats/ min. No significant differences ($P > 0.05$) were found in heart rate in those subjects who completed a further 10 min period of play after completion of the first period (first period : 179$\pm$8, second period : 181$\pm$5 beats/min; n=5).

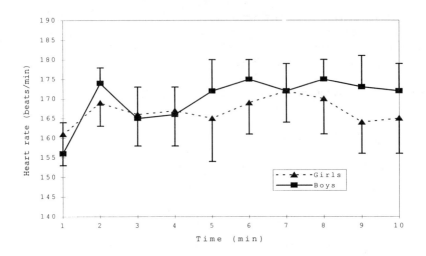

Figure 1. Mean heart rates ± S.E for 10 min small-sided-games for both male and female players.

Table 2 shows the correlation matrix for both male and female and the pooled data for heart rate response, BMI and playing experience. No correlations (P > 0.05) were observed between heart rate and body mass index or playing experience.

Table 2. Correlation matrix for the data of boys, girls and the pooled sample

	Pooled	Boys	Girls
HR-BMI	0.33	0.34	0.31
HR-playing experience	0.04	-0.04	0.19

4 Discussion

The mean heart rate observed during 10 min games was 169±6 beats/min. Seliger (1968) used 10 min model games to assess cardiovascular strain on adult male players and observed a mean heart rate of 160 beats/min. Data on adult top class male players in 11-a-side games (Bangsbo, 1994) have produced figures of 173 beats/min for first half play and 169 beats/min for the second half . Such data highlight the usefulness of small-sided games as a training tool not only in a coaching sphere but also in a conditioning context. Bar-Or and Unnithan (1994) argued that the use of such games for youngsters is to reduce the total energy expenditure of the game compared with adult play. This is intended to prevent problems associated with the unique exercise-related characteristics of children (e.g. the higher metabolic demands of walking and running) causing injury or burn-out in later life. It seems that the high intensity, intermittent nature of the game remains the same as in 11-a-side contests. No significant difference was observed between the boys and girls in heart rate responses, indicating a high physiological demand irrespective of sex.

The heart rate range (36±18 beats/min) illustrates the maintenance of a high heart rate throughout the period of the match. The high heart rates are preserved due to the short recovery period occurring in the game (Reilly, 1990). The heart rate range is comparable to the average heart rates (147 to 187 beats/min) detected by Klimt et al.(1992). No significant differences were evident in the heart rate response to a second period of play following the initial session. Van Gool et al. (1988) witnessed declines in mean heart rate of University players during the second half of matches and attributed this in part to fatigue. It is likely though that the game employed in the present study was not of sufficient duration to induce fatigue and thereby affect heart rate responses.

The altered running economy observed in children as a result of factors such as differences in stride frequency, body composition and gait mechanics (Wilmore and Costill, 1994) could be responsible for the failure to find a significant relationship between heart rate and body mass index. Additionally, the lack of correlation between playing experience and heart rate demonstrates the high physiological demand of the activity independent of any previous experience in the game. It implicates a high physiological demand associated with exercise "off the ball".

The heart rate responses observed during small-sided games reflect the high intensity nature of soccer. This, as a consequence, places high demands on players irrespective of sex or playing experience. Techniques of motion analysis could be included in future work to provide another index of energy expenditure and yield time-motion characteristics of the children's games.

5 Acknowledgements

Thanks must be given to British Soccer Camps and all the children involved in the study for their help in the collection of the data.

6 References

Ali, A. and Farrally, M. (1991) Recording soccer players' heart rates during matches. **Journal of Sports Sciences**, 9, 183-189.

Bangsbo, J.(1994) **Fitness Training in Football - A Scientific Approach.** HO + Storm, Bagsvaerd.

Bar-Or, O. and Unnithan, V.B. (1994) Nutritional requirements of young soccer players. **Journal of Sports Sciences**, 12, S39-S42.

Klimt, F., Betz, M. and Seitz, U. (1992) Metabolism and circulation system of children playing soccer, in **Children and Exercise XVI : Paediatric Work Physiology** (eds J. Coudert and E. Van Praagh), Maason, Paris, pp. 127-129.

MacLaren, D., Davids, K., Isokawa, M., Mellor, S. and Reilly, T. (1988) Physiological strain in 4-a-side soccer, in **Science and Football** (eds T.Reilly, A. Lees, K. Davids and W.J Murphy), E. and F.N. Spon, London, pp. 76-80.

Reilly, T. (1990) Football, in **Physiology of Sports** (eds T. Reilly, N. Secher, P, Snell and C.Williams), E. and F.N. Spon, London, pp. 371-425.

Rohde, H.C. and Espersen, T. (1988) Work intensity during soccer training and match-play, in **Science and Football** (eds T.Reilly, A. Lees, K. Davids and W.J Murphy), E. and F.N. Spon, London, pp. 68-75.

Seliger, V. (1968) Heart rate as an index of physiological load in exercise. **Scripta Medica,** Medical Faculty, Brno University, 41, 231-240.

Van Gool, D., Van Gerven, D. and Boutmans,J. (1988) The physiological load imposed on soccer players during real match-play, in **Science and Football** (eds T. Reilly, A. Lees, K.Davids and W.J Murphy), E. and F.N. Spon, London, pp. 51-59.

Wilmore, J.H. and Costill, D.L. (1994) **Physiology of Sport and Exercise.** Human Kinetics, Champaign, IL.

DEVELOPING AND ACQUIRING FOOTBALL SKILLS

LES BURWITZ
Division of Sport Science, Crewe+Alsager Faculty, the Manchester Metropolitan University, Hassall Road, Alsager, Stoke-on-Trent, ST7 2HL, England

1 Introduction

In this review, the development and acquisition of football skills are considered from a multidisciplinary perspective. The emphasis is on goal-oriented skills that are not innate or developed naturally. Specifically technical, mental, physical, tactical and social skills are addressed through a consideration of various football-related problems. The solutions to such problems are considered using general principles developed from Social Learning Theory and, in particular, Bandura's Contiguity-Mediational Theory which stressed the importance of attention, retention, ability and motivation. The benefits of developing decision making skills and individualised approaches to training are discussed and the relevance of communication between the player, coach and support staff highlighted.

2 Classification of Football Skills

Football involves a multiplicity of skills. Some of these are basic skills (e.g. running) whilst others may be referred to as technical (e.g. passing) or goal-oriented (e.g. scoring a goal) skills. Basic skills are assumed to be innate or developed via a process of maturation whereas all other skills have to be learned through practice or past experience. Whilst technical skills are accepted as a fundamental part of any footballer's repertoire, emphasis is placed on those skills which enable goals or specific targets to be achieved with maximum certainty and a minimum outlay of time, energy, attention or any combination of these (Knapp, 1963). It is suggested that, in football, achieving a goal (such as being able to make a good quality pass consistently) is relatively more important than exhibiting the textbook technique.

Reports on the characteristics of elite team games players can be divided into five main areas, namely technical, mental, physical, tactical and social factors. Technical factors typically include such skills as passing, receiving, dribbling (where relevant) and defending. The mental category often incorporates aspects such as confidence, anxiety control, concentration and motivation. Physical qualities include strength, endurance, power and flexibility. Tactical aspects are often under-represented but anticipation, pressurising, creating space and support are worthy of mention. Finally, under the social category are cohesion, leadership, governing body or club support and access to support facilities.

3 Football-Related Problems

A multidisciplinary perspective on football-related problems involves several disciplines simultaneously and in parallel (Burwitz et al., 1994). This is a precursor to interdisciplinary work which would involve contemplating the various relationships between the disciplines from the outset. An example illustrates the concept.

Consider a situation where a player was deemed to have a problem with passing the ball. This was normally considered to be a technical problem in that the player did not possess the necessary technical skill to pass the ball successfully on a consistent basis. Other disciplines should not be ignored. The player may have a problem with passing because:-
a) he or she could not make a correct decision about when to pass the ball between two defenders (mental factor);
b) he or she had insufficient power to weight the pass correctly toward the end of a tiring game (physical factor);
c) he or she was not able to evaluate whether it was appropriate to attempt a penetrating pass at a specific time during a game (depending on the score and the time to the final whistle) and in particular areas of the field of play (tactical factor);
d) there was no support communication from team mates (social factor).

Adherence to fitness training is deemed to be the province of an exercise physiologist. Adherence to aerobic, anaerobic and strength training programmes is often different for female amateur players (see Figure 1). In particular, adherence to the aerobic aspects of training is generally very good whereas compliance with anaerobic and strength training is relatively poor. Ongoing research indicates that this is partly due to mental factors such as motivation and/or fear of injury, tactical issues relating to the player's perception of position-specific requirements and social variables such as access to appropriate training facilities and/or group support. Evidence indicates that these problems could be overcome with a training programme that was based on a multidisciplinary perspective and incorporates aspects relating to appropriate physical, mental, tactical and social factors.

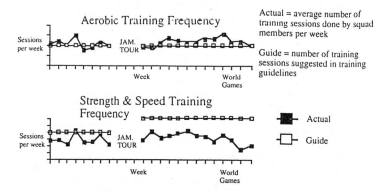

Figure 1. Training adherence.

A similar problem was posed with respect to "goal" scoring however it was defined in the various football codes. If a team managed to create as many "goal scoring" opportunities as the opposition but failed to score as many "goals", why was this? Was it a function of the lack of technical competence, mental confidence, physical power or tactical decision making relating to shot selection or did it involve a combination of these factors to a greater or lesser extent?

4 Football-Related Problems - Multi/Interdisciplinary Solutions

The solutions to football-related problems stress the relevance of learning in the development of football skills. Some general principles of learning rely heavily on Social Learning Theory and, in particular, Bandura's Contiguity-Mediational Theory (Bandura, 1969). This is pertinent given the nature of football, namely a team game involving invasion of the opponent's territory in order to score. Specifically, there are four crucial factors. These are attention, retention, ability and motivation. Learning in a social context requires that the player attends to crucial aspects of the game, makes correct decisions, retains relevant information and has the ability and motivation to reproduce the desired skill at any given point in time.

Attention and retention have been considered in some detail in recent research (Williams et al., 1993, 1994 and Williams and Davids, 1994) which used a variety of 11 vs 11, 3 vs 3 and 1 vs 1 soccer situations. The anticipation (often both accuracy and speed of response) of relatively skilled defenders was compared with that of less experienced individuals and an eye mark camera was used to track and plot eye movements. In the 11 vs 11 situation, "experts" watched both the ball and the movements off the ball whereas "novices" tended to focus more on the ball and the ball carrier. When the display was much simpler (1 vs 1), "experts" concentrated on the hip, knee and ball in order to predict the direction of the opponent whereas "novices" spent a lot of time looking at the upper body as well as the ball.

With respect to learning, an earlier study of penalty shooting (Williams and Burwitz, 1993) also showed that "experts" appeared to use the hip to provide early information about the likely direction and height of the ball. In that study a "novice" group of goalkeepers was split into an experimental and control condition with the former group receiving advice and training relating to which aspects of the display they should concentrate on at particular times. Results revealed that the experimental subjects improved significantly more than the control group, indicating that aspects of anticipation can be learned.

Another aspect of coaching attention and retention refers to the "decision web" (Royce, 1994). For example, Rugby League decision making practices progress from 2 vs 1 through 3 vs 2 and 3 vs 4 to 7 vs 7. Emphasis is placed on both the structure of the drills and also on methods of coaching decision making at crucial points during open field play such as pre-scanning (before the ball arrives), post-scanning (after the ball has been received) and scanning whilst in possession. In addition, creating space by movement with and without the ball is featured in relation to the type of opportunities that such movement provides. Whilst the decision web (Figure 2) mainly concentrates on offensive tactics, defensive decision making is also relevant.

Skill acquisition may not be apparent even if a player has attended to and retained the relies pre-requisite information. Players may have the innate ability to reproduce required skills or they may have to develop this ability over a period of time. Progression is made from sound basics to more advanced skills at key times when the player is ready. Progression heavily on observation and analysis of an individual's readiness using a triangulation approach incorporating the player's self-rating, the coach's considered opinion and, where relevant, objective information extracted from tests or match analysis. The potential for problems to occur because of a lack of attention to sound basic principles (e.g. decision making skills) at an early stage and de-motivation, due to creating a challenge which was either too great or too little, was noted.

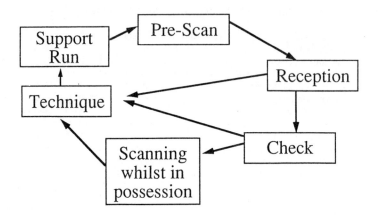

Figure 2. The decision web.

Finally, motivation is important. It is suggested that players who are well aware what they were supposed to be doing and capable of reproducing desirable of skills may still fail to do so if they lack the necessary motivation. Experience from over six years of sport science support had revealed that motivation could be enhanced by using the RIM. This acronym stood for Records of Achievement, Interventions and Monitoring.

The Record of Achievement (REACH) refers to an individual player's progress over a period of time. It comprises several components. Firstly, there is an individual position-specific profile which takes account of the player's perceptions about those characteristics which are required at elite level in the sport as well as a self-rating on each quality (Butler and Hardy, 1992). A second component is the coach's independent rating of the player on the same qualities. The coach might also be asked to discuss with the player any discrepancy between the two ratings and also any aspect that the coach would have included or excluded from the profile. A third aspect of the REACH is based on quantitative data extracted from appropriate technical/fitness/psychometric tests and, more importantly, match analysis of an individual player's contribution both on and off the ball including reference to decision making. The relevance of communication must be stressed. The REACH would have little, if any, benefit to motivation and player development without good quality communication and agreed goal setting.

Consideration of the relationship between interventions or training programmes and motivation raises a number of issues. Conceptually, individualised "contracts", which are agreed a priori on the basis of the REACH, provide the "ownership" that should enhance commitment. In practice, certainly in amateur football, this is often difficult to achieve as it is in direct conflict with the requirements of the club, county or region. "Over-competition" leaves inadequate time for skill development. The importance of players accepting responsibility for aspects of personal development, coaches concentrating on decision making within squad sessions and good quality communication is highlighted.

Regular monitoring is also highly relevant. This should take account of updating and analysing the reasons behind any changes to various aspects of the Record of Achievement. Ideally it would involve analysis of players' daily diaries/logbooks and interviews or consultations with individual players. An impartial support person (e.g. physiotherapist, sport scientist) in this role may be a benefit, as such an individual may act as an "honest broker" were referred to. Communication is a fundamental aid or block to motivation and this is often an area in need of attention.

5 Conclusion

Goal-oriented skills are important in football and it is opportune to adopt a multidisciplinary and, ideally, interdisciplinary approach to problem solving. Wide-ranging skills are required to be successful in football and consideration should be given to the impact of the interaction between technical, mental, physical, tactical and social factors. A wide ranging perspective of skill acquisition and development is crucial with particular attention devoted to decision making during the game, observation and analysis of relevant characteristics, techniques which can be employed to maximise motivation and communication between players, coaches and support staff.

6 Acknowledgements

The author wishes to acknowledge the support of the following in the preparation of this paper: Andy Borrie and Mark Williams (both Liverpool John Moores University); Dave Collins and Keith Davids (both Manchester Metropolitan University); John Kerr (Director of Coaching, Rugby League); Claire Palmer (Manchester Metropolitan University); Jon Royce (England U21 Hockey Coach) and the Sports Council.

7 References

Bandura, A. (1969) **Principles of Behavior Modification.** Holt, Rinehart & Winston, New York.

Burwitz, L., Moore, P.M. and Wilkinson, D.M. (1994) Future directions for performance related sport science research: an interdisciplinary approach. **Journal of Sports Sciences,** 12, 93-109.

Butler, R.J. and Hardy, L. (1992) The performance profile; theory and application. **The Sport Psychologist,** 6, 253-264.

Knapp, B. (1963) **Skill in Sport: The Attainment of Proficiency.** Routledge & Kegan Paul, London.

Royce, J. (1994) How do you coach decision-making? A case study: passing and receiving. **Coaching Focus,** 26, 20-22.

Williams, A.M. and Burwitz, L. (1993) Advance cue utilisation in soccer, in **Science and Football II** (eds T. Reilly, J. Clarys and A. Stibbe), E. & F.N. Spon, London, pp. 239-244.

Williams, A.M. and Davids, K. (1994) Visual search strategy and anticipation in sport. **Coaching Focus,** 26, 6-9.

Williams, A.M., Davids, K., Burwitz, L. and Williams, J.G. (1993) Visual search and sports performance. **The Australian Journal of Science and Medicine in Sport,** 25, 55-65.

Williams, A.M., Davids, K., Burwitz, L. and Williams, J.G. (1994) Visual search strategies in experienced and inexperienced players. **Research Quarterly for Exercise and Sport,** 65, 2, 127-135.

PART SIX

Match Analysis

USE OF MATCH ANALYSIS BY COACHES

EGIL OLSEN* and OYVIND LARSEN**
* Norwegian Football Association (NFF)
** Norwegian University of Sports and Physical Education (NIH)

1 Introduction

The process of bridging the gap between research and practice, so that scientific knowledge about soccer can be discussed and put into practice, has been going on for years in Norway. Nevertheless there is still some tension between the "academic" and the "practical". Ten years ago match analysis was considered with suspicion; today nearly all the coaches in the premier league use match analysis in one way or another.

Our style of soccer is partly a product of match analysis, but also has roots in both more general experience and Norwegian tradition. The aspect of play least influenced by match analysis is the defence. However, the way of playing in defence indirectly plays an important role, especially in connection with breakdown and regaining possession of the ball. The Norwegian national teams, the first team, the first women's team and the U-21 team, play with a zonal defence in extreme form which means that no marking takes place. The position of the player is nearly totally defined by his team mates, not his opponents. Our principles of defence differ radically from opponents such as Germany and Denmark. Compared with most English teams too, we pay less attention to marking activity. This schism in the theory of defence play is scarcely discussed in the soccer literature.

Norway's way of attacking is far more influenced by match analysis. Reep and Benjamin (1968) awoke a curiosity that has been growing up to the current day. Originally interest was centred at the Norwegian University of Sport and Physical Education (NIH), but interest has gradually spread to clubs and the Norwegian FA.

Four main factors have played a decisive role in contributing to the status of match analysis in Norway today: first of all, the 1987 World Congress of Science and Football; secondly, the subsequent visit of George Wilkinson to NIH in 1987; thirdly Egil Olsen's appointment to the position of analysis consultant for former national coach Ingar Stadheim; and finally, Olsen's subsequent appointment as Norway's national coach. Match analysis is used to evaluate patterns of play, team and player performance and as a way of enhancing the scientific approach to soccer. Today Oyvind Larsen is employed as the senior consultant for match analysis.

The work has a clear pragmatic aim and the outcome of the analysis is meant to be a tool for evaluation and development of team tactics. The analysis has influenced our play, especially in attack. We have asked a lot of questions through which our practice has given the answers. The answers are not supposed to be definite or ever-lasting but are continuously subject to new and critical questions.

The direction in attack has so far gone towards a more and more penetrative way of play. We know there is a limit to how penetrative we should be. We need to take into consideration both the skill of our own players and the opponents, as well as player mobility. This means that the players' running capacity could hinder further development of this style.

Another important task is to identify the demands of the different situations. Here the principles of balance are of great interest. The balance of the opponents' defence decides our tactics. When we meet a more or less unbalanced defence, i.e. after a breakdown, our penetrating approach is evident. We try to finish the attack as soon as possible. The degree of imbalance is not allowed to decrease during the attack. This leads to frequent losses of the ball, but gives us nevertheless more scoring opportunities than a more elaborate way of attacking play. Especially important is the first pass after the breakdown. It should go forward and be combined with great mobility. This pattern of play includes both frequent loss and gain of possession.

Many members of the soccer family dislike this style of play and consider it to be simple and primitive. However, the overall aim of play is to win matches, so that we are willing to sacrifice the fleeting beauty of aesthetic style in the name of efficiency.

Even more controversial than our attacking pattern of play against unbalanced defence, is our play against a balanced defence. When we face eleven players in balance being on the defensive side of the ball, we use the "long ball". It is often difficult to draw strong conclusions from match analysis and put them into practice. We have not found any sign of the analysis which "indicates" that we should gain greater efficiency by playing more through midfield in these situations. We have therefore tried to find methods for how to exploit the long ball. It demands players with special skills, the players have to move forward collectively, and most importantly, it demands players to make runs behind the first attacker who often flicks the ball. Between 33% and 25% of the attacks start this way. With good planning they give us possession in the opponents' half of the field. This tactic also prevents the opponent having frequent attacks starting from our defending half.

So many factors can influence the outcome of a match that there is a danger of making decisions on false or weak premises. On the other hand, such difficulties do not prevent us from trying. Some of our most used analyses are presented with examples of results.

2 Methods

The methods of contemporary notation analysis have their origins from the early seventies in studies of how goals are created (Olsen, 1973). Data were collected at the Norwegian University of Sport and Physical Education in the mid-1980s (Olsen, 1988), and from 1989 onwards all the matches of the national team of Norway have been analysed. Today the national women's, men's and Under-21 teams and their opponents are being analysed.

The methods of collecting, storing, analysing and presenting data have developed from using pen, paper and a calculator to a computerised analysis system. The methods and data presented in this paper are also the result of the Norwegian FA's first step in a three-phase plan to develop an efficient computerised notation analysis program:

i)   to develop a computerised match and player analysis system;
ii)   to make the database of the match and player analysis system and the video/disk interactive;
iii)   to develop a more detailed player analysis system in order to make more valid and reliable player profiles.

2.1 The chosen parameters
In Norway with only 4 million citizens and a winter with snow in most areas for 4-6 months of the year, we obviously have a difficulty maintaining soccer at a top international level. Therefore, it is important in a long term strategy to focus on fields on which we are, or can become, brilliant. Our growing expertise and continued interest in developing further notation analysis may also account for the remarkable success of the Norwegian national teams in recent years. The strong link between the academics (NIH) and the practitioners (NFF and the coaches) has also made this way easier to follow.

The outcome of the analysis depends heavily on what kind of variables is being noted. The goals of the analysis must guide the data collection. The aims of the notation analysis system that have been developed can be listed very simply:

i)   We want to get beyond the match result and measure the team's effectiveness through counting scoring opportunities.

ii)   We want to categorise different types of attacks with the intention of measuring their effectiveness. The analysis includes both a descriptive summary of which types of attacks produce scoring opportunities and the production of an attack's quotient of relative effectiveness (ratio). This information will help in long-term strategy planning and obviously influences player and team building, team-selection and match tactics.

iii)   We want to gain more knowledge of the "match syntax" in general. Firstly, we need to see which parameters in a match or during a season differ from our team's compared with our opponents. Secondly, data from the syntax in general give us a more scientific approach to developing individual skills (i.e. type of passes, technique used when finishing, type of runs) and team tactics (i.e. what kind of space is needed to penetrate with runs and passes).

iv)   After every match the notational analysis includes a detailed player analysis. We analyse which players are involved in both our and the opponents' scoring opportunities. The "player analysis system" also includes an evaluation of every player's involvement with the ball both quantitatively and qualitatively.

When selecting parameters we also have in mind to use the notation analysis system as a critical tool to study our pattern of play. If we only select and analyse parameters which confirm our soccer ideology we run the risk of being undermined by our beliefs. A "winning formula" in soccer will probably never be discovered. The configuration of a soccer match and therefore the outcome depends very much on the interaction of the two teams (Elias and Dunning, 1966). Yet a systematic approach to analysing the syntax in general and of the winning syntax in particular, both at an individual and team level, can help us in picking and using the right elements.

2.2 Match analysis - parameters

Data are collected on 16 match parameters. These are now described.

1.   Match details: - teams, type of tournament, where the match takes place time of event (min: s - 1st or 2nd leg) with the aim of digitizing all the entries.

2.   Total set plays in the match: - with the aim to get the ratio of set plays - scoring opportunities and in general get more knowledge about the set plays - syntax.

3.   Attacks - scoring opportunities

    a)   Break down: i) Winning the ball in play from the opponent with total control.
        ii) Winning the ball in play from the opponent from control to not control.
        iii) Winning the ball in play from the opponent without control.
        iv) Regain possession (2nd ball).

    b)   Set Plays
        i)   Free kicks   -   shooting distance; attacking 1/3; midfield A; midfield B; defending 1/3
        ii)   Corner   -   inswinging
                      -   outswinging
                      -   short corner

    c)   Longer attacks
        i)   After break-down
        ii)   After set play.

4.   Regaining possession in the attack which is not notated and located as the start of the attack

5.   Type of build up of attacks starting from the teams' own half of the field

     a)   Directly over midfield
     b)   Fast move through midfield
     c)   Slow build up of attack

6.   Balance of defence - start of the attack

     a)   Balanced defence
     b)   Unbalanced in position
     c)   Unbalanced in number
     d)   Unbalanced both in position and number

7.   Location - start of the attack

     a)   Defending 1/3
     b)   Midfield "A" - own 1/2 half
     c)   Midfield "B" - opponents 1/2 half
     d)   Attacking 1/3 not including scorebox
     e)   Scorebox.

8.   First pass of the attack

9.   Penultimate pass

10.   The last pass of the attack

     a)   Location
        i) Defending 1/3 - 8 areas; ii) Midfield 1/3 - 8 areas; iii) Attacking 1/3 - 8 areas

     b)   Type of passing. I) Square pass; ii) Supporting pass; iii) Short penetration pass; iv) Long penetration pass; v) Cross which is not penetrating space behind the back line; vi) Early cross; vii) Late cross; viii) Overlap; ix)Wall - pass; x) Goal kick; xi) Shot/shooting attempt

     c)   Which space the pass is penetrating

        i) Space between midfield and the last defending line (central - left flank - right flank); ii) Space in the last defending line; iii) Space behind the last defending line (central - left flank - right flank); iv) Pass which is not penetrating.

     d)   Player (name) and position involved

        i) Keeper; ii) Right full-back; iii) Right central defender; iv) Left central defender; v) Left full back; vi) Right flank; vii) Right inside midfield; viii) Central midfield; ix) Left inside midfield; x) Left flank; xi) Striker; (Flexible to other positions and formations)

11.   Location where the attack ends

a) Outside penalty
   (central-left-right)
b) 16 - 5 m
   (central-left-right)
c) 5 - 0 m.

12.   Player (name) and team position involved in the finish (The same categories as 10 D).

13.   Type of finish

   a)   Shot: i) Instep shot - from ground - air: ii) Inside foot - from ground - air: iii)
   Lofted shot; iv) Volley; v) Half volley; vi) Lobbing;
   b) Heading

14.   Result of the attack

   a)   Shot/header
   b)   Penalty
   c)   Scoring opportunity
   d)   Goal

15.   Location of the finish

   a)   In goal
         i) -x) 10 areas in goal
   b)   Keeper saves
   c)   Blocked by a defender
   d)   In the post or the bar
   e)   Outside/over the goal.

16.   Balance of defence - end of the attack

   a)   Balanced defence
   b)   Unbalanced in position
   c)   Unbalanced in number
   d)   Unbalanced both in position and number.

2.3 Player analysis - parameters

Description of parameter collection for the player analysis is described. This is also called the DOMP analysis.

a) Quantative data

   i)   Every player's ball involvement as 1st attacker and 1st defender in the 1st half,
        2nd half and total.

   ii) The system collects data on ball involvements for player, position, team
        components, in a match, sample of matches, for the whole season and/or for
        years.

b)   Qualitative data

The ball involvements are categorized as follows:

i)   Defending plus: Positive action as 1st
        (D)   defender which includes:
                              -       Tackle
                              -       Winning the ball by reading the
                                      game

ii)   Offensive plus: Positive action as 1st
        (O)   attacker which includes:- Penetration
                                  pass - Passing an opponent with the ball
                                  - Shot or heading

iii)   Offensive minus: Negative action as 1st
        (M)   attacker which includes: - Losing the
                                  ball; - Losing the ball in dribbling
                                  attempt.

iv)   Offensive minus: Negative action as 1st
        (P)   attacker which includes: - Square pass or
                                  back pass to opponent - Inaccurate
                                  penetrative pass - Inaccurate pass.

c)   Quantitative and qualitative data

The "DOMP" (see qualitative data above) player analysis makes it possible to produce both an individual and a team quotient for success (plus-actions) versus failure (minus-actions). This quotient can be related to the result or to the scoring opportunities within the match.

2.4 Entering, analysis, and presentation of data

All our "objective" notation analysis is based on indirect observation. The software system is developed in Microsoft Windows and can be used on IBM compatible personal computers. When entering the data, a specially designed registration sheet is used with all the parameters occurring on the screen. Using both the mouse and the keyboard on the specific parameter, the possible categories come up. Every entry is digitized with the time the action occurs.

The software offers descriptive statistical analysis, correlation analysis and degrees of significance. Both summary analysis and special analysis can be produced.

The validity and reliability of the data have been carefully approached. Through tests and retests of the analyser (s) inter- and intra-subjectivity, we have gained scientifically acceptable correlations. For many of the parameters, and obviously the most important ones, it is difficult to make precise operational definitions in a "quantitative proper way". But in the game of soccer - especially when the outcome of the analysis means three points or not - we must have a phenomenological approach. Therefore, we have to combine both the quantitative and the qualitative method when categorising the actions.

3 Result and Discussion

The relationship between goals scored and scoring opportunities is shown in Table 1. In the 1993 season we were extremely effective; that means we were very lucky. The opportunities (Table 2), here including goals, are distributed on the main categories of attack for the 1993-94 season. The differences between the seasons are significant. The difference between Norway and the opponents are biggest for the 'set play' category. In a match, it is crucial when goals occur. An early goal, or the first goal, seems to influence the outcome of the game. It has also been stated that random choice often plays an important part in goal scoring (Reep and Benjamin, 1968; Bate, 1988). The skill of the finisher will also influence the effectiveness of the team. To count scoring opportunities makes a more reliable measurement of the team's effectiveness than the outcome of the match.

Table 1. Ratio of scoring opportunities versus goals for Norway and opponents (Opps) in the 1991, 1992, 1993 and 1994 season and total

Season	Matches Played	Goal Score Norway	Opps	Score Opportunities Norway Opps		Ratio Norway	Opps
1991	9	9	8	65	49	7.2	6.1
1992	11	23	8	89	38	3.9	4.8
1993	10	25	5	84	54	3.4	10.8
1994	14	14	8	94	45	6.7	5.6
TOTAL	**44**	**71**	**29**	**332**	**186**	**4.7**	**6.4**

Table 2. Types of attack which create scoring opportunities and goals for Norway and its opponents in the 1993-94 season

Team	Season	No. of Matches	Breakdown N	%	Set Play N	%	Longer Attacks N	%	Total N	%
Norway	1993	10	40	47.7	27	32.1	17	20.2	84	100
Norway	1994	14	28	29.8	38	40.4	28	29.8	94	100
Norway	**TOTAL**	**24**	**68**	**38.2**	**65**	**36.5**	**45**	**25.3**	**178**	**100**
Opponents	1993	10	26	48.1	13	24.1	15	27.8	54	100
Opponents	1994	14	21	46.7	11	24.8	13	28.9	45	100
Opponents	**TOTAL**	**24**	**47**	**47.5**	**24**	**24.2**	**28**	**28.3**	**99**	**100**
TOTAL	**1993-94**	**24**	**115**	**41.5**	**89**	**32.1**	**73**	**26.4**	**277**	**100**

Table 3. Types of attack which create scoring opportunities and goals for Norway

| Type of Attack | Norway 1994 | | | | | |
| | Chances | | Goals | | Total | |
	No.	%	No.	%	No.	%
BD - Control	8	32.0	1	33.3	9	32.1
BD - Without Control	3	12.0			3	10.7
BD - From Control to Not	6	24.0	1	33.3	7	25.1
BD 2 Ball	8	32.0	1	33.3	9	32.1
Breakdown Total	**25**	**100**	**3**	**100**	**28**	**100**
SP - Corner Inswing	14	87.4	1	50.0	15	83.4
SP - Corner Outswing	1	6.3	1	50.0	2	11.1
SP - Corner Other	1	6.3			1	5.5
Corner Total	16	100	2	100	18	100
SP - Throw-in Attack	7	77.8	1	100	8	80.0
SP - Throw-in Other Areas	2	22.2			2	20.0
Throw in Total	9	100	1	100	10	100
SP - Free Kick - Shooting Distance	1	12.5			1	12.5
SP - Free Kick - Attacking 1/3	3	37.5			3	37.5
SP - Free Kick - Midfield	2	25.0			2	25.0
SP - Free Kick - Defending 1/3	2	25.0			2	25.0
Free Kick - Total	8	100			8	100
SP - Penalty			2		2	
Set Plays Total	**33**		**5**		**38**	
Longer - Breakdown	9	40.9	4	66.7	13	46.4
Longer - Set Plays	13	59.1	2	33.3	15	53.6
Longer Attacks Total	**22**	**100**	**6**	**100**	**28**	**100**
Total	**80**		**14**		**94**	

Table 4. A strategy chosen from the defending half - scoring opportunities, Norway's matches 1994

| Type of Attack | Norway 1994 | | | | | |
| | Chances | | Goals | | Total | |
	No.	%	No.	%	No.	%
None	57		23		80	
Over Midfield	16	43.2	4	18.2	20	33.9
Through Midfield-Fast	18	48.7	10	45.5	28	47.5
Build up Attack	3	8.1	8	36.3	11	18.6
Total	**94**	**100**	**45**	**100**	**139**	**100**

Table 5. Position involved in 1st, penultimate and the last pass in attacks which create scoring opportunities and goals

Position	1st Pass		Penultimate		Last Pass		Total	
	n	%	n	%	n	%	n	%
No Pass			30		7		45	
Keeper	8	9.3	2	3.1	1	8.1	11	4.6
Right Full Back	12	14.0	9	14.1	4	4.6	25	10.5
Left Full Back	17	19.8	4	6.3	12	13.8	33	13.9
Right Central Defender	9	10.5	2	3.1	5	5.7	16	6.8
Left Central Defender	10	11.6	7	10.9	3	3.4	20	8.4
Right Flank	1	1.2	4	6.3	16	18.4	21	8.9
Inside Midfield - Right	7	8.2	7	10.9	8	9.2	22	9.3
Central Midfield	7	8.2	4	6.3	10	11.5	21	8.9
Inside Midfield - Left	13	15.1	13	20.3	11	12.6	37	15.6
Left Flank	2	2.3	6	9.4	4	4.6	12	5.1
Striker	0		6	9.4	13	14.9	19	8.0
Total	**94**		**94**		**94**		**282**	

We have differentiated the BD - category in relation to degree of control. This is done because the degree of unbalance in the opponents' defence normally will increase with increasing BD - control. Longer attacks after BD includes attacks where the ball goes backwards and then give the opponents' defence time to regain balance. Longer attacks - (set plays) are attacks lasting more than 7 s. Norway's long passing and direct attacking style is illustrated in Table 4. From 37 attacks started from our own half, only 3 are what we can call 'elaborate' attacks. A clear picture of which positions and which players are involved in different periods of the attacks producing scoring opportunities is given in Table 5.

We gained more corners, more throw-ins and more free-kicks in the attacking third than our opponents. This is probably a result of our aggressive and direct style of play, but the zonal defence also plays an important part of that picture.

Table 6. Number of set plays in Norway's matches in 1994 (N=14)

Type of Set Plays	Norway			Opponents			Total	
	Tot.	%	per match	Tot.	%	per match	Tot.	per match
Inswing Corner	73	78.5	5.2	26	49.1	1.9	99	7.1
Outswing Corner	66.5	0.4	15	28.3	1.1	21	1.5	
Corner - Other	14	15.0	1.0	12	22.6	0.9	26	1.9
Corner Total	**93**	**8.7**	**6.6**	**53**	**4.7**	**3.8**	**146**	**10.4**
Free kick								
- shooting distance	15	8.0	1.1	93.4	0.6	24	1.7	
- attacking 1/3	44	23.4	3.1	38	14.4	2.7	82	5.9
- Midfield	39	20.7	2.8	69	26.1	4.9	108	7.7
- own half	88	46.8	6.3	147	55.7	10.5	235	16.8
Penalty	2 1.1	0.1	1 0.4	0.1	2 0.1			
Free Kick Total	**188**	**17.6**	**13.4**	**264**	**23.2**	**18.8**	**452**	**32.3**
Throw in - attack	134	40.5	9.5	100	28.6	7.1	234	16.7
Throw in - the rest	197	59.5	14.1	250	71.4	17.8	447	31.9
Throw in Total	**331**	**31.0**	**23.6**	**350**	**30.8**	**25.0**	**681**	**48.7**
Goal kick (in play),								
- short	113	40.1	8.0	137	50.7	9.7	250	17.6
- long	114	40.4	8.1	79	29.3	5.6	193	13.7
Back pass	55	19.5	3.9	54	20.2	3.9	109	7.9
Total	282	26.4	20.1	270	23.8	19.3	552	39.4
Goal kick - short	29	30.2	2.7	87	57.6	6.2	116	8.3
Goal kick - long	67	69.8	4.8	64	42.4	4.6	131	9.4
Goal kick Total	**96**	**8.9**	**6.9**	**151**	**13.3**	**10.8**	**247**	**17.6**
Offside	**78**	**7.4**	**5.6**	**48**	**4.2**	**3.4**	**126**	**9**
Total	1068	48.5	76.3	1136	51.5	81.1	2204	157.4

In Table 7 the total number of set plays in the match is combined with different types of attacks which produces scoring opportunities (ratio).

Table 7. Ratio between type of set plays and scoring opportunities in the 1994 season for Norway and its opponents

Type of Set Plays	Norway			Opponents			Total		
	Set Plays	Chance	Ratio	Set Plays	Chance	Ratio	Set Plays	Chance	Ratio
Corner Inswing	73	15	1:49	26	2	1:13	99	17	1:5
Corner Outswing	6	2	1:3	15	2	1:75	21	4	1:5
Corner - other	14	1	1:14	12			26	1	1:26
Corner Total	**93**	**18**	**1:52**	**53**	**4**	**1:13.3**	**146**	**22**	**1:6**
Free kick									
- shooting dist.	15	1	1:15	9	1	1:9	24	2	1:12
- attacking 1/3	44	3	1:14.7	38	4	1:9.5	82	7	1:11
- midfield	39	2	1:19.5	69			108	2	1:54
- own 1/half	88	2	1:44	147			235	2	1:11
Penalty	2	2	1:1	1	1	1:1	3	3	1:1
Free kick Total	**188**	**10**	**1:18.8**	**264**	**6**	**1:44**	**452**	**16**	**1:28**
Throw in - attack	134	8	1:16.8	100			234	8	1:29
Throw in - rest	197	2	1:98.5	250	1	1:250	447	3	1:14
Throw in Total	**331**	**10**	**1:33.1**	**350**	**1**	**1:350**	**681**	**11**	**1:62**
Total		38			11			49	

In Table 8 and Table 9 we present some figures from our player-analysis.

Table 8. Player analysis, team components in 1994 - season

Team Component	Involvement Quantitative			Performance Qualitative				Index
	Tot.	1st	2nd	D	O	M	P	
Keeper	438	234	204	23	6	1	10	2.6
Back line	2978	1448	1530	242	170	27	128	2.7
Midfield	3453	1638	1815	237	399	154	193	1.8
Striker	722	344	378	13	113	51	42	1.4
Total	7591	3664	3927	515	688	233	373	1.99

- correlation between ball involvements and scoring opportunities: $r = 0.12$

- correlation between ball involvements and match result: $r = 0.041$

- correlation between index and match result: $r = 0.764$

- correlation between index and scoring opportunities: $r = 0.49$

Table 9. Player analysis, positions in the 1994 season

Team Position	Involvement Quantitative				Performance Qualitative			Index
	Tot.	1st	2nd	D	O	M	P	
Keeper	438	234	204	23	6	1	10	2.6
Right back	786	375	411	45	42	9	40	1.8
Left back	975	504	471	61	69	11	40	2.5
Right centr. def.	604	278	326	62	26	2	23	3.5
Left centr. def.	613	291	322	75	33	5	25	3.6
Right flank	667	317	350	28	73	15	30	2.2
Right inside mid.	683	327	356	66	81	31	36	2.2
Central midfield	657	297	360	53	80	18	44	2.1
Left inside mid.	1069	513	556	71	116	63	62	1.5
Left flank	377	184	193	19	49	27	21	1.4
Striker	722	344	378	13	113	51	42	1.4
Total	7591	3664	3927	515	688	233	373	1.99

4 Conclusions

In conclusion, the systems that have been presented are accurate, valid and easy to use. They are now accepted by the players and the management of the Norwegian national teams. Notation analysis has enabled Norway to maximise its limited resources, in terms of playing population and the extreme weather conditions faced in the country, and compete with the best teams in the world.

5 References

Bate, R. (1988) Football chance: tactics and strategy, in **Science and Football** (eds T.Reilly, A.Lees, K.Davids & W.Murphy), E. & F.N. Spon, London, pp. 293-301.
Elias, N. & Dunning, E. (1966) Dynamics of group sports with special references to football. **British Journal of Sociology,** 17, 388-402.
Olsen, E. (1973) Scoringer i fotball. Masters thesis. **Norges Idrettshoiskole**, Oslo.
Olsen, E. (1988) An analysis of scoring strategies in the World Championship in Mexico, 1986, in **Science and Football** (eds T. Reilly, A. Lees, K. Davids and W. Murphy), E. & F.N. Spon, London, pp. 373-376.
Reep, C. & Benjamin, B. (1968) Skill and chance in association football. **Journal of the Royal Statistical Society,** Series A, 131.

AN ANALYSIS OF THE PLAYING PATTERNS OF THE JAPAN NATIONAL TEAM IN THE 1944 WORLD CUP QUALIFYING MATCH FOR ASIA

KUNIO YAMANAKA, D. Y. LIANG and MIKE HUGHES*

Institute of Health & Sport Sciences, University of Tsukuba, 1-1-1 Tennodai, Tsukuba-Shi, 305 Japan.
*Centre for Notational Analysis, Cardiff Institute, Cyncoed, Cardiff XF2 6XD, Wales.

1 Introduction

In 1992 and 1993, the Japan National Soccer Team (hereafter referred to as Japan) proved its ability to compete on an international level. Japan won the 1992 Dynasty Cup championship, which was hosted by China and the 1992 Asian Cup which was held in Hiroshima. In the 1994 World Cup Asian Qualifying matches (hereafter referred to as AFQM), Japan drew with Saudi Arabia who qualified for the World Cup, and won against Korea. Eventually, Japan was eliminated by goal difference. These results demonstrated the improvement of Japan in technical performance.

Currently, a number of studies using notational analysis (Hughes, 1988; Yamanaka and Liang, 1993 ; Yamanaka et al., 1993a, 1993b) have been reported. Many of them examined the technical and tactical characteristics of games such as how individual skills and team tactics were used in games and how these were correlated with each other, and authors have also referred to how to utilize the results of these studies.

The purpose of this study was to perform a computerised notational analysis of games in the AFQM so that the playing patterns and problems of the respective teams may be examined, with particular emphasis on the Japan National Team.

2 Methods

2.1 Subjects
The following eight games were selected for study from among the games played between Japan, Saudi Arabia, Iran, North Korea, South Korea and Iraq in order to analyze the playing patterns of the respective teams:

1) Japan vs Saudi Arabia (0-0)   2) Japan vs Iran (1-2)
3) Japan vs North Korea (3-)   4) Japan vs Korea (1-0)
5) Japan vs Iraq (2-2)   6) Saudia Arabia va Iraq (1-1)
7) Iraq vs Korea (2-2)   and   8) Korea vs Saudi Arabia (1-1)

2.2 Notational analysis system
The software used to input data was that designed by Hughes et al. (1988). The most recent version was used for this study.

Performance data during games were entered by replaying the videotapes of games a number of times. Thirty-two different actions of players were entered into 'time', 'place', 'player' and 'action' by clicking the mouse.

2.3 Data processing
Using data during a 90 ininute game (excluding extra-time), by dividing the field into six areas horizontally and three areas vertically, the frequency of each action per area was recorded (Fig. 1). For statistical processing, a X^2 test was used.

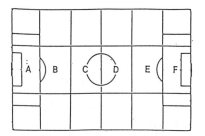

Figure 1. Display of the eighteen division of the pitch.

3 Results and Discussion

Table 1. The mean value for each variable for Japan and its opponent teams in the Asian Final Qualifying matches of the 1994 American World Cup (Frequencies/team/game)

	Japan	Saudi	S. Korea	Iraq
Fouls	19	17	15	18
Dribblings	50	*29	*32	38
Runs	23	13	12	19
Clearing kicks	85	69	63	*54
Passes	334	**270	311	329
Loss of control	35	23	23	36
Throw ins	16	14	16	15
Free kicks	37	24	23	23
Corner kicks	5	7	4	4
Shots on goal	11	16	14	13
Headers	49	35	44	37
Crosses	17	19	22	24
End of poss.	192	164	174	172

Stat. test for Japan and its opponents, *P<0.05, **P<0.01

3. 1 Team performance
Using 13 items processed in this study, Table 1 shows the average values per game for Japan, Saudi Arabia, Korea and Iraq.

Japan employed dribbling as a tactic more frequently than did Saudi Arabia and Korea ($P<0.05$), used more passes than did Saudi Arabia ($P<0.01$), and outnumbered Iraq in the number of times of clearing kick ($P<0.05$). There were no significant differences in the rest of the items.

As previously reported by Yamanaka et al. (1993b), Japan characteristically often used dribbling as a tactic, and made a large number of passes. This result is similar to that of the analysis of the playing patterns of Japan in the Asian Cup. By comparison, the number of passes made by Japan during the game with Saudi Arabia in the AFQM was 366/game, while in the 1992 Asian Cup it was about 30/team/game. Similarly, Japan used dribbling at a rate of 50/team/game during the AFQM and 51/team/game in the 1992 Asian Cup. In other items, Japan increased the number of clearing actions ($P<0.01$), but decreased the number of runs ($P<0.01$). Although there were no significant differences statistically, the number of fouls committed by Japan increased from 12/team/game to 19/team/game as did the number of free kicks from 24/team/game to 37/team/game. It is inferred from these results that the AFQM had more severe playing environments than did the Asian Cup. Compared with the European teams, the South American teams and the British Isles teams in the 1990 World Cup, the number of passes made by Japan in the AFQM was less than that of the European teams(the highest being 376/team/game), but more than that of the South Americans (302/team/game) and British Isles (226/team/game). Japan exceeded the three adversaries in the number of times dribbling was used (38, 35, 22/team/game, respectively) (Yamanaka et al., 1993a). From these results, it is inferred that the defense was more fierce and stronger pressure was applied in the World Cup games than in the qualifying matches. Furthermore, it can be inferred that as team performance increases, the faster are the actions in both offense and defense, and individual players have less time and space in which to play the ball.

The playing patterns of Japan in the AFQM differed from those of Saudi Arabia. This is proved by the fact that though Japan made fewer passes and used dribbling less frequently as mentioned above, Saudi Arabia was much the same as Japan in the frequency of shots, and in the numbers of corner locks and cross kicks. Saudi Arabia used a tactic of carrying the ball to the goal with fewer passes and less frequent dribbling. Using strong defensive performance as its main tactic, Saudi Arabia probably tried to take advantage of limited scoring chances by launching swift attacks on the goal. According to Yamanaka and Liang (1993), Japan's playing patterns in the Asian Cup showed a similar tendency. Therefore, it is concluded that the Saudi Arabia team was strong in defensive performance.

By contrast, Japan, Korea and Iraq have similar playing patterns when comparing the teams' overall statistics alone. However, passes, in particular, must be examined with respect to where in the field they are made. Since a soccer game is performed in a large field, 105 x 68 m, it is difficult to judge the similarity between teams on the basis of the overall statistics alone. To some degree, this can also be stated for the use of dribbling, running with the ball and heading the ball. The four teams listed in Table 1 can be considered to have similar team performance in passing, dribbling, executing corner kicks, crosses and shots on goal, although there may be differences among them in patterns of play.

3.2 The distribution of passes by areas

Japan seems to have given priority to controlling the ball by means of passing, while Saudi Arabia, with the use of fewer passes and less frequent dribbling, seems to have aimed for a more defensive game performance. The game performances of Korea and Iraq may also be examined using passing as a criterion.

Figure 2 shows the distribution of passes by area, obtained by a division of the field into 18 areas, using data from three games between Japan, Saudi Arabia, Korea and Iraq. Areas A-F show offensive directions, with A showing the area in front of each team's goal, and F showing the area in front of the opponent's goal. This Figure also shows that Japan outnumbered the other teams in the number of passes. There is a common tendency among the four teams whereby the number of passes increases in the middle field (CD), and decreases in the defensive (AB) and offensive (EF) areas. This mountain shaped distribution is a general characteristic of soccer game performance. A detailed observation of the distribution of passes revealed that Japan used more passes in offensive areas than did the other teams($P<0.05$-$P<0.01$).

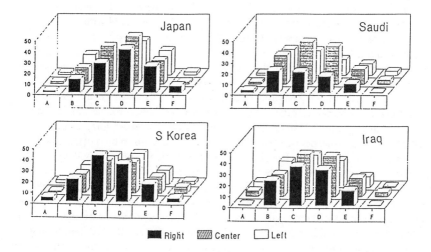

Figure 2. The distribution of the passes for Japan, Saudi, South Korea and Iraq teams (Frequencies/game).

The other three teams made the most passes in area C before the half-way line, while Japan made the most passes in area D within the opponent's half court. Furthermore, Japan made fewer passes in area C than did Iraq, and also made fewer passes in area B than did Saudi Arabia ($P<0.05$). According to an analysis of playing patterns in the World Cup by Yamanaka et al.(1993a), the average numbers of passes used by the European, British Isles and South American teams within their own offensive areas were 79/team/game, 41/team/game and 50/team/game, respectively. In comparison with these top class games, Japan made more passes in the AFQM. Therefore, it is inferred that Japan showed better performance in passing than any other Asian teams in the AFQM.

To evaluate the offensive performance of the team as a whole, however, it must be taken into consideration that making more passes is not necessarily related to a higher scoring ability from shots on goal. In values per area, Japan, Saudi Arabia and Iraq made more passes in the central area, and showed an ideal tactical distribution. This can be supported by an analysis of the playing patterns of teams of the 1986 Mexican World Cup by Hughes et al. (1988) in which, from the distribution of passes per area, it is shown that successful teams (i.e. teams that played in the semi-final or the final) tended to use more effectively the central area in DE immediately in front of the opponent's goal than unsuccessful teams (in the first qualifying round); in contrast, unsuccessful teams tended to use both sides of the field more often than the successful teams. However, the distribution of passes for Korea was lower in the centre than in side areas; passes well distributed more on both sides than in the centre, and passes were biased on the right side in the mid-field, in particular. Furthermore, there was a common tendency for Korea and Japan to make passes in the area of E as often as in the centre of the field. This reflects the fact that both teams used tactics to break through their opponents' line from the beginning. For future improvement, it will be necessary for both teams to foster powerful forward players who can exhibit superior ball control and dribbling tactics and successfully receive through passes even in front of the goal where players are under strong pressure. Team performance to utilize fully these players must also be established.

Table 2. The frequencies of the variables for Japan and its opponents in the Asian Final Qualifying matches of the 1994 American World Cup. The upper line indicates the number of variables of Japan, and the number in partentheses indicates that of the opponent's teams.

	vs Saudi	vs Iran	vs N.Korea	vs S.Korea	vs Iraq
Dribblings	** 61	35	54	46	42
	(30)	(28)	(40)	(30)	(42)
Clearing kicks	64	40	46	87	**103
	(82)	**(70)	(49)	(81)	(46)
Passes	**439	**455	309	324	240
	(309)	(196)	(300)	(303)	**(360)
Free kicks	38	31	21	30	44
	(31)	(32)	(24)	(28)	(28)
Corner kicks	6	8	8	8	1
	(5)	(4)	(3)	(5)	(3)
Shots on goal	14	17	**17	12	7
	(13)	(12)	(6)	(6)	(13)
Headers	34	42	40	48	64
	(28)	(28)	(33)	(52)	(48)
Crosses	24	27	16	17	11
	(21)	(16)	(16)	(17)	**(34)
End of poss	185	168	184	197	193

3. 3 Team performance of Japan in five games

Table 2 shows the team performance of Japan in the five games of the AFQM. Values are obtained for 10 items; the upper values are those of Japan aad those of the opposition teams. From each item, the following findings were obtained. Firstly, Japan used dribbling tactics more often than Saudi Arabia ($P<0.01$). Secondly, Japan cleared the ball less frequently than Iran ($P<0.01$), but cleared the ball more frequently than Iraq ($P<0.01$). Thirdly, it outnumbered Saudi Arabia and Iran in passes($P<0.01$), but made passes less frequently than Iraq ($P<0.01$). Fourthly, Japan out-numbered Korea in the frequency of shots on goal ($P<0.01$). Fifthly, Japan out-numbered Iraq in the frequency of cross-passing ($P<0.01$). The findings illuminate the frequencies of passes, dribbling and clearing plays which characterize the defense-oriented performance of Japan, and also the frequencies of cross-passing and shots on goals which are closely related to scoring. From these findings, it is inferred that the performance of Japan in the five games was unstable, sometimes influenced by unskilled plays.

Lastly, the passing performance of Japan is considered. Table 3 shows the frequency of passes made against its opponents in each of the six-divided areas of the field. It is clear that Japan made more passes in areas D and E and made fewer passes in area B in the game with Saudi Arabia (P<0.01); and that it out-numbered Iran in passes in the whole field except defensive areas (P<0.05) and Korea in passes in the areas D and E (P<0.05). However, no statistically significant difference was found in both areas. In the game with Iraq, Iraq made more passes, having a statistically significant higher number of passes in every area (P<0.01).

Passing patterns vary with games (Figure 3). In the game between Japan and Saudi Arabia, only Japan developed pass performance within the Saudi Arabian territory. In contrast, Saudi Arabia showed an unusual pass distribution with a mountain-shaped distribution at the centre of the field, but terrace-shaped distribution in which the number of passes increases gradually from the opponent's half. From this, it is inferred that Saudi Arabia performed a thoroughly defensive game. In its game with Iraq, Japan showed a very small mountain-shaped pass pattern distribution unlike its original perfomance. In contrast, Iraq made more passes in all areas of the field than Japan, and showed a high mountain-shaped distribution pattern. From this it is inferred that Iraq overwhelmed Japan in passing performance in all areas of the field, and thus had the advantage.

Table 3. The distributions of passes for Japan and its opponent teams in the Asian Final Qualifying matches of the 1994 American World Cup. The upper line indicates the number of variables of Japan, and the number in parentheses indicates the numbers of the opponent's teams. The pitch was divided into six horizontal divisions. Direction of attack is A to F.

	A	B	C	D	E	F
Japan vs	9	64	80	**162	**	19
Saudi	(9)	**(106)	(93)	(58)	(31)	(12)
Japan vs	7	56	**102	**181	**95	*14
Iran	(8)	(60)	(65)	(42)	(16)	(5)
Japan vs	12	68	82	69	63	15
N. Korea	(6)	(64)	(69)	(89)	(55)	(9)
Japan vs	7	46	81	*112	**69	9
S. Korea	(8)	(66)	(98)	(77)	(41)	(8)
Japan vs	3	33	72	78	38	6
Iraq	(12)	**(32)	**(114)	(94)	(54)	(8)

*P<0.05, **P<0.01

4 Conclusion

In this study we performed a computerised notational analysis of eight games between Japan, Saudi Arabia, Iran, North Korea, South Korea and Iraq in the AFQM to examine the playing patterns and the problems of the respective teams, with Japan as the main subject. For statistical processing, the X^2 test was used.

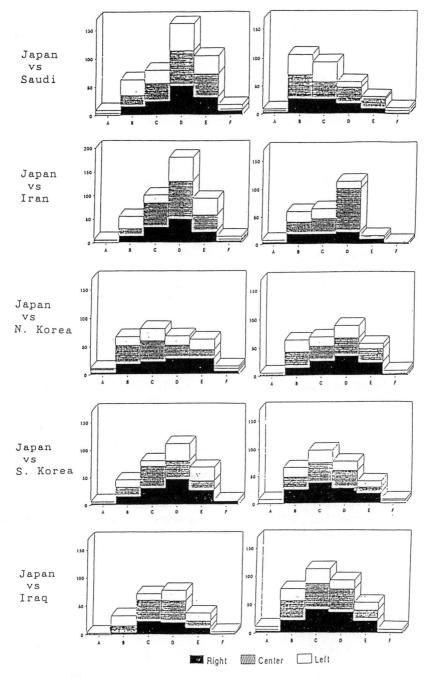

Fig. 3 The distribution of the passes of each match for Japan and its opponents

The results were as follows:

A) For performance of the team as a whole

1) Japan used dribbling tactics more frequently than Saudi Arabia and Korea (P<0.05), more passes than Saudi Arabia (P<0.01), and tried clearing actions more frequently than did Iraq (P<0.05). This shows that the playing patterns of Japan were different from those of Saudi Arabia.

B) From results of games

2) Japan out-numbered Saudi Arabia, Iran and Korea in the frequency of passes in offensive areas (P<0.05 to P<0.01) and used more dribbling tactics than did Saudi Arabia (P<0.01). The frequency of clearing attempts was less than that of Iran (P<0.01) and more than that of Iraq (P<0.01).

3) Japan passed the ball more frequently than did Saudi Arabia and Iran, but less frequently than did Iraq (P<0.01).

4) Japan took shots at goal more frequently than Korea (P<0.01), but it performed fewer crosses than Iraq (P<0.01).

5) We can conclude from the results of our study that it is necessary for Japan to establish flexible tactics in structuring its offense and defense.

5 References

Hughes, M. D. (1988) Computerized notation analysis on field games. **Ergonomics**, 31, 1585-1592.

Hughes, M. D., Robertson, K. and Nicholson, A. (1988) Comparison of patterns of play successful and unsuccessful teams in the 1986 World Cup for soccer, in **Science and Football** (eds T. Reilly, A. Lees, K. Davids, and W. Murphy), E. and F. N. Spon , London, pp. 363-367.

Yamanaka, K. and Liang, D.Y. (1993) A computerised notational analysis of playing pattern the 1992 Asian Cup for soccer. **Bulletin on Sport Methodology**, 9, 57-65.

Yamanaka, K., Hughes, M. and Lott, M. (1993a) An analysis of playing patterns in the 1990 World Cup for Association Football, in **Science and Football II** (eds T. Reilly, J. Clarys and A. Stibbe), E. and F.N. Spon, London, pp. 206-214.

Yamanaka, K., Matsumoto, M. and Uemukai, K. (1993b) An analysis of playing patterns of the Japan National Team in the 1992 Asian Cup for Soccer. **Ibaraki Journal of Health and Sport Sciences**, 9, 17-27.

A NEW NOTATIONAL ANALYSIS SYSTEM WITH SPECIAL REFERENCE TO THE COMPARISON OF BRAZIL AND ITS OPPONENTS IN THE WORLD CUP 1994

Pekka H. Luhtanen, V. Korhonen and A. Ilkka
Research Institute for Olympic Sports, Rautpohjankatu 6, FIN-40200 Jyvdskylii, Finland.

1 Introduction

In international tournaments, teams are judged on their ability to win matches. Behind the wins, the teams must have effective ways to win the ball, create successful attacks first to reach the attacking third of the pitch, create effectively scoring chances and to complete them by scoring goals with a high efficiency. A computer overlay has been used for computerised notational analysis by Hughes (1988), modelled on the playing pitch. The 128 cells were programmed so that with each move the position on the field, the player involved, and the action and its outcome were recorded. This allows observation of the patterns of play and can be utilised by a coach. The number of research results based on the computerised notational analysis systems has increased during recent years (Franks & Nagelkerke, 1988; Hughes et al., 1988; Patrick & McKenna, 1988; Treadwell, 1988; Yamanaka et al., 1993; Partridge et al., 1993).

The purpose of this study was first to introduce a new notational analysis system and second apply it to compare selected team collected for each player of Brazil and its opponents in the World Cup 1994.

2 Methods

A video recording based notation analysis system was constructed to input data for soccer analysis including different time, space and manoeuvre characteristics per player in match conditions. The analysis system consisted of hardware as follows: computer (Pomi 486/66, 16MB), video card (Matrox Marvel) and video recorder (Panasonic VCR AG-5700). Software included in the system was as follows: display driver (Marvel Tseng drivers), overlay driver (Marvel SDK) and videotape driver (Marvel SDK). The programming tools used were Visual Basic 3.0 Professional Edition and Q+E Multilink-VB v2.0.

Four application programmes were developed separately for the system for 1. Data Input, 2. Numerical Data Analysis, 3. Graphical Data analysis and 4. Databasemaintenance. Additional statistical analysis and graphics can be applied with Excel v4.0 or higher and SPSS+ package.

The input data from each matches of Brazil included time of each action with the ball recorded from video frames, spatial situation of each actions as x-, y-co-ordinates (each playing ground was scaled in the system) clicked by mouse in display, selected qualitative manoeuvre variables stoppage and injury time, and time for each team in possession with ball for each player.

The qualitative manoeuvre variables were as follows:

1. the number of successful attacking trials for the attacking third (ATRI),
2. scoring chances created in the vital area (SCHA),
3. scoring trials (STRI) and
4. goals (GOAL) standardised for the normal playing time.

The quantitative variables were as follows:

1. the cumulative time of the ball in possession (TIME) for each team and
2. distance covered by the ball (DIST) under control of each team. The distance was calculated as a "ground" distance without any curvilinear path for each team.

For evaluation of accuracy and reliability a World Cup match (SWE-BGR) was analysed by two independent experienced analysers. The average difference in percentages were in TIME, DIST, ATRI, SCHA, STRI and GOAL 2.1 %, 3.5 %, 3.5 %, 6,4 %, 0 % and 0 %, respectively.

Statistical analysis in comparing Brazil and its opponents employed t- Paired tests for TIME and DIST and Wilcoxon Matched-Pairs Signed Ranks (z) test for ATRI, SCHA, STRI and GOAL.

3 Results

In Figure I can be seen an example of the distance covered by the ball (DIST) in metres under control of Brazil and Italy for the normal playing time. The distance is a "ground" distance for each team.

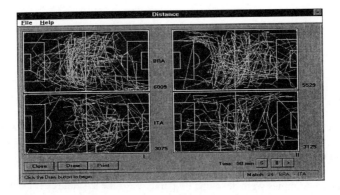
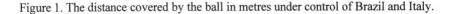

Figure 1. The distance covered by the ball in metres under control of Brazil and Italy.

Brazil (BRA: 6009 m and 5529m) and Italy (ITA: 3075 m and 3125 m) are in Figure I for the normal playing time in each half (1 and 11). In the upper corner left hand side, Brazil attacks from left to right. In the upper corner right hand side, Brazil attacks from right to left. In the lower part, the attacking directions of Italy are contrary.

Table 1. Comparison of selected variables for the normal playing time between Brazil and its opponents (abbreviations, see text, n = number, t- or z-: see methods)

Match	TIME, min	DIST, km	ATRI, n	SCHA, n	STRI, n	GOAL, n
BRA-RUS 39-36	8.6-7.1	50-39	23-10	15-10	2-0	
BRA-CAM 43-38	10.2-6.6	56-37	24-14	12-8	3-0	
BRA-SWE 50-27	13.9-5.1	66-31	31-13	19-8	1-1	
BRA-USA 38-33	8.5-5.2	70-28	28-5	17-3	1-0	
BRA-HOL 39-42	8.2-6.9	49-45	21-15	14-12	3-2	
BRA-SWE 48-32	12.4-5.8	77-27	42-8	27-2	1-0	
BRA-ITA 48-31	11.5-6.2	57-26	23-7	16-4	0-0	

BRA-OPP'S	44-34	10.5-6.1	61-33	27-10	17-7	1.6-0.4
t- or z-:	2.68	4.20	-2.37	-2.37	-2.37	-2.02
P<	0.05	0.01	0.05	0.05	0.05	0.05

----

4 Discussion

According to this analysis, Brazil was the strongest team in the World Cup. Brazil had the highest number of the successful attacking trials to the attacking third (P< 0.01), the highest number of scoring chances in the vital area (P< 0.01) and the highest number of shots for scoring goals (P< 0.05). Relatively, Brazil mastered the matches on average in time 56 %, in distance 63 %, in the number of attacking trials inside of the attacking third 65 %, in the number of created scoring chances in the vital area 73 %, scoring trials 71 % and goals 80 %. The comparison showed that Brazil earned the title also statistically. The most even match was Brazil against Holland in all selected evaluations.

Braking down the dominating attacking manoeuvres of Brazil as compared to their opponents can be seen as follows:
1. the cumulative time of the ball in possession (TIME) and distance covered by the ball (DIST) were based on the successful passing play specially in the middle third, 2. the higher number of successful attacking trials of Brazil for the attacking third (ATRI) were started after interceptions

in the middle third and were more often slow with different passing combinations than their opponents did,

3. for the higher number of scoring chances created in the vital area (SCHA), Brazil used more change over with passing and free style of play and less long passes, long runs with ball, overlapping and wall passing combinations than their opponents;

4. for the higher number of scoring trials into the vital area (STRI), Brazil used more runs with ball for the penetration, wall passing combinations and free style of play and less long passes, centres, passes into depth and set play than their opponents. Brazil had more shots after receiving the ball and direct free kicks and less direct shots and headers than their opponents. The number of the shots after run with ball was equal as compared to their opponents.

This study has shown that notational analysis system based on video recording can be used as tool to analyse objectively own team and to scout opponent teams.

5 References

Dufour, W. (1993) Computer assisted scouting in soccer, in **Science and Football 11** (eds T. Reilly, J. Clarys & A. Stibbe), E. & F.N. Spon, London, pp. 160 - 166.

Franks, I.M. and Nagelkerke, P. (1988) the use of computer interactive video technology in spot analysis, **Ergonomics,** 31, 1593-1603.

Gerisch, G. and Reichelt, M. (1993) Computer and video - aided analysis in football games, in **Science and Football 11** (eds T. Reilly, J. Clarys & A. Stibbe), E. & F.N. Spon, London, pp. 167 - 173.

Hughes, M. (1988) Computerised notation analysis in field games. **Ergonomics,** 31, 1585-1592

Hughes M., Robertson, K. and Nicholson, A. (1988) Comparison of patterns of play of successful and unsuccessful teams in the 1986 World Cup for soccer, in **Science and Football** (eds T. Reilly, A. Lees, K. Davids & W. Murphy), E. & F.N. Spon, London, pp. 363 - 367.

Loy, R. (1990) Entwicklungs tendenzen im Weltfussball. **Fussballtraining,** 9, 23 -3 1. Patrick, J.D. and McKenna, M.J. (1988) CABER - computer system for football analysis, in **Science and Football** (eds T. Reilly, A. Lees, K. Davids & W. Murphy), E. & F.N. Spon, London, pp. 267 - 273.

Partridge, D., Mosher, R.E. and Franks, I.M. (1993) A computer assisted analysis of technical performance - a comparison of the 1990 World Cup and intercollegiate soccer, in **Science and Football II** (eds T. Reilly, J. Clarys & A. Stibbe), E. & F.N. Spon, London, pp. 221 - 231.

Treadwell, P.J. (1988) Computer aided match analysis of selected ball-gaines (soccer and rugby union), in **Science and Football** (eds T. Reilly, A. Lees, K. Davids & W. Murphy), E. & F.N. Spon, London, pp. 282 - 287.

Yamanaka, K., Hughes, M. and Lott, M. (1993) An analysis of playing patterns in the 1990 World Cup for association football, in **Science and Football 11** (eds T. Reilly, J. Clarys & A. Stibbe), E. & F.N. Spon, London, pp. 206 - 214.

BIVARIATE ANALYSIS OF THE REPEATABILITY OF FOOTBALL OFFENSIVE SCHEMES

CHIARELLA SFORZA, GIOVANNI MICHIELON, GIANPIERO GRASSI, GIAMPIETRO ALBERTI and VIRGILIO F. FERRARIO
Laboratorio di Anatomia Funzionale dell'Apparato Locomotore, I.S.E.F. Lombardia, Università degli Studi di Milano, via Corelli 136, 20134 Milano, Italy

1 Introduction

The attacks performed in soccer can follow a pattern. Any action can be divided into single frames or moments, each characterized by a particular arrangement of the reciprocal positions of the players (Ferrario et al., 1994). Indeed, the number, the diversity and the complexity of actions prevent any global analysis, necessitating a piecewise evaluation of the single events (Eom and Schutz, 1992). They can later be included in a model which will help in the optimization of the scheme (Pedotti et al., 1983).

The evaluation of the offensive movements is usually qualitative: indeed, quantitative analyses of these movements, of the time necessary for their perfect repeatability, and of the players' ability to follow them have never been performed. One of the motives could be the lack of adequate statistical tools. In this report, a simplified model was used with only eight offensive players and without defensive players, and a single frame of the action that could characterize the final result of the attack, i.e. a goal, was selected. The variability of the reciprocal positions of the eight football players in this single moment of the offensive scheme was assessed using bivariate analysis.

2 Materials and Methods

2.1 Sample and data collection
Two junior (players aged 15 to 17 years) soccer teams of a different level (one semi-professional, one amateur) were analyzed. A Sony CCD 800E TV-camera operating at 50 Hz (50 frames per second) was positioned 16 m above one half of the field, and the reciprocal positions of the players during two different offensive schemes were filmed (Fig. 1).

Each scheme was repeated 20 times. For each scheme, the single frame corresponding to the cross by player #1 was evaluated, and the position of the eight players (closed circles in Fig. 1) was digitized using a semiautomated instrument (LAFAL Videoanalyzer, CUBE srl, Italy). The position of the goalkeeper was not evaluated. The player position was calculated from the most posterior image of the heels: both left and right heels were digitized, and mean coordinates computed. This position should correspond to an approximate "centre of gravity" of the player on the ground. An algorithm developed for this purpose enabled the correction of parallax. The coordinates of each player were analyzed by bivariate analysis, separately for the two teams and for the two schemes.

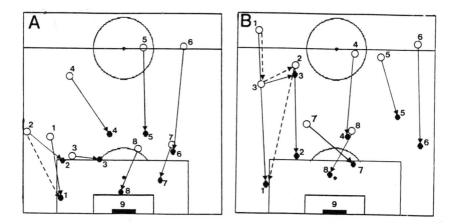

Figure 1. The two offensive schemes: A, throw-in; B, wing attack with interchanging positions. The players' positions at the beginning of the scheme (open circles), their movements (solid arrows), the positions they should have at the end of the scheme (closed circles), and the ball movement (broken arrow) are indicated. The position of the closed circles corresponds to the analyzed frame (cross by player #1). Player #9: goalkeeper. The numbers refer to the position of players not to their identity.

2.2 Bivariate analysis

The mean relative position of each player in the 20 repetitions of each scheme as well as its variability were computed by means of bivariate analysis (Batschelet, 1981; Ferrario et al., 1992, 1993) performed on the x, y coordinates of each player (Fig. 1). Bivariate analysis was used because it provides a more integrated and statistically correct evaluation of positions where the horizontal and vertical coordinates depend on each other. The analysis calculated Hotelling's 95% confidence ellipse and the 90% standard ellipse. The mean position of the player is to be estimated by the sample centre (mean values calculated in the 20 repetitions). The confidence ellipse is a region that covers this centre with a given probability; it is a tool for statistical inference used in bivariate analysis and serves the same purpose as the confidence interval (x ± t • SE) in univariate statistics. On the other hand, the standard ellipse may be compared with the standard interval (x ± SD) in univariate statistics: it is only a descriptive tool used to visualize the variability of the single repetitions, and covers about 90% of the sample variability.

3 Results

The schemes were performed during a standard training session: the coach first explained the scheme, then the players trained for about two weeks before the TV session. The schemes were also performed at a normal playing speed, but without opposing (defensive) players: the following considerations thus pertain to the repeatability of the offensive scheme. A first qualitative inspection evaluated the films: in all the repetitions of the two offensive schemes the eight players moved in the field with an adequate precision, and the frame corresponding to the cross by player #1 was always well defined. Only this frame was further analyzed by bivariate analysis.

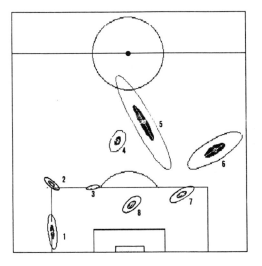

Figure 2. Throw-in of the semi-professional team: 95% confidence (inner) and standard (outer) ellipses of the players' positions in the analyzed frame.

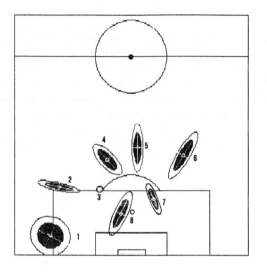

Figure 3. Throw-in of the amateur team: 95% confidence (inner) and standard (outer) ellipses of the players' positions in the analyzed frame.

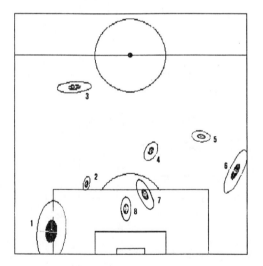

Figure 4. Wing attack of the quasi-professional team: 95% confidence (inner) and standard (outer) ellipses of the players' positions in the analyzed frame.

Table 1. Bivariate analysis of the reciprocal position of the eight players

Player	Throw-in Q-professional	Throw-in Amateur	Wing attack Q-professional	Wing attack Amateur
Ellipse	semiaxes (m)	semiaxes (m)	semiaxes (m)	semiaxes (m)
1 Confidence	1.65 0.42	3.46 3.19	2.88 1.45	6.63 3.78
Standard	4.44 1.14	5.31 4.90	7.74 3.90	10.19 5.81
2 Confidence	0.89 0.27	3.77 0.63	0.65 0.31	6.56 2.34
Standard	2.40 0.74	5.79 0.98	1.75 0.84	10.09 3.60
3 Confidence	0.68 0.17	0.55 0.49	1.70 0.49	4.97 3.44
Standard	1.83 0.47	0.85 0.75	4.57 1.31	7.63 5.29
4 Confidence	1.12 0.66	3.35 1.27	0.92 0.56	5.52 2.34
Standard	3.02 1.78	5.15 1.95	2.48 1.50	8.49 3.60
5 Confidence	5.11 0.93	3.96 0.99	0.90 0.53	3.54 2.21
Standard	13.77 2.51	6.09 1.52	2.43 1.42	5.44 3.41
6 Confidence	3.03 0.98	4.56 1.07	2.23 0.65	4.94 3.47
Standard	8.16 2.63	7.01 1.65	6.01 1.74	7.60 5.33
7 Confidence	1.34 0.46	2.81 0.68	1.54 0.56	4.53 2.10
Standard	3.61 1.25	4.31 1.05	4.13 1.52	6.97 3.23
8 Confidence	1.05 0.49	3.95 1.10	1.17 0.48	7.86 2.29
Standard	2.84 1.32	6.07 1.69	3.14 1.30	12.09 3.52

Table 1 reports the semiaxes of the 95% confidence and standard ellipses, where about 90% of the sample data should be found. The ellipses are shown in Figs 2 to 5. Both teams showed smaller confidence ellipses, i.e. higher reproducibility of the players' positions, in the throw-in routine than in the wing attack practice; the reproducibility was lower in the amateur team. Results showed that the semi-professional team had a higher training level and player coordination than the amateur team, with more reproducible players' positions. The throw-in routine, which was easier to understand and perform even for the less expert players, and implied smaller movements in the field, had the smallest differences between teams.

In the throw-in of the best team, players #1, 5 and 6 had the highest variability (largest semiaxes of both ellipses), players #3, 2 had the lowest (smallest semiaxes). In the same scheme of the amateur team the variability was more distributed among the players: player #1 had a similar variability in both directions (similar semiaxes), while the highest variability of the other players was towards the goal. In both teams, player #3 had a constant position. In the wing attack, the largest ellipses were found for the positions of players #1, 2, 4 (who did not keep their position) and 8 (amateur team), and players #1 and 6 (semi-professional team). Player #2 of the best team showed a small variability in his position.

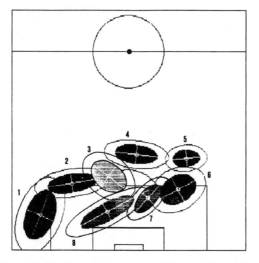

Figure 5. Wing attack of the amateur team: 95% confidence (inner) and standard (outer) ellipses of the players' positions in the analyzed frame.

4 Conclusions

The hypothesis of this investigation was that, in a well functioning team, the offensive schemes in a significant moment of the action, apart from the defensive response, should be the same, i.e. the players should have the same reciprocal positions. The findings confirm that the semi-professional team had a higher level of training and player coordination than the amateur team: the reciprocal positions of the players in the offensive schemes were more reproducible. Moreover, the more or less repeatable positions of the players were well correlated to the "technical maturity" of each player.

The highest differences between teams were demonstrated for the wing attack. Indeed, the throw-in scheme was easier to understand and perform even for the less expert players, and implied smaller movements in the field. Obviously, the presence of opponents would have modified the same offensive schemes: further investigations should analyze the repeatability of more complex schemes.

To the best of our knowledge, this is the first report that analyzed the repeatability of a team play using a consistent number of players, a high speed of play, and a large outdoor field. Apart from considerations of soccer technique, the protocol employed in this study could be used for further quantitative investigations of schemes of play: evaluation of the training (for both the individual players and the whole team), tactics of play and correction of errors, in most team sports (football, handball, volleyball, basketball).

5 Acknowledgements

The artwork by Mrs Paola Raselli is gratefully acknowledged.

6 References

Batschelet, E. (1981) **Circular Statistics in Biology**. Academic Press, London.
Eom, H.J. and Schutz, R.W. (1992) Statistical analyses of volleyball team performance. **Research Quarterly for Exercise and Sport**, 63, 11-18.
Ferrario, V.F., Sforza, C., Miani, A. jr., D'Addona, A. and Tartaglia, G. (1992) Statistical evaluation of some mandibular reference positions in normal young people. **International Journal of Prosthodontics**, 5, 158-165.
Ferrario, V.F., Sforza, C., Miani, A. jr. and Tartaglia, G. (1993) Craniofacial morphometry by photographic evaluations. **American Journal of Orthodontics and Dentofacial Orthopedics**, 103, 327-337.
Ferrario, V.F., Sforza, C., Bazan, E., Mauro, L. and Michielon, G. (1994) The repeatability of the defensive formation in volleyball evaluated by the Morphological Variation Analysis. **Proceedings of the International Congress on Applied Research in Sports,** Helsinki, p. 10.
Pedotti, A., Rodano, R. and Frigo, C. (1983) Optimization of motor coordination in sport: an analytical and experimental approach, in **Biomechanics and Performance in Sport** (ed W. Baumann), V.K. Hofmann, Schorndorf, pp. 145160.

REPEATABILITY OF THE FOOTBALL PENALTY: A STATISTICAL EVALUATION BY THE MORPHOLOGICAL VARIATION ANALYSIS

CHIPARELLA SFORZA, SERGIO DUGNANI, FRANCO MAURO, LUCIANO TORRI and VERGILIO F. FERRARIO

1 Introduction

A style of movement can be decomposed into single frames, each characterised by a peculiar body shape, i.e. a particular arrangement of body shapes can be described by a set of landmarks, and analysed by the classic morphological methods for the quantification of shapes and of differences between shapes (Lestral, 1989). These methods individualise a set of homologous landmarks on the shapes to be compared, and then analyse how the relationships between these points change (Lele, 1991; Lestral, 1989). Players who achieve the best results probably develop a movement pattern which optimises the relationship between the body segments.

The movement patterns, namely the succession of body shapes, that actually lead to the perfect performance of a selected football action could be different between players or in a single player during the training period, but should be highly reproducible within elite players because of their better neuromuscular co-ordination (Pedotti et al., 1983; Sanders and Owens, 1992). The quantification of body shape as described by the reciprocal arrangement of selected landmarks in one particular moment could, therefore provide valuable information for comparison both within individuals (repeatability of movement, modification of movement patterns due to training or to fatigue) and between players.

A recently developed statistical method, Morphological Variation Analysis (MVA), (Ferrario et al., 1994) quantifies shape differences in the reciprocal arrangement of body segments during the execution of sport movements. It has been applied to analyse the within-subject and between-subjects morphological variability of the body pattern in the execution of a standardised soccer penalty kick.

2 Materials and Methods

2.1 Sample and data collection
Three male skilled football players kicked five series of 10 penalties each, which were recorded by a Sony CCD 800E TV-camera operating at 50 Hz (50 frames per second), which was mounted on a tripod, levelled, with the optical axis of the lens horizontal. (Fig. 1). The series were repeated in three sessions; in order to avoid circadian and circaseptan modifications of performance (Reilly, 1994), the sessions took place at the same hour of the day and in the same day of three consecutive weeks. All the players

were right-footed, and were asked to run towards the ball from a 4 m distance, with an angle of 30° relative to the orthogonal line to the goal (Fig. 1). The players were also asked to hit a 60 x 60 cm square positioned on the lower end of the left goal post as shown in Fig.2. The result of each penalty was recorded, and the percentage of successful (inside the square) penalties out of 150 was calculated.

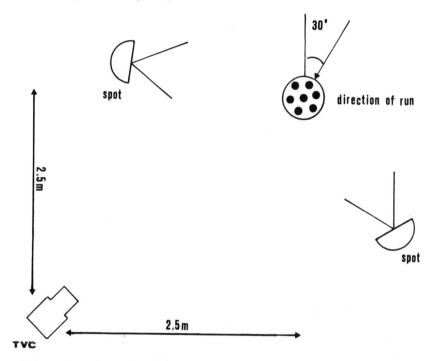

Figure 1. Experimental setting.

Figure 2. 60 x 60 cm square to be centred with the ball.

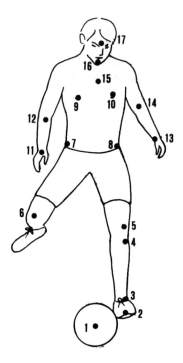

Figure 3. Landmarks identified on the player's body. The scheme is referred to the analysed frame of movement during the execution of the penalty (complctc support on the non-kicking foot before the lower limb is loaded).

1. ball (centre of gravity); 2. non-kicking (left) foot tip; 3. left instep; 4. left tibial tuberosity; 5. superior border of left patella; 6. superior border of kicking (right) patella; 7. right anterior superior iliac spine; 8. left anterior superior iliac spine; 9. right nipple, 10. left nipple; 11. ventral surface of right elbow; 12. ventral surface of left elbow; 13. right radial styloid process; 14. left radial styloid process; 15. body of sternum (half-way between the manubrium and the xiphiod process; 16. gnathion; 17. forehead (half-way between nasion and trichion).

Only the successful penalties were further digitised. For each penalty, the single frame corresponding to a complete support on the non-kicking foot (before the loading of the lower limb) was evaluated, and the positions of 16 standardised body landmarks and of one landmark on the ball (Fig. 3) were digitised using a semi-automated instrument (LAFAL Videoanalyser, CUBE srl, Italy). A reference system allowed for the calibration of both the horizontal and vertical co-ordinates of the films. The landmark co-ordinates were analysed by MVA (Ferrario et al., 1994).

2.2 Statistical analysis: Morphological Variation Analysis

The cartesian x-y co-ordinates of the 17 landmarks calculated in the repeated penalties for each player were analysed by MVA (Ferrario et al., 1994). This method evaluates the global variability between repeated shapes: it first calculates all the possible Euclidean (linear) distances between the selected landmarks on the chosen frame of a single penalty. It thus provides [17 x (17-1) / 2] distances. The corresponding linear distances measured on each penalty were then averaged, and the relevant coefficients of variation (CV) were calculated as CV = Standard Deviation / Mean x 100. The coefficients of variation describe the intrinsic variability of each distance.

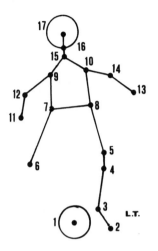

Figure 4. Morphological Variation Analysis for player L.T: mean relative position of the 17 analysed landmarks in the successful penalties.

In order to provide a comprehensive evaluation of the variability of the body pattern in the execution of the penalty, a Morphological Variation Factor (MVF) was further calculated as MVF = mean of the CV. The MVF is a measure of the global variability (for that set of penalties), and it indicates how reproducible a shape is. Low MVFs correspond to highly reproducible body positions.

The method also indicates which distances and landmarks are more or less responsible for the shape reproducibility. The MVF ± 2 x SD interval was calculated; the coefficients of variation outside its limits indicate distances which are relatively reproducible (lower limit) or not reproducible.

3 Results

The percentage of successful penalties was high in all three players (Table 1); L.T. scored both the highest average percentage of successful penalties (68%) and the highest absolute percentage (72%) in his second session.

For all players, the analysis demonstrated a good within-subject repeatability in the arrangement of the body segments during the kicking of the penalty. In all players the MVFs computed in three sessions were not significantly different, and a pooled value was computed (Table 1). Conversely, the between-subjects variability was higher: not only were the MVFs computed in the three players different, but also each player showed a peculiar variability of the body "shape" (Figs 4 and 5). For example, the trunk and lower limbs in players N.F. and G.F. were not orthogonal to the ground, but bent on the left side.

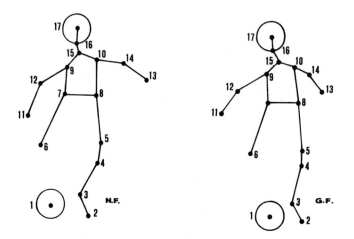

Figure 5. Morphological Variation Analysis for players N.F. and G.F. Mean relative position of the 17 analysed landmarks in the successful penalties.

Table 1. Percentage of successful penalties scored by the three players, relevant Morphological Variation Factors (MVF), and statistical comparison (Student t test for independent samples)

Player		Ist session		2nd session		3rd session		Pooled sessions	
	%	MVF	%	MVF	%	MVF	%	MVF
L.T.	64%	3.31	72%	3.50	68%	3.56	68%	4.05*
N.F.	58%	4.71	70%	5.13	70%	4.66	66%	5.44
G.F.	66%	5.16	54%	3.99	66%	3.69	62%	5.21#

The three sessions were not significantly different.
No difference N.F. vs G.F.
* Significant difference L.T vs. N.F. ($P < 0.005$)
# Significant difference L.T. vs. N.F. ($P < 0.001$)

The lowest MVFs were scored by L.T. In this player the reciprocal positions of upper limbs and trunk explained most of the variability of the movement: this variability did not directly influence kicking, but it was required by postural adjustments. Also the distance of the non-kicking foot (landmarks 1-17) from the football was variable, as well as the position of the head relative to the trunk (flexion/extension).

In the two less skilled players, N.F. and G.F., the highest variability was linked to the positions of the upper limb relative to the trunk, and of the head relative to the trunk (a prevalent right inclination). These variations could be postural compensations due to the non-orthogonal position of the trunk and lower limbs.

In all three players, the distance between the left and right knee (5-6) was highly reproducible (low coefficients of variation in all three sessions).

4 Conclusions

The results showed that a good technique is necessary for a successful performance of soccer penalties. This alone is not sufficient: the player has also to learn and apply good postural control.

The high reproducibility of the right knee-left knee distance in L.T. showed that the neuromuscular co-ordination for this reciprocal position, which greatly influences the result of the penalty, was probably very high in this elite player. This result had not been detected by the first qualitative analysis of films.

The proposed method (recording protocol and MVA) may support the coach with quantitative information about the neuromuscular co-ordination of the player while performing a selected movement such as taking a penalty kick. It would also allow him/her to follow the training progress of a single player, or to compare players of different levels.

5 Acknowledgements

The artwork of Mrs Paola Raselli is gratefully acknowledged.

6 References

Ferrario, V.F., Sforza, C., Alberti, G. and Mauro, F. (1994) Quantative assessment of body shape during the standing long jump test. Proposal of a new method. **Journal of Biomechanics**, 27, 663.

Lele, S. (1991) Some comments on coordinate-free and scale invariant methods in morphometry. **American Journal of Physical Anthropology**, 85, 407-417.

Lestral, P.E. (1989) Some approaches toward the mathematical modelling of the carniofacial complex. **Journal of Craniofacial Genetics and Developmental Biology**, 9, 77-91.

Pedotti, A., Rodano, R. and Frigo, C. (1983) Optimisation of motor co-ordination in sport: an analytical and experimental approach, in **Biomechanics and Performance in Sport** (ed W. Baumann), V.K. Hofmann, Schorndorf, pp.145-160.

Reilly, T. (1994) The human body clock and sports performance. **Coaching and Sport Science Journal**, 1, 1-7.

Sanders, R.H. and Owens, P.C. (1992) Hub movement during the swing of elite and novice golfers. **International Journal of Sport Biomechanics**, 8, 320-330.

ANALYSIS OF GOAL-SCORING PATTERNS IN EUROPEAN TOP LEVEL SOCCER TEAMS

J. Garganta, J. Maia and F. Basto
Faculty of Sport Sciences and Physical Education, University of Porto, Portugal.

1 Introduction

Soccer is an interactive invasive field game where a team's efficiency and efficacy depend largely on tactical performance. Much dissatisfaction in a team's performance arises from the tactics and strategy employed (Ali & Farrally, 1990).

It is often stated about soccer that it is a "game of opinions". Whilst opinions may be respected, much more than opinion is necessary in the mapping out of a strategy for success (Bate,1988). One of the most important aspects of the coaching process is the analysis of individual and team performance (Ali & Farrally, 1990). Match analysis provides a means of quantifying and qualifying some performance variables. In soccer it seems important to know how elite soccer teams play in order to identify patterns and to build up a group of indicators that could be used as references for training. Positive attacking play is an indicative trend in top level soccer and a key point of attractive matches. Players, coaches and spectators get positive experiences when the attacking play is successful. This means a lot of attacking attempts, scoring chances and goals (Luhtanen, 1993). Goals provide objective data about the culmination of attacks. However, to the coach and the researcher, it may be fruitful to attempt to study the antecedents of goal-scoring.

The purpose of this study was to describe and compare positive offensive actions (attacks ending with a goal), from gain or regain of ball possession up to a shot on target, in order to define patterns of play that could be associated with a team's success.

2 Methods

Video recordings were analysed post-event using a hand-notation system. Five European teams (Barcelona, Porto, Bayern Munchen, Milan, Paris Saint Germain) were observed and data were collected from 104 goals scored in 44 matches. Set plays were filtered out. The following key features of play were notated for each scoring movement: i) the sector of the field where the team won ball possession (defensive third, middle third, attacking third); ii) attacking reaction time, defined as the lapse between winning the ball and the shot on target; iii) number of players that touch the ball; iv) number of passes performed.

Statistical procedures involved a Chi-square (chi^2) analysis for independency among observed frequencies of the main actions. Independent chi^2 statistics were used first between Barcelona and Porto, and second among the other teams. The analyses were conducted separatedly for each category of observation. The reason for such an analysis was that for Porto and Barcelona there were 11 and 16 games observed, and for the other teams only 5 to 7 games.

3 Results and Discussion

The observed frequencies are showed for the main actions for defence (def.), midfield (mid.) and attack (att.) in Table 1. All five teams are included.

Table 1. Observed frequencies (%) of team main actions leading to goal

	Ball possession			Att. react. time		# Players		# Passes	
	def.	mid.	att.	0 - 5"	5-10"	1-3	4-6	1-3	4-6
Porto	39.3	28.6	32.1	28.6	21.4	60.7	17.9	67.9	7.1 *
Barcelona	29.5	41.0	29.5	22.7	31.8	47.7	40.9	61.0	29.3 *
Bayern	28.6	14.3	57.1	42.9	21.4	85.7	14.3	92.3	7.7
Milan	27.3	27,3	45.4	45.5	18.2	63.6	18.2	75.0	8.3
PSG	20.0	20.0	60.0	60.0	20.0	80.0	20.0	80.0	20.0

* $P < 0.05$

Concerning movements leading to goal, Figure 1 shows that PSG, Bayern and Milan won the highest percentages of ball possessions in their attacking third (60%, 57.1% and 45.4%, respectively). Porto had its highest percentage in the defensive third (39.3%) and Barcelona in the middle third (41.0%).

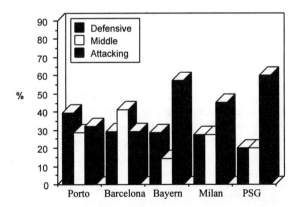

Figure 1. Observed frequencies (%) for goal-scoring actions, concerning field area (third) where the team wins ball possession.

In recent years, several analysts have identified the characteristics of winning team play. A team´s ability to win the ball back in its attacking third is a very important ingredient for winning in soccer (Miller, 1994). A team should put heavy pressure on opposition players in their "back third" to force turnovers of possession in that zone of the field.

Bate (1988) found out that 50-60% of all movements leading to shots on goal had originated in the attacking third of the field. Hughes (1990) claimed that the best and more most positive defensive strategy, is to push up on opponents and pressurise them in order to regain possession of the ball as far up the field as possible.The same author, analysing the frequency of possessions won and the goals scored in top level matches, found that on average a team has to win 34 balls in its attacking third before it scores from one, and it must win 235 possessions in its back third before it can score from one.

In the present study, as we can see in Figure 2, above 50% of offensive actions leading to a goal occur from an attacking reaction time not exceeding 10 seconds. Even when we consider the interval 0-5 seconds, Bayern and Milan teams present values near 50% (42.9% and 45.5% respectively) and PSG reaches 60%.

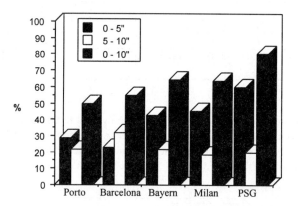

Figure 2. Observed frequencies (%) for goal-scoring actions, concerning attacking reaction time (seconds).

It seems that "attacking" reaction time is an important factor in soccer. Play has become faster in recent years and the player in possession of the ball has less time and space at his disposal (Olsen, 1988). The players, after regaining ball possession, must be able to reach the target faster. Obviously, attacking reaction time depends not only on the player's speed or the velocity at which the ball is circulated, but also on the field area where the team regain ball possession.

Concerning the number of players involved in scoring movements, Figure 3 shows that 47.7 to 85.0% of the actions leading to goal comes from movements performed with 1 to 3 players touching the ball.

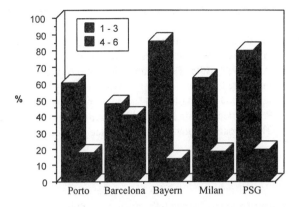

Figure 3. Observed frequencies (%) for goal-scoring actions, concerning the number of players that touch the ball.

Concerning the number of passes performed in scoring movements (Figure 4), 61 to 93% of the actions leading to goal come from movements with no more than 3 passes. A significant difference was only found for Porto and Barcelona in the interval 4-6 passes performed (chi^2= 6.563; P<0.05).

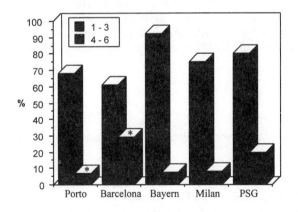

Figure 4. Observed frequencies (%) for goal-scoring actions, concerning the number of passes performed (* P<0.05).

Our results agree with those from other analysts. Olsen (1988) analysing goal-scoring in the Mexico´86 world championship, reported that when penalties are filtered out, only about 20% of the goals are preceeded by five or more passes. Most of the goals are scored after two passes or less.

Hughes (1990) studied 109 top-level matches. He found that 87 % of goals scored came from sequences of 5 passes or less, and 71.5% came from first touches.

Following the World Cup 1982, Bate (1988) had analysed 106 goals. He concluded that: 79% of the goals were scored from movements involving 4 or less passes; no goals were scored from passing movements involving 11 or more passes.

Reep & Benjamin (1968) collected data from 3213 soccer matches between 1953 and 1968. They found that 80% of goals resulted from a sequence of three passes or less.

4 Conclusions

Independent of the number of games observed, the difficulty of matches and style of play, the teams analysed in our study present a similar pattern of actions leading to goal, with respect to selected key features of play. In all but one case (number of passes performed, between Porto and Barcelona), the data present a uniform pattern of behaviour for main actions leading to goals among teams, since chi^2 tests for independency had a P> 0.05.

According to this study we can reach the following conclusions: European top level soccer teams, in scoring movements, often win the ball in their attacking third, reveal a short attacking reaction time (10 seconds or less), involve a few players touching the ball (3 or less) and perform only a few passes (3 or less).

In soccer, a direct style of play seems to lead to a high goal-scoring percentage. Hughes (1990) even recommended *direct play* as the the most productive method of play. However, its efficacy seems to depend especially on the team's capacity to change the rhythm of the game (fast and slow), to vary attacking methods (fast attack and position attack) and to apply different styles of play (direct and indirect) in order to surprise the opposition.

5 References

Ali, A. and Farrally, M. (1990) An analysis of patterns of play in soccer. **Science & Football**, 3, 37-44.

Bate, R. (1988) Football chance: tactics and strategy, in **Science and Football** (eds T. Reilly, A. Lees, K. Davids and W.J. Murphy), E. & F.N. Spon, London, pp. 293-301.

Hughes, C. (1990) **The Winning Formula**. Collins, London.

Luhtanen, P. (1993) A statistical evaluation of offensive actions in soccer at World Cup level in Italy 1990, in **Science and Football II** (eds T. Reilly, J. Clarys and A. Stibbe), E. & F.N. Spon, London, pp. 215-220.

Miller, R. (1994) Charting to win. **Scholastic Coach**, 64 (5), 62-65.

Olsen, E. (1988) An analysis of goal scoring strategies in the World championship in Mexico, 1986, in **Science and Football** (eds T. Reilly, A. Lees, K. Davids and W.J. Murphy), E. & F.N. Spon, London, pp. 373-376.

Reep, C. and Benjamin, B. (1968) Skill and chance in Association Football. **Journal of the Royal Statistical Society,** Series A, 131, 581-585.

A TIME ANALYSIS OF MEN'S AND WOMEN'S SOCCER

SHIGEKI MIYAMURA*, SUSUMA SETO** and HISAYUKI KOBAYASHI***
* Kobe Women's University, 2-1 Aoyama-Higashisuma, Suma-Ku Kobe, Japan 654.
** Otani University, Japan.
*** Tezukayama Junior College, Japan.

1 Introduction

Women's soccer is a fast growing sport throughout the world, clearly demonstrated by the interest generated by the First FIFA World Championship for Women's Football held in 1991 in China. Very little work has been completed on the analysis of women's soccer (Miyamura et al., 1991a and 1991b), particularly with respect to comparison of the time the ball is "in-play" and "out-of-play" in men's soccer. It is the aim of this work to analyse these time variables at different levels of women's soccer, make comparisons, both cross-sectionally with the different groups and also with data previously gathered on the men's game. It is hoped that these comparisons will help with the development of specific coaching and training programmes for women's soccer.

2 Methods

Four matches from the final rounds of the FIFA World Cup for Women's soccer, three matches from the 8th Asian Cup Women's Soccer Championship, the final of the Junior Women's League Cup and the final of the Junior Women's University Cup were all videotaped and analysed post-event using hand notation. The data were then entered into an ACOS 3400 computer for processing. Comparisons were made with previously gathered data from the finals of the 1994 World Cup for men's soccer and the last Asian Cup for men's soccer, using SPSSX.

3 Results and Discussion

The results are divided into six categories.
3.1 Percentage of In-play and Out-of-play times for men and women.
The comparisons made in Fig. 1 show that the men's matches have significantly more In-play time (P<0.001), and each of the women's sets of data are significantly different

(P<0.01). The drop in In-play time from the top international sides through the scale suggests that there is a need for more coaching of technical skills and also raising levels of fitness throughout the game for women.

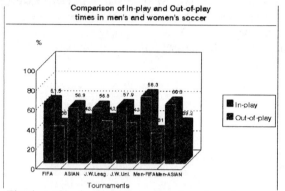

Figure 1. The time play durations for women's and men's soccer matches.

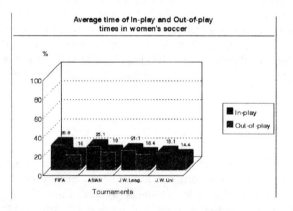

Figure 2. Factors affecting the duration of ball in play time for women's soccer.

3.2 Average time of In-play and Out-of-play
The differences in technical abilities at the different levels of the women's game are further underlined by the presentation, in Fig. 2, of the average times of ball In-play and Out-of-play.

3.3 Factors affecting the Out-of-play times
The comparison of the FIFA and Asian competitions for women in Fig. 3 suggests that the differences between the two groups of nations are mainly in injury times and times spent in scoring (others) and also the times spent in taking goal kicks. This difference is

also noted in the comparison of the men's matches (Fig. 4). The men also spend longer in the other categories - in the men's World Cup it took on average about 49 s to restart after either an injury or a goal, compared to about 35 s for either in the women's game. This could be an area of further research.

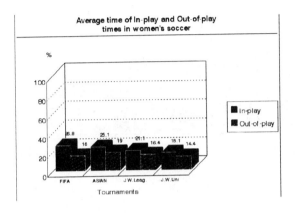

Figure 3. Factors affecting the duration of ball in play time for women's soccer.

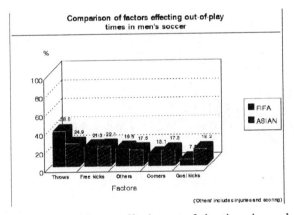

Figure 4. Comparison of factors affecting out of play times in men's soccer.

3.4 Comparison of In-play time and the progress of the match
Figure 5 shows continuous plots of In-play time against match progress in the final round matches in the FIFA tournament for women. The first and second half matches are separated for comparison. The frequency of In-play possessions of over 80 s occurred 5 times (10.4%), over 60 s occurred 7 times (15%) and over 30 s occurred 19 times (40%). Figures in the second half were very similar.

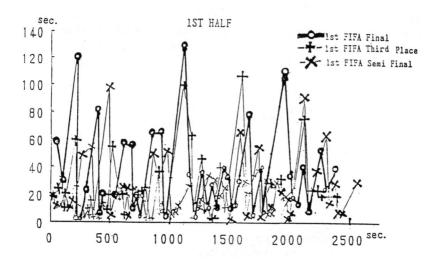

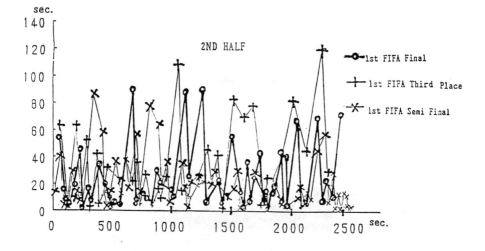

Fig. 5 Plot of In-play time against the match time for the FIFA World Cup for women

Table 1. Analysis of passing frequencies (FIFA competition only)

Frequency	USA				NORWAY			
	1st H	2nd H	Total	%	1st H	2nd H	Total	%
0	57	42	99	46.7	71	60	131	49.1
1	25	35	60	28.3	34	26	60	22.5
2	14	13	27	12.7	24	23	47	17.9
3	6	5	11	5.2	9	7	16	6.0
4	4	3	7	3.3	6	1	7	2.6
5 & over	4	4	8	3.8	5	1	6	2.2

As can be seen from Table 1 the frequencies of 5-pass moves and over are very small, 3.8% and 2.2% respectively for USA and Norway. These are very low compared with the men's game - different researchers (Reep and Benjamin, 196 ; Franks, 1983; Hughes et al. ,1988) concur with an average figure of 12% for the men's game. This again indicates the lower technical and movement skills in women's soccer.

3.5 Frequencies of success and failure at trapping and clearing
The relative performances of the USA and Norway at heading and trapping the ball are shown in Table 2. The higher figures of USA for clearances, in particular heading the ball, reflect the "long-ball" game of Norway. The trapping skills of the teams are similar, USA having slightly higher figures.

Table 2. Frequencies of success and failure at trapping and clearing

			USA			NORWAY		
			Freq.	Total	**Total**	Freq.	Total	**Total**
Clear	Kick	Succ.	10	46		16	38	
	(foot)	Miss	36	(45.5%)		22	(58.5%)	
	Head	Succ.	14	55		8	27	
		Miss	41	(54.5%)	**101**	19	(41.5%)	**65**
Trap	Foot	Succ.	26	34		17	27	
		Miss	8	(52.5%)		10	(50%)	
	Other	Succ.	18	31		23	27	
		Miss	13	(47.7%)	**65**	4	(50%)	**54**

3.6 Distance of ball movement throughout the games
The distance travelled by the ball every five minutes was calculated and averaged for the FIFA and Asian tournaments for women. These distances were then plotted against

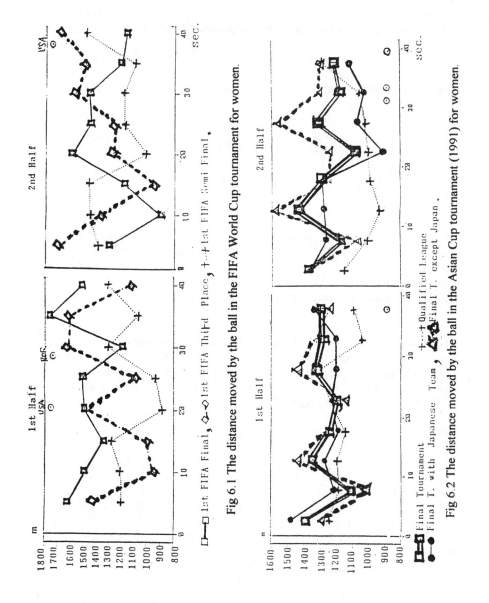

Fig 6.1 The distance moved by the ball in the FIFA World Cup tournament for women.

Fig 6.2 The distance moved by the ball in the Asian Cup tournament (1991) for women.

time in the match, Figs 6.1 and 6.2. The final of the FIFA tournament is notable for the distance covered in the first half; not surprisingly these figures were less in the second half as the players tired. The Asian tournament data had far less variance than the FIFA tournament data.

4 Conclusion

The time of "In-play" for women decreases significantly as the standard of play decreases; it is also significantly less than a selection of men's match data. Continuity of passing moves showed that women do not sustain their passing moves as long as men. There are some notable differences between men's and women's teams in restarting the play after scoring goals, and after injuries, that could warrant further research.

5 References

Franks, I.M. (1983) Analysis of 1982 FIFA World Cup for Association Football. **Soccer Journal**, September/October, 35-43.

Hughes, M.D., Robertson, K. & Nicholson, A. (1988) An analysis of 1984 World Cup of Association Football, in **Science and Football** (eds T.Reilly, A.Lees, K.Davids & W.Murphy), E. & F. N. Spon, London, pp. 363-367.

Miyamura, S., Seto, S. and Kobayashi, H. (1991) The ratio of time for "In-play" vs "Out-of-play" in women's Japan University tournament for soccer. **The 11th Medicine and Science in Soccer Conference**, pp. 55-63.

Miyamura, S., Seto, S. and Kobayashi, H. (1994) A study of time endurance of "Out-of-play", "In-play" and the frequency of players' technique in women's international football matches. **The 14th Medicine and Science in Soccer Conference**, pp 55-63.

Reep, C. & Benjamin, B. (1968) Skill and chance in association football. **Journal of the Royal Statistical Society, Series A, 131**, 581-585.

A METHOD TO ANALYSE ATTACKING MOVES IN SOCCER

J.F. GREHAIGNE*, D. BOUTHIER**, and B. DAVID**
* IUFM de Franche-Compté, Forte Griffon, 2500 Besançon, France.
** Equipe d'Analyse et de Didactique des A.P.S., University Paris-Sud, France.

1 Introduction

Formal configurations of play (e.g. Gréhaigne, 1991; 1992a) may be analysed in order to find promising configurations or successful patterns of play with respect to scoring goals. When players have created a configuration which can permit a goal to be scored, they must then think in terms of exploiting it and making rapid progress toward shooting at the opponents' goal. Time is precious in soccer at such moments.

To emphasise the importance of time in soccer, we have devised a new methodology to analyse the attacking moves and more specifically the transition between two configurations of play in the attack/defence system (Gréhaigne 1992b; Villepreux, 1987). The purpose of this paper is to present our methodology and illustrate it by means of an example.

2 Method of Analysis

2.1 Movement of players and ball

To examine this transition between two configurations of play, the position, the type of move and the speed of the players are first registered, with a video recorder. Since we have 25 images per second, it is easy to establish precisely a diagram of the action. The different lines on the ground are used to obtain the precise position of the players

We employ an index card depicting a standardised half pitch. International match pitches are 112 m by 70 m. Our data collection diagram represents proportionally half a pitch and is covered with a square pattern (Fig. 1). Each square represents two square metres (sometimes, for a precise location we use a square pattern of 1 m) on the ground for greater accuracy in plotting the players' positions. When the pitch sizes are different, the grid is adjusted to the dimensions given by UEFA for the presentation of the European Championship in Sweden (Bietry, 1992).

We note second by second the positions taken up by all the players who participate in the attack or the defence during the pre-goal phase. Depending on available pictures of a successful attack which culminated in a goal, there may be from four to ten topographic diagrams of the precise spot occupied by the players and the ball. For each diagram the speed calculated is the average speed. In using the diagram with the grid, we know the distance covered by a player. With the video recorder, we have the time between two configurations of play. It is then easy to find the speed of the player. The trajectory of the ball is illustrated according to the model presented in Figure 2.

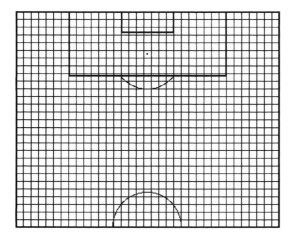

Figure 1. Example of a diagram with grid (square of 2 x 2 m in reality).

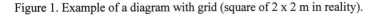

Ball interceptable (< 2 m).

Ball interceptable (> 2 m).

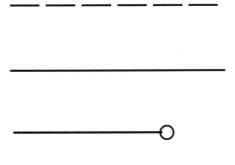

Position of the ball after a time t

Figure 2. Model for the trajectory of the ball.

2.2 Sectors of play and sectors of intervention

Looking for a procedure which would make it possible to pattern the potential sphere of operation of a given player and draw accordingly one's sector of play, 20 P.E. students registered on a soccer course at Burgundy were tested. Each player ran, without the ball, in a straight line over a distance of some ten metres, at a determined speed. Upon reaching a specific area indicated by a marker, he diverted his run to the full and the angle of diversion was registered. This task was realised with various speeds effectively found in a soccer match (Dufour, 1989; Lacour, 1983; Reilly and Thomas, 1976). Knowing the speed of a player, and consequently the distance he would cover in one second, the depth of his potential sphere of action could then be determined (Table 1) and sectors of play, for attackers, or sectors of intervention for defenders (Fig. 3).

Table 1. The potential sphere of action according to the speed.

Speed of the player (m/s)	Angle of degree	Depth of the angle (cm)
0	360	
1	240	0. 35
2	240	0. 7
3	100	1. 0
4	100	1. 4
5	80	1. 7
6	80	2. 1
7	40	2. 45
8 or more	40	2. 8

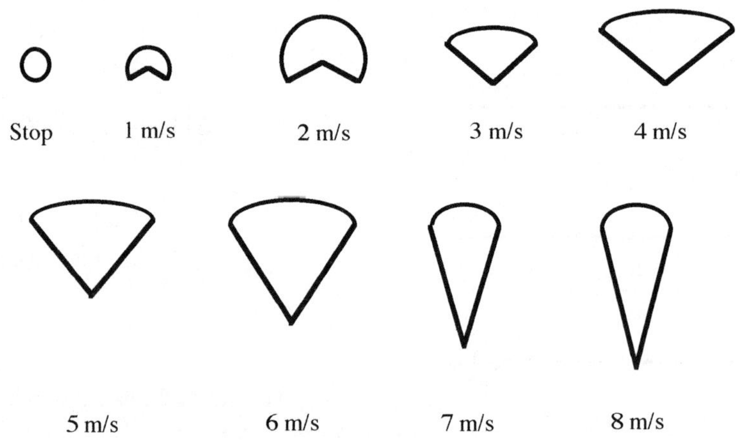

Figure 3. Sector of play or intervention according to the speed.

We can note that it is at a speed of 6 m/s that a player has the greatest potential for manoeuvring, being able to cover the largest area of the pitch.

3 Results

In order to illustrate the kind of result provided by the proposed method, we have analysed the goal of Jensen scored at 19 minutes in Denmark - Germany match in the final of the European soccer championship in Sweden, 1992.

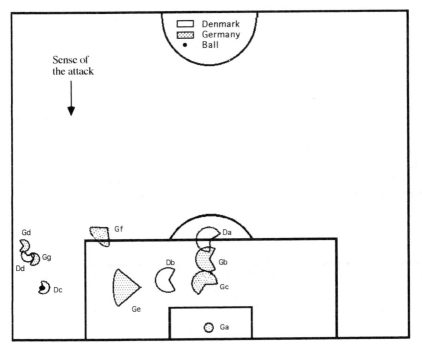

Figure 4a. M -3s: Germany loses the ball.

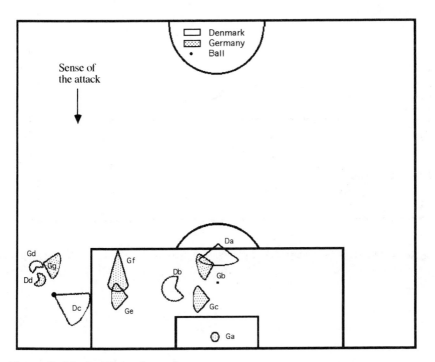

Figure 4b. M - 2s: Denmark attacks.

In Figure 4a, Brehme (Gg) loses the ball after a tackle from Wilfort (Dd). Poulsen (Dc) recovers the ball on the right side of the German defending third. He advances with the ball in the free space. The defence seems to be well positioned.

In Figure 4b, Poulsen (dc) dribbles the ball in the free space until he reaches the side line of the penalty area. Apparently there is no one available to pass the ball to, except to Db (who is free but Gf and Ge are blocked).

As can be seen in Figure 4c, Jensen (De) arrives from the back in an excellent position to receive the ball. Poulsen (Dc) centres the ball back just one metre in front of Jensen.

Being well positioned Jensen (Fig. 4d decides to shoot immediately on goal. The trajectory of the ball does not cross the sector of play of the German goalkeeper (Ga) and the time between the shot and the moment when the ball enters into the target is shorter than the reaction time of the goalkeeper. The first goal of the match is scored.

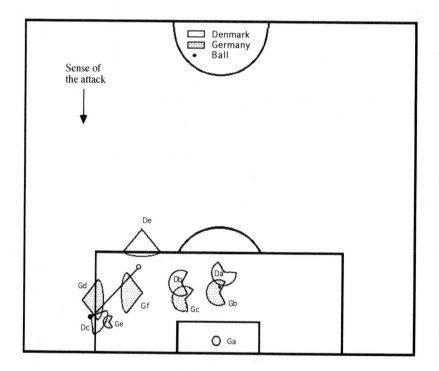

Figure 4c. M - 1s: Jensen supports the player with the ball.

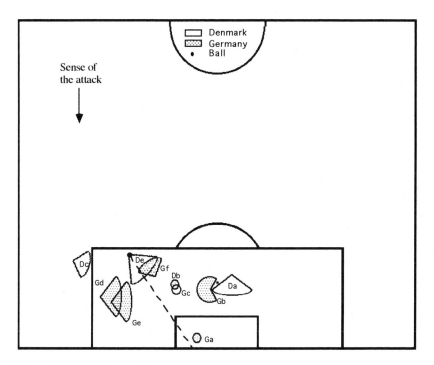

Figure 4d. M - 0: Denmark scores.

4 Discussion

In a complex system like a soccer match all players affect each other in an intricate way; studying them individually often disrupts their usual interactions so much that an isolated unit may behave quite differently from the way it would behave in its normal context. It is, therefore, inappropriate to study the configuration of play in isolation from the environment. From this point of view, the most difficult task in our method so far has been to spot exactly the location and to determine the orientation of each player. With the use of computer analysis systems the task should become much easier.

The analysis of this goal and twenty others (Gréhaigne and Bouthier, 1994) indicates that the different ball players have presented the ball in a free space to their partners. A part of the sectors of play of the receivers is always free in order for them to exchange the ball or to shoot on goal according to their position. When a team is attacking, the object is to create time and space or to keep the amount of time and space available. The ball should be played to the player who is in the best position to penetrate the defence: he is not necessarily the player with the largest space available (Ali and Farrally, 1990; Harris and Reilly, 1988).

Those results show that the positions and the way the receivers move yield important information for the player in possession. The concepts of sector of play and sector intervention can be used to model the attacks. So far we have used a small number of goals and we have only analysed the attacks which culminated in a goal.

Indeed teams can modify their usual style to score in response to the opposition, the players available for a particular match and the state of the game. A larger sample of games is likely to produce more reliable results.

It would also be interesting in the future, using those tools and currently available models, to study the offensive actions that do not end with a goal and try to see if the player in possession makes choices that cause the attacks to fail. We could also try to take into account runs with the ball and the effects of the players on the ball.

5 References

Ali, A.H. and Farrally, M. (1990) An analysis of patterns of play in soccer. **Science and Football**, 3, 37-44.

Dufour, W. (1989) Les techniques d'observation du comportement moteur. **Education Physique et Sport**, 217, 68-71.

Bietry, C. (1992) Présentation du championnat d'Europe en Suéde. **Football, l'année plus**. Paris: Canal +.

Gréhaigne, J.F. (1991) A new method of goal analysis. **Science and Football**, 5, 10-16.

Gréhaigne, J.F. (1992a) **L'organisation du jeu en football**. Paris, ACTIO.

Gréhaigne, J.F. (1992b) A weighted model to analyse the conditions of scoring in soccer. Communication to the **First World Congress of Notational Analysis**, Liverpool, November.

Gréhaigne, J.F. and Bouthier, D. (1994) Analyse des évolutions entre deux configurations du jeu en football. **Science et Motricité**, 24, 44-52.

Harris, S. and Reilly, T. (1988) Space, teamwork and attacking succcss in socccr, in **Science and Football** (eds T. Reilly, A. Lees, K. Davids and W.J. Murphy). E. and F.N. Spon, London, pp. 322-328.

Lacour, J.R. (1983) Aspects physiologiques du football. **L'Entraîneur Français**, 183, 1-6.

Reilly, T. and Thomas, V. (1976) A motion analysis of work-rate in different roles in professional football match play. **Journal of Human Movement Studies**, 2, 87-97.

Villepreux, P. (1987) Rugby de mouvement et disponibilité du joueur. **Mémoire** INSEP, Paris.

PART SEVEN

Psychology and Football Behaviour

USE OF FEEDBACK BY COACHES AND PLAYERS

IAN M. FRANKS
School of Human Kinetics, University of British Columbia, Vancouver, B.C., V6T 1Z1, Canada.

1 Introduction

Performance improvement is a consequence of task relevant feedback. Information that is available to the athlete before, during and after a skilled performance can take many forms and is the product of an extremely sophisticated multi-level feedback mechanism. Several researchers have defined and delineated this mechanism for the practitioner. Magill (1993) offered perhaps the most useful classification of feedback processes. A simple hierarchical family tree describes what Magill terms the "feedback family" (see Figure 1). Whereas sensory feedback encompasses internally generated information, augmented feedback enhances these sensations by providing external information to the athlete.

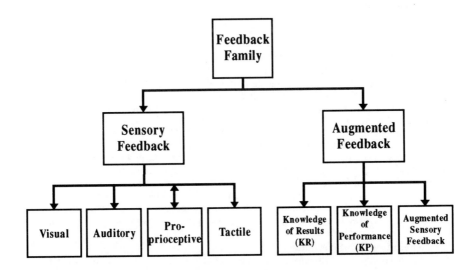

Figure 1. Classification of various types of feedback
(After Magill, 1993, p.306).

During the coaching process augmented feedback is of particular importance if the athlete is to improve. The two most prevalent forms of augmented feedback that are provided by a coach are knowledge of performance (KP) and knowledge of results (KR). Knowledge of performance is information about the characteristics of the skilled movement, while KR is externally presented information about the outcome of that movement. Throughout this review, the content, delivery and utility of various forms of KP and KR that coaches provide and players receive will be discussed within the confines of association football (soccer). Although, some of the findings will be specific to this one particular code of football it will be clear that the general principle under discussion exists for all codes.

2 What Research Can Tell the Coach

Four general findings are applicable to football.

2.1 Relevance of information
The content of the information provided by augmented feedback should be relevant to the skill being learned. Videotape provides the most realistic and understandable form of feedback that an athlete can use. Selder and Del Rolan (1979) demonstrated the benefit of using videotape as a source of augmented feedback. An experimental group of female gymnasts viewed videotaped replays of their own performances, while a control group received only verbal feedback. In addition, both groups were asked to use a checklist for critically analysing their performance and, in the experimental group's case, to guide subsequent viewing of the videotape. Interestingly, there were no significant differences between the groups after the first 4 weeks of training. After 6 weeks the experimental group was superior to the control group in categories such as precision, amplitude and direction of movement but not in rhythm, elegance and coordination. It appears then, that the use of videotaped replays as augmented feedback will benefit athletes who are correcting elements of performance that are easily quantifiable and relatively objective. Also, the benefits of using videotape can be realized only after a period of practice. That is, athletes (and coaches) must learn how to use this particular form of feedback.

2.2 Quantitative and qualitative information
Quantitative feedback is more useful than qualitative feedback. Many studies (Smoll, 1972; Reeve and Magill, 1981; and Magill and Wood, 1986) have shown the superiority of quantitative feedback. This effect is also dependent upon the precision of the feedback and the skill level of the athlete. Skilled performers can modify their movements based upon information derived from a feedback display that offers no apparent advantage to the novice (Franks and Wilberg, 1982). Skilled performers need more precise feedback about the movement than novice performers. If players cannot use feedback to improve performance because it is too precise and not relevant to the players' skill level, then coaches should consider elaborating upon the quantitative feedback they provide. A combination of quantitative and videotaped feedback would possibly ensure the player understands the information and also has the ability to use it to modify subsequent performances. This applies especially if the videotaped instances of performance are based upon and exemplify the quantitative information.

2.3 Scheduling of information
Scheduling of augmented feedback has been the centre of a resurgence in research activity in recent years. Schmidt (Schmidt, Lange & Young, 1990; Winstein & Schmidt, 1990; and Young & Schmidt, 1992) has been the catalyst for much of this renewed interest. The original question posed by Lavery (1962) was "Is it always better to provide KR after every trial?" The general protocol that researchers adopt is

to compare the performance of several groups during acquisition and then after a retention period of a day or week. These retention trials would be situations in which subjects received no information about the produced movement and as such would provide an indication of the amount learned by the subject in a transfer test. This measure of learning is preferable to using only the transitory performance level during acquisition trials. The results from two groups are of interest to the coach:- the "KR after every trial" group and the "summary KR" group. Providing summary KR means that subjects produce movements without KR for several trials and then receive, in summary form, information about the last few trials. The general consensus is that providing summary KR after every fifth trial is probably optimum for learning, whereas the group that receives KR after every trial has superior performance in acquisition but tends to lose that edge after a retention period. Fortunately, in the applied setting of a football coaching practice it is more suitable to provide summary KR than it is to provide KR after every trial, albeit not in a controlled or systematic manner. Some coaches still provide too much information, too frequently during practice sessions (More, 1994). It may be instructive therefore, to stress to the coach that although information given after every trial may yield good results in practice, it may not be the most optimum scheduling of feedback when considering performance on match day.

2.4 Information about error and success

Finally, research may appear to be equivocal on the question of whether to provide feedback about errors in performance or feedback that highlights only correct performance. Early tracking studies (e.g. Gordon & Gottlieb, 1967) tended to agree with Annett's (1959) hypothesis that subjects show performance improvement when supplied with error-based augmented feedback and cannot be expected to improve if they only produce repeated responses that are not accompanied by feedback. Some more recent research findings by Dowrick (Dowrick & Raeburn, 1977; Dowrick & Hood, 1981) in the field of clinical psychology may add a new perspective to the existing literature. Although Dowrick's work is mainly concerned with modelling which presupposes the information precedes performance, the findings have implication for augmentation of feedback, especially in the technical area of videotape. In fact, Dowrick (1991, p.109) used the term feedforward to refer to "images of target skills not yet achieved". Video feedforward and positive self-review refer to compiling selectively the best recorded examples of target skills already manageable but infrequently achieved. These video excerpts are edited such that they present to the subject an image of (the subject's own) correct, achievable performance that he or she has not yet produced. Existing behaviours are recorded on videotape and then the edited tape is compiled. An intervention protocol is undertaken in an attempt to change the target behaviour. Successful interventions have been reported for a wide variety of maladaptive behaviours ranging from selective mutism to depression. What is more relevant to the present discussion is the successful application of this technique in the sport setting. Franks and Maile (1991) described its use with several sports such as powerlifting, swimming, skiing and volleyball. Research is now underway in the author's laboratory to determine if positive self-review and video feedforward can be used successfully in the skill of shooting in association football. The reasons why this form of self modelling may benefit the skill acquisition process is not known. Dowrick (1991) speculated that reviewing videotapes of one's own successful performance is a highly motivating factor that generates interest and enthusiasm for the physical practice setting that is to follow. Nevertheless, it would be prudent of the coach to consider showing some successful performances along with the error-based feedback as a motivating force for subsequent practice.

3 Applied Research on the Utility of Feedback in Soccer

The majority of research that focuses upon augmented feedback is laboratory based. Moreover, the tasks that subjects are required to perform are simple closed skills with few degrees of freedom, either linear movements or coincident timing skills. It is with some caution therefore, that generalizations and recommendations are made to the coach and player based soley on these studies. In an effort to conduct more relevant research into the general area of feedback utility as it applies to the players and coaches of soccer, Franks and colleagues (Franks, 1988 and 1992; Partridge & Franks, 1989, 1990 and 1993) have conducted several experiments that address specific applied questions. Before attempting to modify the process of providing feedback and its content and form, it was necessary to study existing methods.

3.1 Feedback and the coaching process
The traditional coaching process in football has been based upon a simplistic intervention protocol that is cyclic in nature. As can be seen in Figure 2 the coach observes performance and from the information that is gained, decides upon the most effective practice environment for the player. It is in this practice environment that the coach gives feedback to his players in the hope that their performance, both as individuals and as a team will improve. The observations made by the coach are usually subjective, unreliable and often inaccurate (Franks & Miller, 1986 and 1991). This evidence, when combined with many other studies from the field of applied psychology, suggests the processing of visual information through the human information processing system can be extremely problematic (Neisser, 1982).

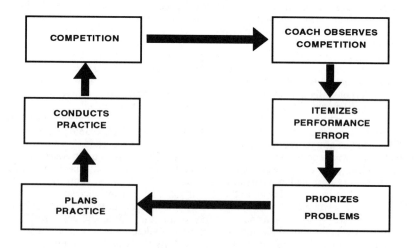

Figure 2. The traditional coaching process

A solution to this problem of unreliable and inaccurate observations lies in the development of an "external memory aid" that can provide objective, quantitative data about individual and team performance. This information should also be linked to a videotape of the performance. From the previous discussion it would seem reasonable to assume that task relevant feedback which is based upon quantitative, objective data leads to improved performance. With the advent of computer and video technology many such systems are now available (Franks, 1992 and Hughes, 1993). The general method of using these systems to collect both quantitative and video information from a match performance is shown in Figure 3.

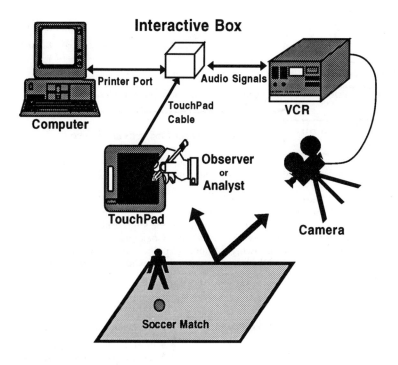

Figure 3. Computer video interactive system used in match analysis.

3.2 Feedback and team performance

A computer-aided match analysis system was developed to collect data of relevant technical events in team play for the sport of soccer (see Figure 4). In addition, it was possible to provide the coach with specific tactical information such as a graphic display of how and where both teams entered the attacking third of the field and also a graphic account of the events leading to shots, goals or crosses. All of these events were collected in real time and synchronized to a videotape recording of the same game. This would allow fast and accurate access to the video image of a particular event via the computer files.

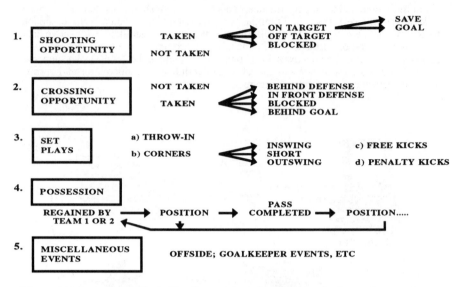

Figure 4. Information collected by the match analysis system for team play events.

Partridge and Franks (1993) used this system to study the efficacy and utility of providing task relevant feedback to soccer players in an international (FIFA Youth World Cup qualifying) tournament. The format of the study followed a simple interrupted time series analysis (see Figure 5) after Cooke and Campbell (1979). This time series analysis involves knowing the specific point in the series when a treatment or intervention took place and the purpose was to infer whether the intervention had any impact upon performance.

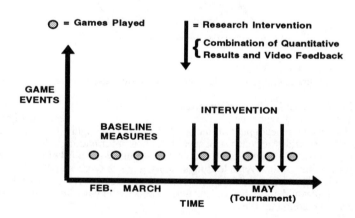

Figure 5. Experimental design for time series analysis.

In the period preceding the tournament an analysis was conducted on four "exhibition games". These games provided the baseline measure of the team's performance. During the tournament quantitative data in tabulated and graphic form were presented to the coach along with an edited videotape of match events. These events displayed both successful and unsuccessful execution of pertinent events that were established as key factors of performance by the coach during previous discussions. In addition, prior to the start of the tournament a summary of the results from the baseline games was presented to the coaching staff. These results then formed the basis of the first intervention with the players. The coaches presented the feedback package to the players in a classroom setting before their coaching practice. Although this appeared to be a limitation in controlling specific variables of the design the need to establish and maintain ecological validity was of concern.

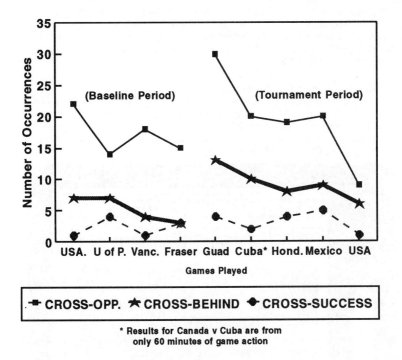

* Results for Canada v Cuba are from
only 60 minutes of game action

Figure 6. The number of crossing opportunities, crosses played behind defenders, and successful (contacted by attacker in the penalty area) crosses.

An example of some results is shown in Figure 6. **First**, it was possible to provide a coach with task relevant feedback on team play during the international tournament (one game every three days). Also the coach was able to base the coaching practice on the information received from the match analysis. **Second**, a stable baseline of performance should be established before any substantial conclusions can be made from this type of time series design. The variability in the performance level of the opposing teams produced an unstable baseline in this particular study. In the normal course of international competition in North America it is difficult to overcome this problem. Perhaps an increase in the number of baseline observations may provide more stable and reliable pre-intervention performance level data. **Third**, within this particular competition format (league followed by knock-out) there is a greater likelihood that as the team advances through to the final the opposition becomes more skilled. Hence, it is more difficult to produce the target performance levels previously agreed upon. One solution is to set varying performance levels through competition based upon the expected quality of the opposition. **Fourth**, variations in technical performance measures may reflect other underlying factors that affect that performance. In this competition the team under investigation suffered many injuries and therefore many of the players either did not train throughout the weeks of the tournament or were replaced by other members of the playing staff. These variables are very difficult to control. Other performance factors must therefore be taken into account before conclusions about team play can be made. **Fifth**, it became clear as the study progressed and as we received comments on the overall process from players and coaches, that there was an obvious need to educate coaches in the appropriate use of this type of feedback. More time should be taken in privately presenting the feedback to individual players who may feel unduly pressured and appear resistant to change when receiving the same information in a group setting. **Finally**, there is a certain amount of empirical evidence to substantiate the claim that both quantitative data and edited videotape recording are beneficial forms of augmented feedback.

3.3 Feedback and individual performance
Coaches spend the majority of their practice time giving feedback to groups of players about team performance. This may not be the most effective method of improving an individual's performance in soccer (More, 1994). If specific, attainable goals are set for individuals and feedback related to these goals is delivered in private, then there should be a greater likelihood of improving performance.

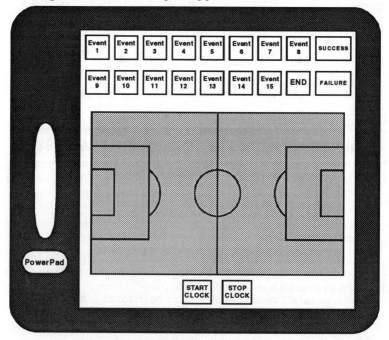

Figure 7. Individual player analysis touch pad.

In order to provide the player with information about his/her performance a specific analysis needs to be undertaken. A computer/video analysis system, similar to that used for team play, was developed for individual performance. This system can be used to record a player's activity and technical performance in real time. The illustration in Figure 7 shows the outline of the data collection "touch pad". The program allows the coach to enter the particular skills to be analysed and also enables a success/fail rating on any technique. Data entry is accomplished by a recorder tracking the player's movement with a stylus on the touch pad and recording selected technical activities as they occur. Video images of the technical behaviours are edited by computer control and displayed to the player at some time following the match. The coach can then use both quantitative information (number of instances of a successful or unsuccessful technique and the path and speed of movement about the field during selected periods of the game) and edited video highlights of both successful and unsuccessful behaviours. Table 1 provides typical quantitative information generated by the program.

Table 1. Technical event selection (success/fail) for the individual player analysis system

PLAYER: 1-KH   TEAM: UBC   END: RIGHT

EVENT	TOTAL	SUCCESS RATIO
1) DEF-POSITION	6	50%
2) DEF-APPROACH	7	57%
3) DEF-TACKLE	1	0%
4) HEADING	6	50%
5) CONTROL-CNT	11	45%
6) CONTROL-1ST TIME	3	100%
7) RUN/DRIBBLE	2	50%
8) ENTERS PEN.AREA	14	
9) SHOT OPPORTUNITY	3	
10) CHALL. CROSS	7	29%
11) RUN DIAG	12	33%
12) RUN STRT	7	100%
13) INFRINGEMENT	3	
14) SHOT RESULT	3	33%
15) SET PLAY RESULT	2	50%

Partridge and Franks (1992) used this individual player analysis system to study the impact such information would have upon the performance of a university soccer player. Since one of the investigators was the coach of the university team, the design of the experiment and the delivery of the feedback were optimized. The subject of this study was a "striker" who had limited but special talents. He was tall and possessed exceptional ability in "heading" the ball. In addition, he was able to recognise and take opportunities to shoot on goal. However, his ability at controlling the ball with his feet was limited. The coach decided upon the most effective way to use the player's strengths and hide the player's weakness.

Before identifying and setting the target behaviours (attainable goals) the coach and player discussed previous performances with the aid of videotape and came to an agreement as to the priorities for player improvement. The data used in these discussions were derived from two "baseline" games. It was essential that the player be an integral part of this negotiation process and as such would be more receptive to "take on board" suggestions for changing his own behaviour. As in the previous study of team performance, a simple time series analysis was used.

1. Baseline Measure **(v CALGARY)**
   Player: KH   Player's Team: UBC   Defending: RIGHT
   Replay Span: 00:00:00 TO 00:15:00

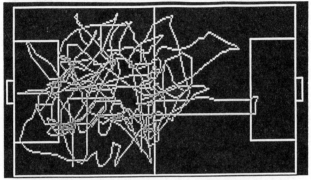

2. Post-Intervention Measure **(v VICTORIA)**
   Player: KH   Player's Team: UBC   Defending: RIGHT
   Replay Span: 00:00:00 TO 00:15:00

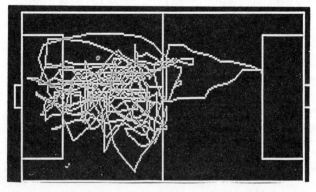

Figure 8. Movement pattern during baseline and following intervention games.

Two general areas for improvement were identified. First, the player's movements "off the ball" were of concern. Since it was necessary to have this player in central attacking areas, movements back into his own half and to the sides of the field ("wings") were discouraged. A comparison of the player's movements between a baseline performance and after intervention can be seen in Figure 8. This was the form of feedback shown to the player. Undesirable movements were first identified using the computer graphic then shown as a video excerpt. The improvement in the player's movement pattern is clearly evident and throughout the intervention period these graphic displays were an important element of the total feedback. They were understandable and relevant.

A second area of concern was the successful completion of previously identified techniques. The definitions of success and failure were clearly explained to the player, using videotape and practical coaching. The task for the player was therefore to recognise the opportunity to perform a targeted skill and then to perform it successfully. Overall success/fail ratios were presented to the player along with particular video instances of the behaviour. The overall success rate of the 15 targeted techniques was analysed and there was a distinct improvement following intervention.

The results of this study were encouraging. The subject became more successful in his performance on the fifteen events that were identified and his movement patterns were considered acceptable. What is more, he contributed significantly to the success of the team (national champions). Also, anecdotal evidence from other qualified outside observers confirmed the conclusions made from empirical data that this player had shown significant overall improvement in performance.

4 Conclusions

Applied research that focuses upon the use of augmented feedback for athletes in general and football players in particular has been conspicuous by its absence. The main problem in conducting ecologically valid research in the football environment is the inability of the experimenter to control all factors that effect performance. In this paper I have described two applied studies that could provide the coach with some practical recommendations with regard to feedback and its use in football. The advent of modern match analysis systems has certainly made it possible to gain an accurate, reliable and objective performance measure of team and individual performance. These performance measures can now be charted over the span of several games and the coach can use various intervention techniques to provide feedback to the players. Thus allowing the coach to make an informed decision about the most appropriate form of feedback and the most effective method of providing it.

5 Acknowledgements

The research reported in this paper was funded by a grant from Social Sciences and Humanities Research Council of Canada.

6 References

Annett, J. (1959) Learning a pressure under conditions of immediate and delayed knowledge of results. **Quarterly Journal of Experimental Psychology, 11**, 3-15.

Cooke, T.D. & Campbell, D.T. (1979) **Quasi-experimentation: Design and Analysis Issues for Field Settings**. Houghton Mifflin Company, Boston.

Dowrick, P.W. (1991) **Practical Guide to Using Video in the Behavioral Sciences**. John Wiley and Sons, New York.

Dowrick, P.W. and Hood, M. (1981) Comparison of self modeling and small cash incentives in a sheltered workshop. **Journal of Applied Psychology, 66**, 394-397.

Dowrick, P.W. and Raeburn, J.M. (1977) Video editing and medication to produce a therapeutic self model. **Journal of Consulting and Clinical Psychology**, 45, 1156-1158.

Franks, I.M. (1988) Analysis of association football. **Soccer Journal, Sept-Oct**, 35-43.

Franks, I.M. (1992) The use of computers in sport analysis: a review, in **Proceedings of the International Conference on Computers in Sport and Physical Education** (eds G. Tenebaum, T. Raz-Lieberman, Zvi Artzi) Wingate Institute Press, Wingate, Israel, pp. 5-21.

Franks, I.M. and Maile, L.J. (1991) The use of video in sport-skill acquisition. in **A Practical Guide to Using Video in the Behavioral Sciences** (ed P.W. Dowrick), John Wiley and Sons, New York, pp. 231-243.

Franks, I.M. and Miller, G. (1986) Eyewitness testimony in sport. **Journal of Sport Behavior, 9**, 38-45.

Franks, I.M. and Miller, G. (1991) Training coaches to observe and remember. **Journal of Sports Sciences, 9**, 285-297.

Franks, I.M. and Wilberg, R.B. (1982) The generation of movement patterns during the acquisition of a pursuit tracking task. **Human Movement Science, 1**, 251-272.

Gordon, N. and Gottlieb, M.J. (1967) Effect of supplemental visual cues on rotary pursuit. **Journal of Experimental Psychology, 75**, 566-568.

Hughes, M. (1993) Notation analysis in football, in **Science and Football II** (eds T. Reilly, J. Clarys and A. Stibbe), E & F.N. Spon, London, pp. 151-159.

Lavery, J.J. (1962) Retention of simple motor skills as a function of type of knowledge of results. **Canadian Journal of Psychology, 16**, 300-311.

Magill, R.A. (1995) **Motor Learning: Concepts and Applications.** Brown & Benchmark, Madison, Wisconsin.

Magill, R.A. and Wood, C.A. (1986) Knowledge of results precision as a learning variable in motor skill acquisition. **Research Quarterly for Exercise and Sport, 57**, 170-173.

More, K. (1994) Analysis and modification of verbal coaching behaviour: The utility of a data driven intervention strategy. **Unpublished Masters Thesis**, University of British Columbia, Vancouver, Canada.

Neisser, U. (1982) **Memory Observed: Remembering in Natural Contexts.** W.H. Freeman and Company, San Francisco.

Partridge, D. and Franks, I.M. (1989) A detailed analysis of crossing opportunities from the 1986 World Cup. **Soccer Journal, May-June**, 45-50.

Partridge, D. and Franks, I.M. (1990) A comparative analysis of technical performance: USA and West Germany in the 1990 World Cup Finals. **Soccer Journal, Nov-Dec**, 57-62.

Partridge, D. and Franks, I.M. (1992) The use of computer-video interactive analysis in the sport of soccer: changing individual performance by providing quantitative and qualitative feedback, Communication to **The First World Congress of Notational Analysis of Sport**, Burton, England.

Partridge, D. and Franks, I.M. (1993) Computer-aided analysis of sport performance: An example from soccer. **The Physical Educator, 50**, 208-215.

Reeve, T.G. and Magill, R.A. (1981) Role of components of knowledge of results information in error correction. **Research Quarterly for Exercise and Sport, 52**, 80-85.

Schmidt, R.A., Lange, C., and Young, D.E. (1990) Optimizing summary knowledge of results for skill learning. **Human Movement Science, 9**, 325-348.

Selder, D.J. and Del Rolan, N. (1979) Knowledge of performance, skill level and performance on the balance beam. **Canadian Journal of Applied Sport Sciences, 4**, 226-229.

Smoll, F.L. (1972) Effects of precision of information feedback upon the acquisition of a motor skill. **Research Quarterly, 43**, 489-493.

Winstein, C.J. and Schmidt, R.A. (1990) Reduced frequency of knowledge of results enhances motor skill learning. **Journal of Experimental Psychology: Learning, Memory, and Cognition, 16**, 677-691.

Young, D.E. and Schmidt, R.A. (1992) Augmented feedback for enhanced skill acquisition, in **Tutorials in Motor Behavior II** (eds G.E. Stelmach and J. Requin), North Holland, Amsterdam, pp. 677-694.

EFFECT OF EXERCISE ON THE DECISION MAKING OF SOCCER PLAYERS

TERRY McMORRIS and JAN GRAYDON
Chichester Institute of Higher Education, College Lane, Chichester, West Sussex PO 1 9 4PE, England.

1 Introduction

It has long been accepted that the skill of the team games player lies not only in the possession of technical ability but also the ability to make quick and accurate decisions (Crossman, 1959). Good decision making is thought to be at least as important as good technique (Smith, 1976). These decisions must be made while the player is engaged in physical activity, often stressful physical activity.

Exercise induces increases in heart rate, respiratory rate and sweating in a comparable manner to that exhibited when somatic arousal level increases due to emotions (Cooper, 1973). Furthermore, increases in plasma levels of adrenaline and noradrenaline are thought to be indicative of an increase in these neurotransmitters in the central nervous system (Chmura, Nazar and Kaciuba-Uscilko, 1994). Thus it has been claimed that increases in exercise intensity are synonymous with increases in arousal. Temporowski and Ellis (1986) drew upon Easterbrook's (1959) Cue Utilisation Theory to hypothesise an inverted-U effect of exercise on the performance of cognitive skills. According to Easterbrook (1959) at low levels of arousal attention is too wide and irrelevant cues are attended to. At moderate levels of arousal attention is optimal, while at high levels of arousal, attention becomes too narrow and relevant cues are missed. McMorris and Keen (1994), however, suggested that it may be unsound to equate exercise induced arousal with emotionally induced arousal. They reasoned that the physiological changes accompanying exercise reflect the way in which the organism maintains homeostasis. On the other hand, emotionally induced somatic arousal destroys the organism's state of homeostasis. Therefore, while exercise is undoubtedly a stressor and does increase arousal, it may affect performance differently from emotionally induced arousal.

Douchamps (1988) also claimed that arousal induced by emotions would have a different effect on performance to that induced by exercise. Douchamps (1988) argued that arousal has three components, the emotional, energetical and computational. According to Douchamps (1988) changes in energetical arousal would only affect that component of performance. Oxendine (1984) argued that the key factor was not so much the stressor but the nature of the task. According to Oxendine (1984) the performance of complex tasks would be enhanced by moderate levels of arousal and adversely affected by high levels of arousal. Simple tasks would require high levels of arousal before facilitation would be exhibited.

Most previous research has used tests that required vigilance, attention or short term memory recall (see McMorris and Keen 1994, for a summary). Such tasks are not as complex as making decisions in soccer. They do not require the same amount and rate of visual search, or provide the same amount of cues, relevant and irrelevant. Nor do they have the same amount of possible responses or the same need to compare the present situation with similar situations held in long term memory. It is possible then that exercise will affect decision making in soccer in a different way to how it affects non-sports specific tasks. The only research that has examined decision making in soccer while under stress of exercise (Marriott, Reilly and Miles, 1993) found that running on a treadmill at a heart rate of 157 beats/min for two bouts of 45 min did not affect the accuracy of decision making of experienced and inexperienced soccer players. This result would suggest that decision making in soccer is not affected by exercise but that may not be the case if speed of decision is measured as well as accuracy. Similarly changing the nature of the exercise may alter the way it affects performance (Tomporowski and Ellis, 1986). The purpose of the present study was to examine the effect of exercise on both the speed and accuracy of decision making in soccer.

2 Method

2.1 Decision making test

Following a comprehensive review of the coaching literature and discussion with a panel of eight experienced coaches, ten situations that were considered to be typical of attacking situations found in football, were identified. These were set up on half a standard sized table-tennis table (1.37 m by 1.52 m) using model soccer players (6.4 cm high). The half table-tennis table was marked out as half a soccer pitch, using white tape and the areas were in proportion to a real pitch on a scale of 2.54 cm to 0.91 m. Each of the situations was set up in three displays that were "identical", except that they were positioned in different areas of the pitch. Each situation contained thirteen players, a goalkeeper, four back defenders, two midfield defenders, four front attackers and two midfield attackers. The situations were photographed using a camera mounted on a tripod so that the view was from the centre of the half way line. Colour slides were produced and the three versions of the test were designated the titles A, B and C.

The slides were projected onto a screen using a slide projector fitted with a tachistoscopic timing device. The slides were illuminated for two seconds. The tachistoscope initiated a voice reaction timer when the slide was illuminated. The subject had to state what action the player in possession of the ball should take. The subject had four choices, pass, shoot, dribble or run. (Run referred to those situations where the player could run forward unopposed, unlike the dribble situations where an opponent had to be beaten for forward movement to be successful.) The answer was made into a hand held microphone which stopped the reaction timer. Subjects were instructed to answer as quickly and accurately as possible. Accuracy and speed of decision were measured. The number of correct responses was one dependent variable while speed of decision was divided into two dependent variables. These were speed of decision for all responses, regardless of whether they were correct or incorrect, and speed of decision for correct responses only.

In order to demonstrate the reliability of the test, a group of male amateur soccer players (N= 18), who had played soccer at school and had continued playing since leaving school, for a mean of 5.94 (S.D. 1.86) years were administered the three versions of the test. Subjects had ten habituation trials before taking the test. Order of presentation of trials A, B and C was randomised. Reliability was measured using the Intra-Class Test of Reliability by Analysis of Variance (see Baumgartner, 1989, for a description of this test).

In the experiment, each subject was to be tested at three levels of exercise. Although the three different versions of the test would be randomly assigned to different intensifies for each subject, there was a possibility that a learning and/or habituation effect may be demonstrated. In order to examine this possibility a group of male subjects (N=12), with similar experience to those to be used in the main experiment, a mean of 5.45 (S.D. 1.42) years of playing football since leaving school, was tested on the three versions of the test. The order of presentation of the three versions of the test were A, B and C for four of the subjects, B, C and A for another four, C, A and B for the other four. A one-way MANOVA (with repeated measures) was used to compare performance on trials 1,2, and 3 .

2.2 Subjects
The subjects (N=16) were experienced male soccer players. All had played soccer at school and had continued playing since leaving school. The mean number of years of playing since leaving school was 5.56 (S.D. 1.23) years. They were majors in physical education or sports studies. The subjects trained regularly and had experience of working to exhaustion on a cycle ergometer.

2.3 Procedure
On day one, the subjects were given a habituation period for the decision making test. This consisted of twenty situations that were similar to those to be used in the experiment. Following the habituation period, the subject's maximum power output (MPO) was determined using an incremental test to exhaustion (McMorris and Keen, 1994). Subjects pedalled a Monark 814E cycle ergometer at 70 rev/min with a resistance of 0.5 kg. After every 2 min, 0.4 kg was added to the resistance until the subject failed to maintain the required pedal rate. The subject's work output was calculated. Heart rate was taken every 2 min using a short range telemeter, while rate of perceived exertion (RPE) according to Borg (1973)was also measured every 2 min.

Forty-eight hours after the MPO test, the subjects were measured on the decision making test at three levels of exercise. On entering the laboratory, the subject was fitted with the heart rate monitor and told to sit on a chair and read the instructions for the test. These were then repeated orally by one of the experimenters. The subject then sat on the cycle ergometer, which was 5 m from the screen. The subject's heart rate was recorded. The lights were switched off and the subject was shown five habituation slides. Following this the first set of trials was administered. This was designated the "at rest" condition. The protocol for this test was the same as had been used in the reliability and habituation studies, except that the microphone was mounted on a stand in such a way that it was immediately above the handlebars of the cycle ergometer.

After being tested "at rest," the subject began pedalling the cycle ergometer and the same procedure was used as for the MPO test except that slight alterations in the increments had to be made so that each subject would spend 2 min cycling at 70% of his MPO. When the subject reached 70% MPO, he cycled for 30 s before the second trial was administered, again in blacked out conditions. Subjects continued cycling during testing. The same procedure was undertaken when maximum workload was reached. Trials A, B and C were assigned to each subject in different orders of presentation.

3 Results

Intra-Class Reliability Coefficients of R= 0.94, R= 0.79, and R= 0.91 were found for accuracy, speed of decision for all responses, and speed of decision for correct responses, respectively, for versions A, B, and C of the test. When the learning or habituation effects were tested without exercise, a one-way ANOVA (with repeated measures) showed no significant difference between the three trials 1, 2 and 3.

Table 1. Mean (and Standard Deviations) scores for accuracy, speed of decision for all responses (SAR) (s), speed of decision for correct responses (SCR) (s), Heart Rate (beats/min) and RPE (Borg scale) "at rest," 70% and 100% MPO

		Exercise Intensity	
	"at rest"	70% MPO	100% MPO
Accuracy	7.81 (1.33)	8.13 (1.50)	8.06 (1.44)
SAR	1.53 (0.21)	1.36 (0.17)	1.31 (0.20)
SCR	1.48 (0.24)	1.33 (0.15)	1.28 (0.20)
Heart Rate	77 (17)	153 (16)	180 (12)
RPE	6.00 (0.00)	15.38 (1.02)	19.56 (0.51)

Bartlett's Test of Sphericity showed that for heart rate and RPE the correlations matrix was an identity matrix; therefore the differences at each exercise intensity were analysed using a one-way ANOVA (with repeated measure). Significant differences were shown, Wilk's $\lambda= 0.006$, $F_{4,58} = 178.67$ (P<0.001). Tukey tests confirmed that heart rate and RPE significantly increased as exercise intensity increased.

When performance on the decision making test "at rest", during moderate and maximal exercise were analysed, Bartlett's Test of Sphericity showed that the dependent variables were acting independently; therefore the results were examined using separate univariate one-way ANOVAs (with repeated measures). No significant difference was found for accuracy between the conditions. A significant effect was found for speed of all responses, $F_{2,30} = 22.07$ (P<0.001), and speed of correct responses, $F_{2,30} = 12.81$ (P<0.001). Tukey post hoc tests showed that, for both variables, performance "at rest" was significantly slower than during the two exercise levels.

4 Discussion

The results of the two preliminary studies showed that valid and reliable tests of decision making could be developed. Also, no learning or habituation effects were demonstrated when the three trials were performed one after the other. The results from the main experiment showed that although the type of exercise used in this study differed from that used by Marriott et al. (1993), the results for accuracy of decision support those of Marriott et al.(1993). No effect of exercise was demonstrated. These results do not support Oxendine (1984) who claimed that performance on complex tasks would be aided by moderate levels of arousal and impeded by high levels of arousal. The fact that both speed of all responses and speed of correct responses showed significant decreases during exercise compared to at rest, while accuracy was unaffected would support Douchamps (1988), who claimed that when exercise is the arouser only the energetical component of a task will be affected.

That speed of decision making should decrease with moderate levels of arousal is not surprising and supports inverted-U theorists but there was no deterioration in performance during maximal exercise. If, however, the increase in speed of decision was due to a speeding up of visual search rather than an improvement in the quality of information processing, then the results could be accounted for by Oxendine's (1984) theory. Visual search is a simple process and, therefore, according to Oxendine (1984) would demonstrate an improvement at high levels of arousal. It is possible though that the decreases in speed of all responses and speed of correct responses were due to a speeding up of the whole process of decision making rather than just speed of visual search.

While it has previously been hypothesised that increases in arousal would lead to increases in the quality of cognitive functioning (Tomporowski and Ellis, 1986), this reasoning has been based on tasks that are less complex than the one set in this study. If increases in arousal during exercise are due to increases of catecholamines in the central nervous system, then one would expect an increase in the speed of processing. It is difficult, however, to see how changes in arousal would affect quality of central nervous functioning. Easterbrook (1959) claimed that at rest attention to irrelevant cues would affect performance. This would only be true if the subject was not motivated. It is very likely that the subjects in this study wanted to perform well even at rest and there appears to be no reason why a motivated subject could not focus attention onto task relevant cues. At maximal exertion, according to Easterbrook, perception would narrow, too much, possibly onto perceptions of distress (Tomporowski and Ellis, 1986). Experienced athletes, however, are used to performing under physical stress and may well have discovered coping strategies (Landers, 1980). Thus accuracy would not be altered by exercise because attention had not been affected. Speed, however, would be affected because of the increases in speed of nerve transmission and concentrations of central nervous system levels of adrenaline and noradrenaline.

To summarise, exercise had no effect on the accuracy of decision making but speed of decision making was enhanced during exercise. The results provide some support for Douchamps' (1988) contention that when the stressor is an energetic one then only the energetic component of performance will be affected. From a practical point of view the results suggest that warm-ups of moderate intensity would aid speed of decision making.

5 References

Baumgartner, T.A. (1989) Norm referenced measurement: reliability, in **Measurement Concepts in Physical Education and Exercise Science** (eds M.J. Safrit and T.M. Woods), Human Kinetics, Champaign, ILL., pp. 45-72.

Borg, G. (1973) Perceived exertion:a note on history and methods. **Medicine and Science in Sports,** 5, 90-93.

Chmura, J., Nazar, K. and Kaciuba-Uscilko, H. (1994) Choice reaction time during graded exercise in relation to blood lactate and plasma catecholamine thresholds. **International Journal of Sports Medicine,** 15, 172-176.

Cooper, C.J. (1973) Anatomical and physiological mechanisms of arousal, with special reference to the effects of exercise. **Ergonomics,** 16, 601-609.

Crossman, E.R.F.W, (1959) A theory of acquisition of speed skill. **Ergonomics,** 2, 153-166.

Douchamps, J. (1988) A metatheoretical approach of operational performance, in **Vigilance: Methods, Models and Regulation,** (ed J. P. Leonard), Long, Frankfurt, pp. 23-34.

Easterbrook, J.A. (1959) The effect of emotion on cue utilization and the organisation of behaviour. **Psychological Review,** 66, 183-201.

Landers, D. (1980) The arousal-performance relationship revisited. **Research Quarterly for Exercise and Sport,** 51, 77-90.

Marriott, J., Reilly, T. and Miles, A. (1993) The effect of physiological stress on cognitive performance in a simulation of soccer, in **Science and Football H** (eds T. Reilly, J. Clarys and A. Stibbe), E. and F.N. Spon, London, pp. 261-264.

McMorris, T. and Keen, P. (1994) Effect of exercise on simple reaction times of recreational athletes. **Perceptual and Motor Skills,** 78, 123-130.

Oxendine, J.B. (1984) **Psychology of Motor Learning,** Prentice-Hall, Englewood Cliff, CA.

Smith, M. (1976) Control, pass and support. **Soccer Insight,** 2, 14.

Tomporowski, P.D. and Ellis, N.R. (1986) Effects of exercise on cognitive processes: a review. **Psychological Bulletin,** 99, 338-346.

STRESS MANAGEMENT IN MALE AND FEMALE SOCCER PLAYERS

IAN W. MAYNARD*, MARTIN J. SMITH* and LAWRENCE WARWICK-EVANS**
*Chichester Institute, College Lane, Chichester, West Sussex, P019 4PE, UK.
**University of Southampton, Dept.of Psychology, Highfield, Southampton, S017 1BJ, UK.

1 Introduction

Based on the conceptualisation of state anxiety into at least two components, Martens et al.(1990) developed a sport specific multi-dimensional state anxiety inventory known as the Competitive State Anxiety Inventory-2 (CSAI-2). The CSAI-2 differentiates between cognitive and somatic components as well as assessing state self-confidence, and has been shown to have good internal consistency and construct validity (Jones and Cale, 1989)

Certain investigators (Maynard and Cotton,1993) have recently argued that the CSAI-2 is limited in its appeal as it fails to measure the directional perceptions of particular anxiety symptoms and cognitive intrusions. As Feltz (1988) suggested, some individuals may interpret increases in their physiological arousal as fear that they cannot perform the skill successfully, whereas others may interpret this state as being 'psyched up' and ready for performance. Jones and Swain (1992) thus proposed that future research should examine how performers perceive their anxiety symptoms in terms of their likely effect on performance.

Jones and Swain (1992) have recently developed a directional scale that can be used in conjunction with the CSAI-2. The direction scale measures the extent to which the experienced intensity of each symptom is perceived as being either facilitative or debilitative to subsequent performance. Maynard, Hemmings and Warwick-Evans (1994) have suggested that sports performers' directional perceptions of their anxiety symptoms may provide further understanding of the competitive anxiety response.

The most recent trend in sports stress management research has been to directly examine the efficacy of the 'Matching Hypothesis'. The Matching Hypothesis states that a cognitive intervention technique , such as positive thought control, should be more effective in reducing unwanted cognitive anxiety, and conversely, that a somatic procedure, such as applied relaxation should have a primary effect on unwanted physiological symptoms (Davidson and Schwartz, 1976). These authors also noted that the two systems interact, therefore interventions aimed specifically at one component, indirectly facilitate relaxation through the other system. Maynard and Cotton (1993), in their study on male field.hockey players, concluded that the best approach was indeed, to reduce anxiety with a method directed at the dominant type of anxiety being experienced by the performer.

Therefore the aim of this investigation was to assess the efficacy of allocating male and female subjects to intervention groups based on the principles of the Matching Hypothesis and the subjects' own perceptions of the stress response. It was hypothesised that a compatible treatment is most effective at reducing the type of state anxiety it was targeted towards. Secondly, it was hypothesised that the reductions in state anxiety intensity are evaluated by subjects as being more facilitative to subsequent performance.

2 Methods

Subjects
The sample consisted of 12 male (mean age = 26.14, S.D.= 4.14 years) and 12 female (Mean age = 24.93, S.D.= 4.23 years) recreational level soccer players.

Instrumentation
Competitive State Anxiety Inventory-Two (CSAI-2) Modified Version. Pre-competition levels of state anxiety and self-confidence were measured via the CSAI-2 (Martens et al., 1990). The CSAI-2 is a sport specific, self-report inventory that has been demonstrated to be a valid and reliable measure of cognitive and somatic state anxiety and selfconfidence in competitive situations (Jones and Cale, 1989). The scale is comprised of twenty seven statements, with nine statements in each of the three sub-scales. It should be noted that several of the CSAI-2's statements were slightly modified to make them soccer specific. A scale recently developed by Jones and Swain (1992) relating to direction, was utilised in conjunction with the CSAI-2's twenty seven items. The scale requires subjects to rate the extent to which the experienced intensity of each symptom is perceived as either facilitiative or debilitative to subsequent performance. The direction scale is measured on a seven point Likert format ranging from 1 (very detrimental) to 7 (very helpful).

Treatments
Applied Relaxation (AR) (somatic intervention). There are two main purposes to the technique of AR. Primarily, the subject must be able to recognise the early signals of anxiety and secondly to learn how to cope with the anxiety so that it does not have a detrimental effect upon performance. Therefore the aim of AR is to learn the skill of relaxation, which can be applied very rapidly and in practically any situation (Ost, Jerremalm and Johansson, 1988) At each of the six stages of AR the time taken to relax becomes less, and the skill becomes easier to use in the soccer situation.

Control Group
As with the AR experimental group, the control group met the experimenter in group sessions every week during the eight week period of the intervention. Tasks not thought to be relevant to anxiety reduction, involving soccer specific fitness and skill exercises were carried out.

Procedure
Subjects were required to respond to a modified version of the CSAI-2 prior to a home league fixture against opponents of similar ability. This type of match was selected throughout the study to control for the possible influences of venue, competition and opponents' ability. Based on the modified CSAI-2 directional responses given by each individual, subjects were placed into either the experimental or the control group. The six males and six females who perceived their levels of somatic anxiety as being most detrimental to subsequent performance, were placed into the experimental group. The remaining six males and six females formed the control group. All subjects followed an eight week intervention.

Members of the experimental group were taught the AR technique and members of the control group were given soccer specific fitness and skill exercises, not thought to be relevant to anxiety reduction. Modified CSAI-2 intensity and direction scores were further obtained after eight weeks (post-intervention), twenty minutes prior to home fixtures, against opponents of similar ability.

3 Results

Evaluating the effects of the stress management intervention

Cognitive and somatic anxiety, intensity and direction scores, were compared between the two treatment groups, the pre- and post-intervention matches and between genders using four, three-way analyses of variance (group, event and gender) with repeated measures on the second factor. To protect against increased error due to a series of analyses being computed the Bon-Ferroni correction was applied. Hence, within this study $P<0.0083$ (0.05 divided by six) was deemed to indicate significance.

Cognitive Anxiety Intensity. The treatment group by event interaction for cognitive anxiety intensity tended towards significance ($F_{1,20}= 6.86$, $P = 0.016$). Cognitive anxiety intensity decreased by 14.57% in the male experimental group, by 16.67% in the female experimental group and by 3.65% in the male control group, but increased by 5.52% in the female control group, over the course of the intervention.
Cognitive Anxiety Direction. The treatment group by event interaction for cognitive anxiety direction was significant ($F_{1,20} = 14.05$, $P<0.0083$). The cognitive anxiety direction scores were significantly higher in the control group prior to the intervention, but were not significantly different following the intervention. The male and female experimental groups reported their decreases in cognitive anxiety as being facilitative, with increases in cognitive anxiety direction of 22.89% and 12.18% respectively, over the course of the intervention. The male control subjects viewed their slight increase in cognitive intensity as being slightly debilitative with a decrease of 4.47% on their direction scores, whereas the female controls reported their slight decrease in cognitive intensity as being marginally facilitative, with a 1.25% increase in the direction subscale.
Somatic Anxiety Intensity. The treatment group by event interaction was also significant for somatic anxiety intensity ($F_{1,20} = 13.26$, $P<0.0083$). The somatic anxiety intensity levels of the experimental group were significantly higher than the control group prior to the intervention, but were not significantly different following the intervention. The male experimental group decreased by 29.73% over the course of the intervention and the female experimental group decreased by 25.69%. In contrast, the male and female control groups reported slight increases in somatic anxiety intensity levels of 3.25% and 2.98% respectively, over the course of the intervention. A significant main effect also emerged for gender ($F_{1,20} = 11.23$, $P<0.0083$), with female subjects consistently reporting higher somatic anxiety intensity scores throughout the intervention.
Somatic Anxiety Direction. A significant group by event interaction was also obtained for somatic anxiety direction ($F_{1,20} = 37.79$, $P<0.0083$). The somatic anxiety direction scores of the control group were significantly higher than the experimental group prior to the intervention, but were not significantly different following the intervention. Both the male and female experimental groups reported their decreases in somatic anxiety intensity as being

facilitative to subsequent performance with increases in the somatic direction subscale of 37.31% and 49.35% respectively.

4 Discussion and Conclusions

The aim of this study was to investigate the efficacy of allocating male and female subjects to intervention groups based on the principles of the matching hypothesis and the subjects directional perceptions of the stress response. The first hypothesis, which suggested that a compatible treatment would prove most effective at reducing the state anxiety component it was targeted towards, was supported. This was because the somatic intervention (AR) significantly reduced the somatic anxiety intensity levels of both the male (29.73%) and female (25.69%) subjects in the experimental group, over the course of the intervention. Although the cognitive anxiety intensity levels of the experimental group also decreased over the period of the intervention (males by 14.51% and females by 16.67%), a significant group by event interaction did not emerge. These findings suggest that stress management techniques specifically aimed at one state anxiety component will indirectly facilitate relaxation through the other system. This interaction between the two systems may have important implications for soccer practitioners. If this principle could also be replicated, and this pattern was found to occur consistently, a multimodal intervention may become redundant for many subjects who perceive a smaller reduction in the less dominant form of state anxiety, to suffice.

The second hypothesis which suggested that reductions in state anxiety would be evaluated by subjects as being facilitative to subsequent performance was also supported. The somatic anxiety direction scores significantly increased in both the male (37.31%) and female (49.35%) subjects within the experimental group, over the.course of the intervention. Furthermore, a significant group by event interaction also emerged for cognitive anxiety direction (males increased by 22.89% and females by 26.18%) indicating that subjects in the experimental group perceived their decrease in cognitive anxiety intensity to also be facilitatiive to future performance. These findings seem to indicate that the modified CSAI-2 may be a useful aid to intervention prescription in allowing both the selection of strategies based upon the soccer players' own perception of the stress response, and giving the sports psychologist the ability to ensure that interventions are perceived by subjects as facilitative to subsequent performance.

Throughout the study female soccer players scored themselves higher on state anxiety intensity, lower on self-confidence intensity, lower on state anxiety direction and lower on self-confidence direction, than their male counterparts. However, variations over the course of the intervention were similar for females and males, indicating that the intervention was as equally effective for female soccer players as it was for males.

5 References

Davidson, R.J. and Schwartz, G.E. (1976) The psychobiology of relaxation and related states: A multi-process theory, in **Behaviour Control and Modification of Physiological Activity** (ed D.I. Mostofsky), Englewood Cliffs, New Jersey: Prentice-Hall, pp.87-115.

Feltz, D. (1988) Self Confidence and sports **performance.Exercise and Sport Science Reviews, 16,** 423-457.

Jones, J. and Cale, A. (1989) Relationships between multi-dimensional competitive state anxiety and cognitive and motor sub components of performance. **Journal of Sports Sciences,7,129-140.**

Jones, J.G. and Swain, A. (1992) Intensity and direction as dimensions of competitive state anxiety and relationships with competitiveness. **Perceptual and Motor Skills,** 74,467-472.

Martens, R., Burton, D., Vealey, R., Bump, L. and Smith, D.(1990) Development and Validation of the Competitive State Anxiety Inventory-2, in **Competitive Anxiety in Sport** (eds R.Martens, R. Vealey and D. Burton), Champaign, Ill: Human Kinetics, pp. 117-170.

Maynard, I.W. and Cotton, P.J.(1993) An investigation of two stress management techniques in a field setting. **The Sport Psychologist, 7,** 375-387.

Maynard, I.W., Hemmings, B. and Warwick-Evans, L. (1994)The effects of somatic intervention strategy on competition state anxiety in non-league soccer players. **Proceedings of the 10th Commonwealth and International Scientific Congress,** Vancouver Island, Canada, pp. 382-387.

Ost, L., Jerremalam, A. and Johansson, J. (1988) Individual response patterns and the effects of different behavioural methods in the treatment of social phobia. **Scandinavian Journal of Behavioural Research and Therapy, 19,** 1-16.

IMPROVING ANTICIPATION OF SOCCER GOALKEEPERS USING VIDEO OBSERVATION

TERRY McMORRIS and BRYN HAUXWELL
Chichester Institute of Higher Education, College Lane, Chichester, West Sussex, PO 19 4PE, England.

1 Introduction

The penalty shoot out in soccer has become very important in recent years as more and more games are being decided in this way. Indeed the final of the 1994 World Cup ended in a penalty shoot out. When facing a penalty kick the goalkeeper has several problems. First of all the laws of the game dictate that he must stand on the goal line and cannot move until the penalty taker strikes the ball. Furthermore he does not know in advance where the player will kick the ball nor how hard the ball will be kicked. Kuhn (1988) showed that if the ball was kicked at a speed of 20.83 m/s, as many penalties are, then the keeper would have to initiate his movement at the moment of contact if he was to stand any chance of saving the penalty. This would require the keeper to make a decision about where to move before the player kicks the ball. Indeed, observation of games shows that many goalkeepers actually move before the ball is kicked.

In order to decide where to move, the goalkeeper may simply guess and hope to be correct. Most goalkeepers, however, try to guess or rather anticipate the direction of the shot (Kuhn, 1988). According to Kuhn, goalkeepers take into account such factors as the angle of the run up, the position of the foot at the time of contact with the ball and the angle of the kicker's trunk. Goalkeepers in a study by McMorris et al. (1993) claimed to focus on similar cues to those outlined by Kuhn. The purpose of this study was to examine the possibility of using a training video to improve the ability of novice goalkeepers to anticipate the direction of penalty kicks.

Experience is generally thought to be crucial in aiding anticipation (Abernethy, 1989); therefore it would appear logical that observation of videos of penalties could provide experience and thus result in an improvement in anticipatory performance. There is evidence from other sports (Christina, Barresi and Shaffner, 1990) to show that watching videos does help improve performance. It was, therefore, hypothesised that observation of videos of penalties being taken results in an improvement in anticipatory performance of novice goalkeepers.

The study also set out to find out if there would be a difference in learning between a group of subjects who watched 250 penalties and one that watched 500. There is intuitive appeal to suggest that subjects watching 500 penalties would learn more than those watching 250. Indeed it is possible that 250 observation are insufficient to produce a learning effect. On the contrary, however, the possibility that after observing 250 penalties, further observation becomes redundant should not be discarded. The lack of research on this issue makes it impossible to predict the results of this part of the study.

2 Method

2.1 The task
Three semi-professional footballers were videoed, using a Hi-8 video camera, taking a series of penalties with their right foot. The camera was positioned 1 m behind the centre of the goal, at a height of 1.75 m so that the view from the camera would be the same as that of a goalkeeper standing in a crouched position, ready to save a penalty. A canvass cloth covered in chalk was hung from the goalpost, either side of the camera. When the ball hit the cloth, it made a mark in the chalk. The distance of the mark from the goalpost and crossbar was measured. Ninety penalties were filmed and forty-five were chosen the final test.

The film was edited so that the forty-five penalties could be shown with the action occluded two frames before foot-ball contact (-2), at contact, two frames after contact (+2) and after the ball had reached the goal (full flight). The order of presentation of the 180 penalties was randomised and there was an interval of 5 s between each penalty. The film was presented to the subjects using a V.H.S. video recorder on a 56 cm television screen. The subject's task was to mark with an "X," on a scaled map of the goal (45.75 cm wide and 15.25 cm high), where he thought that the ball would cross the goal line. This was compared with the actual position which had been ascertained during the original filming. Radial, vertical and horizontal error were used as separate dependent variables. Radial error measured the distance away from where the ball actually entered the goal. Horizontal error measured errors in predicting distance from the goalpost, regardless of height of the ball. Vertical error measured errors in predicting the height of the ball regardless of the horizontal error. It was decided to examine all three variables because although radial error is the sum of horizontal and vertical error, previous research has shown that results vary accross the three variables (McMorris et al., 1993). Furthermore, information concerning horizontal and vertical error will highlight the specific areas in which the goalkeeper has difficulty in anticipating.

2.2   Subjects and procedure
The   subjects (N=30) were male college soccer players, mean age 19.93 (S.D. 0.79) years, who   had played soccer for a mean of 4.21 (S.D. 0.65) years since completing their fifth year at secondary school, at the age of 16 years. None of the players had played in goal in competitive football. The subjects all underwent a pre-test on the anticipation test. They were then arbitrarily divided into three groups of ten, a control group and two experimental groups. One day after the pre-test, Experimental Group One watched a video of 250 full flight penalties taken by the same three players who were used to make the test video. Experimental Group Two watched a video of 500 full flight penalties taken by the same players. Both groups were given written instructions to look for certain precontact cues. These cues were angle of run up, the point of foot-ball contact and angle of the kicker's trunk at contact. One day after watching the training video the two experimental groups undertook the post-test. This was the same as the pre-test, except that the order of presentation of the penalties was altered. The control group took the post-test two days after completing the pre-test.

3 Results

Table 1. Mean (and Standard Deviations) scores radial error (mm) for the Control Group (CG), Experimental Group One (Exp. 1) and Experimental Group Two (Exp. 2) pre-test and post-test, at each occlusion point.

Group	Occlusion Point			
Test	-2	Contact	+2	Full
Control	28.01	33.77	28.10	26.87
Pre-test	(3.40)	(2.40)	(1.00)	(1.30)
Control	35.32	28.95	27.92	26.37
Post-test	2.60)	(1.30)	(0.79)	(0.95)
Exp. 1	32.75	34.90	31.31	25.96
Pre-test	(2.10)	(1.70)	(0.73)	(1.90)
Exp. 1	27.12	26.86	24.42	23.00
Post-test	(1.50)	(1.60)	(1.40)	(1.00)
Exp. 2	26.74	27.42	26.11	25.23
Pre-test	(0.82)	(1.00)	(1.50)	(0.78)
Exp. 2	20.44	21.46	20.93	21.97
Post-test	(1.00)	(0.77)	(1.00)	(1.90)

A series of three-way (Group x Test x Occlusion Point) ANOVAs (with repeated measures on Test and Occlusion Point) showed main effects for group, for radial error ($F_{2,27}=35.64$, P<0.001), horizontal error ($F_{2,27} = 26.02$, P<0.001) and vertical error ($F_{2,27} = 8.68$, P<0.00 1). There was a main effect for pre-post test for radial error only ($F_{1,27} = 5.18$, P<0.05). Main effects were shown for occlusion point for radial error ($F_{3,81}=11.71$, P<0.01) and vertical error ($F_{3,81} = 7.56$, P<0.01). These main effects, however, were superseded by three way interaction effects which were found for radial error ($F_{6,81} = 3.46$, P<0. 0 1), horizontal error ($F_{6,81} = 2.45$, P<0.05) and vertical error ($F_{6,81} = 7.43$, P<0.0 1). Tukey post hoc tests showed that for all three variables there were no significant differences between the groups pre-test. Post-test, both experimental groups were significantly better than the control group at the -2 occlusion point, for radial error. For horizontal error, post-test results showed that the two experimental groups were significantly better than the control group at all occlusion points. For vertical error, post-test, both experimental groups were significantly better than the control group at the point of contact.

When comparing pre-test to post-test performance at each occlusion point for each group, Tukey tests show that for radial error, both experimental groups improved significantly at all occlusion points except full flight. The control group improved significantly at contact but performed significantly worse at -2. For horizontal error, both experimental groups improved significantly at all occlusion points, while the control group showed no significant differences. None of the groups showed a significant pre-test to post-test improvement in vertical error at any occlusion point.

4 Discussion

The results for radial and horizontal error support the hypothesis that observation of a video of players taking penalties results in an improvement in anticipatory performance. The results for vertical error, however, do not support this hypothesis. The contradictory nature of the results may be due to differences in the quality and quantity of pre-contact cues available for the different variables. Radial error is a combination of both horizontal and vertical error and therefore the results for that variable must be due to improvements in horizontal error.

Horizontal error refers to judgements of the position of the ball with reference to how close to the goalpost it would be. Previous research (McMorris et al., 1993) has shown that it is easier to determine the horizontal position than to judge the vertical position or height of the ball. This finding is not surprising when one considers that angle of run up is thought to provide a great deal of information concerning the horizontal position (McMorris et al., 1993; Williams and Burwitz, 1993). This information is available to the goalkeeper from the beginning of the run up until the moment of foot-ball contact and is comparatively easy to perceive. The crucial information as far as height of the kick is concerned, however, is angle of the trunk and the position of the foot at ball contact (Hughes, 1980). This information is only available for an instant during contact and indeed the position of the foot may be hidden from the keeper's view by the ball itself.

The fact that it is easier for the goalkeeper to anticipate the horizontal position of the ball compared to the vertical means that goalkeepers will make more errors concerning the height of the ball than its horizontal position. This would suggest that most penalties would be scored with the golakeeper diving under or over the ball. Observation of games shows that this is not the case. This is probabaly due to the fact that most players when taking a penalty aim for the bottom corners of the goal. This is because diving downards and that distance takes time; therefore the goalkeeper, even if he anticipates correctly, will find it difficult to make the save if the ball is struck hard (Kuhn, 1993). The results of this study, however, suggest that penalty takers who vary the height of their kicks could be well rewarded.

The fact that observation of 500 penalties did not produce significantly more learning than the observation of 250 penalties suggests that there may be a threshold level at which observation can provide no more significant information. One must not discount, however, the possibility that a plateau had been reached and observation of even more penalties may result in a further improvement. While observation, alone, proved successful in this experiment, common sense would suggest that observation should merely augment practice of the actual task.

To summarise, observation of videos of players taking penalties proved successful in improving the anticipatory skills of novice goalkeepers. The observation of 500 penalties was no more useful than observing 250, suggesting that there may be a cut off point at which further observation is irrelevant.

5 References

Abernethy, B. (1989) Expert-novice differences in perception: how expert does the expert have to be? **Canadian Journal of Applied Sports Sciences,** 14, 27-30.

Christina, R., Barresi, J. and Shaffner, P. (1990) The development of response selection accuracy in a football linebacker using video training. **The Sports Psychologist,** 4, 1 I17.

Hughes, C.F.C. **Soccer Tactics and Skills.** BBC, London.

Kuhn, W. (1988) Penalty kick strategies for shooters and goalkeepers, in **Science and Football** (eds T. Reilly, A. Lees, K. Davids and W.J. Murphy), E. and F.N. Spon, London, pp.489-492

McMorris, T., Copeman, R., Corcoran, D., Saunders, G. and Potter, S. (1993) Anticipation of soccer goalkeepers facing penalty kicks, in **Science and Football 11** (eds T. Reilly, J. Clarys and A. Stibbe), E. and F.N. Spon, London, pp. 250-253.

Williams, A. and Burwitz, L. (1 993) Advance cue utilisation in soccer, in **Science and Football II** (eds T. Reilly, J. Clarys and A. Stibbe), E. and F.N. Spon, London, pp. 239243.

PHYSICAL PLAY, FOUL PLAY AND VIOLENCE IN FOOTBALL: COMPARATIVE ANALYSIS OF VIOLENT PLAY AMONG PROFESSIONAL SOCCER PLAYERS IN ITALY AND ENGLAND

BENNY J. PEISER and THOMAS MADSEN
Liverpool John Moores University, School of Human Sciences, Byrom St., Liverpool L3 3AF

1 Introduction

Over the last twenty years there has been a tenfold increase in cautions in professional soccer in England (Peiser, 1996). The reasons for this dramatic increase are still undetermined. As a consequence, a series of research projects on player violence has been initiated at Liverpool John Moores University.

The primary aim of this study is to examine the relationship between physical contacts and foul and violent play in soccer. It was hypothesised that there is a positive correlation between the number of physical contacts and the number of aggressive and violent acts.

2 Methods

In order to test our hypothesis, we compared present player violence in professional soccer in two different soccer cultures. The degree of physical contacts in relation to violent play in Italian and English professional soccer was analysed. Twenty video-taped matches were analysed by means of a notation system. In this way, a system for observation and notation of the number and character of violent behaviours exhibited by players was developed.

Violent play was defined as any injurious behaviour which intentionally or recklessly interferes with the health or comfort of another individual. A "contact situation" was defined as any bodily contact between two or more players. When the contact was illegal according to the laws of the game it was classified as an "illegal contact situation". Actions which were identified as likely to cause harm or injury were notated as "serious fouls", whereas the category of "deliberate fouls" was defined as an obviously *intentional* tackle.

Ten video taped soccer matches from the Italian Serie A (n=10) and ten matches from the English Premier League (n=10) were analysed by means of a hand notation system. Video analysis was performed by counting all situations of i) bodily contact, ii) illegal contact (fouls), iii) serious fouls and iv) deliberate fouls.

3 Results

The results show that a very high number of contact situations (254.2 ± 33.8 per game) occur in Italian and English professional soccer, i.e. one incident every 20 s. Significantly more contact situations were observed in the English matches (273.4 ± 27.6) than in the Italian matches (234.9 ± 29.7). Nevertheless, significantly more illegal contact situations and fouls occurred in the Italian matches. On average, 73.7 ± 20.6 illegal contact situations and 13.2 ± 4.8 serious fouls were observed in the Italian matches compared to 65.6 ± 20.8 illegal contact situations and 9.0 ± 4.9 serious fouls in the English matches. More deliberate fouls were detected in the Italian (25.6 ± 12.1) than in the English matches (22.3 ± 9.0). This was reflected by a significant increase in cautions per game in the Italian matches (4.3 ± 1.6) compared with the English matches (0.9 ± 1.0).

Table 1. Matches analysed in the Italian and English Leagues

Italian Serie	English Premier League
Parma - Sampdoria (Genoa)	Manchester City - Oldham Athletic
Inter (Milan) - Lazio (Rome)	West Ham United - Norwich City
Napoli - Roma	Liverpool F.C. - Aston Villa
Torino - Inter	Aston Villa - Queens Park Rangers
Lazio - Milan	Southhampton - Newcastle United
Juventus (Torino) - Parma	Arsenal - Tottenham Hotspurs
Milan - Parma	Arsenal - Sheffield Wednesday
Juventus - Roma	Swindon - Sheffield Wednesday
Napoli - Milan	Oldham Athletics - Tottenham Hotspurs
Sampdoria Juventus	Blackburn Rovers - Leeds United

4 Discussion

The results confirm that top level soccer is a highly interactive game with a high degree of bodily contact. It can only be speculated as to why fewer fouls were committed in the English matches despite higher levels of physical contact. English players seem to accept physical contact as an integral and legal part of soccer. They may be used to tougher physical play since most players used to play also rugby in school. Accordingly, English players do not appeal for a free-kick every time they are challenged physically. Probably suited to the player's acceptance level, English referees seem to allow more physical play than their Italian colleagues. The English referees also seem to allow players to make more use of their bodies - including their arms - in contests for possession of the ball. Although the overall number of contact situations is considerably higher in English soccer, the number of illegal contacts and the frequence of serious and deliberate fouls are significantly lower. The hypothesis that the more contact situations occur the more fouls are committed could not be substantiated. Despite the fact that soccer is played according to the same rules in both countries, it would appear that professional soccer in England is more physical but has fewer fouls than in Italy.

The findings suggest that the different levels of foul and violent play in English and Italian professional soccer are related to different national traditions and concepts of soccer. This may also be true on a national level among different soccer clubs. Since long held traditions and concepts can be changed over time, the governing bodies of soccer have every chance to reduce player violence further by introducing more law-adjustments and new regulations. The new FIFA regulations, therefore, are a step in this direction.

5 References

Peiser, B.J. (1996) Football violence. An interdisciplinary perspective, in **Science and Soccer** (ed T.Reilly) E .& F.N. Spon, London, pp. 327-340.

PART EIGHT

Management and Organisation

THE EXPECTED ECONOMIC EFFECTS OF FOOTBALL SPECIAL EVENTS

Stephen Thompson
University of Technology, Sydney

1 Introduction

Sport managers are working in an ever increasing competitive environment. There are more rival sports, playing for longer seasons with both the consumer dollar and the Government's dollar being harder to extract. Government agencies in particular are less willing to see the "intrinsic worth" of sport and its concomitant future health benefits due to what is considered to be age of economic rationalism. Sporting bodies are now regularly being asked to justify their demands on the public purse for demonstrable community benefit, economic soundness and profitability. Good health, fun and the odd win are not seen as either politically correct or adequate performance indicators when compared to cold indicators.

Economic impact statements, to be accurate, must be *post hoc*. Rarely do sport managers have the opportunity to analyse fully the results of an event or carnival. The need is to have some expectations **before** the event so governmental and private backers, as well as one's own committee, can be convinced and feel justified in giving agreement for the special event to happen.

This paper seeks to translate data from Australian examples into some generalisation that can provide benchmarks for further work both nationally and internationally.

2 Economic Impact Analysis

The area of economic impact, particularly in sport is receiving greater analysis than before (Cobb, 1994; Fox and Murray, 1994; Turco and Navarro, 1993; Soloff, 1993). For a manager to describe an event as a financial success usually means that there is money left over at the end of the event. This is an accounting procedure that takes into focus all costs and revenues. In fact other economic activities are taking place at the same time, or in near time, as the event. It is regularly seen that an event, or more likely, a facility may make an 'accounting' loss but has a real contribution to the economy of an area, region or country. By attracting visitors who spend money in an area the overall economic benefit may fully justify expenditure from public monies. The justifications can be measured in a number of ways; an awareness of these different analyses can help any managers of football events in deciding the efficacy of the particular event.

2.1 Benefit / Cost Analysis

In its most basic form, the cost of staging an event is set against the revenues (gate income, raffles, TV, merchandising, sponsorships etc.) and a profit or loss is declared. Costs can also legitimately include the capital costs where this is considered reasonable. This method is not always clear when the intangible costs/benefits are discussed, especially when no quantitative value is placed on these. Such intangibles can be community pride, public relations, national or international recognition, political exposure, and so on. The Mayor of New Orleans regularly commented that the benefit of the Superdome is greater than its annual profit and loss statements (Hefner, 1990). Mayor Landrieu stated 'The Superdome is an exercise of optimism. A statement of faith. It is the very building that is important, not how much it is used or its economics'

2.2 Input - Output Analysis

The model is extremely popular with the Australian Government and attempts to measure the movement of funds between sectors of the economy. This movement can take the form of capital works or recurrent expenditure. The Australian Bureau of Statistics produces input-output tables on a national basis and most European Union nations do so as well. The impact of additional expenditure is calculated on the value added, income and employment. From figures such as these Multipliers and Multiplier Ratios can be calculated.

The multiplier measures the impact of extra expenditure introduced into an economy. A stadium vendor who earns, say $10 from a spectator may spend $5 of that $10. If this $5 is spent locally, it is considered to be an input of $5 to local income, half of which may be spent locally, and so on. Adding up this flow of money, the total economic activity in the region is $20. Thus, $10 has generated $20 and the multiplier would be considered to be 2.00. The usual formula here is $M=1/(1-c)$ where $M=$ the multiplier; and $c=$ the marginal propensity to consume.

The input-output analysis can take many forms, including the following:

* spending on goods and services by spectators visiting the area

* investment by external sources (e.g. sponsorships)

* government infrastructure spending

* export of goods stimulated by the event (e.g. Sydney Olympic F.C. shirts)

The expenditure can be assessed as follows:

* direct expenditure- goods and services at hotels, the football venue, transport;

* indirect expenditure- this covers the rounds of inter - business transaction such as the purchase of food and beverages by the event caterer, materials by the T shirt makers, paint by the signwriters, tickets for the raffles etc.;

* induced expenditure- this is the increasing consumer spending resulting from the additional personal income generated by the direct expenditure. For example, players may use their wages for purchasing goods and services.

Indirect and included expenditure are together called *secondary expenditure*.

The four types of multipliers that result from the above are linked intrinsically which can cause some internal conflicts and confusion. The four multipliers are:

i) Sales transactions - the extra business turnover per spectator / player both created (direct and secondary).

ii) Output - this is similar to the above but takes into consideration the inventory changes such as stock increases by local shops taverns/clubs, the ground caterers, the merchandisers.

iii) Income - this measures the income generated by players / spectators. There is some confusion over the definition of income(as also with both Australian and British soccer managers), it can be seen as disposable income flowing to households within the area, which is available to be spent. The confusion can occur as to where the money is spent, for example international players often return a portion of their income (including transfer fees) to their home country.

iv) Employment - These are expressed as the employment created by football events per unit of spectator expenditure. Generally one needs to be wary of these as most workers are casual and only employed for the time of the event. The Sydney Olympic Games have projected an employment of 156,000 person years for the period leading up to 2004 due to the Olympic Games.

There are several criticisms of multipliers and Gamage (1991) highlighted these as:

* date deficiency
* restrictive assumptions and limitations
* speed of transactions within the economy, and
* increased incomes outside the area of study which generate spending

It is not possible to state categorically that football based events have a multiplier of 1.83. There are differences between localities national income. Gwynedd in north Wales has a tourism multiplier of 0.37 and Sydney has 1.34, while the UK generally has between 1.77 and 1.90, the type of event (Gay Games, Masters Games, U12 State Championships) and the type of management (public or private). Each event must be analysed separately and with fairly rigorous procedures.

3 Methodologies - Recommended

There is a general acceptance that economic impact is expenditure driven, The bulk of studies to date argue on how to calculate the expenditure, while falling into two classes: i) Examination of those doing the spending (organising committees, sponsors, athletes, accompanying persons etc.), and ii) Examination of the receivers of the money (shops, retailers, hotels, transport, paid athletes, winners)

Clearly both methods are desirable, although in Australia the predominant technique is to focus on the spenders (Burgan and Mules, 1988). The Los Angeles Olympic simply focused on the accommodation and restaurant industries due to the relative ease of calculation. Areas of concern, which can be added to the multiplier issues above, are listed below.

* Expenditure switching - no extra funds spent but money spent on an alternative event, or spent earlier/later than planned. Sydney travel experts are concerned that visitors will switch their travel plans from 1999 to 2000 thus resulting in a poor year before a year with unsatisfied demand.

* Government fast track certain capital projects (It is salutary to talk to the citizens of Montreal regarding the capital expenditure on their Olympic facilities instead of schools, hospitals).

* Determining the amount of tax revenues that allow extra future capital expenditure on the part of government.

* Categorising the operational expenditures. Much of the local expenditure is switched from other activities thus producing no benefit, especially if the event is not a success and there is an operational loss.

Some locals may decide to stay for a local event rather than travelling out of the region. This also is a type of positive switching which adds to the local domestic economy.

In the early 1970's the Australian government of the day brought in a 'holiday leave loading' of 17.5%. For their four weeks annual leave workers were given a "bonus" of 17.5% of the month's salary to compensate for overtime losses and the anticipated higher costs of holidays. Some local economists have argued that what should be measured is the difference between normal or regular expenditure and the monies expended during the visit or event over and above the normal.

At this stage there is no definitive measure of the economic impact of a football event. Focus should be on costs and benefits and the determination of assumptions for measuring the benefits. The acceptable method for this is the input-output model. Most state and national governments have tables for describing these relationships between various sectors of the economy.

The example of the event attendee purchasing a commemorative ring can describe the input-output model. The output of the ring involves inputs from mining, metals trades, transportation, communications and retailing. Each of these industries need to purchase inputs of its own to produce the commemorative ring and these suppliers to the industries will need inputs of their own. Adding up all these inputs enables us to discover the multiplier impact of the purchase of the ring. Measurements can be from the data on gross output, wage income, employment or value added. The short run nature of football events precludes economies of scale (even the Olympic Games are a one-off for merchandising).

The intangible impacts have been well researched by Getz (1994) and the effects of disruption, pollution, noise and negative lifestyle changes which often accompany visiting crowds need to be balanced against the increased publicity for the region, the boost in activity (more South African children playing Rugby since the 1995 World Cup win; greater international sales of the Springbok jumper), regional pride and in England's case - hosting the European soccer championships in 1996) - a sense of the future being good, and a large part of the population sharing the vision of EURO'96.

The data in Table 1 are based on sporting events in Australia over the last 10 years.

Table 1. Averages for events with up to 10,000 spectators - average 4750 - (Mules, Burgeon and Molloy, 1988)

REVENUE	$ AUD
Tickets	11,801
Sponsorship	59,149
Gov. Grants	26,581
Entry Fees	18,173
Other Sales	13,272
Other revenue	1,131
TOTAL	153,365
EXPENDITURE	
Capital	2,455
Admin./organ	29,271
Operating	34,544
Pub./marketing	13,776
Travel/Accom - O/S part	22,983
Other	1,754
TOTAL	147,823

Table 2. Example calculations of the variables contributing to the capital expenditure multipliers

Average expenditure per day	$100.00 (Aus)
Average accompanying persons	0.5
Average extra nights	2
% from O/S	20-40%
Tourism multiplier	1.221 - 1.35
Capital expenditure multiplier	1.39 - 2.228

Table 2 was gleaned from the work of Mules et al. (1988) and the following studies:-
> 2000 Bid Documents
> 1990 Masters Games - Alice Springs
> 1991 Master Games - Brisbane
> 1991 Australia Day Sports Carnival - Canberra
> 1991 Tooheys Motor Cycle Grand Prix - Eastern Creek, Sydney
> 1992 NSW v's West Indies - Lismore, NSW
> 1993 Youth World Cup - Australia
> 1994 World Masters Games - Brisbane
> 1994 Tooheys Bathurst 1000 - Bathurst, NSW
> 1995 Southern Cross International - Sydney Olympic Park

To the football manager, those figures can form a basis for predicting the expected benefits for an event. A three-day event in Australia could result in $500 expenditure per person, including the two extra days. Every two athletes would bring one accompanying person, thus 100 athletes for a three-day event could produce $75,000. income for the region, or an impact of $97,500 (M=1.3).

4 Conclusions

There are at least four considerations in running an "event" in the football industry:

> i) the direct revenue projections;

> ii) the indirect multiplier benefits;

> iii) the booster benefits - the event may act as an attraction to draw people into the area and thus boosting the economic activity of the area (Hong Kong Sevens, World Cup);

> iv) the intangible benefits.

Brade and Dye (1988) found no real economic effect of the booster benefit nor could they measure the intangibles. However, in recent times the body of work in these areas has increased and documents similar to Sydney's 2000 Bid two volume economic analysis cover these areas and give appropriate methodologies (KPMG, 1993, Vol 2).
Most of the benefits fit into the intangible category but where they can be measured they should be in a consistent manner. Generally it should be noted when planning or evaluating a potential event that:

> i) sports people travel cheap, ii) early notice of the event allow for family holidays, iii) older athletes stay longer and bring more followers, iv) overseas visitors stay twice as long as locals, v) journalists spend ½ as much as normal visitors.

Revenues that should be included in the analysis include: sponsorship, Government funds, TV rights, registration fees, ticket sales, catering rights, ground signage, programme sales. When determining costs the key areas are: organisational costs (staff, marketing, promotion, interest charges), capital cost of upgrading or building, operational costs (event administration, transportation, catering for VIP's).
The promoter of a football event who can display financial professional as well as promoting the social and cultural benefits of the event should be better placed to achieve both public and private support.

5 References

Brade, R. and Dye, R. (1998) An analysis of the economic rationale for the public subsidisation of sports stadiums. **Annals of Regional Science,** 23, 37-42.
Burgan, B. and Mules, T. (1988) **Economic Multiplier Impacts of Sporting Events.** University of Adelaide: Centre for South Australian Economic Studies.
Cobb, K. (1994) Sports in La Crosse deliver clear - and tangible benefits. **Fedgazette,** 6(1), January, 1-3.

Fox, W. and Murray, M. (1994) Economic effects of the University of Tennessee Athletic Department on the Knoxville MSA. **Survey of Business,** 28(2), Fall, 20-23.

Gamage, A. (1991) **Differential multipliers for the tourism industry in Queensland.** Footscray: Univ of Technology - Faculty of Business Research Papers.

Getz, D. (1994) **The intangible benefits of hallmark events.** An address to the School of Leisure and Tourism, Faculty of Business: University of Technology, Sydney, Kuringgai Campus, September.

Hefner, F. L. (1990) Using economic models to measure the impact of sports on local economies. **Journal of Sport and Social Issues,** 14(1), 1-13.

KPMG Peat Marwick (1993) **Economic impact of the 2000 Olympic Games on Sydney, Australia.** Sydney: KPMG Peat Marwick.

Mules, T., Burgan, B. and Molloy, J. (1988) **Financial and economic modelling of major sporting events in Australia.** Univ. of Adelaide: Centre for Economic Studies.

Soloff, C. (1993) The economic importance of sport and recreation, **Australian Economic Indicators,** Canberra: Australia, June, xi-xvi.

Turco, D. M. and Navarro, R. (1993) Assessing the economic impact and return on investment of a national sporting events. **Sport Marketing Quarterly, 2,** (3), September, 17-23.

ISSUES OF MANAGEMENT AND BUSINESS ARISING FROM THE TRANSFORMATION OF THE SOCCER INDUSTRY

EDMUND D. ALLCORN

Department of Business and Management, Portsmouth Business School, Locksway Road, Milton, Southsea, Portsmouth, Hampshire, PO4 8JF, England.

1 Introduction

As recently as October 1986 the objectives of the professional clubs in the Football League were described as being `generally thought to be utility rather than profit orientated` (Arnold, Benveniste and Collier, 1986). Davies (1995) accused Manchester United and other top clubs of `ignoring the community and abandoning sport to the relentless pursuit of profit`. Davies went on to suggest that;

> "In just 20 years, money has taken over completely in football, dominating all decisions, corrupting and perverting traditional values. Manchester United, with its great history and inspiring legends, has grown cynical and arrogant in its mad pursuit of money, assuming that the feelings and loyalties of its hard-core fans hardly matter any more. They are in danger of cutting themselves off from their own roots and losing their soul." (Davies, 1995).

The last five years have seen unprecedented changes take place throughout the professional soccer industry in England and Wales. The impact of the Taylor Report (1990), the introduction of satellite television and the increase in commercial opportunities have had far reaching consequences for the traditional philosophies and methods employed in running the industry. It is with this in mind that the under-researched areas of the management, organization and development of the soccer industry are addressed.

This work derives from the early stages of a research programme focusing on the role of key decision-makers in the industry, their functions, aims, and their vision for the future. In particular the aim is to focus on the issues of policy formulation, strategic decision-making, styles of leadership and management and the processes and dynamics of change within the industry. This will lead to an exploration of the contrasts and similarities between soccer clubs and other businesses, and then a preliminary outline of the issues arising from the findings.

Before addressing the changes that have affected the industry and the implications they have had, it is first necessary to examine the origins of the industry's development which made it such an unusual business in the first place.

2 Historical Context

Following the founding of the Football League in 1888, four crucial controls over the industry were developed. The result was that for much of this century there were strict rules regarding dividends payable to shareholders, directors' pay, players' wages and freedom of contract. These conditions greatly influenced the development of the soccer industry because the end result was `...to prevent clubs from being operated for merely financial gain` (Arnold, 1991).

From 1919 onwards the Football League also operated a system of cross-subsidy. This involved revenue sharing between home and away sides, a pooling of a percentage of gate receipts and later an equitable distribution of television and sponsorship monies. With so many restrictions on profiteering from soccer clubs, it is no surprise that the dominant philosophy at clubs was indeed one of `utility rather than profit` maximization (Arnold et al., 1986).

In their analysis of the structure of the Football League, Arnold et al. (1986) investigated the objectives of league clubs and found that playing success dominated clubs' objectives (44%), while financial success was only of secondary importance (26.1%). Financial stability came a distant third (11.4%). At no club were ground improvements a primary objective.

Clearly there were other reasons for getting involved in the industry. Arnold (1991) mentioned the `pleasing local prominence` that directors can feel when involved in a club, while Davies was more forthcoming when he stated that `...it's all about glory and excitement, about loyalty and legends... none of which can be computed on balance sheets`(Davies, 1995).

The emphasis at many clubs may appear to have changed quite recently, but the pressures and tensions that seem to have propelled the industry into a more commercial era were first realised in 1961 when the maximum wage was abolished, and then in 1963 the restrictive retain and transfer system was ended. This allowed the larger and more successful teams to attract the best players with higher wages; it was also easier for players to move clubs, and so an elite began to emerge.

By the mid-1980's the tension between the self-styled elite and the rest of the League raised the spectre of a breakaway. Attendances had fallen to a post-war low, the outcome of the 1985 Bradford fire, in which 57 supporters died, meant that many clubs had to upgrade their ancient facilities. Hooliganism still plagued the game; the Heysel disaster in 1985 led to a ban of English clubs from European competitions and the financial consequences increased the pressures on the cartel. Tomlinson (1991) suggested that by 1985: "...the metaphor of the benefit society or the extended family was giving way to that of the League as Robin Hood.". A super-league was only averted in 1986 by changes to the established cross-subsidies and voting structures and the elite simply grew more powerful and wealthier.

In 1989 ninety four spectators died in the Hillsborough disaster, and the resultant Taylor Report (1990), with potentially ruinous financial implications, impacted upon the entire industry. By 1991-92 the richest clubs in the top division had had enough of 'giving to the poor' by subsidising the rest of the League and with the blessing of the Football Association broke away to form the Premiership.

3 Implications

Having covered the context in which recent changes within the industry have taken place, it is now necessary to draw out the factors that perhaps single out soccer clubs as unlike more conventional businesses, before focusing on three particular areas of interest.

3.1 Particular characteristics

The fundamental objective of all professional soccer clubs, despite being small firms, is to achieve success on the playing field. The pursuit of profit, although increasingly important and potentially helpful in securing playing success is not the sole aim.

Not fitting easily into the usual profit-maximizing business model, many clubs are controlled by a small number of individuals. This allows them to pursue policies that could not be described as rational in the strict business sense. As the then chairman of Aldershot explained in 1990:-

> "In a business sense they (directors) act illogically, irrationally - you do so because it's football, and that's part of the romance of football." (Tomlinson, 1991).

A further unusual aspect is the nature of the customers - the supporters - who have very strong 'brand-loyalty'. The emotional commitment to the organisation can be fanatical but this can also bring complications.

Recently a tension has developed between many of the more traditionalist supporters and owners and the business-orientated modernisers that have come into the game. The industry is now faced with striking a fine balance between the 'glory' and the need to change and generate income. The crucial future debate will be over which path to pursue in order to secure playing success.

3.2 Management

The Taylor Report required a sudden huge financial investment by all clubs in new facilities. This meant that the commonly held practices of 'short-termism', day-to-day crisis management and adhoc policy formulation had to be abandoned. What is of particular interest therefore, is how clubs are incorporating long term planning, strategic decision-making and a more business-like approach to their operations, and in particular how this change is managed with respect to dealing with the complex nature of the relationship with the supporters.

3.3 Organisation
Firstly the emotional commitment expected within any club is very high. Secondly, the core operation is still to achieve success on the playing field, but many clubs now have a second administrative and commercial arm that, although not directly involved in matters on the pitch, impinges upon the ability of the club to improve its chances of playing success. Crucially though it must be noted that this interaction of finance and player investment is unpredictable. Success cannot be guaranteed by spending money on players. The commercial and administrative sections of the organisation can only seek to maximise the likelihood of playing success by generating funds to buy players and pay higher wages; it cannot be certain of the outcome.

3.4 Commercialisation
The crucial debate within the soccer industry at the moment is how far should it embrace commercialisation, which option should it take? Should clubs concentrate on playing success, and several club owners have gone down a path of utility maximization, or should they fully exploit their commercial potential? The decision for many clubs is how to steer a successful path between the two extremes.

4 The options

The clearest way to set out the options available is with the use of a simple typology using the twin dimensions of business (profit-maximisation), and playing success (utility-maximisation), to map out the position of individual soccer clubs (Figure 1).

4.1 The typology
The typology can be used to classify soccer clubs according to their business orientation, using the degree to which they attempt to maximise profits, and their playing success, which can be seen as maximising their utility. The result is four broad categories into which a cross-section of clubs can be placed.

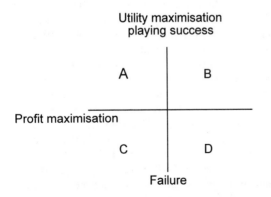

Fig. 1. Typology of soccer club management - based on the two dimensions of business and utility.

Clubs in Section A are both engaged in maximising their profits and are achieving success on the field of play. Manchester United is the clearest example. In the 1993-94 season it turned over £44 million, made profits of £11 million and won both the Carling Premiership and the F.A. Cup.

Clubs in Section B have managed to achieve playing success without, or despite not, maximising their potential commercial revenue. The most notable example is unfashionable Blackburn Rovers, the champion club in 1994-95, on whose team Jack Walker had spent £22 million of his own personal fortune of £400 million by June 1994 (Management Today 1994 p.111). Add to that a further £30 million on the stadium and his input tops £50 million. The aim though is to maximise the club's utility and it seems Mr. Walker is prepared to finance the move from "D" TO "B".

In Section C are the clubs that are now business-orientated, but are yet to reap the rewards in terms of playing success. Coventry City as members of the Premiership is relatively unsuccessful, but still profitable.

A large majority of the smaller League clubs find themselves in Section D, having failed to make it into B. Typically they are in debt, historically they have under-achieved, traditionally they have not been run along business lines. Gillingham of the Third Division, currently in receivership, is a cautionary example.

4.2 Plotting Paths
The paths that various clubs have followed, or are aiming to follow when trying to move out of "D", or from "B" to "A" can be traced using the typology. It may also be applied to examine what issues arise when they adopt different strategies.

For example in the case of Arsenal, in 1983 David Dein the now vice-chairman, joined the board of a moribund club (in "B") and set about transforming the club with '...an entrepreneurial zest previously unseen at this most staid and traditional of clubs.' (Campbell and Shields, 1993). Dein's philosophy was that 'business comes first'. By 1993 the club's turnover had risen from £2 million to £16 million and it was established in "A". The developments did not all go smoothly and the issues raised include the way the change was managed, conflict with the traditional supporters, the role and influence of key decision makers, policy formulation, and the motivation of owners.

Further down the scale is Walsall which was on the verge of bankruptcy in 1988. It was in "D", but has since sold its ground, moved to a new site, pursued a policy of diversification and is now well on its way to self-sufficiency. Two thirds of income now comes from commercial activities and a weekly loss of £11,000 has been transformed into an annual profit of £87,000 in 1993-94. (Walsall Football Club Accounts, 1994). Crucially the directors seem to have transformed the club's position without antagonising the supporters. Walsall is now moving towards "C" with a realistic aim of achieving modest sustainable success ("A"). Walsall is perhaps a role-model for clubs in "D", who wish to move to "A" via the business-orientated route of "C" rather than rely on a wealthy individual to fund them.

5 Conclusion

The impact of the Taylor Report forced clubs to change fundamentally the way that they are run. The varied strategies they adopt are of great interest, and the typology will help to map their paths, but all clubs must be wary of maintaining a balance between profit and glory or risk alienating their customers, the fans.

6 References

Arnold, A.J. (1991) Rich man, poor man: economic arrangements in the Football League, in **British Football and Social Change** (eds J. Williams and S. Wagg), Leicester University Press, Leicester, pp.48-63.

Arnold, A.J. Benveniste, I. and Collier A. (1986) Cross subsidisation in the English Football League. **Discussion Paper Series,** 302, Department of Economics, University of Essex, November.

Campbell, D. and Shields, A. (1993) **Soccer City, The Future of Football in London.** Mandrin , London.

Davies, H. (1995) A new set of goals, in **The Guardian** (in Section two, April 4th, pp. 2-3).

Management Today (1994) **Fat cats and sick parrots,** June, 111.

Taylor, Lord Justice. (1990) **The Hillsborough Stadium Disaster, 15th. April 1989: Final Report.** HMSO, London.

Tomlinson, A. (1991) North and South: the rivalry of the Football League and the Football Association, in **British Football and Social Change** (eds J. Williams and S.Wagg), Leicester University Press, Leicester, pp. 25-47.

Walsall Football Club (1994) **Annual Report 1993/94.**

THE IMPACT OF 'YOUTH TRAINING' ON THE STOCK OF 'CONTRACT PROFESSIONAL' PLAYERS IN SOCCER IN ENGLAND AND WALES

JOHN SUTHERLAND, GERRY STEWART and CHRIS WOLSEY
Leeds Metropolitan University, Calverly Street,
Leeds LS1 3HE, United Kingdom

1 Introduction

The Youth Training Scheme (YTS) became operational in September 1983. In May 1990, Youth Training (YT) was introduced to replace YTS. Throughout the British economy, substantial numbers of young people in apprenticeships were subsidised by these schemes. In professional soccer in England and Wales, the former 'ad hoc' system of "apprenticeships" was replaced by a more uniform, systematic programme of both general and specific training compatible with the aims of the YTS then YT schemes.

Empirical studies of the operation and consequences of YTS/YT have indicated that the schemes had important quantitative effects (see, for example, Chapman and Tooze, 1987,) The aim of this paper is to examine the extent to which the 'Trainee' system in professional soccer in England and Wales has had a similar impact on the stock of 'contract professionals'. It does so by comparing and contrasting player statistics for two seasons, 1982-83, the last season before the advent of the new 'trainee' system, and 1993-94, the last season for which near comparable data are available.

2 Methods

Data for season 1982-83 were extracted from Williams (1983). These were cross-sectional data as recorded at the end of that season. Data for season 1993-94 were extracted from Williams (1994). Again, these were cross-sectional data but recorded this time from the base of the players' club of registration for season 1994-95.

The variables used in this investigation, and their several value labels were as follows:
1.Year: as explained above, there were 2 years of record: 1982-83 and 1993-94.
2.Division: clubs with whom players were registered were classified according to a four-fold division: Division 1, Division 2, Division 3 and Division 4 for the earlier season, and Premier, First, Second and Third for the latter season.
3.Age: this identified the age of the player at the year of record.
4.Mode of entry into the 'Football League': a four-fold base for entry into the occupational internal labour market of, what is termed for convenience, the 'Football League' was used: as an apprentice; as a trainee; from a non-League club (e.g. Altrincham) or as a contract professional (e.g. from a League club in Scotland/France).

Table 1. 'Age', 'games played for the current club', 'games played in total' : some descriptive statistics

	1982-83	**1993-94**
Age of player (years)	25.7 (0.1)	24.9 (0.1)a
Games played for current club	85.4 (2.4)	55.3 (1.7)a
Games played in total	166.8 (3.8)	153.8 (3.6)a

Standard Errors of the Mean are given in brackets. 'a' denotes significant (P <0.01)and 'b' denotes significant (P <0.05) between 1982-83 and 1993-94 seasons.

5. Only status of the club on entry into the 'Football League':a two-fold classification was employed. If the club on entry into the 'Football League' was or had been in Division 1 or the Premier League at any time during the 13 year period between season 1982-83 and season 1993-94, it was classified as "major". Otherwise, it was classified as "other".
6.Number of clubs played for since entry into the 'Football League': a self explanatory four fold classification was used: One; Two; Three; or Four or More.
7.Mode of entry into the club of current registration: a four-fold classification was used to denote entry: from apprentice/trainee status; following a transfer; following a "free" transfer; or "other".
8.Games played for the club of current registration: this denoted the number of games played for this club.
9.Games played in total: this denoted the number of games played in aggregate during the spell/spells the player was registered with a Football League club.

Some descriptive statistics for the three non-categorical variables (ie 'Age', 'Games played for the club of current registration' and 'Games played in total') are reported for the two years of the record in Table 1. In each instance, there was an observed decrease between 1982-83 and 1993-94. The mean age of the player decreased, from 25.7 to 24.9 years: the mean number of games played for the current club of registration decreased, from 85.4 to 55.3 (although this may be attributable, in part, to the timing of the record for the second period): and the mean number of games played in total decreased, from 166.8 to 153.8.

3 Results and Discussion

The extent to which there have been changes in some of the categorical variables between the 2 seasons were examined. In all, 4 themes were explored: entry into the 'Football League'; the role of the "major" clubs in this process; the number of clubs for which the contract professional has played and mode of entry into the club of current registration.

3.1 Entry into the 'Football League'
Table 2 shows the changes which have occurred with respect to mode of entry into the 'Football League' for the two seasons. For example, for the stock of 'contract

Table 2. The distribution of 'mode of entry into the 'Football League", at the 1982-83 and 1993-94 periods

	1982-83 (%)	1993-94 (%)
Apprentice	67.1	20.0
Trainee	00.0	50.2
Non-league	28.9	23.9
Contract professional	4.0	5.9
Number	1829	2442

professionals' as a whole, whereas those recruited from 'non-league' sources decreased by -4 percentage points, those recruited as 'contract professionals' increased by +1.9 percentage points.

For these two particular modes of entry, however, there were inter-divisional differences. Although mode of entry from 'non-league' sources increased (by 3.3 percentage points to 21.4 percent of the total) for Division 1/Premier League clubs, it decreased for each of the other divisions: by 7.7 percentage points for Division 2/First Division clubs (to 22.2 percent of the total): by 5 percentage points for Division 3/Second Division clubs (to 27.1 percent of the total): and by as much as 14.4 percentage points for Division 4/Third Division clubs (to 26.2 percent of the total). Entry via the 'contract professional' mode increased from 7.7 percent of the total to 10.2 percent of the total for clubs in Division 1/Premier League. There was a greater percentage point increase (3.8) (if from a lower initial base of 3.1 percent of the total) in this mode of entry for clubs in Division 2/First Division. For clubs in Division 3/Second Division, there was a marginal increase of 0.7 percentage points to 2.3 percent of the total. There was, in contrast, a marginal decrease of 0.2 percentage points to a total 2.3 percent for clubs in Division 4/Third Division.

These statistics illustrate the extent to which recruitment from (subsidised) traineeships has had a particular impact upon the stock of contract professionals in clubs in the lower divisions. For example, for clubs in Division 3/Second whereas recruitment from apprentices constituted 66.3 percent of the total in season 1982-83, recruitment from apprentices and trainees constituted 70.6 percent of the total in season 1993-94. The corresponding percentages for clubs in Division 4/Third were 56.9 and 71.5, respectively.

3.2 The role of the "Major" club in recruitment into the 'Football League'
The distribution by 'status' of the clubs originally responsible for recruiting players into the 'Football League' has changed between 1982-83 and 1993-94. As seen in Table 3, in the latter season, the "major" clubs no longer recruited the majority of players.

Moreover, when the stock of contract professionals as a whole was examined by division, there were important inter-divisional differences. For Division 1/Premier clubs, "major" clubs were responsible for the original recruitment of the substantial majority of their registered contract professionals. Between 1982-83 and 1993-94, this majority decreased by 8.9 percentage points. Conversely, over the same period, the extent to which clubs in Division 1/Premier recruited via transfer players who had their initial introduction into the 'Football League' via an "other" club increased. By way of contrast, although clubs in both Division 3/Second Division and Division 4/Third employed a significant minority of players who had their initial introduction into the 'Football League' with a

Table 3. The distribution of 'status of club on entry into the 'Football League", by period

	1982-83 (%)	1993-94 (%)
"Major"	54.1	47.7
"Other"	45.9	52.3
Number	1855	2455

Chi-Square value 17.45 (P < 0.01)

"major" club, the percentage of players in this category decreased.

Thus far, this analysis of the role played by "major" clubs has been undertaken for contract players as a whole. To what extent has the role of this particular category of club changed when the total is disaggregated by mode of entrance into the 'Football League', to focus on apprentices in the 1982-83 season and trainees in the 1993-94 season?

In 1982-83, of the 1,228 contract professionals who had been formerly apprentices, 60.1 percent had entered into the 'Football League' via "major" clubs (See Table 4). Again, there were important inter-divisional differences when the stock of Division 1 clubs was compared to the stocks of clubs in Divisions 3 and 4. For clubs in Division 1, 90.9 percent of the 405 who had been formerly apprentices entered via "major" clubs". Of the 295 in Division 3 who had been formerly apprentices, 36.6 percent had been recruited by "major" clubs. The corresponding percentage for the equivalent group in clubs of Division 4 was 41.6 (of 202).

This examination of the comparative role of the "major" club was replicated for season 1992-93, this time to focus upon those who entered the 'Football League' as former trainees. Percentage distributions for the four divisions as a whole are presented in Table 5. Altogether, 46.1 percent of the 1,226 who were formerly trainees were recruited originally by "major" clubs. Again there were important differences observed when clubs of the Premier were compared to those of Second and Third. 82.3 percent (of the 368) of the contract professionals with clubs in the Premier had been recruited into the 'Football League', originally, by "major" clubs. The corresponding percentages for Second and Third were 26.1 (of 291) and 26.2 (of 256) respectively.

It is difficult to make a direct comparison of the role of the "major" clubs over the two seasons because of the complicating presence of 'apprentices' as well as 'trainees' in

Table 4. The distribution of 'mode of entry into the 'Football League" by 'status of club', 1982-83

	"Major" (%)	"Other" (%)	Row Total
Apprentice	60.1	39.9	1228
Non-league	37.3	62.7	528
Contract professional	79.5	20.5	73
Column Total	993	836	1829

Chi-Square value 96.66 (P < 0.01)

Table 5. The distribution of 'mode of entry into the 'Football League" by 'status of club',
1993-94.

	"Major" (%)	"Other" (%)	Row Total
Apprentice	63.3	36.7	488
Trainee	46.1	53.9	1226
Non-league	34.1	65.9	583
Contract professional	66.0	34.0	144
Column Total	1168	1273	2441

Chi-Square value 111.23 (P < 0.01)

season 1993-94. "Change", however, is perhaps seen best from the perspective of clubs of
Division 1/Premier. In 1982-83, only 13 percent of their stock of (546) contract
professionals came from "other" clubs. Of this minority, 9.1 percent were former
apprentices. In 1993-94, however, of the stock of (723) contract professionals registered with
Premier clubs, 21.4 percent had been recruited originally by "other" clubs. 61.6 percent of the
total (of 155) so recruited had been either apprentices or trainees with "other" clubs.

3.3 The number of clubs with which the contract professional has been registered
The increased frequency with which Premier clubs have been seen to recruit players from
"other" clubs is illustrative of the potential returns to be made from human capital
investments in trainees by "other" clubs. If, following initial recruitment, selection as contract
professionals and training, "other" clubs succeed in transferring (some) players to other,
especially "major" clubs, financially it is equivalent to earning a return on investment capital.
Further, this apparent increased propensity to buy and sell players suggests, 'a priori', that the
mean number of clubs with whom the contract professional has been registered will have
increased between 1982-83 and 1993-94. Table 6 demonstrates that this has been the case. In
comparison with 1982-83, for 1993-94, a relatively smaller percentage of contract
professionals have played with only one club: and a relatively greater percentage have played
for three or more clubs.

Table 6. The distribution of 'number of clubs registered with', by period

	1982 -83 (%)	1993 -94 (%)
One	51.2	45.3
Two	24.9	22.5
Three	13.1	13.8
Four or more	10.8	18.5
Number	1855	2463

Chi-Square value 52.18 (P < 0.01)

Table 7. The distribution of 'mode of entry into the club of current registration', by period

	1982-83 (%)	1993-94 (%)
Apprenticeship/trainee	40.9	36.2
Transfer	33.8	38.2
Free transfer	18.7	22.8
Other	6.6	2.8
Number	1811	2359

Chi-Square value 51.16 ($P < 0.01$)

3.4 Entry into the club of current registration

Much of the foregoing analysis would suggest that the mode of entry into the club of current registration would have changed between season 1982-83 and season 1993-94, with proportionately more players entering via some form of transfer in the latter season. Table 7 demonstrates that this has been so. The percentage recruited from apprenticeship/traineeship decreased by 4.7 percentage points. By comparison, the percentages acquired via transfer and free transfer increased by 4.4 and 4.1 percentage points respectively.

There were important inter-divisional differences in experiences. For the top 2 divisions, the percentage recruited via apprenticeships/traineeships was lower: but the percentage recruited following transfer was higher in 1993-94. For the lower 2 divisions, there was little change in the percentage recruited from apprenticeships/traineeships. The percentage recruited from (cash/player exchange) transfers was lower and the percentage recruited via 'free' transfer was higher for 1993-94.

4 Conclusions

There were several statistically significant differences observed in central variables between the two periods. These suggest that the implementation of the YTS/YT schemes in professional soccer in England and Wales has had considerable "quantitative" effects. Important among these would be the following :

* the increase in the number of contract professionals registered
* the reduction in their mean age and in the mean number of games they have played
* the increase in the mean number clubs with which they have been registered
* the increased importance of the "trainee" route into the 'Football League' for clubs in the lower divisions, referred to as the "other" clubs in this analysis
* the increased propensity for "major" clubs to recruit from "other" clubs, via transfer, contract professionals who had been recruited originally into the 'Football League' from traineeship status by these "other" clubs.

5 References

Chapman, P.G. and Tooze, M.J. (1987) **The Youth Training Scheme in the United Kingdom**, Avebury, Aldershot.

Williams, T. (1983) **'Rothmans' Football Year Book, 1983-84**, Queen Anne Press, London.

Williams, T. (1994) **'Endsleigh' Football Club Directory, 1995**, Harmsworth Active, London.

COMPARISON OF AUSTRALIAN RULES FOOTBALL AND GERMAN PROFESSIONAL SOCCER WITH REGARD TO PLANNING AND EXECUTION OF TRAINING AND COMPETITION

W. KUHN
Institute of Sports Sciences, Free University of Berlin, Germany

1 Introduction

One major characteristic of the past two decades has been the emergence of science as a potent factor in coaching football. Consequently, the level of play has been raised in many aspects. The purpose of this study is to gain insight into the application of sports science by the modern day coach in two codes of football. Whereas soccer is a truly international game with FIFA comprising almost 200 national federations, Australian Rules Football (ARF) is mainly confined to Australia. A few teams have developed in England, Canada and the USA as a result of promotional matches being played in these countries. Further, up to 1992 a hybrid game was played between Ireland and Australia. Starting out with a demand profile of each code, the focus will be on the following aspects:- planning and execution of training and competition, diagnosis and evaluation of performance.

2 Methods

Data were collected from clubs in the top professional soccer league in Germany and from clubs of the Australian Football League (AFL) beween 1990 and 1992. In German professional soccer 16 out of 18 first division teams and in ARF 9 out of 14 club teams were investigated. Interviews were conducted with head coaches, assistant coaches, conditioning coaches and players from both codes of football on the basis of a comprehensive written guideline. Besides, training sessions and games were observed to verify parts of the interviews. One of the limitations of this study is that it focuses only upon present-day conditions of professional soccer in Germany. There are many other successful nations with professional soccer leagues displaying a different structure and different training programmes.

3 Results and Discussion

3.1 Game demands

An important training principle is that planning of training should be related to the game demands. Therefore, coaches of both codes of football were asked to rate nine components for good performance from zero (completely unimportant) to ten (extremely important). There were striking similarities and differences between the two codes (Table 1). In ARF skills were considered most important for obvious reasons: an oval-shaped ball is much harder to control for kicking, handling, bouncing and catching than a round ball. Psychological abilities were ranked second, followed by endurance, speed, discipline, tactics, strength, flexibility and constitution (body build). Speed was mentioned first in soccer, followed by psychological abilities, endurance, skills and tactics (both at the same level), flexibility, strength, discipline and constitution. Specificity of position was regarded as important only in ARF for the components constitution and endurance. The smaller players usually play as rovers, the taller ones as full-forward or full-back. The nomadic positions (centre, rucks, rovers) have a higher level of endurance than the set positions (flankers, full-back, full-forward). The expected distances covered during a game can vary between 5 km and a half marathon (21 km) in ARF. In soccer the range is between 6 and 14 km. Effective game time in ARF is almost 100 min compared to 60 ± 10 min in soccer. Blood lactate levels in ARF fluctuate probably between 4 and 10 mmol/l as in soccer.

Table 1.   Ranking of components of good performance between ARF and professional soccer in Germany

Components	ARF	Soccer
Skills	1	4.5
Psychological Abilities	2	2
Endurance	3	3
Speed	4	1
Discipline	5	8
Tactics	6	4.5
Strength	7	7
Flexibility	8	6
Constitution (body build)	9	9

3.2 Planning of training and competition

In both codes of football, training takes place over the whole year. In ARF a single type of periodization is used with one peak per year (i.e. making the finals); in soccer a double type of periodization is applied (Table 2).

Table 2. Periodisation of the year in Australian Rules Football (above) and soccer (below)

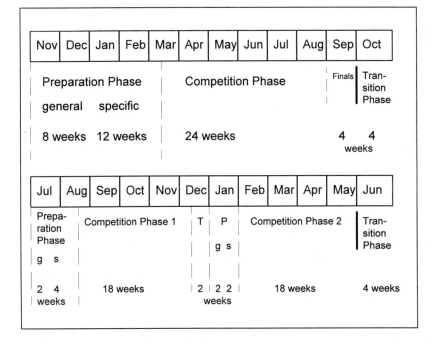

Due to adverse weather conditions in winter, the competitive period is split into two parts. Thus, there are two competitive periods per year. As a result of this fractionisation the soccer coach is under heavy time constraints in the first pre-season period. He is forced to overlap the off-season with the first phase of the pre-season period (emphasis on basic endurance) and also the second phase of the pre-season period with the first phase of the competitive period (emphasis on specific conditioning). In ARF the situation is almost ideal as 12 to 14 continuous weeks (sometimes even more) are available for pre-season training.

The major difference in the pre-season period between the two codes is its duration and number of training units per week (Table 3). The fact that the volume of training per week is much less during the pre-season period in ARF can be explained partly with its length and partly with the semi-professional status of ARF players. In ARF there are three distinct phases, emphasizing first endurance, then skills and afterwards strategy. In

Table 3. Pre-season characteristics of ARF and soccer

Parameter	ARF	Soccer
Duration	12-14 weeks	10-12 weeks (split)
Phase 1	Endurance, strength, skills	Endurance, strength, skills, tactics
Phase 2	Skills, endurance, strength	Speed, tactics, skills
Phase 3	Strategy, skills, endurance, strength	---
Execution of microcyles (training units)	Mixed	Mixed
Number of training units	5-7	7-15
Average length	90-120 min	65-100 min
Ball work in conditioning	30-70%	0-80%
Number of games	1 game per week, second and third phase	2 games per week
Training camp	0-10 days	14-28 days (split)

soccer there are only two shorter phases: endurance and strength in the first phase, speed and tactics in the second phase are dominant. The execution of microcycles and training units is generally mixed and not directed to one specific aspect (e.g. only strength or skills training) in either code. The number of training units per microcycle differs largely between the two codes: 5 to 7 for ARF and 7 to 15 for soccer. There is a trade-off between the number of training units and their average length: in ARF 90 to 120 min, in soccer 65 to 100 min. In soccer two friendly games per week are played on average during the pre-season period, in ARF one game per week only during the second and third phase. Two training camps lasting from seven to 14 days are the general rule in soccer; in ARF training camps are the exception as many players pursue a part- or full-time professional career at the same time.

The duration of the in-season is much shorter in ARF with 24 weeks (plus four weeks for finals) compared to soccer with 34 weeks. In ARF several coaches tend to divide the competitive period into four macrocycles of six weeks (Table 4). In the first and third macrocycle conditioning, skills and tactics are emphasized in this order, in the second and fourth macrocycle skills, tactics and conditioning are stressed. In soccer the microcycle concept is dominant. The order of tactics, skills and conditioning remains stable for the two competitive periods. This code-specific approach can be explained by a different peaking strategy for the season. In soccer there is primarily week-to-week peaking, whereas in ARF the majority of teams aim for the highlight of the year, the finals in September. As in the pre-season the execution of microcycles and training units is generally mixed in both codes. This demonstrates that both versions of football are in favour of an integrated approach to training, i.e. emphasizing the functional integration of all game-related components.

Table 4. In-season characteristics of ARF and soccer

Parameter	ARF	Soccer
Duration	26 weeks	34 weeks
Phase 1	Conditioning, skills, tactics	Tactics, skills, conditioning
Phase 2	Skills, tactics, conditioning	Tactics, skills, conditioning
Phase 3	Conditioning, skills, tactics	---
Phase 4	Skills, tactics, conditioning	---
Execution of microcyles (training units)	Mixed	Mixed
Number of training units per week	4-6	7
Average length	90-120 min	60-80 min
Ball work in conditioning	70-90%	0-80%

The number of training units in ARF varies between four to six per week, in soccer it averages about seven per week. Again, the average length is much shorter in soccer (60 to 80 min) than in ARF (90 to 120 min). There is a tendency in soccer towards short high-intensity workouts to simulate game demands. In both codes a considerable amount of time is devoted to special training (individual or small group approach) with regard to contents and physical demands. In both codes there is a high variation in microcycle planning with regard to load structure and content. For example, most Victoria-based clubs have an optional training day on Wednesday. Besides the emphasis on match play in weekends, most soccer clubs emphasize a pronounced second peak at mid-week with a subsequent tapering phase. One training unit on Wednesday is usually devoted to a full squad scrimmage of 60 to 75 minutes. Some ARF clubs also do a considerable amount of "water work", not only for rehabilitation but also as part of the weekly training routine.

Table 5. Off-season characteristics of ARF and soccer

Parameter	ARF	Soccer
Duration	5-10 weeks	6 weeks (split)
Planning & Supervision	Yes / No	Yes / No
Breakdown in different phases	No	Yes / No
Contents	Skills, conditioning, other sports	Endurance, skills, other sports
Number of training units	3-4	4-7
Average length	60 min	30-70 min
Execution of training units	One specific aspect or mixed	One specific aspect or mixed
Recommended activities	Swimming, Surfing, Squash, Cycling, Tennis, Basketball, Triathlon, Weights	Swimming, Squash, Cycling, Tennis, Volleyball, Cross Country Skiing

The duration of the off-season is five to ten weeks for ARF and six weeks (four weeks in the summer, two weeks in the winter) for soccer (Table 5). Only around 50 per cent of the coaches in ARF and soccer plan and supervise this period. In soccer this is extremely difficult as most players spend their holidays abroad. The majority of soccer coaches hand out individual training programmes, emphasizing basic endurance training. Two series of 3000 m or three series of 2000 m runs three times a week are usually prescribed as a minimum requirement. The "anaerobic threshold" test at the beginning of the pre-season period is used as an indicator of whether the homework was done or not.

3.3   Execution of training
There are only minor differences between the two codes with regard to execution of training (Table 6). With regard to endurance training the steady pace, fartlek and interval methods are used. In accordance with the demand profile, the distances run in ARF are on average higher than in soccer. Strength training is considered important in both codes and is geared mainly to the development of power and "strength endurance". Some coaches in ARF also prescribe "reactive strength training" (maximal strength training). Speed is developed with the repetition method (maximal speed with long intervals for recovery) and intensive interval method (submaximal and maximal speed

with short intervals for recovery) in ARF, only with the repetition method in soccer. From the observations in ARF, it can be concluded that most coaches prefer the intensive interval method. The approach to speed training with the ball is mixed: it varies in ARF from zero to 50%, in soccer from zero to 60%. Coaches either prefer one method of flexibility training or use a mixed approach (dynamic stretching, static stretching, PNF-techniques). Dynamic stretching is not very common, but those coaches who apply it justify it with game specificity. In training skills and tactics all coaches in ARF and soccer rely mostly on active training (90% and 80%-100%), and to a smaller extent on mental training (0 and 0-20%).

Table 6. Execution of training in ARF and soccer

Parameter	ARF	Soccer
Endurance training		
steady pace	7-12 km	3-10 km
fortlek	4-10 km	3-10 km
interval	5x200/5x300/5x400	different programs
Strength training		
maximal strength		
power	xx	xx
reactive strength	xx	
strength endurance	xx	xx
Speed		
repetition method	xx	xx
intensive interval method	xx	
with ball	0-50 %	0-60%
Flexibility		
dynamic stretching	xx	xx
static stretching	xx	xx
PNF-Techniques	xx	xx
Skills, tactics		
active training	90%	80-100%
mental training	10%	0-20%

3.4 Diagnosis and evaluation of performance
There are remarkable differences between the two codes with regard to game evaluation (Table 7). Each ARF team employs several statisticians who keep track of individual game performances. In soccer most coaches still rely entirely on their subjective impressions of the game. Some coaches also use the individual and team statistics

provided by the communication media. The highly objective approach in ARF is also seen in fitness testing. For indices of endurance the "anaerobic threshold" and VO_{2max} are measured in laboratory conditions, distances covered in the 15 min run (or time trials over 4000 to 5000 m) and 5 min run (or time trials over 1500 to 2000 m) are registered in field conditions. The only endurance parameter in soccer is the "anaerobic threshold". Fourteen clubs use lactate tests, one club uses the test of Conconi et al. (1982) and one coach thinks this is not important. Speed testing is comparable in both codes. In ARF (and in soccer) 40 m (30 m) from a standing position with breakdowns of 10/20/30 m (5/10/20 m) are preferred. For speed endurance the times of 40 m repeats (ARF) and of five maximal repetitions of 30 m (soccer) are measured. In ARF an agility speed test is also very common. Flexibility for the lower back and hamstring groups is only tested in ARF. Strength testing in ARF is very comprehensive; it incorporates one repetition maximum of clean, bench press and squats as well as the number of chins, dips and press-ups. Vertical jump performance is measured by most ARF coaches and a few soccer coaches. Only in ARF are specific skills tested. In soccer endurance and speed tests are performed about 3-6 times a year, depending on how well the team is doing. Tests at the beginning and at the end of the pre-season periods are considered essential for setting up individualized training plans.

4   Summary

Both ARF and soccer have similar structural characteristics, such as continuous activity, passing instead of running with the ball, positions spread over the playing area and kicking as the primary method of transporting the ball. This is also reflected in the planning and execution of training.

German professional soccer could benefit from ARF practices in applying a more objective game analysis, a more offensive approach towards the game and aqua-jogging/aqua-walking in normal training and for rehabilitation. Besides, the implementation of a salary cap and a player draft should be seriously considered in the future as these measures could contribute to a more balanced competition. At the moment five teams either fight for the title or for relegation, the remaining teams in the league are neither championship contenders nor in danger of being eliminated from the league.

On the other hand the AFL might consider field tests for estimating the "anaerobic threshold", variable sprint tests and variable sprint training instead of emphasizing speed endurance, lactate analyses in regular matches as well as in training for checking the efficiency of common drills and a more balanced microcycle with one mid-week peak. Further, it should be mandatory for head coaches working in the AFL to hold the highest coaching certificate.

Table 7. Evaluation of performance in ARF and soccer

Fitness Component	ARF	Soccer
Endurance	Anaerobic threshold VO_{2max} 15 minute run or 4000-5000 m 5 minute run or 1500-2000 m	Anaerobic threshold
Speed	40 m from a standing position (breakdown 10/20/30 m) 40 m repeats agility speed	30 m from a standing position (breakdown 5/10/20 m) 5x30 m
Flexibility	For the lower back and the hamstring groups	---
Strength	1 RM of Clean, Bench press, Squat, number of chins, dips, press-ups, vertical jumps	vertical jumps
Skills	all specific skills	---
Medical tests	blood profiles	blood profiles

5 Reference

Conconi, F., Ferrari, M., Ziglio, P.G., Droghetti, P. and Codeca, L. (1982) Determination of the anaerobic threshold by a noninvasive field test in runners. **Journal of Applied Physiology,** 52, 869-873.

RUGBY'S PENALTY PROBLEM - MYTH OR REALITY?

C. THOMAS
166 Albany Road, Cardiff CF2 3RW

1 Introduction

It is thought that the majority of rugby matches, including and especially internationals, are won by penalties. Coaches select their teams on this assumption, and the major rugby-playing countries are continuously seeking methods by which the importance of the penalty can be minimised.

The idea that most matches are won by penalties is, however, based on one observation - that more penalties are being kicked now than previously - and no further research or investigation has ever been made to justify it. Because of this, it was decided to analyse all Five-Nations internationals played since 1945 (N=478), and all other matches between International Board countries including those involving the British Lions (Total N= 836). The aim was to investigate the relative contribution of the penalties kicked in a match to the outcome of the match.

2 Methodology

The source of data for this research was from the Rothmans Rugby Union Yearbook 1989/90 (Jones, 1989), Guiness Rugby Union Fact Book (Rhys, 1992) and the Save and Prosper Rugby Union Who's Who Yearbook (Spink, 1995) in which full analysis of points scoring in internationals was presented. Each match was examined, the number of penalties kicked was extracted, and the total number of penalties kicked in the Five-Nations Championship in each decade since 1947, and in the 8 years to 1994, was established.

3 Results and Discussion

The results, when grouped into decades, showed an increasing number of kicks being converted (Table 1). There was little difference in the decade 1957 - 1966, but in the subsequent two decades, and up to 1994, the numbers of penalties kicked, increased by two and a half times, and almost four times respectively.

This is a considerable increase in numbers, but it still does not show the actual effect of such penalties on the result of the game. The next step therefore was to examine the result of each match and evaluate the effect of the penalties kicked on the final score. There are four possible effects that penalty kicks can have on the result of a game.

i)   A team scores fewer tries than the opposition but still wins through penalties. This is the most obvious situation and arises, for example, when a team scoring a goal and 3 penalties beats 1 goal, 1 try and 1 penalty goal (e.g. England beat France 16-15, in 1993).

ii) The number of tries scored is equal, but one team wins because it kicks more penalties e.g. 1 goal, 1 try, 4 penalties beats 1 goal, 1 try, 1 penalty (e.g. Wales 24 v.France 15 in 1994).

iii) The team scoring fewer tries draws because it kicks more penalties e.g. 1 goal, 1 penalty = 3 penalties (Ireland 9 v.Wales 9 - 1974 - try value 3 points)

iv) There are no tries scored, or the number of tries are equal, and the result is a draw with a penalty or penalties cancelling out a drop goal e.g. 2 penalties, 1 drop goal = 3 penalties. (England 9 v. Ireland 9 - 1968)

Table 1. Total number of penalties kicked in each decade since 1947 and the eight years to 1994

Penalties kicked	Five Nations	Average number per match
1947 - 1956	115	1.1
1957 - 1966	125	1.2
1967 - 1976	289	2.9
1977 - 1986	432	4.3
1987 - 1994 (8 years)	348	4.3

Working within the above definitions, an analysis was made from the four categories listed above. In addition the data were examined in two groups to determine if there was any ethnic effects on the way in which matches were won and lost. The two groups were defined as:-
Group A: matches played in the 'Five-Nations' Championship
Group B: all other matches between International Board (IB) countries

3.1 Group A - 'Five-Nations' matches
An analysis of the 478 matches produced the results shown in Table 2. This combined table shows that penalties have had some sort of effect in only 81 games out of 478 - i.e. some 17% of all Five-Nations matches - and the percentage has not varied greatly in any decade since 1947/1956, with the last 8 seasons showing a total that was substantially less than in the previous decade, and at a rate no worse than 40 years ago. It appears therefore that despite a considerable increase in the number of penalties being kicked, very few Five-Nations matches are won through penalties and the figure is declining.

Table 2. Total number of matches, effects of the number of penalties kicked, in the Five-Nations Championship in each decade from 1947 and the eight years to 1994

Category	1	2	3	4	total
1947 -1956	4	5	3	1	13
1957 - 1966	4	9	3	1	17
1967 - 1976	6	3	4	1	14
1977 - 1986	7	14	2	2	25
1987 - 1994 (8 years)	5	5	2	0	12
TOTAL	26	36	13	6	81

3.2 Group B - matches between International Board countries

Table 3. Total number of penalties kicked in matches between member countries of the International Board, outside the Five-Nations Championship, in each decade from 1947 and in the eight years to 1994

Category	1	2	3	4	Total
1947 - 1956	4	4	0	0	8
1957 - 1966	1	11	2	0	14
1967 - 1976	5	4	3	0	12
1977 - 1986	10	11	2	0	23
1987 - 1994 (8 years)	3	2	1	0	6
TOTAL	23	32	8	0	63

The same analysis was completed on the 358 matches played between members countries of the IB not involving the Five-Nations Championship, but including matches played by the British Lions. Following the same four categories defined earlier, the analysis is presented in Table 3.

These results are remarkably similar to those for the Five-Nations matches - with the combined figures showing that in only 17% of all IB international matches, world-wide, did penalties have an impact on the make-up of the final score. But why should this be, especially when four times as many penalties are being kicked than in earlier decades? Perhaps referees award penalties in such a way that balances the effect of the penalties to each team. The data were further examined and it was found that if one team kicks 3 penalties, then the other team is almost certain to kick 2, 3 or 4. In other words, the penalty differential has changed very little. This is shown in Table 4.

Table 4. The percentage breakdown of penalty differentials in the four full decades included in the review

	Five-Nations			
	1947/56 %	1957/66 %	1967/76 %	1977/86 %
1 matches where each team kicked the same number of penalties	47	42	26	27
2 where one team kicked one more than the other	44	49	41	42
3 where one team kicked two more than the other	8	9	22	15
Sub-total	99	100	89	84
4 where one team kicked three or more than the other	1	0	11	16*
Total	100	100	100	100

* 8 of which were kicked by the losing team

Penalties kicked by one team are largely cancelled out by the penalties kicked by the other and this can be clearly illustrated by examining the matches played between Ireland and Wales over the last 20 years, when one team has kicked 3 or more penalties. The differentials in these matches were as follows: 5 - 4, 4 - 3, 4 - 3, 4 - 3, 4 - 3, 3 - 3, 3 - 3, 3 - 3, 3 - 3, 3 - 2, 3 - 2, 3 - 1. In 11 matches out of 12, therefore, the differential was one or none - and it is this that is happening on the international scene world-wide.

It would appear that referees, consciously or unconsciously, use the penalty as a method of levelling out the game. To examine this a detailed analysis of 21 international matches, selected at random, was completed. This analysis showed that the team that is behind on points during the game is given almost twice as many penalties as the team that is in the lead (see Table 5).

Table 5. Comparison of the numbers of penalties awarded to winning and losing teams in 21 matches selected at random

Winning Team	Losing Team	Total
117	221	338
35%	65%	100%

Whatever the reasons for such partiality, it shows penalties being awarded against a winning team. The net result of this is likely to be that teams losing during the game are allowed back into contention by being given an over-generous number of penalties, or the margin of points between the winning team and the losing team is kept artificially low through penalties. Teams that are in the lead are being prevented, by the referee, from pressing home an advantage and scoring additional points so that their true superiority is distorted.

During this analysis, it became apparent that the home team seemed to be receiving proportionately greater generosity from the referee than the away team. This resulted in extending the examination of the data to examine this phenomenon. Of the 478 Five Nations matches since 1947, 81 results were affected by penalties as shown above, 70% (57 matches) of these went to the home team, whereas in examining all matches, however, the winning percentage of the home team was only 58%.

Analysis of the 358 other IB matches replicates almost exactly the analysis made of Five-Nations internationals, the corresponding figure being 72%. The analysis of all the matches produces similar data - of 836 internationals the away team has won on only 42 occasions, through penalties, as opposed to 102 times by the home team. When penalties affect the result of a game, the home team appears to be at a great advantage.

This is further highlighted if the spectrum of the IB games are examined more selectively. In all there are only 18 fixtures; Table 6 presents the results of the 149 matches played in just 9 of these fixtures. It shows that in as many as 50% of the fixtures, the away team has never benefitted from penalties - and of the remaining 9 fixtures, the balance of benefit went to the home team in 3 fixtures, to neither team in 3, and to the away team in just 3.

The evidence would seem to indicate that referees are unconsciously, or consciously, favouring the losing team and/or the home team in their allocation of penalties within international matches. While the benefit of penalties may favour the home or the losing team, what also must be accepted is the fact that the figures showed that tries win matches. This is, after all, the main objective of the game. It is with this aim that the rule changes have been made over the last ten years - but Table 7 shows how little has changed over the last 40 years. Over the last 8 years, no less than the previous 40 to 50 years, the team scoring the most tries wins on 70% of occasions. If it is accepted that tries should win matches, then, in the great majority of games, these data suggest that the "right" team wins.

Table 6. Benefit from penalties in a selection of International Board fixtures excluding the Five-Nations Championship

	No. of Matches	Matches affected by penalties	Benefit to home team	Benefit to away team
France v. Australia	17	7	7	0
France v. New Zealand	21	2	2	0
England v. New Zealand	12	2	2	0
British Lions v. N Zealand	24	3	3	0
England v. Australia	11	2	2	0
Scotland v. Australia	10	2	2	0
Wales v. Australia	10	4	4	0
Ireland v. South Africa	7	1	1	0
South Africa v. N Zealand	27	6	6	0
TOTAL	149	29	29	0

Table 7. Matches won by the team scoring the greater number of tries

Period	Percentage of matches %
1947 - 1956	74
1957 - 1966	61
1967 - 1976	76
1977 - 1986	62
1987 - 1994	76
(8years)	**Average:- 70**

5 Conclusions

The analysis work undertaken has produced evidence that contradicts the universally held view that penalties win matches. It was concluded that:

i) despite a four-fold increase in penalties being kicked, no more matches are being won by penalties than 40 year ago;

ii) the results of matches affected by penalties amounted to only 17%;

iii) penalties appeared to be used by referees as a method of balancing differences in the score;

iv) when penalties affected the result of a game, there was a heavy bias in favour of the home team;

v) in 70% of matches, it is the team that scores the most tries that wins.

It is recommended that further work could explore attitudes of referees to penalties, winning, losing and home teams, and examine whether the effect of penalties early in a game then effect the later scoring patterns. It may be that the losing team is pressured into playing a more expansive game and either score tries, or concede them through making errors.

6 References

Jones, S. (1989) **Rothmans Rugby Union Year Book,** London: Queen Anne Press, pp. 59-86.

Rhys, C. (1992) **Guinness Rugby Union Year Book,** Enfield: Guiness Publishing, pp. 23-87.

Spink, A. (1995) **Save and Prosper Rugby Union Year Book**, London: Harper Collins, pp. 24, 37, 48-49, 61-62, 78, 91-92, 106, 118.

Index

Accident and emergency 156
Accumulated oxygen
    deficit 21
A.C.L (anterior cruciate
    ligament) 150, 162
Acromio-clavicular injury 132
Adherence 201
Adiposity (see body fat)
Adolescent players 185-201
Aerobic fitness 7, 27, 106, 196
Aerobic metabolism 43
Aerobic power
    (see also VO_2max) 3-11, 32, 112
Age 145, 185-201
Aggression 295
Agility 7, 112
Alcohol 77
American Football 132-142
Ammonia 43
Anaemia 81
Anaerobic metabolism 43
    power 32, 125
    testing 21, 37
    threshold 321
Ankle injuries 181
Anthropometry 3-7, 37, 103, 112
Anticipation 290
Anxiety 285
Apprenticeship 314
Arousal 290
Asian Championships 229
Attack 258
Australian Rules 321

Back strength 16
Bandura's theory 201
Behaviour analysis 89-94, 267
Behaviour change 89-94
Bench press 16
Bivariate analysis 233
Blood analysis 190
Blood lactate 7, 43, 103, 118
Body clocks 125
Body fat 7-11,27-37,81,112
Brazilian soccer 229

Carbohydrate metabolism 43, 66
Carbohydrate supplements 66
Cervical spine injury 132, 145

Children 185-201
Cholesterol 72
Circadian rhythms 125
Clinical examination 150
Coaching 201-209, 267, 321
Cognitive function 54, 279
Commercialisation 308
Computerised analysis 209, 229, 267
Concentric exercise 168
Concussion 156
Contracts 314
Cooper's test 3, 32
Coping strategy 279
Cost benefit analysis 301
Cruciate ligaments
    (see also ACL) 150
Cue utilisation theory 279

Decision making 201, 267
Dehydration 54, 190
Development 201
Diagnosis of injury 142
Diffusion of innovation 89
Diurnal rhythms 125

Eccentric exercise 168
Economics 301
Efficiency 168
Electrolytes 190
Electromyography 168
Endsleigh League 112
Endurance capacity 106
Energy drinks 54, 66
Environmental conditions 54, 118, 190
Epidemiology 132, 156
Estimated VO_2max 3-7, 27, 81
Event management 301
Eye movements 201

Fat metabolism 43
Fatigue 43, 125, 162
Feedback 267
Female soccer 37, 162, 196, 251, 285
Field tests 21-27, 106, 321
Fitness 3-37, 98-118, 168
Five-nations
    Championship 330
Flexibility 27-32, 112

Flexor - extensor ratio   162-168
Fluid loss   54-60
Fluid replacement   54-60
Foot injuries   185
Fouls   295
Fractures   168, 185

Gaelic football   3
German soccer   321
Girls' soccer   (see female)
Glucose   43
Glycogen agility test   7
Glycolysis   7, 43
Goalkeeping   290
Goal scoring   201, 240-246
Grid-iron football
    (see American Football)
Grip strength   16, 32
Groin injury   176

Haematocrit   81
Haemoglobin   81
Hamstrings/Quadriceps
    ratio   7-11
Heart rate   37-43, 106, 118, 196
Heat   54, 190
High intensity shuttle
    run test   21
Hillsborough   308
Hip injury   132
Hooliganism   308
Hormones   43
Hypoxanthines   43

Illness   156
Injuries   132-139, 150-156, 168-176
Innovation   89
Intermittent exercise   43
Intermittent tests   106
International Board   330
Iron   190
Iron supplements   81
Isokinetics   7-11, 112, 162-185
Italian soccer   295

Japanese soccer   221
Jet-lag   125
Jump performance   3, 32-37, 112, 125

Kicking   240, 285, 321, 330
Knee injury   132, 150-156, 185

Lactate threshold   118
Leg injuries   132

Lewis nomogram   32
Limb dominance   176
Lipid profile   72
Lower back injury   139, 185
Lumbar spine
    abnormalities   139
Lung function   37

Management   308
Match analysis   209-229, 246-251, 330
Maximal oxygen uptake   3, 21, 32, 185
    (see also aerobic power, VO$_2$max)
Medial collateral knee
    ligament   150
Meniscus injury   185
Middle-aged players   145
Morphological Variation
    Analysis   240
Motion analysis   209-229, 246-258
Motivation   201
Motor learning   201
Multiple sprints   60-66
Muscle strength   7-11, 32, 125, 162-176

Naps   125
Norway   209
Notational analysis   209-229, 246-251
Nutrition   54-66, 81

Osgood Schlatter's disease 185

Paediatric physiology   185-196
Passing   233, 246
Patterns of play   209-251
Penalty kicks   240, 285, 330
Percent body fat   27-32
    (see also body fat)
Periodisation   89
Physiotherapy   168
Plasma resin   190
Pneumothorax   142
Positional role   11, 72
Posterior cruciate ligament 150
Premier League   54
Pre-season training   89, 98-118
Profits   308

Quadriplegic   132, 156

Radiography   139, 145
Range of motion   162
Recruitment   314
Rectal temperature   125
Refereeing   77, 295, 330
Rehabilitation   94, 150, 168-176

Rehydration   54
Relaxation   285
Resistance training   89-94
Risk   132
Rugby League   11, 176
Running economy   196

Seasonal variations   118
Shoulder injuries   132
Shuttle runs   21-27
Skills acquisition   201
Skinfold thicknesses   7-11, 27, 37, 112
Sleep loss   125
Small-sided games   196
Soccer camp   196
Social learning theory   201
Sodium   190
Somatotype   37
Speed   7, 32, 60-66
Speed endurance   27, 321
Spinal injuries   132-139, 145
Sprinting   3, 32, 43, 112
Statistical analysis   233-240, 330
Strength training   89-94, 168, 321
Stress   279-285
Stress fractures   185
Stress management   285

Tactics   209, 233-246
Taylor report   308
Team performance   267
Time analysis   251
Time of day   125

Touch football   7
Training   21, 89-118, 168,
                          196, 201, 321
Transactional model   94
Travel fatigue   125
Turf toe   132
Turkish soccer   32-37, 103

Upper body strength   16
Uric acid   43

Variable resistance
          training   168
Vertebral disc disease   139
Vertical jump   3, 27, 37, 112
Video analysis   246
Video interactive systems 267
Violence   295
Vital capacity   37
VO_2max 32-37, 81, 321
    (see also aerobic power)

Water-jogging   150
Weight loss   54, 190
Women's soccer   37, 162, 196, 251,
                          285
Work-rest ratio   106, 156

X-ray
    (also see radiography) 139, 145

Youth soccer   32, 185-201
Youth Training Scheme   314